Roger C. Sullivan and the Ma
of the Chicago Democrati
Machine, 1881–1908

Roger C. Sullivan and the Making of the Chicago Democratic Machine, 1881–1908

RICHARD ALLEN MORTON

Foreword by ROBERT McCOLLEY

McFarland & Company, Inc., Publishers

Jefferson, North Carolina

Names: Morton, Richard Allen, 1951– author.
Title: Roger C. Sullivan and the making of the Chicago Democratic machine, 1881–1908 / Richard Allen Morton.
Description: Jefferson, North Carolina : McFarland & Company, Inc., Publishers, 2016. | Includes bibliographical references and index.
Identifiers: LCCN 2016025515 | ISBN 9781476663777 (softcover : alkaline paper) ∞
Subjects: LCSH: Sullivan, Roger C. (Roger Charles), 1861–1920. | Politicians—Illinois—Chicago—Biography. | Democratic Party (Chicago, Ill.)—History. | Chicago (Ill.)—Biography. | Chicago (Ill.)—Politics and government—19th century. | Chicago (Ill.)—Politics and government—20th century. | Chicago (Ill.)—Ethnic relations—History—20th century. | Cook County (Ill.)—Politics and government—19th century. | Cook County (Ill.)—Politics and government—20th century.
Classification: LCC F548.45.S88 M67 2016 | DDC 324.2092 [B]—dc23
LC record available at https://lccn.loc.gov/2016025515

British Library cataloguing data are available

ISBN (print) 978-1-4766-6377-7
ISBN (ebook) 978-1-4766-2378-8

On the cover: Thomas Taggart (left), senator from Indiana, and Roger Sullivan, member of the Cook County Democratic Organization, at the 1916 Democratic National Convention in St. Louis, Missouri (Library of Congress)

Printed in the United States of America

McFarland & Company, Inc., Publishers
Box 611, Jefferson, North Carolina 28640
www.mcfarlandpub.com

For Paul and Viola Dunlap
Faith, Family, and Farm

Table of Contents

Acknowledgments

There have been myriad good people who have lent me their time, expertise, and assistance in pursuit of this project. At the top of the list must go Professor Emeritus Robert McColley of the University of Illinois, who has always been a source of encouragement, and who manfully waded through endless pages of drafts on my behalf and has been a steadying rock of common and professional sense. John M. Andrick, a friend and true scholar, made a tremendous contribution to facilitating the writing of this manuscript, and I cannot thank him enough. A special expression of gratitude also must go out to George W. Gibson, Boone County historian, who graciously allowed access to his considerable collection of local newspaper sources. John Hoffmann of the Illinois Historical Survey of the Library of the University of Illinois has never failed to respond to even my most unusual request for bibliographical direction and source material. No less important has been the enthusiasm of Frank J. Sullivan (Roger C. Sullivan's grandnephew), and the access I have been granted to Sullivan family history research as compiled by Helen Sullivan McKinley (my subject's granddaughter). The willingness of the Sullivans to open their personal archives and access fading memories has enhanced and facilitated this study beyond measure. Thank you so much. The staff of the Woodruff Library of the Atlanta University Center has been unstinting in their professionalism, without which nothing could have been accomplished. Deserving special mention are Monica Riley (thank you for your patience), Olafare Ijimayowa, Helen Threatt, Charles Ambrose, and Oscar Daniel. Also deserving inclusion are my colleagues and students, who have tolerated my endless prattling on about Roger C. Sullivan and Chicago politics, as has my friend Mrs. Claudia Combs. Other special people deserving mention in no particular order are Tamara Botkin, Tatiana Palacios Chapa, Claudia Miranda Monroy, Lisa Broehl, Dan Tobias, I. Bruce Hoffman, Stephanie Hahn, Jill Howe, Richard Shoemaker, Tina Shoemaker, Joel Shoemaker, Veronica Shoemaker, Laura Labno, David Swain, Buffy, Willow, and Winnie Morton, Becca Dunlap, John Dunlap (both of them), Donald Dunlap, Jacob Dunlap, my sisters Julie Hepler and Rebecca Blosser, and, most of all, my wife Sharon.

Foreword
by Robert McColley

In this book, Richard Allen Morton demonstrates that there was a full-fledged Democratic political machine in Chicago more than four decades before the consolidation of the Kelly-Nash machine in the 1930s. Roger Sullivan (1861–1920) and John Patrick Hopkins (1858–1918) created the machine and shared in leading it, though after serving one term as mayor, Hopkins allowed Sullivan to become the *de facto* boss.

The United States, some conservatives contend, is a republic, not a democracy. They are half right; in fact the United States from its inception has been a democratic republic—democratic in that we began with the widest suffrage of any nation on earth, and have expanded it ever since; republican in that we must elect representatives to make our laws and administer our national, state, and local governments. Any citizen not disqualified from doing so may vote, but common sense dictates that only specially qualified citizens can make, enforce, and administer our laws. We choose them by elections, but above the village level, we rely on political parties, other voluntary organizations, and journalists to introduce, praise, or warn against our candidates. By the time Sullivan and Hopkins became political players there was no way a candidate for mayor could meet and talk with every voter. A city-wide party could help neighborhood politicians running for alderman, who in turn could help the party, with its slate of candidates, win control and administer government.

Perhaps the reason why this first Democratic machine in Chicago has previously gone unrecognized is the preference in newspapers and history books for high-intensity conflicts, crimes, reformers real or bogus, and of course scandals. To be sure, savvy reporters left a rich account of the Sullivan-Hopkins machine; their newspaper stories have been an essential source for Morton's history. But Sullivan and Hopkins preferred to keep themselves in the background rather than make headlines, and, apart from Hopkins's single term as mayor, neither of them held high offices. The professional historians who write about American cities in the Gilded Age and Progressive Era—a span of time that almost exactly covers the entire lives of Sullivan and Hopkins—are inevitably impressed with the huge growth in wealth and population during that period, but also tend to think that growth mainly served to enrich capitalists while oppressing farmers and laborers. They do not look for heroes among wealthy and successful businessmen who, also inevitably, profited by their political connections, even if their businesses were honest and useful.

One may ask why there is not in this book more about the parochial Irish concerns of Sullivan and Hopkins. The reason is that this is a study of a political machine, how it

1

started, how it functioned, and how it grew. It was no more inclined to favor Irish-Americans than any other group that enjoyed the benefits of education and opportunity presented by a growing and thriving city. It is interesting that the Irish, more than any other immigrant group, were successful in urban politics, but we are too likely to think that the Irish-Americans did not need to learn a new language as did most of the immigrants of this era. Those who came from Ireland in the 19th century were British citizens, however much they resented the fact. Indeed, most of the descendants of their kinsmen still live quite successfully in English-speaking nations. Apart from going to different churches on Sunday mornings, they blended in as well as they chose in our fast-growing cities. The Irish-Americans have unquestionably been prominent in the Chicago Democratic Party, but they would lead the way in welcoming everyone else. As Morton proves, the distinctive thing about the leading Democrats of this era was that they were successful businessmen.

Short histories of Chicago in the Gilded Age and Progressive Era tend to emphasize class conflict and various catastrophes, even looking for dark aspects of the wonderful Chicago World's Fair and Columbian Exposition of 1893. Who can forget the great railroad strike of 1877, the Haymarket Riot and subsequent trials of 1886, the Pullman Strike of 1894, and the election for one term of a liberal governor who was foreign-born, John Peter Altgeld?

The careful, prudent, and sustained politicking of Roger Sullivan, however admirable, has been neglected because it does not contain the standard heroics of popular American history. For careful readers, however, the chronicle of Sullivan and his associates does not lack excitement. Readers should discern that these politician-businessmen were also essential in the rapid and mostly admirable growth of Chicago over half a century.

Robert McColley is a professor emeritus at the University of Illinois, Urbana-Champaign. He is the author of numerous works on American history and has been the president of the Illinois State Historical Society as well as the editor of the Journal of the Illinois State Historical Society.

Preface

This study has its foundations in earlier research that became a book on Edward F. Dunne, the only man to be mayor of Chicago (1905–07) and governor of Illinois (1913–17). The Windy City's only genuinely reformist chief executive and the state's most progressive governor, Dunne's importance was self-evident, and fit neatly into the tendency within the historical profession to focus upon reformers and reform in this period. Yet even as that inquiry moved forward, it became apparent that real power within the contemporary Democratic Party of Illinois and Chicago lay not with the man elevated by the electorate into the highest administrative positions, but instead with a historically obscure figure who held no office (save for one term as Cook County probate clerk in the 1890s) named Roger Charles Sullivan. Labeled the "boss" by his contemporaries, a title he despised, Sullivan ultimately exercised a proprietary influence over the affairs of his party unmatched in the history of his city and state. Simultaneously, he became a figure of national stature able to fend off the repeated efforts by William Jennings Bryan, thrice the Democratic presidential nominee and the most prominent Democrat of the age, to unseat him from a position of paramountcy.

One immediate result of this discovery was an article on the 1914 Illinois senatorial election. This campaign saw Sullivan brush aside the united opposition of Bryan, then serving as Secretary of State, Dunne, the Democratic governor, the Democratic United States Senator J. Hamilton Lewis, and the Democratic mayor of Chicago, Carter H. Harrison, Jr., to easily win the primary for his party's nomination for the Senate. Though losing narrowly in the general election to his Republican opponent, Sullivan emerged with an enhanced status even as Bryan, Dunne, and Harrison soon fell into politically irrelevancy. After this, Sullivan remained virtually unassailable until his death in 1920.

Adding interest was the subsequent revelation that Sullivan's organization was the actual source of the famous Chicago Democratic machine that found full fruition under Mayor Richard J. Daley in the latter decades of the twentieth century. Sullivan's leadership saw not just the development of a structure with an informal but well-understood hierarchy, but, more importantly, it was during his time that the idea of the machine as an enduring and broad set of alliances of political leaders operating for the general benefit took hold. Perhaps not surprisingly, the machine found its direct inspiration in the commercial culture that was at the heart of Chicago's massive economic development, and found its leadership—including and especially Sullivan, who was independently successful as a businessman—among entrepreneurs who saw in politics a means of financial advantage. The machine as a concept proved itself to be a workable and lasting solution to the problems emerging in Chicago's ever more complex political landscape; after Sullivan's death, there was a direct line of succession, first to his chief lieutenant, George Brennan, who served as "boss" until passing in 1927, then to Anton Cermak, whom Brennan had first brought into politics in 1903.

The accepted narrative has long been that it was Cermak who, by staging a kind of ethnic coup against the existing Irish elite, originated the famous machine. However, close research related to this project undermines this interpretation by revealing that the machine, as the Sullivan organization, was in evidence as early as 1908. Moreover, there is no good reason to believe that either Sullivan, Brennan, or their associates actively discouraged political participation by those who were not of Irish descent. The Irish predominated in Chicago politics (as they did in other urban centers in the period, for reasons discussed in the text), but they never held anything like a monopoly on political affairs or created a single united coalition. In fact, Cermak, who was Bohemian, rose to political prominence within the organization after 1918 with the backing of many Irish leaders, including most especially Roger Sullivan's son Boetius, and Patrick Nash, Sullivan's special protégé, who served as Cermak's party chief of staff. Well before 1927, Cermak had become something like "inevitable," and stories of a possible rival emerging at the last minute in Michael Igoe (based upon an alleged deathbed diktat by Brennan) as the Irish candidate for boss were found to be greatly overstated. Moreover, while it is demonstrable that non-Irish urban ethnics were more in evidence by the 1930s than previously, this trend was certainly not confined to or politically definitive in Chicago. After Cermak was assassinated in 1932, Mayor Edward J. Kelly and Nash, both Irish-American, exercised a lengthy collective leadership, and were ultimately followed by Daley, whose ancestors were also Irish. All of this, no doubt, will frame a future study.

Once revealed as the principal creator of the Chicago machine, Sullivan assumed an even greater importance as a figure worthy of historical inquiry. An account of his life and career, as well as the political culture in which he rose, offered the possibility of significant new understandings of the sources and patterns of politics in American metropolitan centers, and particularly those of Chicago and Illinois, in the Gilded Age and the Progressive Era. It presented an opportunity to pry beneath the headlines and governmental records to learn how things actually happened, and how power as a daily affair actually worked. Now the true beginnings of the famous Chicago Democratic machine could at last be extricated from a heretofore sparsely examined past.

The immediate challenge was one of sources. Sullivan never held high office; he left no papers. It is precisely for this reason that studies of men like Sullivan and his contemporaries have been generally overlooked by historians. To be sure, there is a body of work on various big-city bosses, but few attempt to delve more deeply than the general outlines of their careers augmented by a collection of apocryphal stories. The greatest detail is usually reserved for their foibles and, where possible, their criminal activities as derived primarily from accessible public records.

Fortunately, Chicago in this period benefitted from a vigorous and competitive newspaper community, and factional politics and the activities of leaders were treated as a type of spectator sport, complete with breathless accounts of proceedings, feuds, alliances, and even private conversations, all colored by endless speculation and commentary. Added to this was a similar interest by the national press in the political doings of the nation's second city and state (or third; Pennsylvania was sometimes accorded the honor of being second).

This has made a coherent account possible. There is also a small library of official biographies and "vanity" books that greatly aid in identifying important players. Once events are understood, government and party documents are frequently helpful. Useful, too, are a body of memoirs and autobiographies. Most of these are inevitably self-serving, but they provide anecdotal information and insight into the personalities of many of the actors. Not a few of the participants and relevant organization left papers. However, these as a rule are of limited value, as they almost always have been culled of anything revelatory. On the other hand, a singular blessing appeared in the active cooperation of the descendants and relatives of Roger C. Sullivan. Priceless family and personal information completely unavailable elsewhere has added considerably to this work's depth and credibility.

While the primary sources are there to use, if one is willing to do the tedious job of searching through them, the body of secondary studies is very limited. As historians of Chicago and Illinois have long conceded, massive gaps exist in the literature. There are general histories of the city and state, biographies of prominent people—usually, but not always, reform types—dry monographs laden with statistics and interpretive rhapsodizing about specific and narrow subjects, and sometimes lascivious popular accounts of corruption and sin that leave little to the imagination even as they excite sparse confidence in their accuracy. But there is not much about the development of the ongoing political culture central to the focus here.

As a consequence, it has proven impractical to attempt to create an account of Sullivan and the course of Chicago Democratic politics without greater in-depth reference to related local, state, and national events than would be otherwise necessary. The accomplishments of Sullivan and his contemporaries cannot be appreciated without an organized understanding of the dynamics and personalities of the political world of their time and place— and this does not exist elsewhere in any compact form. While admittedly there is a risk at times of overwhelming the reader with information, the benefits of creating a more complete historical record (and understanding), where none existed before, would seem to provide ample justification for this approach.

In the end, the reader is urged to remember that as with all history, and for all the effort expended to be accurate, this work remains incomplete. Good history cannot be the accomplishment of a single historian, and must inevitably be the product of collective effort over time. It is this process that brings integrity to historical study. The most important outcome to which this study can aspire, therefore, is that it will serve as a basis for future research.

Introduction:
A Political Commerce

By 1908 Roger C. Sullivan (1861–1920) had become the most powerful Democrat in Illinois, a position he would retain until his death in 1920. The organization he built with his partner, former mayor John P. Hopkins (1858–1918), controlled the state party machinery for decades, while also dominating Cook County and Chicago. No election, no primary, no candidacy, no distribution of government jobs and favors was possible without Sullivan exerting a compelling interest and influence. Moreover, as the state's national committeeman, he was counted as among the top political leaders in the nation.

Like so much else about Chicago in this period, Sullivan and Hopkins's rise came amidst the immense economic expansion that came with industrialization. In the last twenty years of the nineteenth century, the Windy City became the most intensely commercial urban center in America, vast, disheveled, and prosperous. But rapid change also brought political chaos that invited some kind of coordination, if only to prevent anarchy, while also offering opportunities for political advancement for those starting near the lower reaches of society. In the spirit of the times, and with goals of consolidation and efficiency not unlike those of the "trusts" in the economy, Sullivan and Hopkins overcame the challenges of the almost incomprehensibly complex politics of Chicago to achieve a near monopoly of power within the local and state Democratic Party.

Their success in uniting so many of the disparate elements of Chicago's Democratic Party was an achievement of undeniable substance that would come to define the fundamental nature of Chicago organizational politics thereafter. This alone justifies a closer study. However, this was not the limit of Sullivan and Hopkins's prominence and significance, as both were first and last consummate businessmen of a type prominent in this era of relatively unrestrained capitalism. Their economic empires were themselves guarantees of their place among the city and state's leadership elite. In this they were entirely representative of Chicago's emerging politics, in which virtually all of the rising leaders came from among the growing class of young, self-made millionaires (many of whom, like Sullivan and Hopkins, were either immigrants or children of immigrants). Though not criminally corrupt, as businessmen they looked upon politics as a means for economic and social advancement, and their ascendency signaled a new phase in the history of political Chicago.

As a large town in the 1850s, the Windy City's political government was dominated by "segmented" ward leaders, who like medieval lords exercised semi-independent authority over their fiefdoms. Civil War growth and prosperity upset this tidy arrangement and

7

brought increasing power to what would become the "old" native upper class, who pulled the strings of both parties. They in turn were increasingly augmented over time, as the city grew, by local "rings" led by gamblers, saloon owners, and others of shady reputation. After about 1880 a younger generation of "businessman politicians" like Sullivan and Hopkins brought a new modernity (though some of the ringleaders would remain, as would many of their untoward practices), introducing the business values of organization, efficiency, hierarchy, and even some appreciation of public relations in pursuit of that defining goal of American free enterprise, profit.

While this shift towards a more direct business control of politics has long inspired historical study concerning the nation (this also being the period in which the nation's leading businessmen became dominant in the federal government, occasioning a subsequent reform movement), its role in Chicago and Illinois, and by extension to the sources of the other "machines" found especially in Midwestern cities, has never been explicated in depth. Nor have the key contributions of Roger Sullivan and John P. Hopkins to the evolution of Democratic politics in Chicago and Illinois attracted significant inquiry.

For one thing, large gaps have characterized the historical record of the city and state. Moreover, political leaders of Sullivan and Hopkins's ilk have tended to be dismissed as irrelevant to a more general quest by historians of this period for the sources of future reform. Consequently, just a few chapters in Harold Zink's well-known but limited survey of "bosses," and two articles written by this author, have appeared that discuss Sullivan to any degree, while Hopkins has inspired virtually no meaningful attention beyond the passing use of his name in accounts of the Pullman Strike.[1]

Still, Sullivan has not been ignored. Indeed, he has frequently appeared in historical writings—especially for his later part in the nomination of Woodrow Wilson. Inevitably, however, these studios have been very superficial, riddled with unfounded suppositions and clichés, and usually feature distorted characterizations, most of which do not stand up under closer scrutiny. Some of these can be traced to Roger Sullivan himself, who allowed the publication during his lifetime of a biographical sketch that exaggerated the humble conditions of his youth, casting him as a child of poverty compelled to leave school early to support his family. However, among the least supportable, but most universal, is the assumption of Sullivan and Hopkins's (and by extension, the kind of organizational politics they pursued) association with corruption and criminality. So pervasive is this preconception that it initially framed this study.[2]

It is not difficult to understand why a more accurate account of the rise of Sullivan and Hopkins has not been previously available. For one thing, the very fact that so little has been known about them and their accomplishments encouraged a tendency to view them through the prism of the Chicago machine in the 1920s and 1930s, when the Democratic Party was unquestionably laced with corruption and even criminality (and there were indictments, trials, and convictions to prove it). For another, the most accessible contemporary sources come from their political opponents, Mayor Carter H. Harrison, Jr., in particular, and from sometime-reformers less concerned with truth than with a political agenda. It is their often-distorted versions of events that have served as the basis for scholarly assessment. Finally, as Roger Sullivan did indeed become a "boss," who headed an urban machine, and Hopkins was his partner, it has become the course of least resistance in addressing their place in history to cite the easy clichés associated with such aggregations—clichés reinforced by the well-known antics of notorious characters like William Tweed (1823–1878) of Tammany Hall in New York City; Mayor William Hale Thompson (1869–1944), Sullivan's eventual Republican contemporary in Chicago; and others. Political bosses have not inspired good press either in their own time or our own; in this, Sullivan and Hopkins have proved to be no exceptions.

However, closer study has uncovered a more complex reality. In the first place, Chicago before 1920 was not the Chicago of Al Capone and Prohibition, and despite the alleged criminal connections of some of its politicians—like the First Ward's notorious aldermen "Bathhouse John" Coughlin and Michael "Hinky Dink" Kenna—the Windy City's politics then were not especially about serving the needs, in part or in whole, of criminal organizations. There was crime, of course, as in any large city, and it is difficult to conceive that any prominent man in business or politics could have escaped contact entirely, but during Sullivan and Hopkins's lifetimes the underworld was as a rule segregated and controlled.

In the second place, the word almost universally used by contemporaries to describe Sullivan was some variant of "decent," or as his implacable political opponent, the prominent reformer Raymond Robins, phrased it: "a very decent man." Similarly, John P. Hopkins was an object of public respect and even affection (most of the time, anyway) as a celebrity of sorts throughout his life. While it is difficult to prove a negative, the evidence, or its lack, seems clear. Neither Sullivan nor Hopkins was ever indicted for any crime in a time and place when politically inspired indictments were common. No malfeasance was ever seriously alleged against Hopkins as mayor, and when Sullivan left office as clerk of the probate court, a review of the records revealed nothing untoward. Also importantly, the two were never accused, even during the height of the bitterest factional fighting, by anyone—including Carter Harrison II and their most vehement reformist critics—of criminality or any association with criminality.

In a world that thrived upon the red meat of scandal, even if it were decades old, this apparent absence of suspicion would have been impossible if there were any evidence or broad belief to the contrary. John P. Hopkins was a special favorite of President Grover Cleveland, who first became prominent as the reform sheriff of Buffalo, New York, and certainly would not have been so openly associated with anyone with an unsavory reputation. Moreover, it seems unlikely that people of the caliber of George Cole of the Municipal Voters League would openly call a man his "friend," as he did Sullivan, if he believed him corrupt or criminally associated. Similarly, it is inconceivable that if William Jennings Bryan, a man who proudly wore his self-righteousness openly for all to see, had entertained the least suspicion of such associations, he would have permitted a personal reconciliation late in their careers and be seen walking arm-in-arm with the Chicago leader in the streets of Washington, D.C.[3]

While their contemporaries understood that Sullivan and Hopkins were no criminals, they also correctly perceived that they represented a style of politics that unabashedly looked for profit in government. As the historian Forrest McDonald has recognized in his excellent biography of Samuel Insull, Sullivan, Hopkins, and their allies introduced "a new pattern of urban politics," one that "postulated that politicians should keep their hands out of the public till and earn their livelihood from non-civic activities," for which "political power was an indispensible asset." Access to government contracts, bonding, employment, and the like, combined with the ability to affect policy, could pay dividends in business, as it certainly did for Sullivan and Hopkins.

But it was not and never had been illegal, and it certainly was not exclusive to these two, as even their most vociferous critics among the reformers were willing to use "connection" for personal advancement and advantage. In addition, seeking private benefit through the use of public influence has been part of government since the first one was organized. It is difficult, writing from a time when men and women regularly emerge as multimillionaires after "public service," and congressmen have until lately been allowed to invest based upon "insider" information learned in committee, to condemn Sullivan, Hopkins, and their generation of politicians for being more direct and honest about their motives and goals.

To their credit, neither tolerated misappropriation and other criminal practices, and they set limits, as in Sullivan's insistence that the public schools be off-limits to politics and that judges be qualified. To their discredit (at least to their reformist critics), they perpetuated and improved upon an existing exploitive system many felt to be inappropriate for a representative society. If these practices were "boodling" and the returns "boodle," as their opponents defined them, then they were "boodlers," as were a vast majority of political figures in Chicago and the nation at the time. But they were never seriously accused of conforming to the dictionary definition of the term as those engaged in bribery, theft, or unsportsmanlike conduct. It is significant that no one at the time thought to challenge Roger Sullivan's public assertion in 1919 that he was "not in the criminal business."[4]

Substantiating this appearance of relative respectability was the character of their personal lives. Roger Sullivan especially was a paragon of Victorian middle-class values. Passionately devoted to his family, he conceived his primary duty as being the provider for and protector of an extended clan comprising his wife and five children, numerous brothers and sisters, and innumerable cousins, including many in Ireland he had never met. He, for instance, encouraged members of his kindred from the Emerald Isle to stay with him during their first months (sometimes years) in America, and after he became successful, he was unstinting in his generosity to those who remained behind.

His personal habits were appropriately regular and admirable; he rarely if ever swore; he was moderate in his consumption of alcohol; and there was no other woman in his life besides his wife, who ruled their home. He was a devoted Roman Catholic, having boarded with and worked for the local priest in his youth, and he maintained very close ties to members of his church's hierarchy throughout his life; he unashamedly professed his Christian faith. He was also blessed with intelligence, leadership abilities, and natural honesty augmented by a charisma that drew the admiration of other men.

These were the qualities, of course, necessary to his eventual position as paramount leader, which in the final analysis depended upon the respect he commanded among some of the world's most cynical businessmen and politicos. Like them, it was true, he could be ruthless, and he was a scrapper in his youth with a considerable physical presence (as were his equally imposing brothers). However, by instinct he was a "harmonizer," who first developed a political mien by being "helpful" to others, and who sought to build his organization through compromise and consensus based upon mutual interest rather than conquest. He was widely known for the absolute bond of his word, a considerable and well-guarded asset for a politician or a businessman, and he was praised for his generous spirit and for never holding grudges or seeking vengeance; his later title as a "benevolent boss" was from all accounts well deserved. One contemporary description, in the exaggerated tone of the period, praised his "kindly heart, the openness and generosity of which has brought sunshine to many hard lives and lightened many a hard load."[5]

John Hopkins was known as a gentleman, dapper and courteous. He was an object of feminine fascination, but also a confirmed bachelor who lived with and was devoted to his mother and sisters. Like Roger he was a man among men, but also prudent in his habits. In the early years of their association, it was Hopkins who was clearly the more popular and connected of the two, and he, too, was blessed with the ability to charm other men. Undeniably charismatic, he became the successful Democratic candidate to replace as mayor the assassinated elder Carter H. Harrison in 1894.

But any portrait of Roger C. Sullivan, John P. Hopkins, and the early political seas in which they swam that did not refer to the importance of their roles as entrepreneurs would be grossly incomplete and inadequate. Tellingly, one year while between positions in his various enterprises, Roger Sullivan listed himself in Chicago's city directory simply as a "capitalist." Moreover, it was this mix of politics and business that defined Chicago's politics of the period. Increasingly dominated by scores of young self-made millionaires like Sullivan and Hopkins, who lived out the American dream of prosperity, politics in Chicago came to reflect both the vitality and ugliness of industrialization in a city whose chief landmark and tourist attraction was the huge, smelly, dirty, and dangerous, but highly profitable stockyards.

Massive growth brought opportunities for seemingly unlimited economic and social advancement for those with intelligence, luck, and a willingness to take risks. And it was from among these that Sullivan and Hopkins found like-minded allies, men like Frank Stuyvesant Peabody, who inherited a coal business and built it into one of the leading concerns of its type in the United States, or Andrew Graham, who began relatively poor but through his own efforts became a successful West Side banker, or George Brennan, who became rich in the bonding business, and many others of similarly enterprising natures.

Moreover, just as these many young businessman politicians sought entrepreneurial and personal advantages through a political commerce, so the values and influence of business they brought by their participation in matters of state helped in turn to redefine Chicago's political life. It is not entirely unreasonable to find an analogy between the impulse that led the monopolies or "trusts" of the period to consolidate production in individual industries, and the Sullivan organization's drive to absorb—on the basis of mutual advantage—other factions, major and minor, into a massive "corporate" structure. Similarly, the business ethos was eventually to manifest itself in demands for efficiency, and in the creation of clearer hierarchies.

Ironically, it was this business orientation, rather than anything directly to do with politics, that was to be the source of the one scandal that tainted Sullivan and Hopkins's careers. In the spring of 1895, the Chicago city council voted franchises for two new companies, the Ogden Gas Company and the Cosmopolitan Electric Company. It was generally assumed at the time that these were created to compel their purchase by the local utility monopolies, and thus create massive profits for their investors (among whom, allegedly, were many of the leading men in the city and on the Board of Aldermen).

Sullivan's role remains unclear, though it seems certain that he did not instigate the scheme. Hopkins certainly had no direct involvement, but apparently was convinced by his partner not to—as mayor—veto the measures. Regardless, it was Sullivan who emerged effectively the chief operating officer overseeing both enterprises (assuming the title of president of the Ogden Company in 1905), and he unquestionably profited from the connection. For this, however, both men paid a high price in terms of their reputation, and they were forever afterwards vulnerable to attacks as "boodlers" and "gas kings."

Soon the lion's share of the companies' stock was purchased privately by investors in the utility monopolies, and these sales may (or may not) have helped finance Sullivan's chief entrepreneurial investment, the Sawyer Biscuit Company. This became a national concern, marketing Crispo soda crackers, ginger snaps, graham crackers, and other products, and it helped make Sullivan a multimillionaire. Long after Sullivan's death, the firm's successor enterprises became part of the Kellogg Company. He also served as a director on numerous boards, and his investments and business interests included Union Carbide and the Great Lakes Dredge and Dock Company.

There is no evidence that Hopkins ever profited in any way from the Ogden/Cosmopolitan franchises—though this was widely believed. However, he was already a wealthy entrepreneur. His initial business was in the grocery trade around the city, which he undertook after leaving the service of George Pullman. His most lucrative venture was the Great Lakes Dredge and Dock Company (GLDD), founded in 1891 as Lydon & Drews. Another was the Aurora Automatic Machinery Company. He was a major shareholder as well in Union Carbide, while serving on the boards of several other companies over the years.

But it was not all about dollars and business sense, for Chicago's political world of the late nineteenth and early twentieth centuries was also a vast and joyful boys' club. There were picnics, banquets, dinners, marches, meetings, and conventions where men could socialize with other men in a manly environment. There were intrigues, secrets, cliques, and ever-shifting alliances, all exciting aspects of the ultimate boyish game of us-versus-them that with frequent elections and primaries (at least two sets a year) could be played endlessly with no defeat as final, and no victory as absolute. There were impressive titles to which one could aspire, and ornate uniforms for those so inclined in the various marching bands and clubs. For the more pugnacious, there was the attraction of the occasional street brawl. As in any fraternal order, gossip and feuding were rampant, although it was generally considered bad form for a political rivalry to become personal as today's enemy could become tomorrow's ally, and warm friendships often were formed across factional and party lines.

Perhaps not surprisingly, it was a world populated by many colorful and controversial characters. One of these was Robert Emmett "Bobby" Burke, a unique player who would later be the only Democrat at the 1916 national convention to vote against the renomination of Woodrow Wilson (to Sullivan's embarrassment). The hyperactive environment of campaigning and factional discord, as well as the relative absence of the usual distaff restraints, seemed at times to encourage the eccentric and extreme. But it was all great fun, and it was a world in which Roger Sullivan and John P. Hopkins thrived; by Roger's account, it was the "excitement" of politics that kept him involved long after he made his fortune.

As bizarre and sometimes silly as the machinations and personal feuding of Chicago politics could become, they remained mechanisms of public power, and serious issues intruded regularly into this otherwise prosaic and mostly self-contained political universe. In 1896, Sullivan and Hopkins (who was the more prominent of the two at the time) helped lead the National Democratic Party (Gold Democrats), created to oppose the Democratic presidential candidacy of William Jennings Bryan. With close ties to Grover Cleveland, the pair were in the forefront of the national opposition to the man from Nebraska and what he represented. Indeed, Sullivan in particular would become for a time the Great Commoner's designated urban enemy within the party. His and John's success in deflecting the attacks of the most prominent Democrat of the age was testimony to their political skills and popularity, as was their adaptation to the early local expressions of progressive idealism.

Until 1904, it was John P. Hopkins who served as the front man for the faction (he was never actually "boss" in the sense of being the sole director of what was then a coalition), and who very briefly, as mayor, helped achieve that most elusive of ambitions, true local Democratic unity. Nonetheless, Sullivan, though less in the public eye in these years, was steadily building his influence as well as his base in his home ward, and unquestionably was the equal partner. It would be Roger, for instance, who would oversee many of the key negotiations, and the politics of the two were virtually indistinguishable. In the end, in part because he was the stronger personality and in part because Hopkins wished to forego public life, it was Roger C. Sullivan who rose to become the openly acknowledged leader.

By 1908, the processes enabling the modern Chicago Democracy and Sullivan's paramountcy had come to fruition. Chicago was now America's second largest urban center, "the Metropolis of the Midwest," with nearly two million (up from 500,000 in 1870) residents residing within 191 square miles (up from 36 in 1870).[6] Its leaders were major players in national politics, and its elections and power struggles were followed closely throughout the country. However, with growth came complexity, and with complexity the necessity for a more efficient model of governance.[7]

Rising to help "bring order out of the chaos" were the businessman politicians. By 1908, they had become the predominant element in the Democratic Party and in local politics in general. Primarily through what was known as the Sullivan organization, there was something close to an absolute control of events achieved by this generation of public men whose careers straddled politics and the city's bustling commerce.[8]

Symbolically, Roger C. Sullivan's status as "boss" was decisively established in 1906 with his turning back of William Jennings Bryan's crusade to seize control of the city and state democracy. Though the Great Commoner was the most powerful Democrat of his era, and could claim his own legions in the Sucker State, he was outgeneraled at every turn. Within less than two years, in part thanks to this victory, Sullivan would be able to create within the Cook County Democracy a "managing committee," which, added to his influence over the state committee, became the formal mechanism of his singular power. However, Sullivan's success, beyond his immediate political skills, was also founded in the very nature of his leadership, which in itself represented an important departure from the past.

There were, of course, many prominent and influential figures in Chicago Democratic politics before 1908, most of whom until now have escaped historical scrutiny. Most powerful of all were two earlier mayors, a father and son both named Carter H. Harrison. They both headed large "city hall crowds." However, the focus of these groupings was always upon the leader and his political career. When this faltered—as happened when Harrison II lost his position as mayor in 1905—and the sources of patronage and other benefits dried up, things unraveled. Although Hopkins also served as mayor, and Sullivan a term as clerk of the Cook County Probate Court, their organization neither rose nor fell as a result of their degree of success in any primary or election. This had the effect of creating more durable bonds of loyalty and mutual interest, making for a remarkably robust structure. So it was to be among Democrats in Chicago thereafter until nearly the end of the twentieth century. Bosses would come and go, but like a corporation or a great idea, the Sullivan organization, or rather its descendant, endured.

This was a remarkable achievement. It brought order within a political culture that struggled for decades with the increasing contradiction between the need for organization to meet the growing demands upon government brought by relentless growth, and the simultaneously expanding opportunities for political fragmentation. Overcoming and adapting to depression, industrial unrest, assassination, brawls in the city council chambers and the streets, scandals, reformist outrage, personal feuds, the tsunami of the free silver movement and the advent of William Jennings Bryan, the modern Chicago Democracy had emerged as recognizable in 1908. Of its many midwives, none would be of greater importance than Roger C. Sullivan and John P. Hopkins. It was they, more than anyone, who made it like a business.

1

"That bright young democrat"
(1861–1893)

Born into a lower middle-class family of Irish immigrants in a tiny northern Illinois town, and receiving but a basic education, Roger C. Sullivan knew restlessness that drove him at first opportunity to seek his fortune in Chicago. There his skill as a political operative, together with shrewd alliances, brought him by the age of thirty into the highest ranks of the leadership of the Democratic Party of Cook County. Not incidentally, he would also begin to create an extensive and close-knit family, and the basis for a substantial personal fortune

His father, Eugene William Sullivan, immigrated in about 1855 at age 18, from Kenmare, County Kerry, Ireland, to join his older brother, Boetious Henry Sullivan, who had arrived in Janesville, Rock County, Wisconsin, about two years earlier. The brothers emigrated as soon as they were of age to seek economic opportunities that were not available in post-famine Ireland.[1]

In about 1857, Eugene married Mary O'Sullivan, also from Kenmare, who though only sixteen years of age came to America originally to visit uncles living in Massachusetts and Illinois. Her family was, by the standards of nineteenth century Irish Catholics, well off; when her brother Roger O'Sullivan died in 1876, he left the handsome sum of fifty pounds sterling to "my sister Mary Sullivan in America" (perhaps her share of the family property). Sadly, as was often the case of immigrants from Europe in this era, Mary never returned to Ireland.[2]

After a short stay in Janesville, Eugene and Mary set up house in the Belvidere area, and it was in nearby Harvard, Illinois, during the summer of 1859, that their first child was baptized as Boetious Sullivan (an old family name, traditionally bestowed upon the eldest son). About two years later, on February 3, 1861, their second child,

Eugene Sullivan (courtesy Sullivan Family).

15

Roger Charles, was born in Belvidere. Over the next years, seven more children arrived (John, Kate, Eugene, Mark, Maurice, Mame, and Frank), and the family circle was broadened still further when Eugene's younger brother Timothy emigrated from Ireland to the area in about 1862 to begin his own large family.[3]

In 1859, Belvidere was an energetic place that sat on the railroad line and boasted 2,500 residents served by 40 stores, four banks, five hotels, a flour mill, nine churches, a female seminary, two Union schools, a print office, and a brewery. From all accounts, Eugene Sullivan enjoyed a modest prosperity, working first as a section hand on the railroad, followed by stints as a tax collector (something that suggests at least a modest political involvement) and as a notions and linen merchant, peddling goods from the old country over a route that extended back to Janesville. He did well enough to acquire property over time, including a building on a main artery where he operated a tavern with the family living quarters on the second floor. There is very little information about young Roger other than that he was educated in the local public schools and worked at odd jobs in town and on neighboring farms. Later when he became famous there were those who recalled that he was just like all the other boys—"the usual type of boy, with a boy's fun-loving spirit, a keen fertile brain," while others remembered him as "the typical village boy of poor parents [*sic*], bright and quick to learn, but carefree and rollicking." There is also one interesting account that offers a glimpse into his developing personality. "Roger was always a scrapper," a schoolmate recalled many years later. In those days the boys of the town were divided into north-side and south-side "gangs," based upon which side of the Kishawaukee River they lived. Roger, one of the leaders of the south-side boys, was known for always being willing to stand up for his side and for being very good in a rock fight.[4]

Mary Sullivan (courtesy Sullivan Family).

But the Sullivan family was not a brood of hooligans. Eugene enjoyed a respectable status and his eldest son Boetious studied law in Milwaukee and with local attorney Charles E. Fuller, while also teaching school in Argyle, Illinois. By 1880, Boetious had moved to homestead and begin an eminent career in the Dakota Territory. Meanwhile, Roger's spirit and intelligence attracted the attention of his parish priest, Father Patrick McGuire, who employed him as a driver to tend his four horses, among other chores, at the parish house for $5 a month plus board. It was an experience that may have revealed itself over the years in Roger's precise use of logic and structured language that far exceeded what he might have been expected to learn in the local schools. It also was one source of the strong religiousness that was to characterize his life. Later, Sullivan would admit to his friends that his association with Father McGuire "greatly fashioned" him. After completing school, Roger substituted as a teacher for Boetious, but apparently was not impressed with the low status, poor pay, and uncertain future of the educator. About 1879, at the age of seventeen, he hitchhiked to Chicago (to save the cost of a railroad fare), supposedly completing the last leg of his journey on top of a load of hay a farmer was taking to market.[5]

Already a bustling town with a population of over a half a million, the Windy City must have been an impressive place for the young man from rural Illinois who would live to see it grow by nearly six times to almost three million souls. One contemporary observer adroitly captured its boomtown spirit: "First in violence, deepest in dirt; loud, lawless, unlovely, ill-smelling, irreverent, new; an overgrown gawk of a village, the 'tough' among cities, a spectacle for the nation." Fully recovered from the Great Fire of 1871, it was now well on its way to becoming the nation's second

Roger Charles Sullivan, 1872 (courtesy Sullivan Family).

city and the metropolis for a great American hinterland that was extending ever west to the Rockies and south to the Gulf Coast. Sitting at the heart of a widening network of railroads, it was the nation's center for meatpacking, agricultural processing, and mail order. The new technologies, too, were finding a home in Chicago with companies like American Can, AT&T, Diamond Match, Union Carbide, and the McCormick Company eventually employing tens of thousands of workers. By the early twentieth century, the city was responsible for almost six percent of the nation's total industrial production. Riding a wave for decades of unbridled growth, it was a place of seemingly infinite possibility. It was also a kind of economic Promised Land for young men seeking the opportunity to rise in society, becoming known as a "center abounding in self-made men," who in turn would come to dominate the city socially and politically.[6]

Adding to the color and excitement was the growing ethnic diversity of its people, now beginning to be profoundly affected by a new wave of southern and eastern European immigrants arriving in the thousands to join those earlier arrivals coming from places like the British Isles, Germany, and Scandinavia. By 1920, only about 24 percent of Chicagoans were classified as "American," with the remainder being either of foreign birth or the children of those born overseas. Poles, Germans, Russians, Swedes, Irish, and Italians collectively comprised nearly sixty percent of the population, and African Americans, who began arriving in larger numbers after 1910, made up an additional four percent. Chicago was, in short, a place of hustle, opportunity, and risk, ideally suited for a young man of ambition and ability like Roger Sullivan.[7]

Upon his arrival in the big city, the young man contacted Bernard "Barney" McDevitt, a former Belvidere neighbor employed as a master car builder for the West Side Street Car Company. McDevitt boarded Roger at his home, and arranged for his employment in the car barns. After a few months of apprenticeship, he became a journeyman machinist. His earnings of $32.50 a month were more than sufficient for his room at 405 Park Avenue and other expenses, and—ever the loyal son and family man—he was able to send ten dollars of his pay regularly to the folks back home. It was during this time that he first discovered his aptitude for politics, and apparently also learned a hard lesson about the importance of balancing politics with one's "bread and butter."[8]

Barney, who was also Roger's supervisor, was active in the local Republican Party. The political side of their relationship became legendary with a 1914 article in *Collier's* magazine, precipitated by Sullivan's U.S. Senate run. In 1882, so the story goes, McDevitt asked Roger to do some work for the company's candidate for the mayoral nomination in the Republican primary. Although a Democrat, young Sullivan did as he was told and soon revealed a natural affinity for the pavement-pounding and glad-handing of ward politicking. Roger made such an impression that a Democratic operative named Matt Clancy (probably Matthew C. Clancy, a successful pawnbroker and city hall employee) subsequently approached him to help in the campaign of one of the several candidates in the Democratic primary held shortly afterwards. However, the company and McDevitt were also concerned about the outcome of that contest, and they were supporting a different man. When Roger stood by his promise to Clancy, he was summarily dismissed![9]

Unfortunately, like so much that has been written about Sullivan, this account, in detail at least, is of questionable veracity. While Barney McDevitt did board Roger, was his supervisor, and was also involved in the Republican Party, 1882 was not an election year. Instead, it seems likely that it was the 1881 mayoral race to which the article refers. Also, his absence from the Chicago city directory indicates that in 1882 Roger was not in the city. There were genuine races in the Republican primary in 1881, in which he may well have participated (John M. Clark won, though he lost the election); however, there was no contest for the Democratic nomination, and the incumbent mayor, the elder Carter H. Harrison, who was renominated without opposition, would go on easily to win reelection. Whether partially apocryphal or not, the account illustrates Sullivan's quick grasp at an early age of the business of politics.[10]

Adding some substantiation to the account, we know Roger traveled west in 1882 to join his brother in Plankinton, Dakota Territory, where he worked in a lumberyard for the substantial sum of a $1.50 a day (he would claim later he went west to make money), while perfecting his own homestead claim. Boetious was already a major success, and would become one of South Dakota's leading citizens. Ironically, considering his brother's future prominence as a Democrat, Boetious was to serve as a Republican in the territorial legislature and as surveyor general of first the territory and then the state. In 1888 he traveled to Chicago as a delegate to the G.O.P.'s national convention. Like Roger, he was gifted with impressive entrepreneurial instincts, and by his death at the age of fifty-one in 1910, he had amassed a considerable fortune of his own.[11]

By 1883, Roger Sullivan was back in Chicago, boarding again at McDevitt's home and, it seems, working again at the West Side Street Car Company. He also began a course of night study at Bryant & Stratton Business College. The following year he accepted employment as a custodian at the Cook County Hospital. As such jobs were patronage appointments and were more about maintaining hospital records than cleaning floors, this suggests that his work in the 1881 election and its consequences may not have gone unnoticed. He remained almost two years and during this time either met or renewed an earlier acquaintance (the exact details are not known) with the man who was to prove to be his most profound political contact, firm friend, and partner for the next thirty-five years, John Patrick Hopkins.[12]

They had much in common: they were about the same age, both were children of Irish immigrants, both were trained as machinists, and both were driven by the American dream of power and wealth. They shared a geniality and a charisma that made them natural leaders, as well as the element of ruthlessness necessary for success in business and politics, which was, however, tempered by personal middle-class moralities. One contemporary would later speak of Sullivan during this time as "humorous, friendly, and attractively aggressive with a dash and resourcefulness," a description that fit Hopkins equally well. However, there were differences. Hopkins was a handsome, well-appointed man, later said to be the "idol" of Chicago and "of the Apollo figure," who was "finicky" about his clothes and cared very much about making an appearance. This made him, in the early years of the partnership, the perfect front man. Roger could be dapper, but vanity was never his vice. Of the two, Sullivan proved in the end to be stronger, and to be the more aggressive politically. He was also very centered upon his growing family. John, on the other hand, remained a bachelor, devoted to his sisters and mother, for whom he took responsibility when his father died eight months after following his son to Chicago. Ironically, given that John and Roger became notorious (some would even have said infamous),

as "gas kings" for their association after 1895 with the controversial Ogden Gas Company, John Hopkins, Sr., died at age 76 as a result of asphyxiation due to a faulty gas fixture in the family home at 2403 Wabash Avenue. During the earlier years of their affiliation, it was Hopkins who enjoyed the broader connections in business and politics, and he became the leading and more visible partner. Sullivan, on the other hand, increasingly focused during this period upon building his influence in the Third Ward, where he made his home. After 1904, for reasons discussed below, however, Roger would step forward into the public eye as "boss." Such was the compatibility of this political marriage that despite occasional heated discussions, there is no evidence their friendship and alliance ever weakened.[13]

John Patrick Hopkins (*Illinois Political Directory, 1899*).

John Patrick Hopkins was born on October 29, 1858, in Buffalo, New York, as the seventh of twelve children of John and Mary Hopkins (née Flynn). His parents immigrated with their two eldest daughters from Castlebar, County Mayo, to America about 1849 at the time of the famine. John Hopkins, Sr.'s work included running a saloon and a boarding house, as well as some time as a policeman. His son John attended St. Joseph's College for his primary education, completing his formal schooling at the age of thirteen. He then became a machinist's apprentice, heating rivets, and at fifteen weighmaster for the Evans Elevator Company of Buffalo. In December 1879 at just eighteen (about the same age as Roger when he migrated to the Windy City), John visited Chicago, where his older sister Anna Lydon had moved by 1870 with her engineer husband. John spent "four months looking around and arranging for a place for his family." They would join him the following November, and he would fix "up his sisters in the dressmaking business." In April 1880 he appeared at the offices of the superintendent of the Pullman Palace Car Company and within twenty minutes he was hard at work in the lumberyards. By August, his industry and personability brought him a promotion to general work in the storekeeping department of the company (the company had its own town, eponymously named Pullman, in which all services were provided for its employees living there). Just a year from his first employment, he was appointed the timekeeper in the company store, and in 1883, he moved up to become timekeeper for the entire company. It was a position of immense responsibility for a young man, but he met the challenge until resigning five years later to go into business on his own by capitalizing for $10,000 the Arcade Trading Company (later Secord & Hopkins) with Calumet entrepreneur Frederick Secord. He and his new associate eventually established grocery and general goods stores throughout the Chicago area with great financial success. In later years, like Sullivan, he would display an innate talent for business in such roles as president of the Aurora Automatic Machinery Company and director of the Chicago & Great Lakes Dredge & Dock Company (later renamed the Great Lakes Dredge & Dock Company).[14]

John was more than just an unusually successful capitalist; since his arrival in the city, he had become active in local politics, and Chicago and Cook County were places of great political opportunity. Chicago was a large town both before and immediately after the Civil War, and its business community—led by men like Potter Palmer, Marshall Field, and Joseph Medill—dominated Chicago's political life. Daily activity was principally the concern of the semi-independent party leaders of its (ultimately) twenty wards, who worked together in a loose confederation, choosing candidates and distributing patronage and favors. After about 1870, however, tremendous growth dramatically altered this comfortable arrangement. By the end of the century, the city's political culture was so complex that it has been frequently, and accurately, described as Byzantine. This complexity was enabled by a system of governance that had become virtually incomprehensible.[15]

There were, of course, the mayor and the city council of Chicago. The mayor appointed hundreds of city employees and oversaw the street department, public works, and myriad other patronage-rich agencies, and was, as a consequence, potentially a very powerful political figure. The aldermen (though known even in their own proceedings as the city council, they were officially the Board of Aldermen) always had their say about appointments in their wards and among their own followings. There were also a number of independently elected boards and offices like the Metropolitan Sanitary Board, the Board of Review (which reviewed taxes), the city clerk, and the city treasurer. Other entities like the Board of Education and the Public Library Board, while appointed by the mayor, were traditionally independent. Among the richest sources of patronage were the three park boards. The West and North Park Boards were appointed by the governor of Illinois, while the South Park Board, thanks to the curious reasoning of the state legislature in 1869 (the General Assembly always treated Chicago as a private preserve), was appointed by the twenty Cook County judges. The judges themselves also formed a political nexus of considerable influence. Additionally, there were other county officials, including the county commissioners, the sheriff, and the county clerk. Also, each of the suburban towns had its own political hierarchy. Added to all of this were township officials and the various state authorities, including the state's attorney and the state representatives and senators from the city and Cook County. At the top of the heap was a federal layer of congressmen, tax collectors, inspectors, and most important of all (in terms of jobs), the postmaster of Chicago.[16]

Further contributing complexity was the ongoing influx of immigrants, who tended to settle in their own enclaves. Among these, the Irish (like, of course, Sullivan and Hopkins) were most politically successful. With the advantages of having come to America relatively early, of being English speakers familiar with representative institutions, and of celebrating traditions of collective political activity rooted in an ancient resistance to English rule, their importance in politics and government outweighed even their considerable numbers. Indeed, as the historian John Allswang has concluded, the "older" ethnic groups, including the Germans and Scandinavians, but most particularly the Irish, were to be dominant in Chicago politics through the 1920s. "Newer" ethnicities like the Italians and those from the Slavic areas of southern and eastern Europe (which began to predominate in numbers of immigrants after about 1886), generally did not fully organize themselves politically until the 1920s. Instead, while each of these groups and their leaders might cling together socially, they generally voted in conformity with national and local patterns without much reference to ethnicity. There were exceptions, of course, most notably Anton Cermak, who although of Czech or Bohemian descent, would command a considerable personal following and become an important player in, and ultimately head of, the Chicago Democratic organization. Similarly, Adolf Kraus, also an important leader, based his strength in the Jewish-German community. However, in the period in which Roger Sullivan and John P. Hopkins were most active, the Irish predominated in Chicago's political culture, and most of the members of their organization as well as many of their antagonists would share their heritage. This Irish ascendancy was further enabled by familial relationships created as a result of their tendency in Chicago to marry within the Irish community. Even factional enemies could find themselves related by blood or marriage, adding a private and largely unrecorded dimension to the city's politics.[17]

The end result was a political culture that quickly became diffuse with hundreds of private political fiefdoms, each struggling within the two major parties for place, patronage, and power. It was also a natural spawning ground for young politicians like Hopkins and Sullivan. However, mimicking the historical progress of west European feudalism (an useful point of comparison for this phase of Chicago politics) to the later development of nation states, the city's political culture gave way over time to powerful and seemingly inexorable forces of centralization that, by 1920, resulted in single dominant organizations ("machines") within the Democratic and Republican parties.

Among the Democrats the first major step in the direction of consolidation was the formation in 1881 of the Iroquois Club (the name of which may have been inspired by New York's Tammany Hall, the country's most famous political machine), chiefly through the efforts of Erskine M. Phelps. Like so many of his rising generation of Democratic politicians, he was a successful businessman, having established the prosperous shoe concern of Phelps, Dodge & Palmer. His initial concept was an organization for all of the party leadership, regardless of faction, to compete with the Union League, then the association of prominent Republicans. The Iroquois would serve as a focal point for party socializing and politicking until nearly the middle of the twentieth century. Phelps, himself, became a close ally of Grover Cleveland, and would later be loosely associated with Hopkins and Sullivan.[18]

By 1890 the forces for further centralization were attempting to coalesce. In March of that year a group of younger politicians incorporated the Wah-na-ton Club. Its name was inspired by the Iroquois and was said to have been taken from the Lakota language to mean "one who chases his foes." The club was elaborately structured, with ward commanders, a board of directors, vice presidents, and a president. Its purpose was supposedly fraternal, but it was widely understood to be a proto-Tammany or "Little Tammany," as it was labeled by its opponent, the *Chicago Tribune*. By 1891 it was under the control of a faction headed by William C. Asay, and after his fall from grace in 1895, the organization rapidly faded, having never become anything like a dominant power in the Democratic Party. Hopkins was one of the incorporators of the Wah-na-tons, and while he and Sullivan were doubtlessly disappointed by its fate, their involvement signaled their early interest in party centralization.[19]

In the quest for party power, John Hopkins enjoyed an important advantage that would serve his and his partner's interests well: he could claim a connection with the governor of New York and future president, Grover Cleveland. The contemporary Democratic political insider Edward F. Dunne (who would serve as mayor of Chicago and governor of Illinois) writes in his *Illinois, the Heart of the Nation* (1933) that Cleveland and Hopkins had been schoolmates. This is not very likely, as Grover Cleveland was twenty-one years older than John. However, Dunne underscores the broad perception in the city and state of a special bond between the two men, one that would resonate at critical moments. Indeed, during Hopkins's tenure as mayor of Chicago, the prestigious *Harper's Weekly* identified him as a "protégé" of the president, and certainly as events unfolded, John seems to have been blessed with both ready access and support.[20]

When and how this relationship was created is uncertain. It may simply have been that the young politician's energy and travel in high circles made him conspicuous as someone to be cultivated by the president. Another reasonable explanation might be found in the possible activities of the elder John Hopkins, who raised his family in Grover Cleveland's home ward in Buffalo. Saloons like his were natural centers of precinct and ward politics, and the future president in those days was doing "yeoman's service for Democracy at the polls" before becoming district attorney and sheriff of Erie County. Further, the elder Hopkins's time on the police force, which was often made up of patronage jobs and carried electoral responsibilities, also suggests some degree of political involvement. It is, therefore, quite possible that Grover Cleveland knew John's father before his talented son moved to Chicago. Without question, however, at an early date Hopkins enjoyed the regard of the Cleveland administration and this began paying off, and not just for him.[21]

Just months after his appointment as Cook County Hospital custodian, Roger Sullivan felt sufficiently financially secure to begin a family. On February 11, 1885, he married Helen Quinlan, and they set up household at 29 N. Oakley Avenue. Their first child, born that November, was named after Roger's brother Boetious Henry (Bo changed the spelling to "Boetius" in conformity to Latin norms while attending Yale). Over the years, four daughters arrived (Mary Catherine—May 1887; Helen Marie—December 1889; Frances Josephine—September 1890; and Virginia Hopkins, apparently a tribute to John Hopkins—June 1894).[22]

Moreover, the listing for their home at 803 Fulton in the 1885 *Chicago City Directory* confirms that Roger's entire family (except for eldest brother, Boetious) had joined him in Chicago by that date—Eugene Sr., a "commercial traveler," apparently continued a sales route; John, 23, was a machinist and Eugene Jr., 20, a clerk; with the youngest children at ages 14 (Mame) and 11 (Frank) probably still in school. A *Chicago Tribune* article datelined December 15, 1884, Belvidere, Illinois, describing the "destructive flames" of a coal-shed fire that "consumed thirteen buildings" in the business district, including "Sullivan's Saloon," seems to provide the proximate reason for the timing of the family's move. The urban environment, however, may not have been the most healthful for Eugene Sr., and he passed away in August of 1886. It is ironic that the document granting Roger C. Sullivan power to administer the estate of his father, dated December 29, 1886, was signed by Thomas W. Sennott, the man Roger would defeat for the office of clerk of the Cook County Probate Court less than four years later. When his mother Mary O'Sullivan Sullivan died in 1893, Roger's signature would be on the Cook County Probate Court documents as clerk.[23]

In 1887, Sullivan was able to resign his job as custodian to accept an appointment as a federal gauger—an office to regulate the quality and production of liquor. In 1889, he moved up to become a federal deputy tax collector. The Sullivan family continued to establish themselves in the area, and the *Chicago Tribune* (October 24, 1888) included a building permit issued to an "R.C. Sullivan" to construct two 2-story duplexes (costing $4,000) at No. 512 Warren Avenue that became the homes of his mother until her death and other members of the family at least through 1910.[24]

John Hopkins in the 1880s also had a more immediate patron than Cleveland in his employer, George M. Pullman, president of the Pullman Palace Car Company. John's quick ascent was based upon his employer's recognition and approval of his special competencies. For years John resided in the more luxurious section of Pullman, the company town, and generally, he followed Pullman's lead in local politics in the Citizens Party and even the Republican Party, being elected in 1885 as the treasurer of the township of Hyde Park for a term. Pullman's good will extended to a secret agreement to provide a rebate on the rent for four stores in a Pullman building for John's grocery business.[25]

However, "sometime in 1888," there was a falling out with Pullman. Though Hopkins had threatened to resign earlier, reportedly over matters of employee relations, this rift was more serious and permanent. In part, it stemmed from the company's reneging on the Arcade agreement, in part from work for Cleveland in this election year, which would help bring the usually Republican Hyde Park in for the president. Doubtlessly, too, a major cause was simply because John chafed from the restrictions of working under a man who "was pompous ... who could never see any viewpoint but his own"—especially as Hopkins "was the only man in Pullman, who dared call his soul his own!" Though still living in his former employer's town (he would move shortly to nearby Kensington, sometimes called "Bum-town," which was now the site of his main store), Hopkins would demonstrate his new independence by becoming a leader of the movement for the annexation to Chicago of Hyde Park—an idea George Pullman loathed.[26]

In the 1880s and '90s the city of Chicago was engaged in extensive territorial expansion to match its new economic growth and regional dominance. In all, almost 154 square miles were added in this period, including such towns and villages as Gano, Washington Heights, and Norwood Park. It was in the spring of 1889, however, when the opportunity arose for the greatest annexation of them all, comprising nearly 124 square miles. Eyeing greedily the towns and townships of Hyde Park, Lake View, Lake, Jefferson, and parts of Cicero were a cadre of Chicago boosters led by the *Chicago Times* and backed by most of the other newspapers, and they were more than matched in their enthusiasm by local community leaders who saw economic and political opportunity in joining the big city. Others, like the officeholders of the selected areas, were as a group understandably less enthralled at losing their positions.[27]

Hyde Park, directly south of Chicago, was the most tempting prize, with 49 square miles and a rich tax base that included the town of Pullman and the Pullman Company. In April 1889, Hopkins and others began their public work for annexation. Quoted for the first time extensively in any newspaper, John proclaimed the movement to be irresistible: "Opposition is dying out!" Moreover, he dismissed the known opposition of George Pullman as simply a ploy to keep the car builder's taxes low and to maintain hegemony over the township. Subsequently, he directly condemned Pullman for what he claimed were threats against employees and even dismissals for any support of the cause.[28]

Hopkins was not the only leader in Hyde Park, but he was important. He was one of twelve of the "substantial citizens" at the initial meeting of residents on May 3, where representatives were chosen to confer with committees from the other towns and townships. He then served as the representative of the twenty-second precinct (Pullman) for a joint convention on May 11. There he offered the resolution to create an executive committee. He declined a nomination to be its chair, but did agree to sit as one of its members. Though the committee would be pared down at the next meeting, and Hopkins was one of those who withdrew, he would help oversee the campaign in Hyde Park.[29]

In conformity to a recent state law allowing for local elections on the issue of annexation, the executive committee petitioned Judge Richard Prendergast of the Cook County Court to schedule a referendum. Although bitterly opposed by the anti-annexationists backed by George Pullman (but no longer by most local officials, who were placated by a provision that allowed each town temporary continuances of local control, including the election of independent assessors, collectors, supervisors, and clerks until 1900), the judge ruled in their favor and the election was held on June 29. It was a landslide, with 62 percent of the voters supporting the propositions. However, in the twenty-second precinct, Hopkins's special responsibility that included parts of Pullman, the vote was but 51 for annexation to 301 against (such was the company's power). Following a lawsuit that eventually ended up before the Illinois Supreme Court, the election results were at last implemented later in the year.[30]

Sullivan's role in the annexation movement was not reported. However, it is difficult to imagine that he did not take part. What is clear is that this was a decisive moment in the political careers of both men. Hopkins was soon selected to serve on the Cook County

Democratic Central Committee, and in 1890 he became vice chair of the County Executive Committee. At the 1889 County Democratic Convention in October, he was elected as one of the assistant secretaries, and in 1890 he was appointed Democratic campaign chair for city and county, a role he performed until 1892, suggesting an appreciation of his work during the annexation effort. But it was at the County Convention of 1890 that it first became apparent that a potent new force was at large in the party.[31]

By this point, the Hopkins/Sullivan crowd had their own organization of a sort, and one that was not centered upon the career of any member. They called it the Nectar Club in praise of a brand of beer being bottled by one of the members and likened to "the fabulous drink of the gods." As later recounted, there were eleven initially enrolled, mostly young men who were immigrants or of immigrant stock, mostly Irish, and all marked for commercial and political success. Besides Hopkins and Sullivan, the club comprised Col. John Sidney Cooper, who made a fortune first in a teaming business, then in street cleaning (for which he was granted for a period a monopoly in the city), and finally in horse dealing; Daniel Corkery, who became a millionaire in the coal business, and was very prominent in Irish-American activities; and William Charles Walsh, educated at Chicago University and the University of Notre Dame, U.S. mail contractor after 1868, and twice appointed Cook County jury commissioner. The younger members included Frank J. Gaulter, a businessman who served terms as clerk of the circuit court and president of the Cook County Democracy marching club; Stephen D. Griffin, who became clerk of the superior court, clerk of the board of review, clerk of the sanitary district, supervisor of the school census, and later in the 1920s, chair of the Democratic state committee; and William G. Legner, a German-American newspaperman and brewer responsible for the club's name. At the time he headed the West Side Brewing Company, which became part of the City of Chicago Consolidated Brewing Company in existence between 1890 and 1919. When Prohibition arrived in 1920, he was head of the Conrad Seipp Brewing Company, which transitioned into the business of making ice cream. Sullivan had worked with him as deputy collector of internal revenue, and Legner would later honor his friendships with Sullivan and Hopkins by naming his eldest son "Roger Hopkins." Legner regularly served on the Democratic county committee. Others were Frank Stuyvesant Peabody, who entered the coal trade in 1881 immediately after graduation from Yale and would become one the most important coal magnates in the nation, while also remaining active in Democratic politics (although Peabody repeatedly refused nomination for public office); William Henry Rehm, who worked his way up to become president of National Brewing Co., and who was destined to become a wealthy banker as president of the Cosmopolitan State Bank, and director of the Continental Illinois Bank and Trust Company (later he would accept appointment to one of the park boards); and Fred Secord, a pharmacist who was Hopkins's grocery business partner, and also established a chain of pharmacies throughout the city.[32]

The Nectar Club would endure until at least 1898. After 1894, it generally met in the Monroe Restaurant, owned by Hopkins and Secord "on Monroe Street just east of Clark Street." The building featured an eating establishment on the lower floors, but upstairs there were large and small dining rooms that were perfect for meetings, poker games, and other manly activities in which the membership of the club found pleasure and satisfaction. In 1898, a fire broke out at the eatery, and though rebuilt, it went into receivership in 1901 and was sold.[33]

Backed by this circle (with one very important exception), as well as by most South Side Democrats, Hopkins began a campaign in the late summer of 1890 for the nomination for sheriff of Cook County. This was a breathtaking leap—some, like the Wah-na-tons, felt it was too breathtaking for one so relatively young—from his last public office as Hyde Park township treasurer; the job as sheriff was, with its massive patronage, perhaps the second most desirable position after the mayor of Chicago in both city and county. Nor was Hopkins's candidacy spurious. Even before his work in the annexation movement, he was rated a man of respect among important Democratic leaders who first noticed him during the 1888 races and his valiant (but vain) effort that year to unseat one of their number as a delegate to the national convention. The Republican *Chicago Tribune*, for instance, counted Hopkins as the leading contender up to the eve of the convention, reporting him to be the choice of the party leadership. Others like the Democratic *Chicago Times* were not so certain, and they were booming Frank Lawler, a former mailman, liquor dealer, alderman, and a retiring three-term congressman.[34]

Lawler was an imposing political figure with a wide personal following on Chicago's West Side based in large measure upon his custom of attending as many funerals as possible. Recognizing his principal opponent's strength, Hopkins at one point made a special journey to Washington, D.C., where Lawler was visiting, and proposed an accommodation with himself taking the shrievalty nomination, and Lawler running for county clerk. Lawler turned him down cold, claiming that the presence of too many Irishmen on the ticket would sink it at the polls. The ethnic division of the nominees was of real concern this election year, and Lawler's fears were not unique. With any deal out of the question, both men strived mightily to influence the primary elections held to elect the delegates by touring the wards to meet with various coteries of leaders. In small ways, this became ugly, particularly as the Lawler forces were claiming that Hopkins was the candidate of Mike McDonald, a notorious gambling figure who in the past had dabbled in politics as a supporter of the elder Carter Harrison and helped future United States Senator William Lorimer get his start in the Republican party. Beyond the accusations, there is no further evidence of any close association between this notorious figure and Hopkins. For all of the energy of the candidates, however, the results of the primary to choose the delegates were unclear.[35]

Thus, when the convention started on September 30, 1890, at the North-Side Turner Hall, it promised to be a boisterous affair with an ambience enhanced by the many colorful characters present, boasting nicknames like "Little Fly," "Hinky Dink," and "Bull," joined by numerous "Reds." The forty policemen within the hall could barely keep order, while outside mounted officers struggled to contain and control the crowds. Hopkins packed the galleries, which showed no inhibitions in expressing their support with deafening cheers when the man himself appeared or if his name were mentioned. The nomination for sheriff was the first substantial order of business. Joseph Cahill of the Second Ward nominated Lawler, who was then endorsed with elaborate oratory by Alderman Edward "Sly Ed" Cullerton (identified in 1896 by the newly created Municipal Voters' League as the leader of the "gray wolves," or those thought to be corrupt on the city council). Then, following the presentation of his name by James M. Quinlan, a young attorney from the Third Ward, A.W. Green made an impassioned speech on Hopkins's behalf describing his man as "honest, brave, and fearless!" Also nominated was J.W. Richards, but it was the nominations of Hopkins and Lawler that set the convention alight. However, after the first ballot brought Lawler 261 votes to Hopkins's 86, Green rose and withdrew his candidate's name by what seemed to be prearrangement, and the convention nominated Frank Lawler by acclamation. Not all those present accepted this result; for example, a boisterous young man named Marx, posing as a delegate, was escorted forcibly to the street, all the while protesting vehemently the convention's choice for reasons that were not recorded.[36]

Hours passed, and the party's candidates for Cook County treasurer, judges of the Superior Court, and others were named (there was some thought of nominating Clarence S. Darrow for the position of county judge, but nothing came of this). Next the convention moved on to the nominations for clerk of the Probate Court. This was a coveted position, and in the weeks before the convention, there was wide speculation about as many as a dozen different men said to be interested. However, only four names were presented, and among those was Roger Charles Sullivan. He had been briefly mentioned in the newspapers as possibly running for county commissioner, but he was not the subject of anyone's public speculations for the more important position of probate clerk. He had been quietly working for the nomination for months. The first ballot gave him 140 votes, but he was second to Stephen Griffin, who attracted the support of 206 delegates. Before the second round, the two other candidates dropped out, and the final count was Sullivan 247, Griffin 195.[37]

A spirit of amity now prevailed, and Sullivan's nomination was endorsed heartily by the *Chicago Times*, which also strongly supported Lawler. The next day it praised Sullivan as "32 years old ... a contractor" (in fact he recently had assumed the title of president of the West End Building and Loan Association, an outfit he set up with a young lawyer named Edmund S. Cummings, though given his later activities he may have been also involved in contracting at this point). The paper proclaimed Sullivan to be "a man whose popularity is not confined to his own section, for he is favorably known throughout the city as a man of energy and capacities."[38]

The ease of his nomination aided by the timely withdrawal of two candidates, the importance of the office to which he was nominated (it included a significant amount of patronage with which he could barter for power and influence), and the general good feeling after the convention, make it virtually certain that Roger Sullivan received the nomination as part of an arrangement. This was facilitated no doubt by the fact that Sullivan backed Lawler rather than Hopkins for the sheriff's nomination. This was not a result of any falling out, but rather, as it was later recounted, because Lawler approached Roger for support before John decided to enter the race. Feeling obligated and recognizing the political importance of unfailingly keeping his word, Sullivan remained faithful to his pledge. It was the only certain time in the history of their relationship that Roger and John found themselves on opposite sides. There were no hard feelings, however, and Hopkins was supportive of his friend's candidacy for probate clerk throughout.[39]

Unlike John, Roger not had served in office, but any fears that might have existed about his talent for campaigning were soon dissipated when Candidate Sullivan began appearing with Lawler and others on the ticket around the city. Just as important, however, were the efforts of his political circle. As recalled years later, he told his friends: "You fellows go and up and down the city telling people that no matter how things look Sullivan is going to smash the Republican slate and win." Many found his confidence and energy impressive; the *Chicago Times*, for one, noted: "He has been making a splendid canvass." Just as significant, however, was the broad perception that Roger Sullivan was someone whose "integrity has never been questioned."[40]

These perceptions proved for once to actually matter to the voters this year. The outcomes of the November 4 elections were mixed. Incumbent Republican County Clerk Henry Wulff easily retained his job against his Democratic opponent, and Mrs. Marian A. Mulligan (widow of Col. James A. Mulligan, who organized the city's Irish Brigade during the Civil War), the Democratic choice for superintendent of schools, lost. But these were minor setbacks compared to the surprising defeat of "Our Frank" by the G.O.P.'s James H. Gilbert in a close contest that apparently turned upon issues of corruptibility. More happily, "that bright young Democrat" Roger Sullivan easily carried his race by a vote of 72,471 to 61,434 given to his Republican rival, Tom Sennott. Hopkins as campaign chair was accorded much of the credit for the generally positive outcome.

Lawler's loss signaled the beginning of his decline; in the years that followed, he would fail in subsequent attempts to become postmaster of Chicago and to return to Congress. He did manage to get himself reelected to the city council in 1895, only to die early the next year. However, while the campaign of 1890 witnessed the descent of one rival, it also brought the reemergence of former Mayor Carter H. Harrison, the most dynamic figure in local Democratic politics in recent history and a far more potent threat to the ambitions of Hopkins and Sullivan than Lawler ever could have been.[41]

Harrison was born in 1825 to a prosperous family in Kentucky. He studied law and passed the bar in his home state, but devoted most of his time to his diverse and successful business interests, one of which led him in 1855 to visit Chicago. Impressed with the city, the vitality of which matched his own, he made it his home and began investing in real estate, becoming ever wealthier. In 1870 he entered politics as a Cook County commissioner, followed by a term in Congress (where he proposed an amendment to limit the president to a single six-year term and making the retiring chief executive a senator for life). In 1879 he was elected to the first of four successive two-year terms as mayor, during which he waged a strong but unsuccessful fight for the Illinois governorship. He retired in 1887, in part because election scandals that had little to do with him personally undercut the chances for victory. For the next two years he became a world traveler, and upon his return in 1889, he agreed to chair the October 1890 county convention. Harrison was known for his strong opinions and irascibility. Nicknamed "the Eagle," he inspired passionate positive and negative emotions—Joseph Medill, the legendary publisher of the *Chicago Tribune*, judged that Harrison's chief personality trait was his "colossal egoism" (and this was just after the Eagle's death!). Now in 1891, he decided it was time to return to the mayor's office.[42]

The problem was that the incumbent mayor, Dewitt C. Cregier, was a Democrat who was performing reasonably well in office. Like so many political figures in the city, he was born elsewhere, in his case New York City. He came with skills as a mechanical engineer, and became Chicago's Designing Engineer and then Commissioner of Public Works. In 1886, he was superintendent of the West Division Street Car Railway, where Sullivan had worked earlier. Originally loosely associated with Harrison (though apparently there were no personal affections), he displeased many of the Eagle's followers by ignoring them in his appointments. What emerged was a situation remarkably analogous to that confronted by the Republican Party in 1912, with Harrison playing the role of Theodore Roosevelt, the celebrated former chief executive determined to regain office, and Cregier as William

Howard Taft, the former minion equally dedicated to retaining his party's nomination. Just as would occur in 1912, the established leadership rallied to the incumbent, while popular support fell to the challenger.[43]

Hopkins and Sullivan were firmly embedded in the regular leadership and stood behind Cregier. Hopkins now wore the grand title of president of the Cook County Democracy or head of the party's famous marching club, known for their uniforms of dark suits, white ties, and top hats (these would be updated over the years). Roger served upon its executive committee. John's job had, of course, no governing function—it only made him an *ex officio* member of the county executive committee from which he had recently departed after a term—but it spoke volumes about his and his partner's popularity among the party faithful. Over the course of the next two years, he became the party's ceremonial face, and would be prominent in such affairs as the elaborate welcome back to Chicago in the spring of 1891 of his friend, Illinois' newly elected senator, John McAuley Palmer. For his part, Sullivan as probate clerk stood behind the county executive committee and declared for the mayor.[44]

What followed was a lively campaign for delegates to the Chicago city convention. Managing Harrison was Adolf Kraus, city drainage commissioner and leader of the Jewish community, but his most influential supporter was Frank Lawler. "The Eagle" and "Our Frank" made speeches to large and enthusiastic crowds throughout Chicago. Cregier also ran a spirited campaign, and counted among his ranks the Iroquois Club, the Wah-na-tons, the city Democratic executive committee, John M. Palmer, and Clarence S. Darrow (who would eventually become the most famous attorney in the United States, but who at this point was an important local Democratic figure, included in most conventions and meetings).[45]

The primaries held on March 20 seemed to signal a clear Cregier victory. At least his people said so. But the Harrison crowd cried fraud. One piece of good news for both Hopkins and Sullivan was the landslide vote given to the mayor by Hyde Park, at this time their primary political base. At the convention, the parallels to what would later transpire during the famous 1912 presidential election became even more apparent. The Harrison forces claimed that machine tactics were being used to give disputed delegations to Cregier. "Boss Hopkins" (this was the first time the title was ever bestowed by the press either sarcastically or seriously upon either John or Roger, and it was a sign of their growing influence) was given some of the blame (or credit), for it was he who led a successful effort to keep Harrison from being allowed to enter the hall. As a result, 47 of Harrison's 99 delegates withdrew—as had been rumored for weeks they would do—even before the balloting, making the results inevitable. The mayor was renominated by a vote of 311 to 52. The Harrison delegates by then had gathered at Uhlich's Hall to the accompanying sounds of a pre-arranged brass band. They proceeded to unanimously proclaim their hero as the true "regular" Democratic nominee.[46]

Now things began to echo more closely the disastrous 1860 national elections; besides the two Democratic nominees, and the previously nominated Republican, Hempstead Washburne, an important fourth candidate with a name confusingly similar to that of the G.O.P.'s man was already in the field. This was Elmer Washburn, formerly warden at Joliet State Penitentiary, Chicago chief of police, federal secret service man, and currently president of the Stock Yard Bank. He was being run by the "Citizens Party." This moniker had been used over the years by various supposed reform efforts, but was sported now by a group created in February by such "silk stockings" as Potter Palmer, Marshall Field, and P.D. Armour, operating through the Union League. It represented the last substantial attempt of several over the years by the city's old elite to regain control over local politics and supposedly bring clean and efficient government (and reduced taxes). Washburn lacked in neither financial resources nor in publicity.[47]

The short election race was, as expected, intense. All sides engaged in vituperation and slander, but Harrison directed most of his fire at Cregier, Cregier towards Harrison, Washburn against both Democrats, and Washburne against all comers. Things became ugly enough that at one meeting Harrison literally was pelted with mud! Cregier was declared incompetent with shady connections, while his forces claimed that "the Eagle" was connected through Lawler to Charles Yerkes, whom nobody liked because he ran most of the street railways, which were felt to be uncomfortable, inconvenient, and a source of corruption.[48]

Mayor Carter H. Harrison, Sr. (Library of Congress LC-USZ62-134211).

The results were quite close. Washburne, the Republican, won with 46,967 votes, or 28.8 percent; Cregier came in second with 46,588 votes, or 28.6 percent; Harrison took 42,931, or 26.4 percent; Elmer Washburn was given 24,027 votes, or 14.8 percent; and the Socialist-Labor candidate, Thomas Morgan, tallied 2,376 votes, or 1.5 percent (all percentages round up). The Harrisonites maintained that the election was stolen by a nefarious collusion between the Cregier crowd and the Republicans through their control of the election judges. For their part, Mayor Cregier's supporters dismissed Carter Harrison as a mere "Benedict Arnold."[49]

In the end, what mattered more even than the loss of the mayor's office to the Republicans was that the Democratic Party was rent asunder into acrimonious factions that now must be reunited. After passions cooled, the regular and Harrison executive committees of the Chicago and Cook County Democracies appointed a reconciliation panel to include representatives from both camps. Among those serving were John P. Hopkins and Adolf Kraus. In August the Joint Committee presented a new party constitution. It eliminated the separate City and County Central and Executive Committees and created a new, more accessible and inclusive method of choosing the Cook County Central Committee by stipulating that elections every fall use the Australian method (secret ballot). Each precinct would select five precinct committeemen. The precinct representatives would in turn elect two ward committeemen to serve upon the central committee. The "towns," or those areas of Cook County not incorporated into the city, would be allotted one central committeeman each. No committeeman at any level could be an appointed official, and acceptance of an appointive office was tantamount to resignation. The central committee would in turn select the executive committee.

County convention delegates would continue to be elected. In the primary (also now using the secret ballot), a "regular" ticket of candidates was to be presented by the precinct committees, but any of these could be challenged by anyone with the backing of fifty local Democrats in good standing, who would pay a proportional measure of the cost of the election.[50]

This charter for the "United Democracy of Cook County" attracted almost universal support, and in short order it was ratified by both the Cook County and Chicago executive committees. Frank Lawler "aided materially in quieting" such opposition as existed among the irreconcilables in the city party who were disinclined to forgive what they believed was Cregier's stolen nomination. Adolf Kraus and Hopkins among others also brought their influence to bear. This irenic spirit found further expression in a more-or-less equitable division between the Harrison men and the regulars of candidates for the upcoming county elections, a division ratified by the September 26 county convention (elected under the old rules).[51]

Things became somewhat confused as the primary to select precinct committeemen and to ratify the new constitution was scheduled to be held simultaneously with the general election. Unity, however, did prevail, and even Carter H. Harrison took the stump to appear with many of the same men he had so recently excoriated. However, the results were disappointing. Only two Democrats won: Jonas Hutchinson, who also was nominated by the Republicans, and a single candidate for the drainage commission. Some blamed low Democratic turnout, which was even lighter for the primary and ratification. The new constitution was, however, handily endorsed, failing only in the Eleventh Ward to gain a majority. Interestingly, some cited the introduction of the secret ballot as frightening voters away because of their unfamiliarity with its use. Still, the Democratic Party was restored, and with it came an enhancement of John P. Hopkins's position and therefore that of Sullivan.[52]

Accordingly, 1892 was to be the year in which the two partners emerged as major local political leaders. The immediate occasion for this was their local participation in Grover Cleveland's bid to return to the White House. Roger especially would benefit, becoming for the first time a figure publicly recognized as a political sachem in his own right.

As the New Year dawned, it was not written in stone that Grover Cleveland would be the Democratic presidential candidate. The former chief executive was at first of mixed emotions about making the run. He knew that many eastern Democrats had not forgotten how as governor of New York, he backed significant reduction of the tariffs—something they opposed as harmful to their business interests—while most western Democrats were antagonized by his public opposition to the free coinage of silver, an issue of growing potency in the American West and South. Further, there were other candidates afield. Chief among these was Governor David B. Hill of New York, a former Cleveland associate, who unlike the ex-president was truly a man of many sentences but few convictions.[53]

In the Illinois Democracy, the man of the hour was John Peter Altgeld, who was embarked upon an irresistible march to the gubernatorial nomination. He held ambivalent opinions about Cleveland. Although he was almost never truly dominant in the party's internal governance or in the Cook County party, Altgeld's hesitation, together with the uncertainty of Cleveland's cause, convinced the state Democratic convention, held in late April in Springfield, to hedge its bets. It instructed the Illinois delegation to vote for Senator John M. Palmer as a favorite son. Palmer repeatedly expressed his friendship for the former president and the majority of the 48 chosen were Cleveland men, including Palmer's allies and friends, John P. Hopkins (in the First Congressional District), who first had worked with the senator during the elections of 1888, and Roger C. Sullivan (in the Third). Underscoring the ambiguity of the state convention was its adoption of a platform that included a plank in favor of the free coinage of silver, something, of course, that Cleveland opposed.[54]

Illinois was the second or third state in the nation in terms of political influence, and its importance was enhanced by the fact that the Democratic national convention was held—as it frequently was—in Chicago. Thus the first caucus of the Sucker State's delegation on June 18 attracted more than usual interest. It was revealed that there was a core of ten members who insisted that they all vote for Palmer as instructed. By this point the Hill candidacy had collapsed, and Cleveland was a clear front-runner. The former president's opposition now attempted to use favorite sons in as many states as possible to force multiple ballots and stop the Cleveland bandwagon. Hopkins, for one, was having none of it. He explained his position in practical political terms: "We are for Cleveland because he is strong in Illinois. It may be selfish of us to say so, nevertheless it is a fact." Palmer, the object of the dissident delegates' "affections" in his own state, was even more emphatic in arguing against obeying the state convention's instructions to vote for him. Using slightly distorted reasoning, he explained that the state body actually supported Cleveland all along, but wanted his own name presented only if no "eastern man" were nominated![55]

The Illinois dissidents, and most notably Congressman Lawrence B. Stringer, labored mightily, making the argument that Cleveland could not be elected. It was reported that many delegates in fact wavered, but were kept in line by the strident efforts of Hopkins (now an assistant sergeant at arms of the convention), Sullivan, and Palmer. The trio, when called in to confer with the former president's campaign manager, William C. Whitney, made clear they expected the credit for bringing Illinois over, as well as the right to be consulted in the distribution of "lucrative offices."[56]

They kept their part of the bargain: when the balloting began, Illinois gave all 48 votes (the unit rule being invoked) to Grover Cleveland. The final tally was Cleveland, 617½; Hill, 114; and 103 for Horace Boise of Iowa. Now came Illinois' reward. Nominated for vice-president was the chairman of the state delegation, former Congressman and Assistant Postmaster General Adlai E. Stevenson of Bloomington. As a westerner generally supportive of the free coinage of silver, he was a good choice to placate those uncomfortable with Cleveland's conservatism on the issue. In addition, he would help carry an important state. At the request of the Cleveland managers, Roger Sullivan served with four others as a steering committee to manage the vice-presidential vote.[57]

As the campaign began, John and Roger's heightened status became ever clearer. Shortly after the national convention, Sullivan put in an appearance with others before the County Executive Committee, now chaired by Hopkins, to discuss how best to win the local elections in November. It was concluded that an early Cook County convention meeting August 20 would help maintain the current spirit of harmony and ensure that only the "best" candidates were selected. Just a week before the county gathering, the Cook County Central Committee conferred further on the question of the ticket with "prominent and active Democrats," again including Roger Sullivan. A committee of twenty-five was appointed as an advisory body, with both Sullivan and Hopkins as members. Its report never became fully public, but a full slate was produced, save only a candidate for state's attorney. This was an issue of some controversy, as the man in the lead for this nomination was Jacob Kern, a rising star of the party currently occupying the office of city attorney, whom the committee had originally opposed, apparently because he was disliked by Governor Altgeld and because of corruption in office. His followers threatened war, and in an effort to achieve peace no recommendation was made. In the end the convention nominated Kern while accepting all of the committee's choices except one candidate for county commissioner.[58]

In the event, 1892 was a Democratic year. Cleveland won Cook County by over 30,000 votes, and virtually all of the Democratic county ticket was elected by substantial pluralities. This inspired euphoria, and the party held a massive celebratory march that supposedly included 100,000 Democrats and 300,000 spectators. More importantly, the election seemed to encourage the centralization of authority in the party, which at this point served the interests of both Hopkins and Sullivan. Hopkins went so far as to predict that the Democratic organization could be made as effective as Tammany Hall (the famous Democratic machine that dominated New York City for decades).[59]

Within days of this interview, on December 11, Hopkins and Sullivan were parties to what was supposed to be a secret meeting of leading Democratic operatives and officials at the Great Northern Hotel. John was one of the fourteen who issued the invitation, and Roger was one of the more than 100 who attended. Prominent names included Johnny Powers, Walter S. Bogle, Jacob Kern, Edward Cullerton, Thomas A. Moran, Alfred S. Trude, and William Loeffler. Moran did much of the speaking, and explained that their purpose was to discuss the creation of an "auxiliary Democratic organization," that would expand and "perfect" the circle of the party's influence and would make possible continued victories by "vigilance, discipline, and fair dealing," through the selection of good candidates. The majority present, who argued that the voters would not accept a Chicago Tammany, was unimpressed and shouted down the idea of an auxiliary organization. Among the other ideas that were floated in its place were increasing the number of committeemen in each ward to help "keep close to the voters." There was also a consensus that party loyalty should be the basis of all rewards and that patronage should never be given to someone "who had not been a worker in the ranks or who was not identified with some recognized democratic [sic] organization." In the end, however, it was merely agreed to appoint a committee of 21 to find ways to strengthen the county central committee. This group in fact never met, and the energy to create a single centralized political machine dissipated, if only temporarily, but it was clear that Hopkins, Sullivan, and their allies were already thinking in those terms. It would, in fact, take them another fourteen years to achieve this goal.[60]

One immediate source for the relative failure of the cause of consolidation was implied in the conspicuous absence from the Great Northern Hotel conclave of Carter H. Harrison. Nor were any of his major supporters like Adolf Kraus, Frank Lawler, and the West Side leader Robert Emmett "Bobby" Burke present. Harrison had, it was true, rejoined the "regular" Democrats, supported Cleveland, and allowed this meeting to pass without public comment. However, he was even now building his own organization in a two-front offensive. First, in late 1891, he purchased the *Chicago Times*, which became his official mouthpiece and advocate. Second, the Carter H. Harrison Democratic Association was organized. Presented as a high-minded endeavor to encourage good government, it was in fact a Harrison political combination that was to evolve eventually into the bitter factional rival of the more informal organizations of Hopkins and Sullivan.[61]

Carter Harrison's immediate goal was to secure the Democratic nomination for mayor, and in early 1893, his campaign was fully active with Adolf Kraus reprising his role as manager. This time special attention was paid to stoking the popular passions for the Eagle at the ward level through the local branches of the massive Harrison Democratic Association, and soon his momentum began to assume the appearance of irresistibility. This was of great concern to many regular Democrats like Hopkins and Sullivan, who feared the charismatic Carter Harrison could become dominant in the party should he win—a possibility that was becoming ever more likely. Moreover, there were larger concerns; Harrison's relationship with Cleveland had always been little more than lukewarm, but now the two men fell out over the silver issue, to which the president was vehemently opposed. As leader of the Cleveland wing of the local party, it fell to Hopkins, backed by Sullivan, to assume leadership of the effort to defeat the former mayor.[62]

But whom should they choose to run? Dewitt Cregier was making noises about trying again, but he was given little chance of victory. Other names were discussed, but eventually Washington Hesing, editor of the *Staats-Zeitung*, and former deputy sheriff of Cook County, was given the nod. Hopkins became his manager, while Sullivan used his special political magic to work the wards. But as the Harrison bandwagon rolled on, even Walter Bogle and Edward Cullerton, who generally were friendly with John and Roger, knew a winner when they saw one and stood with the former mayor. Rumors began circulating that Hopkins was in desperation, contemplating a search for some other man to back. When the primaries were held on February 27, 1893, the Harrison crowd crowed victory, claiming at least three-quarters of the delegates.[63]

They became so confident that they did not even bother to select their own candidate for the chair of the convention held the following day at the Central Music Hall. Nor were they especially aggressive in the credentials committee, where some Hesing delegates were seated (Sullivan was appointed to a committee of three to assure all those claiming to be delegates were present). Three candidates were nominated: Harrison, Hesing, and Cregier. Hopkins conferred frantically in the hallways with leaders, while Sullivan, chair of the delegation of the Third Ward, roamed the floor. What appeared to be a hail–Mary strategy emerged when Cregier spoke before the vote in an apparent attempt to stampede the delegates. He claimed Harrison to be a "friend," but also one who, because he broke his word to him by running, could not be trusted. He was repeatedly interrupted with catcalls and shouts and was only able to finish because of the intervention of Harrison leader Cullerton. It was no contest. Harrison won with 531 votes to Cregier's 93 and Hesing's 57. Even in Sullivan's Third Ward, eight of its fourteen votes were cast for the former mayor (with the remainder going for Cregier, perhaps indicating that the earlier rumors about Hopkins and company seeking another candidate might have been true). In Hopkins's home ward, the Thirty-Fourth, nine of twenty-one votes were for Harrison with twelve for Cregier.[64]

The Republicans nominated George B. Swift, and yet another Citizens Party, which was formed in a movement led by *Chicago Daily News* publisher Victor Lawson, nominated Cregier but inspired almost no support. In the first week of March, a general exodus of

Democrats to Washington, D.C., to witness the inauguration of Cleveland truncated the campaign, and neither Swift nor Cregier excited much enthusiasm with their attempts to tar the former mayor with the brush of corruption. Hopkins and Sullivan appear to have sat things out (at least publicly), which followed from their prominence as Harrison opponents and the fact that John was no longer general campaign chairman. Carter H. Harrison returned to office in triumph, winning easily with 114,237 votes to Swift's 93,148, and Cregier's unimpressive 3,033.[65]

Within weeks Hopkins and Sullivan's worst fears came to be realized as Harrison began to appoint hundreds of his followers to various offices, creating an instant "city hall crowd." His strength at the polls and his excellent organization made him so powerful that only a greatly depleted cadre of regulars remained with Hopkins and Sullivan outside of his camp. Their one unassailable source of power, however, was the increasing public support of President Cleveland, who consented to a very well-publicized interview with Hopkins at the White House during which a discussion was held about a new postmaster for Chicago. Hopkins and Sullivan wanted Washington Hesing for the job. Harrison, who had come to dislike Hesing personally, and doubtlessly wished to control the extensive patronage and local party power associated with the office, vehemently objected, and the conflict would not be resolved until the end of the year. Despite some show of perfunctory unity, chiefly at an elaborate Democratic picnic, the ongoing disputes over patronage between Harrison and the dwindling number of regulars became acrimonious.[66]

For all of that, Mayor Harrison became ever stronger within the party. The onset of the worst economic depression in American history to this point diverted the president's attention and eroded his status. Governor John Altgeld, who was generally not involved in Chicago factional issues but who was a potential obstacle to Harrison's ambitions, effectively destroyed his own political future in June by pardoning several of the anarchists condemned for the 1887 Haymarket Riot. The Columbian Exposition, for which Harrison could actually claim very little credit, redounded to his benefit as it focused positive national attention upon the city and its mayor. By early fall it was commonly understood that Harrison was intent upon taking control of the county party as a step to becoming Illinois' senator in 1895, to be followed by a possible bid in 1896 for the Democratic nomination for president or vice president. His confidence was such that he became openly disrespectful towards President Cleveland. In early October it was reported in the *Chicago Record*, and significantly reprinted in Harrison's *Chicago Times* without comment: "The most powerful political machine Illinois has ever known is gradually being formed by the merger of two forces," in reference to a meeting of minds between the mayor and Senator Palmer. Harrison forgave Palmer for his opposition, and the two most significantly agreed to oppose Cleveland's known inclination to appoint Hesing as postmaster of Chicago.[67]

Harrison's growing control of the local party became indisputable when he and his city hall crowd, now increasingly dominated by his "Big Four"—Henry F. Donovan, William C. Asay, Patrick McCarthy, and Bobby Burke (all members respectively of the county executive committee)—successfully dictated the slate of nominees for the upcoming October county convention. A meeting was held on September 16 in Corporation Counsel Kraus's office with John McGillen (chair of the county executive committee), Asay, Hopkins and others in attendance. Things were apparently sedate, but the mayor's forces emerged with their slate intact. Mayor Harrison then sought to bring John into his camp, or at least keep him from open opposition, by insisting that the executive committee of the county party give him one of the sixteen vacancies on the central committee. Recognizing his importance as a leader, Harrison explained: "Mr. Hopkins' democracy is built upon too solid of a basis to be ignored in the councils of the party." Despite some opposition from his own friends, John accepted the appointment.[68]

The October 3 primaries only reaffirmed the mayor's strength and assured his control of the county convention held the next day, which promptly nominated his choices. Hopkins and Roger Sullivan were elected to the campaign committee, which made them *de facto* members of the executive committee at least until after the election. However, any illusions the mayor might have entertained about the two were soon to be shattered when Hopkins went to Washington, D.C., to consult with the president and to urge the appointment of Hesing. Despite this, it appeared unquestionable that Carter H. Harrison was on the verge of mastering the Cook County Democratic Party and creating a single ruling organization for the first time in history.[69]

So things stood on October 28, 1893. Mayor Harrison spent the day delivering a speech before other American mayors at the fair during this, its last weekend. There was every reason for him to be content with his political progress and his personal life; he recently had become engaged to a comely lady who was not only 37 years younger, but was also a multimillionaire. That evening at about 8 o'clock found him napping, tired from his exertions at the fair, when he was called to meet an unexpected visitor. Upon entering his front hall, he confronted the caller, a deranged young man named Patrick Eugene Prendergast, who opened fire, striking the mayor with four shots. Within the space of fifteen minutes Carter H. Harrison was dead from internal bleeding, and the political future of Chicago and the Cook County Democratic Party was altered forever.[70]

2

In Power
(1893–1894)

The assassination of Mayor Harrison plunged the city into a state of despair such as it had not experienced since the death of Abraham Lincoln. The unexpected and pointless nature of the tragedy, combined with its occurrence at precisely the moment of the climax of Chicago's greatest triumph to date, the closing of the Columbian Exposition, made it especially difficult to bear. Overnight the frequently controversial Carter H. Harrison was transformed into a saint beloved by almost all. In keeping with the emotional depths stirred by the event and the dramatic proclivities of the age, a "Pageant of Grief" was planned by the city council that climaxed on November 1, 1893, with a huge procession in which over 20,000 people, representing every conceivable group in the city, marched before a crowd estimated to exceed half a million people. John Hopkins appeared as a leader of the County Democracy, while Roger Sullivan rode in a carriage as one of the delegation from the Iroquois Club.[1]

Grief-stricken though they may have been careful to appear, the leading politicians, with scarcely a pause, began plotting to seize control of the office of acting mayor now to be selected by the city council. At stake was not just the temporary position itself, but also, it was felt, some measure of influence over the oncoming county contests and the required election of a more permanent chief executive. The Democrats, not unnaturally, felt that as Mayor Harrison had been overwhelmingly elected just that spring, morally the job should fall to one of their own. The Republicans, less impressed with this particular interpretation of morality, found their confidence and justification in the fact that they enjoyed a majority of 38 to 30 on the Board of Aldermen.

On November 2, or the day after the funeral, the Republican council leadership caucused at the Great Northern Hotel, and agreed that George B. Swift would be their standard-bearer for acting mayor. Swift was 48 years old and was born in Cincinnati. He had served three nonconsecutive terms on the city council, interrupted by a stint as Commissioner of Public Works under Republican Mayor John Roche (1887–89). In his private life, he was the vice-president of the Frazer Axle Grease Company—yet another businessman politician.[2]

Leading the Democrats was Harrison's "city hall crowd," who dominated the party caucus held on November 4 at the Sherman House. They specifically requested the help of Hopkins and Sullivan in convincing the Democratic aldermen to go along with their plan—such was the pair's influence. It was agreed to back Alderman John McGillen of the Twenty-First ward, who was also chair of the county executive committee. The hope was to secure victory through parliamentary maneuver and the seduction of as many Republican aldermen as possible.[3]

Following an abortive attempt by a minority of Republican aldermen to call an early special meeting to circumvent possible Democratic machinations, the council convened on November 5. What ensued was a remarkable demonstration of the sometimes passionate nature of representative government in Chicago: things quickly devolved into the kind of anarchy more usually associated with a barroom brawl than with the supposedly somber deliberations of the people's tribunes. The moment reading clerk John G. Neumeister called the meeting to order, the council chamber echoed with shouts as both sides attempted to claim the speakership (that had to be first selected before the election of an acting mayor could proceed). The names most frequently called out were John McGillen and Republican J.W. Hepburn. Both men rushed to the front of the chamber noisily proclaiming their election based upon an inaudible viva voce vote. McGillen arrived first at the speaker's chair, where he seized "the sacred emblem of authority" (the gavel). Hepburn sought to confront McGillen but was blocked by Neumeister, who pushed him back and hurriedly called for an official voice vote. Neumeister immediately declared McGillen elected over the vociferous protest of the Republicans who responded by proclaiming Hepburn the victor.

In the confusion, McGillen began reading the Democratic resolution calling for the election of a temporary mayor, and then quickly called another questionable voice vote. As he was doing this, Alderman Swift sent the Republican version of the same resolution to Hepburn, who remained at the front of the room. Before Hepburn could begin reading, Neumeister seized the paper from his hand, angrily ripped it into pieces, and threw the shards on the floor, stamping upon them. "Maddened with rage," Swift jumped at the clerk, but such was the force of his leap that it "carried him clear over Neumeister's head." The much smaller Swift was restrained by friends from further attack. Hepburn next went after McGillen, attempting to remove him from the chair and bum-rush him from the room, but the Democrat resisted. Thereupon, Neumeister reached for some kind of weapon under his desk, but was restrained by a reporter.

Pandemonium ensued. Democratic Alderman Tom Carey, "with blood in his eye," shed his coat, and began "throwing Republicans right and left," while Alderman John "Bathhouse" Coughlin was seen swinging a chair. Alderman Stanley Kunz picked up a former councilman named Jake Miller, who was present observing, and bodily threw him over the railing. Six police guards led by an inspector rushed into the room and were ordered by several Democrats to remove Hepburn, who was immediately surrounded by a protective phalanx of six of his fellow Republicans. The police then turned their attention to the belligerent Carey, who stood coatless, spitting defiance, and brandishing a water pitcher. Swift saved the day by leaping upon the podium, where McGillen had been frantically pounding for order, and grasping the Democrat's hand in a token of unity. This had the desired effect, and amidst "blushes of shame," quiet was restored with both men remaining at the front of the room, effectively sharing chairing duties.[4]

In the relative calm, the council voted to accept motions declaring the office of mayor vacant and calling for a special election. McGillen and Swift were then nominated. The Democrats insisted upon a secret ballot (which would shield any Republican defectors), but were disappointed with the outcome of 34 votes for Swift and 33 for McGillen, with one left blank. Confusion reigned because McGillen (still acting as chair) decided that the abstaining vote meant that Swift had not received the necessary majority of the 68 aldermen. Hearing this, the Republicans immediately withdrew (overwhelming attempts to block their passage at the door), declared their man the winner, and began drawing up a bond of election. The Democrats voted to adjourn and instructed the Democratic Commissioner of Public Works to post a guard on the chambers and the mayor's office to prevent Republican seizure.[5]

This "Mexicanizing" and "Hoodlumism" of the city council, using the "Tactics of the Thug," took place even as the black crepe of mourning still adorned the chamber and the city. The untoward events unsettled even some Democrats. Tempers cooled, reason prevailed, and a mood for compromise soon emerged as Corporation Council Adolf Kraus and noted Democratic attorney Alfred S. Trude (who was especially prominent at the moment, as he was acting as chief prosecutor of the late Mayor Harrison's assassin), advised that the original secret vote had been legal and Swift elected. McGillen wanted to fight on, but found his support dwindling. On November 6, when the council came together again, by previous agreement McGillen was unanimously chosen as temporary chair to salve his pride, and by a vote of 50 to 18 Swift was officially elected (or reelected).[6]

Adding insult to injury, the Republicans the following day swept the county judicial elections. Gloom and doom briefly settled over the Democratic camp as they attempted to explain their defeat away in terms of President Grover Cleveland's growing unpopularity, the general economic crisis, its being an "off year," and a "demoralization" caused by the death of Carter H. Harrison. In truth, things were not as bad as they appeared, as the party had still won in the city of Chicago, albeit by a reduced majority, only to be overwhelmed by the lopsided vote of the towns of Cook County.[7]

It quickly became apparent that George Swift intended to seek the mayor's office permanently despite his earlier pledge to the contrary. He began appointing as many Republicans to city jobs as possible while allowing his friends to build a campaign organization. Although there was some thought that the allies of former Mayor John Roche might back Henry Wulff instead, Swift was easily nominated by his party's convention.[8]

Among the Democrats things were much more complicated. Harrison's death left the city hall crowd without an obvious leader. They were actually, in any case, little more than a collection of disparate elements that had been held together by the Eagle's charisma and success. Speculation was rife and numerous names were mentioned including the late mayor's son, Carter H. Harrison II. However, the smart money began to center upon three men: Alfred S. Trude (known as "A.S."), president of the Board of Education; Frank Wenter, president of the Sanitary District Board and leading Harrisonite; and John P. Hopkins.[9]

Of the three, Hopkins was the immediate front-runner and the one "looked upon with fear and trembling by the city hall Democrats." No one, however, wished to appear overly eager or to make himself a target for concentrated opposition, so none of the trio at first openly campaigned for the nomination. Trude flirted for weeks with both his supporters and the city. But for the rather specious reason that his choice would compel his brother George to resign and be replaced as an election commissioner by a Republican, he ultimately withdrew his name from consideration. Wenter, on the other hand, was in it to the end, and he became the great hope of the dwindling remnants of the city hall crowd and their mouthpiece the *Chicago Times*. At one point the paper hopefully proclaimed him the likely victor based in part upon the support of the important Democratic leader, Roger C. Sullivan![10]

But it was Hopkins who played the game masterfully. While admitting that "like every man in Chicago," he would not mind becoming mayor, he withheld permission to use his name until nearly the eve of the city convention (which did not prevent ward organizations forming on his behalf). This compelled the backers of the other candidates to disperse their fire. At the same time, John did his best to present himself as the choice for all Democrats, going so far, in a very public attempt to avoid factional association, as to quash an attempt by the County Democracy marching club to acclaim him as their candidate. At the heart of his appeal, however, was the perception that he could offer something for everyone through his special relationship with the Cleveland administration, which had been conspicuous in withholding federal patronage under Harrison. Even his opponents privately conceded that if he were able to secure the postmastership for his ally, the local German-American icon Washington Hesing, the contest was effectively over. Accordingly, November 15 found Hopkins in Washington, D.C., conferring with the president, who was favorable to the idea of replacing the late and hostile Harrison with his young protégé. Hesing's appointment was announced on December 27, which caused "the Germans to fall in line," and began a general, if quiet, stampede to the Hopkins camp.[11]

The opposition became desperate. Following a clear Hopkins victory in the primary on December 1, Chairman John McGillen, who was backing Wenter, attempted to appoint himself as chair of the convention. This would give him control over the credentials committee, which could, presumably, disqualify a sufficient number of Hopkins delegates to give his man the victory. However, Hopkins's support among the regulars was irresistible; McGillen was overruled in the full executive committee by a vote of 7 to 2, and the Republican *Tribune* now estimated that John could count upon 80 percent of the 624 delegates.[12]

They were not far off. Despite "strategy, artifice, threats, and all like resources" chiefly exercised in the credentials committee, the Hopkins candidacy kept gaining support. He was nominated by A.W. Green, to great applause, as a self-made success who had brought victory to the party in 1892, and as a businessman who was a friend of labor. The names of Sanitary Board President Wenter and John A. King were also presented to the convention, but when the balloting began, they received hardly a vote. At the end of the first round, but before the totals could be announced, King and Wenter's candidacies were withdrawn, and Robert Emmett "Bobby" Burke, a major city hall leader, emotionally moved to nominate John P. Hopkins by acclamation. A committee of five, including Washington Hesing, Frank Lawler (who had worked diligently against Hopkins) and others, was appointed to bring the man of the hour into the hall. Exactly two minutes and thirty seconds later, he entered and gave a very short but rousing speech that praised both President Cleveland and Harrison's memory, and concluded with the remarkably unoriginal promise of "malice towards none, charity to all."[13]

The next day he began organizing his campaign in a private meeting with Sullivan and other Democratic leaders as a preliminary to a much larger and representative gathering on December 4, at which all the factions would be represented. A close ally, former judge Lambert Tree, was appointed campaign manager, and a "field marshal" was chosen for each ward. The remnants of the Harrison faction came on board as Frank Wenter and Bobby Burke pledged their support, as did the many of the more reform-minded, like Clarence S. Darrow. Among the groups offering their endorsement was a delegation of "colored" Democrats from Alderman "Bathhouse John" Coughlin's First Ward (interesting because in this time and place African American Democrats were relatively rare). The meetings were amiable and a spirit of unity prevailed as reflected by the decision to postpone the elections for the Cook County Democratic executive committee until after a mayor was elected. This unusual unanimity was rooted in the backing Hopkins enjoyed from the Cleveland administration, his consequent likely control of the local federal plums, his own strident efforts to reach out to those who had been lately his opponents, and the equally cogent reality that the Republicans were united behind Swift in the firm expectation that the deepening economic depression guaranteed them the victory.[14]

The Democratic platform, with its call for strict municipal bookkeeping, the elimination of needless city employees, the removal of political influence from police operations, and the abolition of railroad crossings through the elevation of tracks, was virtually identical to that proposed by the Republicans. With little of substance separating the parties, the campaign was undistinguished by the extraordinary.[15]

There was an attempt to spice things up by connecting Hopkins with the pending Wilson law in Congress to lower the tariffs and supposedly affect the jobs of workingmen, but this had little apparent impact. Two days before the election, the *Chicago Tribune* sought to sway the voters with an "October surprise" by breathlessly reporting that Hopkins had helped secure a city contract to extend the "Hyde Park tunnel" for his nephew's firm, Lydon & Drews (only five years younger than Hopkins, William A. Lydon was the son of John's sister, Anna, and boasted his own political contacts, having been city assistant engineer between 1886 and 1891 while Republican Hempstead Washburne had been mayor). Supposedly the specifications were not followed, work was not done on time, and there was overcharging (all due, according to the company, to unexpected subterranean rock formations), alleged facts ignored by the city after Harrison became mayor. With only his wealth offered as evidence, Hopkins, it was implied by the *Tribune*, profited greatly from the transaction. Even worse, it was alleged that non-union labor had been utilized on this project as well as others in which he had a hand. However, the story appears to have had no effect on the voting, and it disappeared without a trace after the election. Nor was the religious issue, often powerful in urban politics, entirely ignored. Although with Chicago's large Catholic population it was always a dangerous card to play, circulars mysteriously appeared at Protestant churches emphasizing Hopkins' "Roman" and Irish heritage.[16]

Most of the real excitement was in the energy (and money) expended by both sides in the candidates' personal appearances. John, contrary to his claim that "I am no orator," was an exciting speaker who appeared to relish his contact with the public in rallies around the city. He excoriated Swift for using the police to promote his cause and for padding the city payroll. He could also count upon the vigorous efforts of his party's other stars, including Frank Wenter and "Our Frank" Lawler (but not Sullivan, who did his work behind the scenes), as the Democrats proved that, for once, they were united in fact as well as word. Swift and his campaign cohorts fought with at least equal intensity, and the outcome was never certain.[17]

Ultimately, it was party loyalty and turnout that were decisive. Though Democratic support had eroded steadily since the onset of economic downturn the previous summer, the recent county judicial elections confirmed the likely Democrat majority in the city. On December 19, 1893, Hopkins was elected mayor with 112,959 votes to 111,669 for Swift. This compared unfavorably to Harrison's plurality of 21,000 votes just eight months before, and a change of fewer than two votes per precinct would have spelled defeat. However, with the clear growth of Republican strength nationally and locally, even this slim victory was welcomed by Democrats everywhere.[18]

Within days, the mayor-elect departed for the nation's capital to confer with President Cleveland, chiefly about patronage matters. For the president, Hopkins's victory amidst the growing economic distress and his declining political base was a truly welcome event. The meeting was convivial, and on December 26, John returned to Chicago with federal patronage in hand to prepare for his inauguration the following day.[19]

It was a joyous but restrained affair. The podium was festooned with floral bouquets including one made of "blushing" roses from Mrs. Washington Hesing inscribed "The Race Is Not Always to the Swift," and another far more elaborate arrangement above the mayor's chair featuring a great sun of chrysanthemums within an enormous horseshoe from Hopkins's home ward. Mrs. Roger Sullivan, Mrs. Daniel Corkery, and Mrs. Thomas Gahan sent a white chrysanthemum chair with the floral inscription "The Rising Sun" on its back. The crowds filled the corridors and rushed the doors when they opened at 7:00 p.m.[20]

Such was the press that it required the energetic efforts of over a dozen burly policemen to put one tardy and quickly disheveled alderman into his seat. Present were such leading political allies of the new mayor as Washington Hesing, A.S. Trude, Daniel Corkery, and Roger C. Sullivan. Roger's wife, Helen Quinlan Sullivan, accompanied John's "venerable mother," Mary Flynn Hopkins, and the new mayor's sisters, Misses Adelia, Julia, and Kate Hopkins (who, with their mother, still shared a home with their brother), Mrs. Anna Lydon, Mrs. Mary Bonfield, and Mrs. Josephine McCormick, to their seats of honor in the right balcony. There was "thunderous" applause when the man of the hour arrived at 7:15 p.m. nattily dressed in a black Prince Albert coat, sporting a black necktie, and carrying a black silk hat. He and the increasingly restless crowd waited for over thirty minutes while other business was conducted before he was able, at last, to take the oath, and then turn to speak to the assemblage.[21]

His address was described as "short and simple," with an appropriately somber tone, given the growing effects of hard times upon the people in Chicago. As he phrased it, he took office with the "resolute purpose to meet as far as within my powers the demands of the situation rendered more difficult because of widespread distress in commercial and industrial affairs." This task was going to be especially challenging as the city's finances were in a mess, with a $2,719,000 deficit, and no effective system of accounting in place, facts confessed in a committee report delivered to the city council immediately before the new mayor took his oath. Accordingly, Hopkins promised to "place the finances in absolute order," and to introduce spending for only specifically appropriated purposes. With an eye to his workingman constituency, he also suggested that "useful public works" on the city's streets might be introduced to alleviate unemployment. He proposed to reform the police force by eliminating "incompetents, drunkards," those "who trespass wantonly upon the personal rights of citizens," and politics and party affiliation from hiring and promotion. Lastly, he called for an end to railroad grade crossings to spare the citizenry "murder and menace to life and limb." His speech was a success and was met with resounding cheers and applause. It was a good beginning.[22]

However, his primary concern over the next months was not to be city business at all. Instead, the new administration would be first preoccupied by the consolidation and organization of power within the party that had been implied by his nomination and his very public endorsement by President Cleveland. Hopkins, Sullivan, and their allies of mostly self-made entrepreneurs brought their business acumen to the task and by late spring a new and efficient structure was up and running. Ostensibly a campaign organization and an appendage of the County Committee, it was in fact a "machine" designed to control the Democratic Party as surely as any "trust" was designed to control a particular industry. Much of the credit for the details of its arrangements was given to Hopkins/Sullivan ally Daniel Corkery.[23]

The city's 34 wards were divided into eighteen districts, each with a headquarters under the command of a chairman and secretary. These district leaders were usually a local alderman and/or some other locally powerful Democrat. Each district was in turn divided into precinct organizations under a precinct captain. Shrewdly, those in the city cabinet who could claim their own independent political support, like City Attorney A.S. Trude, were not included as key members, which diminished the possibilities of a serious public rival to the mayor emerging. Instead, the "inner circle" was made up of loyal and seasoned political and business operatives, and counted among its number Roger C. Sullivan as well as Thomas Gahan, a member of the Railroad and Warehouse Commission; Thomas Byrne, Gahan's business partner who shared city contracts for the maintenance of "sections G and H of the sanitary canal"; John S. Cooper, a contractor who enjoyed a monopoly on the city's street cleaning; Stephen D. Griffin, clerk of the Superior Court; and State's Attorney Jacob J. Kern. Others reported to be in the alliance were City Prosecutor William Asay, Superintendent of Streets John McCarthy, and former alderman William Loeffler. In its structure, purpose, and function, it was an unabashed political "machine," which took its immediate inspiration from New York City's Tammany Hall. It was very much like similar organizations appearing elsewhere in Northeastern and Midwestern cities.[24]

Political combinations to secure power and remuneration have existed since human social and political structures became complex enough to support them. The job of politician, therefore, may well be the second oldest profession (some might find irony in this). Certainly in traditional societies shifting alliances among courtiers that were centered upon obtaining favors from the monarch characterized court affairs; the political histories of such countries and empires have been in fact focused almost exclusively on these types of intrigues. In the West, as societies became more democratic, such

Mayor-elect Hopkins (*Chicago Eagle*, 1893).

associations became more inclusive and the "modern" political machine with its roots extending down to the humblest of voters first found full fruition in the American experience. Indeed, the very nature of American politics, with its steadily broadening franchise as well as vast increases in the size and power of government, invited the creation of organized coalitions whether for a specific set of political goals or for the benefits of power themselves.

From the beginning, much to the dismay of the nation's first president, "factions" emerged nationally that were to become the political parties. Although created with ideological contexts, these parties were also "machines" in the purest sense as affiliations held together by a common goal of achieving and benefiting from office. As the system of two major parties became stable, vehicles of governmental empowerment in the United States, they in turn became the arenas of factional competition among aspiring machines and machine politicians that could be found both in the innumerable "court house gangs" in rural counties and in broader statewide and urban organizations.

However, it was in the late nineteenth and the early twentieth centuries down through the 1930s that the classic big city machines of notorious repute and infamous reputation—with their elaborate, if nebulous, hierarchy headed by an openly proclaimed "boss"—exercising, at times, nearly absolute power over urban political life came into their own. This was largely a function of the immense growth in size and population of Northeastern and Midwestern metropolitan areas fueled by industrialization and the influx of millions of immigrants from Europe and the American countryside after the Civil War. As the urban areas grew, so did the complexity of their governments, creating myriad niches for informal political alliances to arise that could be eventually welded into one or more organizations. Nowhere were these conditions more fully present than in Chicago, and, as discussed above, the forces of consolidation of these myriad associations became in the latter half of the nineteenth century the ongoing theme of the city's and Cook County's political culture.

In this context the creation by Hopkins, Sullivan, and their allies of a political organization in the spring of 1894 that sought to be a Chicago "Tammany," and, for that matter, the thwarted attempt just months earlier to achieve something similar by the elder Mayor Carter H. Harrison, was entirely consistent with the dominant trends in America's and Chicago's urban politics. In detail, the new Hopkins organization did differ initially in its formal affiliation with the Democratic Party; more usually machines were either entirely informal or merely linked together through some private club. However, in its elaborate structure based first in the precincts, then in districts made up of one or more wards, culminating in a leadership elite fronted by Mayor Hopkins, it was virtually an archetypical political establishment. This was equally true in its actual operation, which, as was the case in all machines of this type, was founded upon the most obvious of goals: winning elections to achieve the enrichment and empowerment of its membership through a profitable influence within government.[25]

The idea that the people's government could be a fertile source of remuneration and advancement was not especially shocking and was even defensible to many Americans. In this age of unfettered capitalism in which fortunes were made ruthlessly, and those who made them were celebrated as leaders and even, under the dictates of Social Darwinism, as superior beings, the application of the same capitalist principles to government did not seem inappropriate. Indeed, the machines themselves could be seen as near cousins to the "trusts" that were monopolizing production and profits in most major industries, in the process transforming the country into the world's leading economic powerhouse. Unlike the "trusts," however, machines actually engaged and arguably served to benefit the growing urban working masses.

An added and not inconsequential factor in the creation of machines in this period was the usually urban ethnic status of their creators. These immigrants often lacked the Yankee "conception of public service as a duty to be undertaken for the good of the community; they expected to be rewarded for their services." Some of this may be attributed to differing religious orientations. The native-born Protestant elite were mostly raised in a Calvinistic and pietistic tradition with an emphasis upon the imperative of personal and social perfectibility. In this view, sin might be inevitable, but never tolerable. However, many immigrants, and especially the Irish, came from a ritualistic Roman Catholic background that took a more flexible—some would say more realistic—view of man's foibles. Because sin was inevitable as a function of man's imperfect nature and of a world tainted by evil, it must be expected, confessed, and then forgiven. But there was no expectation that it could be eliminated through any agency of human endeavor (and it was futile to try).[26]

However, a certain acceptance of personal profit from government was certainly attributable to more than religion or confined just to Catholic immigrants. Indeed, according to some, it was implicitly American. Lincoln Steffens, a radical socialist and progressive critic of urban politics of the time, for whom capitalism was the root of all evil, contemptuously and adroitly articulated this attitude as founded in the belief that "there is no essential difference between the pull that gets your wife into society or a favorable review for your book, and that which gets a heeler into office, a thief out of jail, and the rich man's son on the board of directors of a corporation; none between the corruption of a labor union, a bank, and a political machine; none between a dummy director of a trust and the caucus-bond member of a legislature...."

Of course, to reformers like Steffens, all of this appeared to be self-serving and specious. However, for the immigrants, and sons and grandsons of immigrants like Hopkins and Sullivan, hungry for advancement upwards beyond their initial status near the bottom of the social ladder, the contention by comfortable middle-class reform types that there was significant difference between seeking personal economic gain in business and achieving the same thing in government remained unimpressive.[27]

And it was almost invariably the Irish (like Hopkins and Sullivan) of all the many immigrant nationalities flocking to American cities, which would organize and lead the machines. Speaking English and with traditions of political activism originating back in Ireland, they were able to seize quickly the opportunities for advancement in America's accessible governments. In Chicago, though never exceeding about 10 percent of the population, their political dominance, while never absolute, was pervasive. Indeed, the Irish-American political involvement was so omnipresent that at no point in this era could they boast anything like complete ethnic solidarity. In virtually every factional battle, Irish politicians could be found on all sides.[28]

For Roger Sullivan and John Hopkins their Irishness (both of them probably spoke with a brogue, while Sullivan was a founder of the Irish Historical Society, and on rare occasion he agreed to speak for Irish rights) unquestionably contributed greatly to the shape and success of their public careers. However, beyond the simple fact of their ethnicity was the important factor of their economic success and capitalist orientation. As early as the late 1880s, both men could be counted among the upper two percent in income of Chicago's Irish community, and this served their leadership.

As one historian has pointed out, the pair were representative of a new breed of Irish political leader that would dominate the political culture of urban America—and Chicago in particular—as the new century dawned: the businessman politician (contrasting sharply to the more stereotypical model of the working-class Irish ward heeler). This interpretation is compelling; virtually all of the leading Democratic politicians with whom Sullivan and Hopkins were to ally were self-made capitalist millionaires, whose successes often preceded or were at least in part independent of their political activities. Both Sullivan and Hopkins achieved a degree of economic success (albeit aided by political contacts) before becoming major political players. Nor is it an overstatement to say that the orientation of the businessman politicians melded well with the innate character of political machines, especially in a city as commercially defined as Chicago.[29]

No business could ever boast greater productivity than an aggregation that could run the political life of a city of more than a million with only a membership of a few hundred leaders and operatives. Relatively small size was no handicap if everyone did his job—and no one was long accorded a position of responsibility unless he did. This was possible because political realities dictated that most elections attracted just a fraction of potential voters to the polls. For this reason, while a precinct captain might only be able to count upon as few as a hundred or so votes from among his family and acquaintances, or a ward or district leader a few thousand, he could still help win the election or exercise great influence locally if he could guarantee this turnout. This was especially true in primary contests, where the electorate was smaller but the stakes were even higher, because while a machine could still retain some patronage even if it lost some elections, its entire purpose was undercut if it could not demonstrate electoral power within its own party. Thus it was that the single most important gauge of a local leader's success and the best basis for advancement in the organization was his ability to get out his vote.

While all American urban political machines were structurally and operationally similar, their individual cultures, like that of any business, were shaped by local conditions that reflected most obviously the personality and circumstances of the current boss. Standing at the apex of the organization, the boss set policy, determined which candidates and issues to support and oppose, rewarded and promoted friends, punished and demoted enemies and traitors, and generally held things together. He did not have to hold a public office—some bosses, in fact, preferred to remain shadowy personages to the public—but he had to be gifted with political savvy and ruthlessness, as well as charisma and leadership ability. His political instincts were the basis to a large extent of the machine's success, and too many tactical and strategic mistakes could bring about his overthrow. At the same time, without his willingness to use his power to punish those who opposed him or who broke ranks, he would lose respect and become an easy target for those who coveted his position.

Lastly, it helped his cause greatly if he were blessed with an instinct for personal interaction, for being a "man among men," who could command not just the fear but also the respect of those he led. It was these management skills that brought his success and advancement through the ranks in the first place. They were probably his most important asset, as the boss usually owed his status almost entirely to the allegiance of a relatively small group of major figures in the top tier of the machine. In fact, sometimes the leadership could be so collective as to make the leader little more than the first among equals. This was the case with the new Democratic organization led by businessman-politician John P. Hopkins in 1894, which depended upon the support and wisdom of the men of his "inner circle," like Roger C. Sullivan. On the other hand, the boss was not just the most powerful member of the organization; he was also the one who largely set the agenda for profit, and the opportunities for profit were plentiful.[30]

Regrettably for the historical record, most of these activities were informal; negotiations, arbitrations, requests, and complaints are generally not recorded, or have been long lost. Fortunately, two letters have survived that illustrate how influence was exercised. Both were written by Sullivan as a ward leader to Robert "Bobby" Burke, a chief lieutenant in both of the Carter Harrison administrations, and both concern the extension of favors. One was a simple request for salary increases for John J. Sullivan (Roger's brother) and others who had been promoted to detective sergeant on the Chicago police force. Written in April 1900, the letter is formal but friendly in tone. Though Burke and Sullivan had long been friends, it is addressed to "Mr. Burke," and politely inquires "that [as] there is an opportunity now [because of budget increases] … if you will not do what you can towards securing for them their regular salaries to-wit [sic]:- $100 a month, and by doing so conferring a great personal favor upon me and our ward." It is significant that, though Sullivan and Hopkins were formally out of the Democratic Party at this time, much of their power remained intact.[31]

In contrast, an earlier missive reveals something of the iron hand in the velvet glove that would characterize of Roger Sullivan. Writing on August 26, 1899, with a degree of frustration, Roger asks "Dear Bob" for a job for "Mr. Edward Dunn, a young man of our ward, who is very, very deserving, and of whom I have spoken to you before." An earlier conversation between Sullivan and Mayor Carter Harrison, Jr., apparently had not brought results, despite the fact that "some of the limitations of the civil service men would expire." Sullivan had no specific placement in mind—"Most [sic] any position will do for him"— but this was something "we need very, very badly [as] everyone in the ward is as anxious as I am to see that he gets a place." Moreover, it is made clear that this was a favor that could not be refused if Burke wished to keep Sullivan's friendship: "It is very necessary that we do something for this man…. I assure you I would not call upon you to bother you now, if this were not necessary … do this for me, by all means." Regrettably, research does not reveal the ultimate disposition of this matter, but given the generally cordial relations of the two men thereafter, there is little doubt that a favorable outcome was reached.[32]

Where the exchange of such favors was a well-accepted and legal practice, some machines were entirely corrupt. The most infamous boss of them all, William Tweed (1823–1878) of the Tammany machine, was notorious for his villainy and plunder of New York City in the mid-nineteenth century, as well as for his subsequent downfall and imprisonment. Similarly, Chicago's Republican Mayor William Hale Thompson (1915–1923, 1927–31) and his cronies openly colluded with gangsters.

But Chicago's most overt period of "boodling" in the spirit of Boss Tweed came before the emergence of Sullivan and Hopkins, when the still growing city could boast its own share of local legends and colorful characters on the margins of its political culture. These invariably were criminally connected, relatively petty in their ambitions, and usually focused upon outright theft. Sometimes they were caught, and this phase climaxed with the Great Boodle Trial of the summer of 1887. This saw seven members of the Cook County Commission and a number of county employees dragged into court accused of conspiring to profit from false and illegal transactions in the supply and maintenance of the County Normal School and the County Hospital.[33]

The two most prominent were William J. McGarigle and Edward McDonald. McGarigle, no businessman, had risen through the police force to be appointed in 1883 as warden of the Cook County Hospital. McDonald began as a machinist, then worked as a fireman for a railroad and then on a tugboat. Eventually he became a ship's engineer before returning to Chicago to enter business as a furnace manufacturer. Apparently not achieving much success, he found employment as a cashier in a saloon owned by his brother, Michael McDonald, a well-known gambler, political manipulator (he was an associate of Alderman Johnny Powers), and the city's most widely recognized "boodler." He had barely avoided indictment with his sibling. All the defendants were found guilty, with four paying a fine, and six sentenced to two years in the state penitentiary. McDonald (the brother) and McGarigle were ordered to serve three years. McGarigle fled to Canada (he returned to Chicago after cutting a deal and avoided incarceration with a payment of a $1,000 fine), while McDonald managed to win on appeal.[34]

The boodle trials and their outcome were a great source of satisfaction for the good people of Chicago. Some felt that future disgrace could be avoided by the elimination of "the apathy for politics shown by successful men particularly in large cities," which followed from the fact that "a majority of capitalists and professional men seem to regard 'politician' as little more than an opprobrious epithet." The *Chicago Tribune* explained: "In all other important undertakings practical business methods are necessary to success. Why should one [government], which involves far more than any individual enterprise, be an exception?"[35]

But the times were changing and even now, the businessman politicians like Sullivan and Hopkins were on the rise. They avoided illegality and found the most profit in so-called "legal graft," or monetary gain that, while not overtly illegal, was founded upon their special influence in government. At the heart of operations was the business of distributing patronage positions. There was nothing more compelling to political operatives than the prospect of a lucrative government job for themselves or their followers. In Chicago, where the possibilities of public employment as yet remained largely unhindered by civil service examinations or other impediments, patronage was always a primary political focus. Those gaining such favors were expected in return to contribute liberally to party funds and to obey instructions.

Another lucrative practice for the boss and the machine was to facilitate matters for firms doing business with the city. A boss and machine could help with the acquisition of contracts as well as influence their terms. They could also offer relief from burdensome regulation. Consultation fees and other forms of direct and indirect recompense could bring a considerable profit. At the same time, there was general acceptance of the idea that the municipality could do business with concerns in which the boss or some other powerful member (or their relatives and friends) had an interest as long as the services themselves were provided in a reasonably honest manner. However, if the charges for goods and services were too untoward, or if the results were undeniably poor, public outrage could follow. This happened, for instance, during the administration of Mayor Fred Busse (1907–1911), who as a former postmaster headed a "federal faction" within the Republican Party. Chicago found itself billed for inferior manhole covers at possibly three to four times the going rate by a firm recently created by a close friend of the mayor. Indictments and convictions soon followed.

Beyond these more general practices were myriad lesser sources of profiting, some "legitimate," some less so. Machine leaders could rake off a percentage of campaign contributions from the membership. They might assess a regular fee from the salaries of public officials who secured their jobs, sinecures, or promotions through the organization. Public funds were sometimes routed to a friendly bank for lines of credit and a percentage of the interest. Protection from the law or tax adjustment was a ready source of cash, and not the least was the advantage of "emoluments arising from official position, such as loans, market tips, real estate information, and business favor and patronage of miscellaneous and varying forms; law practice, contracts, and good turns."[36] Neither Roger Sullivan nor his partner John Hopkins appeared to have made a custom of profiting directly from the sale of government jobs or contracts. Indeed, Sullivan was to claim later in his career that there was no money in politics! Still, there can be no debate that both men used their political contacts to facilitate their business enterprises for their own enrichment, acting first and last as businessmen. Not unexpectedly, the details of most of these kinds of deals have disappeared over time, either because they were not recorded in the first place, or because they are buried in usually incomprehensible and incomplete business reports. However, the eminent historian Joel Tarr has recovered once such transaction.

Sometime before 1904 the Chicago National Bank, run by controversial banker John R. Walsh, lent substantial sums of money to a number of leading political figures including Sullivan, who was a shareholder and down for $80,000, and Hopkins, who received $50,000 (and there were numerous others receiving similar or even greater amounts). It seems that these loans, which were only discovered when the bank failed, were a *quid pro quo* for the deposit of public funds. "Many of the loans were extended on signature alone, or on poor security, although most of them were eventually repaid." It is not clear whether interest was charged, but easy access to this kind of capital was an obvious advantage, and was also as much a reflection of the ethics of the contemporary commercial culture as of those of political corruption. This was, after all, an era in which, before the federal government stepped in, large companies like Standard Oil regularly extorted "rebates" from railroads by threatening to withhold their shipping with the effect of raising rates for competitors and costs for consumers. Still, neither Sullivan nor Hopkins were ever charged by their political enemies, who were as a group unrestrained in their accusations of wrongdoing (the one exception was William Randolph Hearst, who never hesitated to vilify anyone with ugly charges, including at one point William Jennings Bryan), with any illegal activity, or of receiving payoff or kickbacks from either jobs or contracts they helped secure for others.[37]

For all of the machines' self-serving entrepreneurialism, however, it has been long recognized by historians that they also served several positive purposes. Perhaps most importantly, they provided social services, especially for the new immigrants, in a time when government had yet to assume such responsibilities. In return for political allegiance, an immigrant could count on the local representative of the machine for help finding a job, for assistance with the judicial system, or even for a small loan.

No less important was the fact that machines provided an avenue of empowerment for those who otherwise were shut out of the existing elites. Certainly, Hopkins and Sullivan are cases in point of young men rising from relatively impoverished immigrant backgrounds to positions of influence through participation in organized politics. In this sense, political machines could function as engines of democracy, bringing people otherwise merely governed into the ranks of the governing. It was perhaps no accident, then, that so many of the reformers most offended by machines were found among the native-born hailing from social circles that had long been predominant in American life; not a few of them were overt in their nativist discomfort with the influx and rise of so many "foreigners." Ethnic and religious baiting, whether covert or overt, against machine candidates were never uncommon in urban elections.[38]

Events in the early months of 1894 underscored the efficacy of the machine structure for conditions in Chicago and Cook County. The deepening depression, it was true, helped bring a fattened Republican majority to the City Council of 23 to 11 in the unruly April elections. However, earlier in February, the organization's and the mayor's control of federal appointments was made clear to all as the Cleveland administration began announcing its choices. One man who was keenly disappointed was Frank Lawler, who had been led to believe that he would become a United States Marshal in return for his support of Hopkins. "Our Frank" saw his hopes shot down by the intervention of Senator John M. Palmer, who apparently held a personal grudge. As there was no effective protest by his backers in the party, clearly the previously potent power of Lawler and his following had severely diminished. Others of greater standing, on the other hand, were well pleased by the distribution of spoils, and a general spirit of harmony—or at least acquiescence to the new realities— seemed to prevail.[39]

Accordingly, the machine swept the primaries for the delegates to the county convention held in early June 1894, where its "armor plated" will was overwhelming in the nomination without meaningful opposition of an approved list of men for the county offices. Among those named was Roger C. Sullivan, who won the party's endorsement for the important position of Cook County Clerk. His victory could help bring direct control of both the city and Cook County governmental apparatus (and patronage). The delegates also followed Hopkins, Sullivan & Company's lead in their selection of the members of the Cook County Central and Executive Committees. Lastly, a slate for the upcoming state convention was chosen, comprising mostly machine men, including Hopkins and Sullivan themselves, with the remainder hemmed in by the imposition of the unit rule.[40]

When the state's Democrats met in Springfield, "Mayor Hopkins ... ruled as absolutely and completely as he ruled the Democratic convention of Cook County." The platform reflected his influence in its support of President Cleveland's calls for tariff reform and in its very general commitment to bimetallism. However, it included no specific endorsement of the free coinage of silver. Also included was a brief statement of confidence in Governor John P. Altgeld, whose influence at the convention was limited. He did, however, meet and cooperate with Mayor Hopkins in securing the United States Senate nomination for Franklin MacVeagh over the strong candidacy of Congressman John C. Black, a war hero who held the Congressional Medal of Honor, and who would go on to become commander-in-chief of the powerful Civil War veterans' association, the Grand Army of the Republic. In contrast, MacVeagh's public record was limited to a single term as one of the government's directors of the Union Pacific Railroad during a period of receivership. His prominence came from the fact that he was yet another of the self-made millionaire businessmen, and that he was said to be also a favorite of the president.

Born in Pennsylvania, and trained in the law, he came to Chicago in 1865 and became wealthy in the wholesale grocery business with his brother. He originally was a Republican but broke with the GOP in 1884 over the issue of tariff reform and the nomination of James G. Blaine, whom he despised, for president. He served as one of the original trustees of the reformist Chicago Civic Federation that was organized in 1894, but also had devoted himself heart and soul to the election of his friend, John P. Hopkins. The mayor now returned the favor, and his success in "putting MacVeagh over" for the nomination was another strong signal to the party of his dominance (a fact also affirmed by his election by the convention to the state committee). It was thus a happy group of machine politicians who boarded the train to Chicago after adjournment, confident of their continued hegemony. Alas, as must happen in life, not everything went right; during a stop at the Bloomington station, a box of fireworks exploded that burnt several of the party and singed the mayor's carefully groomed mustache![41]

Behind this façade of success and solidarity were the "outs" fuming in their frustration. During the primaries for the Cook County convention and at some of the local delegate conventions there were spontaneous rebellions against the machine rule and even some violence (at the Twenty-third Ward Convention, pistols were fired!), though this had little impact upon the results. Articulating their unhappiness, and in effect presenting himself as a rallying point of the opposition, was young Carter H. Harrison, Jr., the son of the late mayor. Before the county convention, he used the family newspaper the *Chicago Times* (which was going broke and would be sold within a year) to describe the situation in the local Democratic Party as "desperate" because "a few politicians of small-caliber and wholly selfish instincts have arrogated to themselves the power to dictate the nominations to the county ticket this fall." "These fellows are either blind or mad," Harrison assured his readers, "because the "people will not support a machine-made ticket!"[42]

His motives may not have been as pure as they appeared. At the Cook County convention, he was boomed for the nomination for county treasurer, and later at the state conclave it was vaguely reported that he may have been considered for state treasurer (he supposedly declined, but this is questionable), suggesting some willingness on his part to join the machine. It is possible that the purpose of his tirade was to bring some degree of propitiation by the "city hall gang" of John Hopkins and Roger Sullivan. If that were his intention, it backfired, as neither the mayor nor his allies showed much interest in promoting the career of another Harrison.[43]

Another small, but much more ominous, cloud on the horizon was based in ideology and threatened the hard-won unity demonstrated at the county and state conventions. In this, the third year of the worst depression in American history to date, there was festering dissatisfaction with President Cleveland and his Eastern conservatism. Most immediate was the general disappointment felt over the administration's inability to effect a tariff reduction—a central element of Democratic thinking for decades, which held that high tariffs benefitted big business at the expense of the consumer. Even in the Iroquois Club, safely under the control of its new president, Hopkins/Sullivan ally Lambert Tree, there was a debate in May during which leaders like Clarence S. Darrow attacked the president for his failure to bring the rates down. Earlier, Mayor Hopkins and other sachems were compelled to endure without public comment similar attacks at a club meeting by visiting Cleveland Mayor Tom L. Johnson.[44]

Such small ripples did little for the moment to disturb the placid self-assurance of the machine; however, events outside the narrow and sometimes petty world of party politics were already beginning to alter the confident composure of not just Hopkins and his friends, but the city and nation as well. In early May 1894, the workers at the Pullman Palace Car Company went out on strike.[45]

The Pullman Strike of 1894 was the last and most famous of the great industrial conflicts of the nineteenth century, and it has inspired a library of historical inquiry. At its heart was the explosive question of the proper balance of power between employer and employee in the new industrial setting. Like some other industrialists, George Pullman conceived his responsibilities to his employees in paternal terms, and in the mid–1880s built the town of Pullman. There "his" workers (or many of them) could live while building his famous Pullman Sleeping Cars (which he leased to railroads) as well as other types of railway equipment. With its famous Arcade (a shopping mall with stores and an impressive library for which each worker was charged the considerable sum of $3 a year), parks, schools, churches (which also paid rent), an auditorium, paved streets, and homes with running water, the town was promoted by the company and its owner as a model of progressive capitalist benevolence and order—and one that seemed designed to preempt worker unrest. Within ten years, however, the sheen had worn off as the company town began to be viewed by many as a "civilized relic of European serfdom." The homes that appeared to be the last word when built had become at best average and even substandard, and it became clear that the Pullman Company's hierarchy of concerns put the bottom line at the top, and the needs of its workers and tenants very much at the opposite end. When depression hit the country in 1893, and specifically after June in that year as the workers' savings in the company-owned bank began to plunge, this became painfully apparent.[46]

It was true that the Pullman Car Company diverted operations from places like Detroit to the central plant in the "town" of Pullman (by this time annexed to Chicago), resulting in the rescue of some jobs there, but with receding profits came declining wages and increasing distress. Already the company had introduced in parts of its operation an unpopular piece system that brought more work for less pay, and in September of 1893, it began accepting contracts significantly below its usual prices. The differences were made up with wage reductions that averaged overall at 25 percent, but in some cases were claimed to be as high as 40 percent. Making things worse was that house rents saw no concomitant downward adjustment.[47]

Although the company always claimed otherwise, there is an impressive body of evidence that testifies to its official and unofficial encouragement of workers to take housing within Pullman. This facilitated access to the jobsite, but it also fostered a nearly complete dependency, a dependency the company was fully willing to exploit by charging rents that averaged about 15 percent higher than those in surrounding neighborhoods. Originally, until the practice was outlawed by the Illinois legislature, rents were collected directly from their employees' wages. The Pullman management now refused to recognize any linkage between falling wages and the charges they were extracting. Making the situation more critical, employees were being allowed to fall months behind in their rents to a collective total of $70,000 (a huge figure in that time and place). They were then compelled to accept having repayment squeezed out of drastically reduced wages, or face the prospect of eviction and even dismissal.[48]

Sometimes literally adding injury to insult was an alleged culture of abuse found within the factory grounds. Complaints frequently spoke of verbal and sometimes physical attacks by foremen, minimal compensations for the victims of major accidents, favoritism, outright theft of services, and other practices that fed a smoldering anger among workers. And these resentments were only aggravated by George Pullman's arrogant refusal even to consider negotiations.[49]

By March 1894, local unions began to spring up among the employees in association with a young and vigorous American Railway Union. Organized just the year before as an industrial union independent of the craft networks of the American Federation of Labor, the ARU was headed by the charismatic and talented Eugene Debs. It was currently in the throes of winning a battle against Jim Hill's Great Northern Railroad. The Union stretched its constitution somewhat to allow in the Pullman workers, while urging a settlement without a strike.

The ARU was not alone in backing the workers; such groups as the Civic Federation of Chicago remonstrated with George Pullman for a settlement of the grievances. The union authorized a negotiating committee to discuss the rents and wages, which never met with Pullman himself (who maintained there was "nothing to arbitrate," as he claimed he had no more responsibility towards his tenants than any other real estate owner), but who were as a concession allowed access to the complex and perhaps doctored books of the company. Such goodwill as this gesture might have inspired was shortly thereafter undercut when three members of the committee were almost immediately laid off—something the company claimed was not in any way related to their union work. On May 5, 1894, the local unions called for a walkout and the Pullman Strike began.[50]

From the beginning, the sentiment in Chicago was one of support for the strikers. George Pullman was not a likeable figure and in the public imagination, he fit easily into the increasingly unpopular role of the unprincipled predatory capitalist. John P. Hopkins also held no lingering affections for his former mentor and was even now engaged in a lengthy lawsuit dating back to 1891 against the Pullman Palace Car Company for violating the rental rebate agreement for his store in the Arcade (the dispute was not to be settled—mostly in Hopkins's favor—until 1898).[51]

Since becoming mayor, Hopkins had used his office on at least two occasions to strike out at George Pullman and his company. First, he sought to double the cost of city water to the company on the basis that the town residents were being overcharged. Then he worked to have the town's independent postal status rescinded. Neither effort was successful, but the mayor's enmity was made clear. Moreover, as a former employee of Pullman himself whose home in Kensington was but a block from the company Arcade, he naturally identified with the workers' plight—an identification that was politically advantageous as well.[52]

Thus, Hopkins, Sullivan and their friends joined many of the most prominent citizens in the city in seeking to help the strikers and their families. When the workers formed a relief committee, the mayor's grocery firm, Secord and Hopkins, donated goods, cash, and a seven-room apartment without charge for a union medical committee to care for ill and injured strikers. In June, the mayor issued an official proclamation calling for private assistance for strikers. Hopkins even allowed Southside policemen to solicit donations for the committee among shopkeepers. Others also helped, ranging from various organized bodies of society ladies, the *Chicago Tribune*, and the *Chicago Daily News*, to the Hyde Park Water Department, the Spiegel's Home Furnishing Company, and the German Singing Society.[53]

For several weeks the situation remained relatively tranquil, until the ARU convened a special convention in Chicago on June 21. This was to issue a call for all of the union's national membership to strike in sympathy, while inviting members of other unions to do likewise. The hope was that this might compel Pullman to sit down and talk, but he remained intransigent; at midnight on June 26, 1894, a national boycott of Pullman cars that were leased to the railroads went into effect. Within days most of the railroads of the North and West were affected as were some as far away as California. The success of the call had its roots not just in the sympathy felt for the Pullman employees but also in a simmering resentment among many railroad workers across the nation against their employers who had joined together in the General Managers' Association. On June 22, this association joined with Pullman by going to war using every means possible to undercut the boycott. Within days, local command centers around the country, agencies to hire strikebreakers, and press bureaus to influence public opinion were opened and amply funded. The group also arranged with the Cleveland administration for the mustering of 3,600 new deputy United States marshals (of their own selection) to police the lines.[54]

Violence soon erupted across the United States, although within Chicago the level of disruption at this point was relatively minor and under police control. Mayor Hopkins took virtual personal charge of the force throughout the strike. When appearing afterwards before the investigative Strike Commission appointed by President Cleveland, he insisted proudly that all lawlessness during this phase was outside of the borders of his city.[55]

Grover Cleveland was hearing otherwise, or was choosing to believe differing reports.

He later claimed to have received complaints almost immediately about interference with the mails and interstate commerce in Chicago and elsewhere on the railroad lines. When he received a plea (that may have been arranged) for intervention from an assistant United States District Attorney in the Windy City on June 30, 1893, he ordered the Justice Department to petition the federal courts for an injunction against the strike and boycott. Among other things, it cited violations of the Sherman Anti-Trust Act of 1890 (that prohibited "restraint of trade"). With court order in hand, the president on July 2 directed federal troops into the city and elsewhere to address the "painful emergency."[56]

Governor John P. Altgeld protested vigorously what he saw as an unwarranted intrusion of federal authority into state affairs and a blatant repression of legitimate labor grievances. Mayor Hopkins did not protest, but made it clear at the time and afterwards that he saw no need for federal action. Regardless, the presence of the troops in and outside of Chicago, beginning on July 4, brought the greatest violence. With the unions' ability to exercise its own discipline in the rail yards, floating mobs began invading on a daily basis to loot and destroy.

This represented a significant escalation to the relatively peaceful efforts already made by striking railroad workers to shut down the lines through tampering with switches and other such relatively innocuous methods. Those now threatening chaos, it was generally recognized, had no direct connection with the union leadership (who sometimes assisted the police in their apprehension) and were universally characterized as "hoodlums, women, a low class of foreigners, and recruits from the criminal classes." Clash after clash, some with fatalities, broke out over the next two weeks as troops began escorting trains into the city. Mayor Hopkins, having little influence over the federal soldiers, but being importuned by the railroad companies for still greater protection, was nearly seized and assaulted on July 5 by a hostile mob as he was making an inspection of the yards. The next day he issued a proclamation outlawing riotous assemblies, and calling upon the governor for state troops, who soon added their numbers locally to the federal army, the deputy marshals, and the police.[57]

For all of that, Hopkins's position continued to be perceived as favorable to the strike and the strikers. In mid–July, he was even compelled to deny that he was about to be arrested by the federal government for being an enabler! This was not entirely specious. This much is clear. In July 1894, Hopkins, accompanied by his business partner Fred Secord, met with Debs and other ARU leaders. Debs, during his later trial for contempt, claimed that the possibility of a strike was discussed in detail and a walkout was encouraged by the mayor. Hopkins maintained that the meeting was merely one of courtesy at which matters of substance were not discussed. He directly denied any effort to "prompt" the workers to go out. Regardless, he did lend his office to an attempt at arbitration by Detroit's progressive Mayor Hazen Pingree. Armed with telegraphs from fifty other affected mayors, Pingree went with Mayor Hopkins to a meeting on July 11 with the second vice-president of the Pullman Company, Thomas H. Wicker, to no positive outcome.[58]

By that time the strike was already winding down. On July 7, Debs and his chief lieutenants were arrested for violating the injunction. Five days later, the executive officers of the American Federation of Labor and its affiliated Railroad Brotherhoods denied a request by the ARU for support, and recommended to its membership that they refrain from further involvement. Meanwhile, the long rumored and anticipated prospect of possible rescue by a general strike locally led by the Knights of Labor proved to be illusionary; almost all the city's workers refused to answer the labor organization's call. On July 13, 1894, the ARU offered to declare the strike at an end if the General Managers' Association would arrange for the return of the Pullman workers to their jobs without prejudice. The Pullman Company, as always, refused any negotiation or concession, and for another two weeks some effort was made to keep the boycott going. Essentially, however, the strike was over, and federal and state troops left the city in early August. Pullman workers and former workers now faced a bleak future with further wage cuts, broader blacklists, and the trials and convictions of their leaders.[59]

With not a little symbolism, in the first week of August—just as the troops were leaving—arsonists torched twelve of the city's major lumberyards and destroyed nearly 300 acres of real estate with an estimated value of almost three million dollars. Fortunately, the conflagration was brought under control and the devastation of the Great Fire of 1871 was not repeated. While never directly linked to the Pullman Strike, the fires cast a smoky pall that symbolized well the workers' gloom and the economic desperation stalking the land.[60]

For John Hopkins, Roger Sullivan, and the nascent machine, the Pullman Strike and its result were unmitigated disasters. It was undeniable that the mayor had performed his job commendably during the crisis, and that he had managed the delicate balance between his loyalty to the president and his sympathies for Chicago's workers. However, the local Democratic Party, already saddled with identification with a chief executive blamed by many for the depression, now also bore the stigma of an association with a national administration that was demonstrably anti-labor. With Republicans already riding a tide of resurgence locally and nationally, the Pullman Strike only added to the bleakness of the machine's prospects.

3

…And Out
(1894–1895)

Inside of most professional politicians, though perhaps well concealed, lives an eternal optimist who knows that there is always another election in a few months or years that can reverse the most dismal of defeats. The possibilities of renewal as well as the escape from the routine of life that each campaign offers are among the compelling attractions of a political life. In this spirit the young Chicago Democratic machine marched forward determinedly to battle in the fall of 1894 in defiance of the aftershocks of the Pullman Strike, an ever-deepening depression, and the unarticulated but mounting odds against success. They could do little else; another defeat could fatally undercut the credibility of an organization that had yet to win a single election, while victory would at a stroke assure longevity and the obliteration of past failures.

The first priority was to rally and reorganize the troops. In the late summer of 1894, opposition newspapers were replete with reports of pressure upon Democratic operatives by Mayor John P. Hopkins and his allies. This perception was strengthened during the September conventions held around Cook County to select candidates for the Illinois Senate. At one conclave the mayor himself made an appearance to assure conformity. However, there were signs that not all was well. By October, the officers of the various district organizations were reporting an unusual apathy among the rank and file. Adding to the list of challenges was the local rise of the Peoples' or Populist Party. This prompted a series of maneuvers by Hopkins, Sullivan, and their allies to undercut the new party. While brilliant in conception and execution, in the end these machinations achieved only a mixed success.[1]

Populism was an atavistic movement that looked longingly back upon a disappearing America where agriculture was dominant and traditional rural values were supreme. It was born initially in the frustrations and status anxieties of the farmers in the newly opened western reaches between the Mississippi River and the Rocky Mountains. Facing grasshoppers, prairie fires, harsh extremes of unpredictable weather, and (early on) Indian attacks, they also found themselves at the mercy of an increasingly centralized and monopolized economy. Completely dependent upon railroads and national banks over which they exercised no control, and which often used their influence in state and federal government to deflect any attempt at regulation, farmers suffered further because of steadily falling commodity prices. Ironically, these followed in large part from increased production brought about by the very technologies, like more efficient plows, that made western farming possible. Added to this were the boom/bust cycles of the new industrial economy, and in 1893, the worst economic downturn to date in the nation's history began and would endure for four long years.

In frustration and frequently despair, many came to believe that descending prices and worsening conditions were actually the result of a conspiracy among Eastern moneyed interests to impoverish those tilling the soil. Adding final insult to injury was their growing sense of becoming marginalized in American society, that they were losing their status as the backbone of American life, and were being relegated to the risible roles of "hicks" and "hayseeds."

In the decades after the Civil War, Western farmers—with those of the South, who were also suffering from economic dependency and status loss—began to organize politically. In the 1870s, building from primarily fraternal and social organizations like the Grange (officially the Order of Patrons of Husbandry, founded in 1867), they created various farmers' alliances as political action groups. Their relative success inspired a convention at Omaha, Nebraska, in 1892 that saw the inception of the People's or Populist Party on a reform platform that called for outright governmental ownership of railroads and telegraphs (or, failing this, close regulation), postal savings banks, a graduated income tax, the replacement of the selection of United States Senators by state legislatures with popular elections, and the expansion of the money supply by the coinage of silver at a ratio of 16 to 1 of gold. They nominated James B. Weaver, who won nearly a million and half votes in the election for president, and they elected numerous state officials as well as several congressmen in the West.

Chicago was the obvious focal point for a Populist urban strategy of seeking alliances with workers' organizations. The Windy City was the metropolis for the West to the Rocky Mountains as well as for much of the South, and the source of farm machinery, mail order, and many of the other goods offered farmers by industry. It was, moreover, the hub of western railroads and the principal regional marketplace for agricultural products. After a few years of limited and sporadic activity, by 1894 the Chicago Populists had managed to win over the support of the leaders of a number of local unions. Now they were preparing to make their political presence felt.

This was not a development upon which the Democratic machine looked with complacence. The working men of Chicago were a major center of Democratic strength, and the populist movement threatened to undercut the campaign for the November elections. However, many of those leading the machine, including most especially Roger C. Sullivan (who was known for being helpful to individual workers in assisting them in finding jobs, and other favors), were popular and influential among the unions and their members. They began making conciliatory noises towards populism and the populists even as they sought ways to subvert the burgeoning movement. This alarmed the local leadership of the incipient People's Party, which issued an explicit warning to the membership to avoid Hopkins and the Democrats.[2]

Undaunted, the mayor and his allies began using their contacts and operatives among the unions to infiltrate the upcoming People's Party convention, scheduled to be held on Saturday, August 18, 1894. The Populists placed guards on the door of the Twelfth Street Turner Hall. These disallowed the credentials of "about 149" men said to be close to the machine and representing the American Waiters and Bartenders Local No. 28, the "Carl [*sic*] Marx Club," the Carriage and Cab Drivers Union No. 1, the Socialist Labor Party, the Golden Circle Literature Society, and other groups. Perhaps predictably, what ensued was chaos. Amidst the clamor of large numbers of rejected delegates and their supporters outside, the convention quickly divided over the choice of a temporary chairman. The "city hall crowd" (now defined as those friendly to Hopkins and Sullivan), which, despite all the preemptive efforts, was probably in a majority, began pushing the candidacy of J.J. Ryan, president of the Building Trades Council. Amidst a maelstrom that was threatening to turn into a riot, the Populist central committee quickly adjourned the meeting. With unheard promises to reassemble, they fled the hall as the boisterous crowd began the difficult task of dispersing.[3]

Within weeks any hope of consolidating the two factions faded and they met separately. The Populists and Socialists, dominated by the American Railway Union and a contingent from the Knights of Labor, met quietly on August 24 at the same Turner Hall, and nominated their own county ticket while denouncing both major parties. The "Ryan Faction," meeting as the Labor Party on September 2, was actually just a shadow organization of the Democratic machine. Not surprisingly, three of their nominees had already been chosen by the Democrats: Frank Scales for county judge, Theodore Oehne for treasurer, and Roger C. Sullivan, "a man who has done more to get strikers out of jail than anyone else," for county clerk. From start to finish the new Labor Party did the bidding of the machine, whose interests were capably represented by, among others, Sullivan's chief clerk at the County Probate Office, who was conspicuously present during the convention. However, this attempt to subsume the new movement proved to be pointless as the city hall "populists" were unable to get on the ballot. A true amalgamation of Populists and Democrats would have to wait for another two years.[4]

In September yet another organization appeared to add to the complexity of the situation. Grandly called the Independent American Party, it claimed a voting membership of 37,000 in Cook County, and was closely affiliated with, and in part created by, the American Protective Association, a nativist society that perceived the Roman Catholic Church (and presumably its Irish, Italian, Polish, and German parishioners) as a threat to the nation. The Republicans claimed it was all a ploy of the Democrats to split their vote—a charge that the evidence suggests may have been partially true. Certainly, the Democrats looked upon the group with favor and may have engaged in some private encouragement of one kind or another.[5]

For all of the drama of the preliminaries, the Democratic campaign itself was restrained. Counting upon the organization of the machine, the party forewent most of the usual massive rallies around the city, confining itself for the most part to merely a picnic and two parades. The first procession was held on September 4, when the major unions in Chicago presented a massive triumph in which the Democratic leadership and candidates were prominently featured. This was followed by the annual Democratic picnic held on September 30. Designed to promote party loyalty, it was judged generally to be disappointing in both attendance and in partisan spirit. It was, however, highlighted by the presence of Senator John Palmer, Hopkins, Sullivan, and most of the leadership. Finally, in late October came the largest event, a well-populated procession through downtown. Sullivan's candidacy was noisily endorsed with an enthusiasm exceeded only by that accorded Franklin MacVeagh, the party nominee for the United States Senate.[6]

MacVeagh was in fact the only Democratic candidate to conduct a vigorous speaking schedule, but even he campaigned mostly outside of Chicago. Though taking liberal stances on issues like labor rights, he was unable to escape the label of being Hopkins's creature, which became the focus of the Republican attack. The *Chicago Tribune*, in particular, excelled in its use of ridicule in an ongoing series of front-page cartoons. Featured were caricatures of the mayor as the "young Alexander." This sobriquet was originally coined that fall by Corporation Counsel Harry Rubens in a fulsome speech referencing Hopkins's relative youth. Now it rang with the opposition's biting sarcasm.[7]

More substantially, the mayor was targeted for his alleged tolerance of the extralegal gambling establishments in the city. Led by the Civic Federation and most of the newspapers, the demand for shutting them down as dens of vice bore fruit on September 20, when Hopkins at last ordered them closed. This, together with previous grand jury indictments of many of the owners, did have some stifling effect, though only temporarily; many simply moved their operations into the suburbs or into Indiana, to return when public attention had moved on. Others continued more or less surreptitiously in business, prompting the Civic Federation, which conducted its own raids after the mayor's order, to accuse the administration of bad faith. Under similar pressure, the mayor directed his police chief to enforce the Sunday Closing Laws of the saloons. This, too, brought brief compliance. This tension between the demands of the growing reformist movements in the city, and the vacillations of the professional politicians over issues of private vice and morality, would linger in the years ahead—regardless of who held the reins of power.[8]

In the end, it was all for naught as the election of November 1894 brought nothing but bad news for the machine. Nationally, the Republicans took control of Congress by increasing their numbers in the House of Representatives from 127 to 244 and in the Senate from 38 to 42. Democrats, who had won the presidential election handily two years earlier, were now only able to secure majorities or pluralities in the "Solid South" (though not so solid as usual, because Tennessee moved into the Republican column). In Illinois, the GOP also won the congressional elections, increasing their total from eleven seats to twenty (of twenty-two), while easily enhancing their majorities in the state legislature to assure the success of their candidate for Illinois' next United States senator.[9]

In Chicago and Cook County, the results were equally discouraging. Republicans won all of the county offices with margins ranging from twenty percent to a high of twenty-four percent of the vote. Roger Sullivan ran ahead of most of the slate, but lost his bid for the office of county clerk by a margin of 145,607 to 100,777 votes. Nor could the Democrats blame the Populists. The People's Party candidates garnished respectable returns, but their totals were insufficient to make the difference. No amount of explanation could disguise the fact that the Republicans had returned as the majority party, and the young Democratic machine had lost yet another election.[10]

Behind the disastrous figures, it was true, was some reason for hope. Though the Populists' participation in the elections was not the direct source of defeat; if their numbers were added to those of Chicago's Democrats—a reasonable proposition given the growing ideological compatibility of the two—the margins were very close. Moreover, the results could hardly be interpreted as a rejection of the mayor or of the machine and its leadership. It would have been a political miracle to have won in face of a deepening depression and the increasingly bitter antipathy towards Grover Cleveland and his administration.

Nonetheless, the solidarity of the leaders of the Cook County Democrats began to unravel. Just days after the debacle, Corporation Counsel Rubens and Controller William K. Ackerman resigned. Harry Rubens was one of the mayor's chief advisors, and his departure especially evoked howls of anger. Perhaps in response to the abrupt departure of these two men who had been so lately high in his counsel and as a warning to others, the mayor publicly lashed out days later at unspecified city hall officials for a lack of loyalty. Meanwhile, the effects of the defeat upon his political future, and therefore that of the machine, were becoming fodder for public speculation.

Before the elections it had been assumed that Hopkins would seek reelection in the spring, and that he might even go on to seek the senate seat in place of MacVeagh, the party's selected standard-bearer. Now his every act and pronouncement was scrutinized for some hint of his intentions. For instance, late December found Hopkins, with Sullivan (who often accompanied him on trips and vacations), in New York City having his throat examined by a specialist (Hopkins was to suffer from throat and lung difficulties throughout much of his life). Also present in the city was the representative of the company building Chicago's elevated railways. There was no evidence of any meeting or agreement, but the coincidence created speculation that the mayor might take over the job of running that transportation system currently under construction. For his part, Roger Sullivan made it clear that he was not currently interested in any elective or appointive office, and he quashed any suggestion that he might take over from Ackerman as controller. Instead, he let it be known that with his departure from the probate clerk's office on December 3, he expected "to go into private business." Of course, he was already a very successful businessman with various going concerns, and he certainly had no intention of surrendering his growing influence and power in the Democratic Party.[11]

Optimistic and pugnacious, neither Hopkins nor his associates were at this point willing to surrender quietly to events. Instead, an effort was initiated to burnish the mayor's standing as a reformer, and therefore to create new positive issues to overshadow the election, and his connection with the Cleveland administration and the depression. This was a shrewd move. By 1894, reform was a growing political theme, and already the structures to anchor the progressive movement that would define the nation's politics for the next twenty-odd years were in place.

For nearly a decade "good government groups" had been springing up in America's major cities, a trend finding expression in Chicago with the recent chartering of the Civic Federation. Dedicated to governmental efficiency and honesty, these organizations were created precisely because of the operation of machines like that of Hopkins and Sullivan and of the massive influx of immigrants that formed the basis of their strength.

In 1890, Hazen S. Pingree in Detroit was elected as the first of a series of celebrated and openly reformist mayors around the country (that would include Sam "Golden Rule" Jones in Toledo, Tom L. Johnson in Cleveland, and in 1905, Edward F. Dunne in Chicago, who advocated broadening city government as an agency of the people's welfare). Adding strength to what was becoming a movement were a number of middle-class and native-born citizens who began working among immigrants to assist in their welfare, acclimation, and uplift, a trend that first attracted public attention with the efforts of Jane Addams in Chicago at her famous Hull House (founded on the city's near West Side in 1889). Addams was even at this moment leading a fight for better garbage collection in one of the poorer sections, and engaged as well in a lengthy but ultimately vain attempt to overthrow her ward's notorious alderman, Johnny Powers.

Young investigative journalists were also doing their bit to expose social and political injustice. These "muckrakers," as President Theodore Roosevelt would eventually label them based upon a fictional character from John Bunyan's *Pilgrim's Progress* (1678), began to make an impact in the 1890s as new magazines (*Cosmopolitan* and *McClure's* for two examples) appeared as forums for social debate. Men and women like Jacob Riis in *How the Other Half Lives* (1890), Henry Demarest Lloyd in *Wealth Against Commonwealth* (1894), and Ida Tarbell in a series of articles in *McClure's* subsequently published as *The History of the Standard Oil Company* (1904), indicted in detail many of the more egregious abuses of the new industrial society and helped inspire a growing chorus for change.

Religion, too, played its role as an emphasis on "Social Gospel" emerged in the 1880s among more liberal Protestant clergymen who called for churches to engage in social action and uplift. Further adding to the reformist stew were longstanding crusades for women's rights and the prohibition of the drug alcohol. Not least important was the example of Populism, with which this newer urban progressivism shared a belief in the efficacy of government as a mechanism of social change.

From the beginning of his administration, Hopkins capitalized upon his business background by making much of his advocacy of efficiency and "clean" government. This first came to the fore in a personal crusade to alleviate the city's considerable financial challenges. In a message to the city council in April 1894, he noted that Chicago carried a massive debt of over eighteen million dollars, upon which the city was frequently in default. The situation was in part created by inflated fiscal responsibilities assumed with the large number of recent annexations. With shortfalls of nearly a half-million dollars between expected revenues and monies actually collected, the situation was deteriorating exponentially. Moreover, discounting legally mandated spending for the Library Board, the School Board and the sinking fund, the city had on hand only $560,611 instead of the nearly four million in "ready cash" the mayor felt was needed for anything like financial stability. Contributing to the problem were antiquated methods of assessing and collecting taxes and years of padding the city payroll. Things became so bad that the city council Committee on Finance began calling for salary restrictions and even cuts.[12]

Hopkins was not able to resolve fully these fiscal difficulties, though he and the Democrats were careful to frame them in terms of his predecessors' incompetence and/or corruption. Nonetheless, progress was made. As early as his first week in office, the mayor began reviewing the city rolls and found, among other things, that the street cleaning department was "stuffed beyond a doubt." He even ordered a reduction in the budget of his own office, and by July, it was being reported that the city's financial state had improved considerably in the course of the first six months of 1894. Even his Republican opponents were willing to recognize by their silence that something meaningful had been accomplished.[13]

The Hopkins administration also buffed its reformist halo with a refusal to allow a license for a racetrack in Garfield Park, and with the mayor's veto of an ordinance benefitting the Chicago City Railway, a leading streetcar company, which, in his opinion, offered inadequate compensation to the city. The veto was subsequently overridden by the Republican-dominated council, but the political advantage had been achieved, especially as it was widely believed, though neither confirmed nor denied by Hopkins, that he had turned down a substantial bribe from the company. He also attracted attention in his successful confrontation with the "paving trust," which had outraged homeowners of one neighborhood with what were purported to be exaggerated costs. His zeal was further evidenced after the elections of November 1894, by his proposal to appoint a nonpartisan police commission to remove politics from law enforcement (something he had advocated in his inaugural speech). Hopkins's own father had been a cop who probably held his job as a patronage appointment, and the mayor understood well the political tone of an urban law enforcement community.[14]

Cynically, his political opponents questioned whether his interest in a nonpolitical police department was something that followed from the fact that the elections were over. Moreover, among the professional politicians there was no real consensus that the police should in any case be removed from politics. As a consequence, although the commission was appointed, a city council coalition of Republicans and some Democrats refused to grant it supervisory authority, or even the authorization and funding to investigate. It was to endure—powerless and as eventually an object of ridicule—until just after Hopkins left office.[15]

Hopkins's primary claim to the ever more desirable mantle of a reformer, however, was his response to the operation and expansion of the city's (not so) public utilities. In the late nineteenth and early twentieth centuries, no set of issues inspired such emotions in urban America. As cities grew, so did their need for ever-expanding transportation, gas, electricity, sewage, and garbage disposal services. In this era of open-ended capitalism, these soon became big business, with numerous competing enterprises the unabashed focus of which was profit. Not surprisingly, public dissatisfaction was soon simmering over what was generally perceived as substandard service, and government was increasingly called upon to offer relief through either regulation or outright ownership. In the years ahead, it was public transportation that was to become the primary rallying point for such calls for change in Chicago, but during the Hopkins administration it was the lighting and heating gas industry that attracted the most attention.

Because of the rapid growth, the free-for-all capitalist environment, and the intervention of the courts, efforts to organize fully the production and distribution of lighting and heating gas throughout the city had been repeatedly frustrated. The end result was that the structure and operation of service in Chicago in the last decade of the nineteenth century was a hotbed of economic opportunism and political contention.

It all had begun simply enough: in 1849 a charter was issued to the Chicago Gas Light and Coke Company, which initiated operations the following year. For decades this company enjoyed a near monopoly in the city, having fought off the intrusions of all successive competitors except the People's Gas Light and Coke Company, which went into operation in 1855. Seven years later an agreement was entered into by the two to divide the market with the Chicago Gas Light and Coke Company's "turf" to be the North and South Sides, with the People's confined to the West.

By the late 1870s other providers from Chicago's growing suburbs began to intrude upon the territories of the two older companies. The first of these, the Hyde Park Gas Company, was incorporated in 1871, followed in 1881 by the Lake Gas Company, and in 1884, the Suburban Gas Company. The Chicago and the People's Gas fought back by acquiring the Suburban Company as well as the private gas works of Pullman, which the courts had compelled George M. Pullman to relinquish. However, by the mid–1880s, the period of controlled competition faded away as ever more competitors sprang up in the wake of Chicago's expansion. Much of the growth of the industry sprang from technological innovations that allowed for far simpler and cheaper gas production, which in turn broadened the demand for heating gas.[16]

The Consumers Gas Fuel and Light Company was organized in 1881, then in 1885 the Equitable Gas Light and Fuel Company, and the Illinois Light, Heat, and Power Company (which confined itself to simply manufacturing and selling gas without distribution). Serious incursions were made upon the customer bases of the two original gas giants, and "gas wars" loomed. On April 7, 1887, however, after prolonged negotiations, the Chicago Gas Trust Company was chartered to include the Chicago Gas Light and Coke Company, the People's Gas Light and Coke Company, the Consumers Gas Fuel and Light Company, and the Equitable Gas Light and Fuel Company. It was a combination that also controlled all the other remaining gas producers. Each company retained its corporate identity, but it seemed that the era of coordinated gas service had at last dawned. But it was not to be. All efforts by the legislature and the city council to grant a monopoly to the Gas Trust were undone by court rulings. The forces of consolidation soon found themselves further frustrated by the appearance of yet more competition in the Calumet Gas Company, the Mutual Gas Company, and the Chicago Economic Fuel Gas Company, a paper entity controlled by "Eastern interests" that used the Indiana Natural Gas and Oil Company to bring their product into the city.[17]

So things stood at the beginning of 1894, when John P. Hopkins and his associates came into office. The situation was significantly modified in July of that year by a court-ordered dissolution of the gas trust as an illegal monopoly. Each of the companies was ordered to elect its own board of directors and to set up individual headquarters. Though the trust continued its legal fight for existence, there was a series of attempts to take advantage of the situation by a group of promoters working in collusion with a number of councilmen led by "Little Mike" Ryan and Henry Stuckart. They well understood that any new concern receiving a city franchise to produce and sell gas would be endowed instantly with value that could be sold to the existing companies for a vast profit without the burdensome expense of actually building a plant and providing services. In the late spring of 1894, they rammed through the city council a provision creating the Metropolitan Gas Company, which Hopkins successfully vetoed. They tried again with an ordinance expanding the franchise of the Hyde Park Mutual Fuel Gas Company to include the distribution of gas within Chicago. It also featured the strategic additions of cheaper gas and a deposit of $100,000 for street repair, both issues the mayor had raised in his first veto message.[18]

General skepticism followed, however, led by Mayor Hopkins, who questioned the motives of the backers as well as many of the details of the plan. But the tide of popular opinion against the scheme became overwhelming when one alderman revealed that bribery had been a factor in its approval. The mayor once again used his veto, and once again backed by newspaper and reformist indignation, he was sustained by the city council—though relatively narrowly.[19]

That summer, however, he was less successful in blocking the next attempt by the same "strong men" (including the ubiquitous "Little Mike," the group's floor manager in the council), who were able this time to convince a resounding majority of the city council to enfranchise the Universal Gas Company. Hopkins's veto was overridden by a margin of 53 to 14! This apparently followed from the fact that Universal's backers were able to obtain the acquiescence, or at least nonopposition, of the technically dissolved but still functioning gas trust. The Universal Company never actually distributed the gas manufactured at its massive works opened (to general surprise) later in the year, but instead sold most of its product for a good return to the Hyde Park Mutual Gas Company.[20]

Mayor John Hopkins and his administration thus enjoyed the reputation of being at least moderately reformist guardians of the public interest concerning the question of the gas utilities. Because of this, when the city council unexpectedly revisited the issue in late February 1895, most assumed that the mayor would once again lead the fight against what was to be touted as just another attempt at "boodle" at the city's expense. Instead, what occurred was initially to astound the city, and then to provoke an unprecedented storm of public outrage from which the mayor, Roger Sullivan, and others of their associates were to emerge permanently bearing the label of cynical economic opportunists and machine politicians. The collective and lingering anger that followed the Ogden Gas Scandal (as it became known) also can be reasonably understood as the true beginning of progressive reform as a powerful force in Chicago.

On the afternoon of Monday, February 25, 1895, the city council quietly convened for what was generally anticipated to be a rather dull and ordinary session. Mayor Hopkins, as usual, presided and engaged himself in such routine business as referring to the Finance Committee a report on improving the city water supply and formally presenting a veto message of a measure previously passed authorizing the Chicago City Railway to extend its tracks. To the surprise of observers, the mayor then excused himself and turned the chair over to Alderman "Little Mike" Ryan.

Alderman John McGillen rose and was recognized. He proposed bringing to the floor the Norwood Construction and Electrical Ordinance (originally introduced the previous September and tabled), with the new addition of an amendment to enfranchise something called the Cosmopolitan Electric Company. As an amendment to an earlier proposal, it was not required to go through additional committee review or readings. Featured were unusually broad and generous terms. The new concern was to be granted a fifty-year franchise and to be empowered to build as many generating plants as needed to produce and distribute electricity for virtually any purpose including light, heat, and power as well as the transmission of signals and sound. It was authorized to use the city streets, viaducts, and tunnels and to build poles (required to be made of cedar wood and standing thirty feet high), except in the city's heart and in the tunnels, where the lines were to be laid underground. Construction was to be completed within three years with a bond of $25,000 as guarantee of the restoration of all disturbed city property. Further, when building downtown, all activity was to take place between 9 p.m. and 6 a.m. The maximum that the new company could charge was one cent per hour of sixteen candlepower, and $10.50 a month per 1,600 candle hours; the city was to be compensated at a rate of three percent of the gross after three years.[21]

Immediately the chamber was filled with a cacophony of voices demanding recognition. These "Little Mike" attempted to ignore, but William D. Kent, John W. Hepburn, James R. Mann (who as a congressman would write the Mann Act) and others were able to register their indignant protests. Violently they argued that the proposal was so unrelated to the original ordinance as to constitute a new measure. It, therefore, should be sent to committee for further consideration. Ryan overruled these and other objections and was sustained by a vote of 37 to 24. John McGillen then called for passage and, by a margin of 38 to 22, the measure was approved.[22]

In an environment that was beginning to swelter with charged emotions, Ryan now surrendered the chairmanship of the meeting to McGillen, who immediately recognized Johnny Powers. He used the same maneuver of bringing up for consideration another ancient proposal. This one first came before the council in 1893, and was tabled in January 1895. It provided for the creation of the City and County Gas Company. As before, a sub-stitution was offered. It would now grant a franchise to a new entity to be called the Ogden Gas Company. Like the Cosmopolitan, it was to receive a fifty-year franchise, and unlimited access to the streets, bridges, rights of way, and public property of the city to build its lines. It was not to begin construction without first posting a bond of $20,000 against complete restoration, and it was given three years to complete works that would manufacture five million cubic feet of gas every month. It was to charge no more than ninety cents per 1,000 cubic feet (as opposed to the going rate of $1.20 by the "former" members of the gas trust), and it was to pay the city three and half percent of its gross when it began operations.[23]

Once again, opposition aldermen took issue with the ordinance and the manner in which it was being presented. A particularly passionate speech was made by Mann, who attempted to introduce an amendment that would hand over one-third of the company's stock to the city government (this had been part of the original City and Gas Company proposal). This went nowhere. A vote was called for by Powers and, as before, 38 aldermen voted in support with 22 against. Adjournment was then ordered and the aldermen left the chambers "in a somewhat excited state," with Mann noisily declaring it an "outrage," while promising "they would all be drunk tomorrow!"[24]

By the next day, they had reason to be. Concerned public opinion as expressed in the newspapers was unanimous and heated in its condemnation of the "shameless record" of "boodle ordinances" "recklessly passed" by "the gang"—the universal term of contempt. One problem was that no one seemed completely sure about the identity of "the gang." The nineteen Democratic aldermen and the like number of Republicans who backed the meas-ures were generally, and understandably, unavailable for comment in the days immediately following, but it was widely speculated that forces beyond the council chamber were at work. There was some thought that it might be the Harrison Construction Company, which recently moved into the field of telephone service locally, or perhaps a faction of the stock-holders of Standard Oil (which the company quickly denied), or even that it was a "clique" of Democratic leaders, something that seemed to be belied by the bipartisan support of the ordinances, but which was supported by the fact that John W. Lanehart, Governor John Altgeld's first cousin and law partner, was the attorney who incorporated Ogden Gas.

Altgeld and Lanehart's brothers-in-law Charles J. Ford and Robert L. McCabe, as well as Lanehart's Dartmouth roommate, Elmer A. Kimball, were also listed as incorporators with Charles A. Lark and F.D.P. Snelling, superintendent and agent of Altgeld's Unity Build-ing in Chicago. The Cosmopolitan was incorporated by attorney Albert H. Tyrrell, who in 1890 had organized a printing business with Ford and Kimball. However, no one seemed to know many details and those who did were not talking. Mayor Hopkins was not available to share his thoughts, having traveled to New Orleans with a small retinue (that did not include Roger Sullivan) almost immediately after surrendering the chair of the council. It was not clear why he was in the Crescent City; Mardi Gras had ended the night before his arrival, and he offered no explanation. Finally reached by reporters, he denied he had anything to add about the affair: "Mayor Hopkins' friends were strong in their denial of the statement that he is in any way interested in any of the ordinances." Roger Sullivan said it was foolishness to suppose the mayor was connected with the companies, but he was also accused of being among those involved. This he denied, stating: "I am not. I will admit I am willing to own such valuable franchises as these ordinances grant, but unfortunately I am not interested. I know nothing whatever of the Cosmopolitan company. As to the Ogden Company, I have heard a little gossip, not of a reliable nature. However, I have no means of knowing who is back of it."[25]

Far more definitive in its response was the Civic Federation, which became the fulcrum of protest. Within days, its political committee announced plans for a mass meeting at the Central Music Hall at 3:00 p.m. the following Sunday. Five thousand stuffed themselves into the hall (an additional two thousand, denied entry, marched to the nearby Lake Front Armory, preempted an ongoing Sunday School gathering, elected their own chair, and applauded their own impromptu orators). Chairing was the prominent Civic Federation leader, Lyman Gage, and invited to sit on the platform were luminaries like Marshall Field, Clarence S. Darrow, and even such close allies of the mayor and Roger Sullivan as Lambert Tree and the sitting corporation counsel, John Mayo Palmer. Speaker after speaker rose to condemn the ordinances and all those associated with them. Phrases and terms like "stamped with infamy," "traitors," "microbes," and "Bacillus Aldermanicus" were spat out with contempt from the pursed lips of a bevy of ministers and business leaders, who more concretely called for civil service reform and eradication of corruption. It was not just that the measures were replete with flaws, as, for example, their failure to require insulators for electrical lines running through tunnels, but that they were virtually unrestricted and gave the proposed companies and their capitalist owners (whoever they were) absolute use of the public property without adequate compensation or oversight.

Perhaps the most profound insights came from the noted reformer Henry Demarest Lloyd. He looked beyond the immediate issue at hand to note that while the Ogden Gas ordinance was actually praiseworthy for its provision to lower the cost of gas from the current $1.20 charged by the gas trust to ninety cents, the real question was one of monopoly and the prevalent pattern of the intrusion of predatory business practices into city affairs. What had to be done, Lloyd asserted, was for the city and its utilities to be run solely for the benefit of the citizenry—even if the municipal government had to run the services itself. Following Lloyd's oration, much additional energy was expended in yet more outrage by still more speakers. When the gathering adjourned, the crowd left exhausted but with its need to express its self-righteousness satiated, and with many present, no doubt, reaching for a cigarette.[26]

More concretely, the leadership of the Civic Federation appointed a special committee to draft repeal ordinances and to solicit the cooperation of an obliging alderman to see to their introduction. However, all real hope centered upon the chance that Mayor Hopkins would return vetoes when the council next met. This seemed feasible given the precedent of the Universal Gas franchise. As the week wore on, expectations began to fade as reports emerged from unnamed sources that, at best, he would just offer some amendments. However, the mayor remained as taciturn as possible, indicating in a general way that he would make a decision after conferring with Corporation Counsel John Palmer. By the date of the highly anticipated meeting of the council, he was back in Chicago being besieged by those opposing the ordinances. Among these was Marshall Field, the leading business figure in the city, who advised him to find in his hero Grover Cleveland's model the courage to stop "the boodle." On the same day, reportedly, Potter Palmer, who held a status equal to that of Field in the business community, conferred with Hopkins and presented him with a set of veto messages for possible use.[27]

That the reformers greatly misjudged the situation became clear when the aldermen convened at 7:00 p.m. on Monday, March 4, 1895. Once again "the Gang" "throttle[d]" their opposition. As the first order of important business, Mayor Hopkins rose to deliver his message personally (this was unusual, as customarily it would be read by the clerk or just placed into the record). His intentions were revealed in the first sentences: he was going to approve the creation of the Ogden Gas Company, and was only offering two minor amendments to the franchise of Cosmopolitan Electric. He explained that in so doing, he hoped to overcome the "bondage of trusts" upon the city; the Ogden Company was sure to undersell significantly the alliance of the gas companies and, therefore, to introduce greater competition into the market. He agreed that the ordinances were passed in a questionable manner, but he argued that he was bound to judge them on their merits alone. It was, therefore, irrelevant if "unknown parties" were behind them; moreover, in the past similar ordinances had resulted in positive outcomes. Nor could the fear that the gas trust would simply buy up any new companies be adequate grounds for a veto. Such an apprehension, if taken to its logical extremes, would paralyze any effort to create new competition and would only serve the interests of those already in control of the utilities. He agreed that the procedures themselves for issuing franchises might indeed be flawed, as many argued, but the answer was to seek new laws from the state legislature, not to halt the process entirely. In short: "Every blow to the trust is a blow inflicted in the interest of the public," and his actions were consistent with the "strong sentiment of reform now manifest in the larger American cities."[28]

Throughout the mayor was interrupted with catcalls and laughter from the crowds packing the galleries; at one point in frustration he threatened to clear the chamber. Things now moved forward quickly. As the mayor concluded, Alderman McGillen rose and offered a motion to reenact the Cosmopolitan ordinance with the mayor's amendments: one that redefined the boundaries where poles were required, and another that set a minimum charge (well below that of the Chicago Telephone Company) for the transmission of signals on the lines. All protest by the opposition was silenced and the motion moved forward by a margin of 43 to 17. This increase in support of five votes from the previous week was also present in the subsequent reaffirmation of the Ogden franchise. After accepting some additional amendments from the mayor on the largely irrelevant and minor issue of slightly broadening the rights of the Chicago City Railway, the meeting was precipitously adjourned in an environment of anger, protest, and confusion.[29]

The condemnation was predictably ubiquitous. Typical was the editorial of the *Chicago Daily News*, which called the mayor's message and acts "cheap, shabby, and transparent." More incisively, the *Chicago Tribune* predicted the doom of his political career: "If he had the remotest idea of being a candidate he would not have dared to act as he did last night." Even more devastatingly, his actions, in the newspaper's judgment, forever stripped from him the mask of a statesman and reformer to reveal "an oily hypocrite and a canting demagogue." It explained: "He glorified himself as a reformer.... His real love of reform, if he ever had any, seems to have disappeared with the November election, which showed him that his cake was dough politically, and it was useless for him to dream of re-election."[30]

For all of the opprobrium in print incurred by Hopkins, much of the immediate public outrage was already spent. There were no further massive meetings, or marches, or petitions. Instead, a grim determination to exact revenge at the municipal elections just a month hence seemed to settle upon the city, something that the Republicans were quite eager to encourage.

Meanwhile, the question of who exactly was behind the ordinances remained unanswered. However, just two days after the mayor's messages to the council, Alderman James Mann, in the role of a "concerned citizen," made a shocking accusation. He claimed that on the day of the initial passage of the Ogden and Cosmopolitan ordinances, he overheard a conversation at a restaurant located in the basement of the Stock Exchange Building. Present, at a nearby table, he alleged, were John P. Hopkins, Roger C. Sullivan, former Corporation Counsel Harry Rubens, Felix Senff (the mayor's private secretary), and one other, a private citizen whom he declined to name. According to Mann, the men discussed the franchises and their plans to see them enacted. Moreover, there were apparently allusions that the offending ordinances had actually been composed by Rubens. The alderman concluded, therefore, that a conspiracy was at work that was "headed by the mayor of the city ... [which] organized [the] companies and granted franchises to these companies owned by themselves." He claimed to be revealing this only now because he had felt constrained by the impropriety of disclosing a private conversation in which he was not a party (what exactly had changed his mind about that was not made clear).[31]

The implications of this accusation seemed to be underscored by other reports that unspecified sources in City Hall were confirming that the ordinances had been enacted "in the interest of Mr. Hopkins." For his part, the mayor reacted to Mann's allegations with anger, and with threats of a lawsuit. Harry Rubens admitted that such a meeting took place, and maintained that they had been together for no more than three minutes. Sullivan categorically denied that any such conversation ever occurred. He also said that he had no interest in the ordinances or the companies, and was unconvinced that Mann had been in fact been present at the restaurant as he claimed. When pressed if he had any connection with the Ogden and Cosmopolitan or of having any interest in the ordinances, he repeated: "I have not." When asked if he had any knowledge of who was "behind either of them," he stated that not only did he have no idea, but also that he did not even "care a snap what becomes of them." In face of such heated denials (and threats of legal action), Mann quickly began hedging his accusations, and it was not to become clear who the real beneficiaries of the deals were until after the April elections, and then only in bits and pieces over the course of time.[32]

Adding still further passion was an obviously symbolic attempt by the Civic Federation, in cooperation with another civic group, the Citizens Association, to have Judge John Barton Payne of the Cook County Superior Court overturn the council's actions based upon alleged "irregularities" of procedures. Payne took the case seriously and listened carefully to the arguments. Among those representing the Cosmopolitan Company was Clarence S. Darrow, a former protégé and future law partner of Altgeld. In a few days, the judge dismissed the case as beyond the purview of the judiciary but with the recognition of the untoward nature of events.[33]

Most public attention, in any case, was by now focused upon the elections. For the Republicans, the Ogden scandal was an unexpected gift that encouraged their optimism. For the Democrats the affair created tension and uncertainty. It was representative of the weakening of Hopkins, his allies, and their organization that the Democrats showed such uncertainty about a mayoral candidate. Hopkins had repeatedly stated over the course of the last months that he intended to leave office, but now he began to make emotional noises about seeking reelection to secure redemption from the voters. This idea was quickly laid to rest as cooler heads within his circle prevailed.

Only two other men seemed actually to want the nomination: Washington Hesing, postmaster of Chicago, and Frank Wenter, president of the sanitary board. Hesing's major booster was A.S. Trude, and there were suggestions that the mayor also probably favored him. Wenter, on the other hand, counted upon

John McGillen (*Illinois Political Directory, 1899*).

the strength of the "old Harrison wing," which in the growing power vacuum in the party was now reasserting itself. Among its leaders were some of the most notorious Democrats including Alderman Edward "Sly Ed" Cullerton, Robert "Bobby" Burke, and William Loeffler (all of whom were to be identified by the Civic Federation in the years ahead as undesirables and enemies of reform).[34]

On the evening of the primaries, a major caucus was held at the Champlain Building with about thirty leading Democratic sachems in attendance. Among these were Hopkins and Sullivan. Both Hesing and Wenter made their pitches, and while no formal decision was made, the smart money was now on the president of the Sanitary Board. And so it was to be. When the convention met, Frank Wenter was easily chosen by acclamation. Hesing withdrew before the nominations were even completed.[35]

The remainder of the conclave was, on the surface anyway, a love feast as all proclaimed their support and admiration for the candidate. Significantly, Hopkins did not attend (though Sullivan was present), and contented himself with a message of congratulations predicting rather cynically an overwhelming Democratic victory. The platform was a recitation of virtually every reformist position (with a few important exceptions) on every urban reform issue, and included support of the introduction of civil service into all city departments, shorter time limits on city utility franchises, improved railroad crossings, and as the special concern of the candidate, promises of still better sanitation.[36]

Frank Wenter did his best against the Republican nominee, George B. Swift. He sought to present himself as someone who was not a "machine politician" and who was "not running on the record of the present administration." He argued that the real issue of the campaign should be "competence," contrasting his fine record heading the Sanitary Board with

that of Swift's brief and controversial term as interim mayor in 1893. Substantial financing was raised and a huge campaign committee was assembled that pointedly did not include Hopkins—though, with Sullivan, he openly supported his party's candidate. On their side, the Republicans counted upon the general dissatisfaction that came with the depression, the lingering effects of Cleveland's action in the Pullman Strike, and the passions of the Ogden scandal. They were not disappointed. On April 2, 1895, Swift was elected by a margin of 143,884 to 103,125 votes.[37]

The results could not have been a surprise to the mayor or to his friends. To his credit, Hopkins maintained good humor and "pleasantly" introduced his successor in the council chambers on April 8, as a man "who well deserves the most flattering majority, which the citizens of Chicago have given him." However, neither the mayor nor his allies allowed the election to interfere with business; on the election eve (in a move that became public knowledge only after the results were counted), permits were issue to the Ogden Gas Company and the Cosmopolitan Electric Company to begin tearing up the streets.[38]

4

Good as Gold
(1895–1897)

Having ridden into office on a tide of public indignation, the new Swift regime immediately began to paint the Hopkins administration as criminally corrupt to justify its attempts to remove all traces of Democratic rule. The Police Commission created in 1894, ostensibly to look into ways to remove politics from law enforcement, was summarily dissolved. Large numbers of Democratic police officers were either fired or forced to resign, even as Democrats employed elsewhere found themselves ruthlessly removed from the city rolls. This was presented as a reform measure in preparation for the implementation in August 1895 of a civil service law recently enacted by the state legislature. In truth, it was simply an excuse to fill as many expiring patronage positions with Republicans as possible.

A grand jury controlled by the GOP began an investigation into the financial practices of the Hopkins administration, and a number of indictments and warrants for arrest were issued against associates of the mayor amidst allegations of millions of missing dollars. However, no trials were actually held. There were even reports that the former mayor would be indicted for "gross mismanagement," though nothing came of this either. Swift also moved against the Ogden and Cosmopolitan companies by revoking their construction permits. But both companies won court victories upholding their rights.[1]

Throughout Hopkins maintained a discreet silence. There was little else he could do; it would serve no purpose to fuel controversy by answering Swift. Later, once the immediate fervor had diminished, he would return to active politics and edge his way back into the public spotlight. Roger C. Sullivan, on the other hand, perhaps more wisely, chose to maintain the relatively low profile that he had been affecting since losing his 1894 bid for county clerk. Astutely, for the next nineteen years he focused his efforts within his party and his business ventures. While his power within the Democratic ruling circles would eventually grow exponentially, and his name would become familiar to the public at large, at this point he largely disappeared from press reports. He would not allow himself to become a fully public figure again until 1914.[2]

John Hopkins and Roger Sullivan now bore some of the stigma of defeat and corruption, but it is unclear to what degree it was deserved. Concerning the election, they could hardly be held responsible for the Republican tide across the nation. On the other hand, while there is no evidence that Hopkins was ever a shareholder in either the Ogden or Cosmopolitan companies, Sullivan became closely identified with both, and benefited from some degree of partial ownership. Beyond this, the historical record is murky. It seems unlikely that Sullivan (or Hopkins) was an instigator of the scheme; Sullivan was not closely connected with John W. Lanehart, the principal promoter or his circle, and he may well have been accurate in his initial claims of disinterest. However, what is equally apparent is that it was extremely unlikely that he could become a beneficiary without some degree of participation in the passage of the ordinances. Neither the press at the time nor the subsequent accounts make clear what role he might have played, but it seems most probable that he was decisive in assuring that Hopkins did not exercise his veto. It might well have taken Sullivan's influence to bring him around, especially as the mayor was on record as opposing similar measures earlier. The importance of Sullivan's probable participation was possibly suggested by the subsequent course of the management of the two companies.

When the favorable franchises were initially brought before the city council, they were designed to be run by men most closely associated with and related to Governor John P. Altgeld. By September 1896 (after the July 16, 1896, death of John W. Lanehart, primary promoter of Ogden and Cosmopolitan), it was Sullivan's friend and mentor Thomas A. Gahan who became effectively the chief executive officer of both concerns. In 1897, Sullivan became their secretary and treasurer, as well as of the Western Republic Construction Company, created to build the Ogden Gas Company's physical plant. Sullivan was then to shepherd both the Ogden and Cosmopolitan firms (becoming their president in 1905, following Gahan's death from Bright's disease) until 1913, when they were finally sold off.

It is equally unclear to what degree any of the participants profited from the franchises. Carter H. Harrison claims in his autobiography that Sullivan (and Hopkins as well) were compensated by as much as $666,666 (whether the figure was symbolic or not is not known). However, it is virtually certain that Harrison was not a party to the deals, and that the five-term mayor was probably basing his figure upon rumor and speculation augmented by a desire to inflate the foibles of the man who ultimately ran him out of politics, Roger Sullivan. In fact, as the subsequent financial history of the two companies is obscured by years of myriad private and complex agreements concerning sales and leasing of property, one of which extended compensation to 1945, it will probably never be known how much remuneration was secured. That said, it cannot be denied that it must have been substantial.

Much more certain is the likelihood that Sullivan and the others did not anticipate the violent public reaction that followed. They may well have expected some protest, as had occurred months before with the creation of the Universal Gas Company, but the relatively short outburst of public acrimony then would not have been subsequently daunting. In that light, the creation of the new companies made some political sense.

What was not counted upon was the strength of a growing reformism in the city and the nation, which correctly discerned the franchises as exemplifying the kind of politics-for-profit that many were growing to abhor. The end result was to contribute to massive Republican victories. Still it was not a total loss for men who regarded politics as appropriate for entrepreneurial enterprise, and Roger C. Sullivan in particular had the significant consolation of having entered permanently into a much more rarified strata of financial security.

The public only gradually became aware of the identity of most of those involved in the companies, and after a time, they no longer seemed to care that much. There was to be no dramatic moment when those concerned were suddenly revealed. Instead, it became self-evident through such things as Sullivan's appointment as secretary of the Ogden Gas Company, a position he would hold for well over a decade. Apparently, with the elections won, and the "rascals thrown out," the press and public were not nearly as offended as the professed anger during the campaign would have had everyone believe. Perhaps also dampening the expressions of outrage, at least from among Democratic reformist circles, was that so many of the men who initially incorporated Ogden Gas and Cosmopolitan Electric and who applied for the related franchises were closely connected to Governor John P. Altgeld, and included the aforementioned John W. Lanehart, Altgeld's first cousin and law partner, and Charles J. Ford (brother of Altgeld's wife Emma). While there is no evidence that the governor himself was part of the scheme, he, too, was one of the many rising young businessman politicians so present in Chicago and Illinois politics of the era, and he was perfectly willing to accept his relative's share as a bequest (worth little at the time) following Lanehart's death. In the years ahead, as Sullivan and Hopkins would endure the permanent stigma of being "gas kings" and "boodlers," this connection to the former governor, a man who would be increasingly lionized as a kind of martyr for reform, would be conveniently ignored. It seems certain, however, that neither Lanehart nor Altgeld reaped the benefits of the riches said to be made possible by the Ogden and Cosmopolitan franchises; both men endured financial embarrassment before their deaths in 1896 and 1902, respectively.

For all of the initial and lingering controversy that the deals created, there emerged in the remaining months of 1895 an issue that would so dominate the political conversation in the city and the United States for the next years as to relegate the alleged foibles of the former mayor and his associates to relative insignificance. It was also to affect significantly their careers. This was the debate over the free coinage of silver. It was to help shape America's political culture for years, while evoking the most extreme passions on both sides. At its simplest, it concerned the coinage of silver to supplement the gold-based supply of money in circulation; at its more complex, it represented a fundamental division between those who championed the new industrial economy (mostly found in the East), and those who believed the nation had been hijacked by powerful Eastern interests to the detriment of the American promise, and more specifically of Western and Southern agriculture (see Appendix).[3]

The passion for free coinage began to appear among Chicago Democrats almost simultaneously with its inclusion in the 1892 planks of the new People's (or Populist) Party. Many factors played a part in its growing local influence, including the fear of the potential strength of the Populists, the Democrats' self-identification as the party of working and average people, the political expediency of breaking with the unpopular fiscal and economic policies of the Cleveland administration, and simple raw ambition. As early as 1893, the elder Mayor Carter H. Harrison had embraced the silver position, and the evidence suggests that he may have planned a bid for the presidency based upon his advocacy. With his assassination, leadership of the cause in Illinois fell to the state's controversial governor, John P. Altgeld.

The Democratic Party's first chief executive in the state since the Civil War, Altgeld has become a figure of legendary dimensions whose life was, like those of Sullivan and Hopkins, an affirmation of America as a place of possibility. He was born on December 30, 1847, in Niederselters, then located in the Grand Duchy of Hessen-Darmstadt of the German Confederation. He was the son of an illiterate agricultural worker. When he was but one year of age, his family migrated to the United States. At the age of sixteen, he joined the Union Army, where he compiled an honorable record of service as a private soldier. Returning home after the war, he attended high school and became a teacher in Woodville, Ohio. Thwarted in love because of his lowly status (temporarily, as it proved), he found employment as a railway worker in Missouri and Arkansas. He eventually returned to teaching even as he was successfully completing legal studies.

In 1875, he arrived in Chicago to practice law, and soon developed a reputation for defending the downtrodden and disadvantaged. He achieved some prominence with the publication in 1884 of his book, *Our Penal Machinery and Its Victims*, which argued the existence of vast disparities between rich and poor in the implementation of justice. In the years ahead, the tome was highly influential among reformers across the nation. He next turned to capitalism and achieved considerable wealth engaging in real estate speculation. Articulate, authoritative, wealthy, charismatic, and endowed with impeccable credentials as a working man, he was nominated in 1892 by both the Democrats and the United Labor Party for the office of governor. He won by the narrow plurality of 48.74 percent of the vote.[4]

In office, he supported prototypal progressive reforms, including attempts to limit child labor, to grant recognition to labor unions, and to regulate the factory workplace. His efforts helped solidify his support among the working people of Chicago as well as the emerging body of middle-class reformers dedicated to their uplift. In 1893, he took the politically courageous step of pardoning three of the anarchists sentenced to death following an explosion at an anarchist rally in Haymarket Square in Chicago on May Day, 1889. This won applause among his laboring and reformist allies, but attracted the worst kinds if imprecations from the city's and the nation's more conservative circles. The following year, he further courted fame and controversy by openly breaking with the Cleveland administration with a public protest at the use of federal troops to break the Pullman Strike.[5]

In 1895, the governor began maneuvering for reelection. His support among urban workers in the state after the Pullman Strike was immense, though achieved at the cost of alienating other more prosperous citizens, but his rural appeal was limited. Regardless of the actual depth of his commitment to the silver cause, the issue unquestionably offered a golden opportunity to draw the state's farm vote to his banner. Early and cogent advocacy, moreover, would help make him a rallying point for the opposition to the conservative Cleveland Democrats, and possibly also endow him with a major voice in the selection of the presidential nominee in 1896—though, being foreign-born, he could not run himself. Finally, because Altgeld was without affiliation to the former Democratic machine or other groupings of professionals within the party upon whom he could count unconditionally for support and votes (he would never have an enduring voice in the Chicago or Cook County party internal governance), he needed silver as a means to channel to his candidacy some of the passionate reaction against the abuses of the new industrial order and the attendant demands for reform.[6]

On March 4, 1895, a group of Democratic silverite congressmen in Washington, D.C., issued a formal appeal to those favoring free coinage, urging them to seize control of their local and state Democratic parties and, in effect, to repudiate the leadership of Grover Cleveland. Within weeks Governor Altgeld and the Illinois central committee responded with a call for a special convention to meet on June 5, 1895, to deliberate upon the Illinois

Democracy's position on the money question. Hopkins as a member of the state committee initially opposed the idea. However, against the overwhelming sentiments of his colleagues and following nearly three hours of debate, he acquiesced and agreed to cooperate. For the forces of silver, it was a politically brilliant move. Such a conclave, with a guaranteed free silver majority, would be an ideal mechanism: (1) to seize control of the movement in Illinois and thus forestall the Populists and the recently created National Silver Party that had just met in convention in Washington, D.C., (2) to break formally with the Cleveland administration, and (3) to create an irresistible momentum for silver and Altgeld's gubernatorial candidacy within the state party.[7]

Overseeing the hastily improvised selections of delegates, chosen at a ratio of one representative for every 300 Democratic voters in the 1894 elections, was Altgeld's myrmidon, Illinois secretary of state and chair of the State Democratic Central Committee, William H. "Buck" Hinrichsen. He was also to serve as permanent chair of the Illinois Currency Convention, as it was to be titled. In the environs of the Windy City, former Mayor John P. Hopkins, who was believed to have become "infatuated with the silver craze," and who still controlled the county committee, led "the Hinrichsen forces in Cook County." Primaries were held on May 3, 1895, and the following day those chosen met, elected 337 men for the state conclave, and voted 706 to 23 for an endorsement of silver.[8]

The presence of Hopkins and Sullivan in the ranks of the silver rebellion, despite an apparent initial reluctance, was not especially surprising, although subsequent events do cast doubts upon the depth of both men's ideological commitment. As with most of the leaders of the Chicago party, from "reformers" like Clarence S. Darrow to the notorious Johnny Powers and "Bathhouse" John Coughlin (the latter two especially targeted by the Civic Federation as "gray wolves," or aldermen thought to be corrupt), they saw in the silver movement a chance to reinvent the party as something other than a creature of the depression and the unpopular Cleveland. Intelligent politics mandated that something had to change after the disastrous elections of the fall and the spring. In consequence, most members of the ruling circles of the Democratic Party in Illinois and Chicago, with a few important exceptions, initially seized upon the silver movement with the desperate grasps of drowning men. Close involvement, and the alliance with Altgeld it would bring, also carried the possibility of a reaffirmation and even an enhancement of the power of Hopkins and Sullivan within the party.

The former mayor did not attend the state convention. This was not political; when announcing in December 1894 that he would not be seeking reelection, he also indicated his intention at the end of his term to depart for Europe for his health. On May 5, 1895, he left to seek treatment in Germany for his chronic throat condition.

During his absence, Hopkins was represented by proxy as a delegate-at-large to the silver convention. Roger Sullivan attended and was elected to the Resolutions Committee. Even without Hopkins, it was a boisterous and happy affair with only a tiny minority present that had not embraced the now sacred cause. Impressive speeches were delivered to noisy acclaim by Hinrichsen, former Judge S.P. McConnell of Chicago, Governor Altgeld, Richard Michaelis, editor of the Chicago *Freie Presse*, and one William Jennings Bryan, lately a congressman from Nebraska (he had been a principal in the Congressional appeal of March 4), who was becoming "famous throughout the nation for his fearless, able, and eloquent advocacy of the restoration of silver as primary money." He treated the audience to an excellent address attacking Cleveland, leaving them cheering his promise, "Truth is right, and will prevail!"[9]

Before adjourning, the convention passed a series of resolutions that endorsed free silver, instructed the state committee to work further for the cause, called upon the Illinois congressional delegation to use "all honorable means" in its support, and petitioned the national committee to organize a national Democratic silver convention in August. Hopkins was elected to the proposed Illinois delegation, but thanks to the influence of the Cleveland administration, it would never be held.[10]

As Altgeld, Hopkins, and their compatriots were moving forward to capture the state party for silver, a sizable body of respected local men were heeding President Cleveland's call to opposition, issued in a vehement public letter on April 13, 1895. Soon, a number of state politicians, led by Senator John M. Palmer and Chicago Postmaster Washington Hesing, created the Honest Money League. Members came from all factions: Hesing and Palmer had been strong allies of Hopkins and leading lights of the Cleveland wing, but also among their number, for example, was Adolf Kraus, a key player in the Harrison administration. Backed by the advice, direction, and patronage of the president of the United States, the League soon became highly visible and unfailingly vociferous.[11]

The Democrats naturally became increasingly polarized. The Iroquois Club, the social organization of the local Chicago Democratic leadership, found itself in the awkward position of having voted by a margin of 47 to 27 to oppose free silver, even as its president, J.P. McConnell, was speaking out in its support and attacking Cleveland. Introducing the resolution was Attorney Stephen S. Gregory, who now found himself on the opposite side from his friend, Clarence S. Darrow, with whom he had been co-counsel in defending Patrick Eugene Prendergast, the assassin of Mayor Carter Harrison. McConnell responded by announcing his resignation from his office, only shortly to change his mind at the urging of the membership, which still was seeking some semblance of Democratic unity.[12]

However, the heated rhetoric only intensified. Leading the attack for the cause of gold was Postmaster Hesing, who targeted Altgeld, characterizing him as a "good hater" who "hates the president." But it was Hopkins for whom the greatest scorn was reserved. John had been an integral part of the Cleveland wing, and received favors of support and patronage from the president, but he also had been decisive in the endorsement of silver by the county convention. Now the former mayor was therefore judged as the worst kind of traitor.[13]

At one point the antagonisms nearly became violent. Following a luncheon at the Iroquois Club on April 24, 1895 (before the trip to Europe), Hopkins and Hesing, previously close, became engaged in a bitter exchange. The Postmaster, his massive mutton-chop whiskers bristling, lost all control. Red-faced and sputtering, he accused his erstwhile friend of being a "coward," "unprincipled," and "no democrat [sic]," who, moreover, had been elected in any case through "depraved methods!" He became so furious that he slipped into his native German with words that "sounded to the apostle of silver [Hopkins] like this: ------xvzkq taoxzn xx zxx!!!!!—XXXXxxft bgk xvxxzy!!!! [nineteenth-century equivalents to "expletive deleted," apparently]." Never nonplussed, Hopkins easily won the argument with his furious former friend as to which was the better Democrat by pointing out that Hesing had been a delegate to the 1880 Republican National Convention that had nominated James Garfield.[14]

The storms quieted over the long and politically inactive summer months, and for some the pause lent hope that things would yet hold together. It was somewhat in this spirit that a grand party was thrown for John Hopkins in late September on his return from Europe "severely bruised" from a rough trip across the north Atlantic. Present were most of the county's leading Democrats (excluding most of the leadership of the Honest Money League), including Roger Sullivan, Clarence S. Darrow, Thomas Moran, Alfred S. Trude, judge and future mayor and governor Edward F. Dunne, Harry Rubens, and William Bogle. Washington Hesing, the man who had publicly excoriated Hopkins just months before, but with whom he was now reconciled, offered the primary peroration praising the ex-mayor for his "stalwart loyalty to his friends" (!), while chiding him gently for being a bachelor.[15]

Hopkins gave every appearance of being greatly moved; according to one report, it was "no exaggeration to say it was the happiest day of his life." Though spending time denying rumors that he had left town because he was suffering from cancer, he had a fine time with the 150 or so of his friends present. Chairing the event was Franklin MacVeagh, and the guest list included most of the old gang and then some. Prominent political men like Robert Emmet "Bobby" Burke, William Loeffler, Thomas Gahan, and Frank Peabody crowded into Kinsley's Restaurant and indulged themselves in an epicurean repast featuring blue points, radishes, celery, strained chicken gumbo, franked whitefish, cucumbers, hollandaise potatoes, sweetbreads à la cigale, French peas, barons of beef, baked tomatoes, browned sweet potatoes, golden plover, asparagus vinaigrette, glacés, cake, coffee, crackers, cheese, sherry, sauternes, claret, champagne, cognac, and liquor. Cigars were then smoked, toasts offered, and songs sung. A special ditty in which all joined with boisterous enthusiasm had been prepared for the occasion:

> Oh Johnnie, Oh Johnnie Hopkins, here's a welcome, full and free
> We're proud to have you home again, from o'er the stormy sea,
> May your shadow n'er grow stronger,
> Oh Johnnie, Oh Johnnie Hopkins, here is friendship's hand to you.

For all the conviviality, the conclave was inevitably political. Most obviously, it proclaimed that despite electoral defeats and accusations of scandal, Hopkins retained the respect and affection of most local Democrats. It also made clear his intention to assert his influence over the city and county parties in time for the upcoming November election campaigns.[16]

Certainly not all of the kind words and sentiments offered at the coming-home party were entirely fulsome or expedient. Because of his youth and charm, Hopkins was viewed by many with the same kind of fond indulgence often extended in Victorian families towards a roué uncle or brother. Of special interest was his status as a bachelor in an age when almost all public men liked to portray themselves as happily married and devoted to family. Handsome and wealthy, he had long been the object of interest for "the fair members of St. James' Parish." So when he was observed (by none other than Roger C. Sullivan) just before Christmas leaving Schubert & Gallagher's, a florist shop on Washington Street, and it was learned that he had purchased sixteen baskets of roses at the hefty cost of $10 each, it made the front page of the *Chicago Times-Herald*. Some of the baskets were for his mother, sisters, and other female relatives, but as to the others, even his partner and friend professed to be mystified.[17]

John's months of absence in Europe also helped turn public attention towards Roger

Sullivan, who would be increasingly perceived as an independent force within the party in his own right. Since leaving office as probate clerk (on December 2, 1894) and the end of the Hopkins administration (April 9, 1895), he had consolidated his position as leader of his home Thirteenth Ward. Located northwest of downtown and prosperous, it was dominated by the middle class and the well-to-do "lace curtain" Irish. It was to prove to be a reliable base for his ambitions. He always maintained a special relationship with the Democratic constituency in his ward; when he moved from the West Side to the North Side in 1919, there was real apprehension expressed about the local impact of his departure in terms of governmental services. The ease of his relatively rapid rise as ward boss was founded upon the political techniques and personal skills that eventually were to carry him to a position of close to absolute leadership within the state and local Democratic Party. As one editorial writer explained years later when discussing his appeal within his ward, it was his use of "patronage, friendship, and helpfulness, which in America's chief melting pot ... were the magnets, that attracted a Pied Piper retinue of followers." While the same observer wrote, "there may have been a lack of idealism" in Sullivan's politics"—at least in this early stage of his career—"there was no lack of gratitude and confidence."[18]

However, as Sullivan understood, sometimes helping someone could backfire, human ingratitude being what it was and is. He once made this point ironically by professing to be exasperated with a defecting political operative because after all he "had never done him a favor." However, for the most part, people liked Roger Sullivan, respected his judgment, and accordingly accepted his leadership. In politics, as elsewhere in life, the personal esteem he inspired among politicians and ordinary citizens alike was everything.[19]

John and Roger naturally, therefore, excelled at the social side of politics. They were regulars at the yearly Democratic picnics, which were still being held in the 1890s before the city's growth made them impractical. Roger was especially good at baseball, and in 1891, he captained his team to victory. John could be counted upon to be among the most active participants at these gatherings, which provided an opportunity for factional rivals to meet in a playful and pleasant setting. Nor did the pair neglect the many banquets and dinners that were then characteristic of the city's political culture. Their visibility and personal popularity were considerable political assets to be cultivated and maintained.[20]

In the months ahead, John and Roger would need all their friends. In a reversal so common to Chicago and Cook County politics of the period, they were to find themselves embroiled in a major political battle with John P. Altgeld. The background against which this drama was to be played was the ever more emotional silver-versus-gold controversy, but its real theme was the control of the Democratic Party of Cook County and of Illinois.[21]

Hopkins and Sullivan had originally partnered themselves with the governor and the silver movement because the alliance promised continued and even increased power within the party both locally and statewide. Altgeld had relied upon the former mayor and his circle to assure a solid return in Cook County for the unprecedented Silver Convention in June 1895, and at that point there seemed to be an understanding regarding the division of power between the state faction and the forces of "Hopkinism."

However, in the late fall of 1895, the governor began encroaching upon the Chicago and Cook County Democracies, heretofore within the ambit of the Hopkins/Sullivan circle. This became clear when, after yet another Republican landslide in the November elections, Francis S. Peabody, an ally of Hopkins and Sullivan, stepped down as chair of the county

Democrats. To their discomfiture, Alfred S. Trude, now having firmly tied his wagon to Altgeld, led a successful effort to elect Thomas Gahan, who, though personally and politically very close throughout the years to Hopkins and Sullivan, was at this moment prepared to join forces with the state's chief executive. At just about the same time, charges emerged from Alderman Johnny Powers and Michael Cassius "never-give-a-sucker-an-even-break" McDonald (both in the Altgeld camp) that three-quarters of a million dollars were missing from the party funds for the period dating from the elections of 1893 through the spring of 1895. Since Hopkins had been instrumental in all these campaigns, the implications were obvious. The former mayor briefly dodged reporters, while Sullivan "laughed" at the statements. The charges were never substantiated and faded away, which made their political nature all the more apparent.[22]

Adding to the growing rift between the governor on the one hand and Hopkins and Sullivan on the other, was President Cleveland, who was doing all he could, including the use of threats and patronage, to sweep back the silver tide. Neither the ex-mayor nor his chief partner had actually broken with Cleveland personally or ever uttered a public word against him. Their involvement with Altgeld and silver had been strictly political expedience.

Now it was becoming evident that the president and his supporters in Illinois were doing their best to woo the pair back into the ranks; stories appeared of presidential backing for Hopkins as a possible candidate for the Democratic National Committee. By the fall of 1895, some degree of reconciliation was achieved, as attested to by the presence of Washington Hesing as toastmaster at Hopkins's welcome-home party. But Governor Altgeld, even as he was attempting to seize control of the Cook County party as part of his vision of a personal statewide "machine," continued to fragment the Democrats with his ever more strident condemnations of his nation's chief executive, even going so far as publicly to blame Cleveland by name for the Democratic defeats of November.[23]

The end result was that by February 1896, cautious speculation began to appear that Hopkins and his circle might be moving away from the governor and the silver movement, speculation that Altgeld felt compelled to deny. By mid–April this belief seemed to be substantiated by Hopkins in an interview conducted by the *Chicago Tribune*. He explained: "I never was a free coinage, at the ratio of 16 to 1, Democrat. My idea is the Democrats of Illinois should drop this money question and go to fighting the Republican Party. By talking of nominating Presidential and Gubernatorial candidates on a silver platform, they are simply fighting one another and splitting their own party." He went on to deny any interest in becoming national committeeman, especially as he would have to spend "$8,000 or $10,000 a year" for the job![24]

Hopkins's change of heart was further confirmed by Roger Sullivan's attendance at a meeting of thirty-six leading gold Democrats on April 17 at the Palmer House (location of the headquarters of the Honest Money League), where a Committee of 100 was appointed to promote the hard currency cause throughout the city and county. Hopkins was "conspicuously absent," although physically present downstairs. Presumably, this was a ploy to express his interest while avoiding commitment until the exact terms for his support had been negotiated. One of these appears to have been an endorsement of Altgeld, whom the former mayor reportedly did not wish to offend unduly, for reelection as governor. This achieved, Hopkins let it be known that he would clarify his position on the money issue in the near future. It was widely believed that he, with his "genius for organization," would take on the task of campaign manager for the cause.[25]

The proclamation, at the urging of Hopkins, of support for the governor by those appalled by his advocacy of silver and his attacks on the president was not as mysterious as it might first appear. Altgeld, in a clever political move, was presenting himself as the indispensable man, as the only one able to retain the governorship for a party battered by recurring defeat and hungry for victory. To drive this point home, he had announced coyly in February—even as he was doing everything possible to gain greater power in the Democracy's ruling circles—that he might not be a candidate after all for reelection in the fall. Hoping at this point to avoid breaking the party apart and the stigma of treason, the Honest Money League accordingly offered their backing for the man, if not for the cause he had so fervently embraced.[26]

The governor was having none of it; he declined their endorsement, dismissing them as being little more than the pawns of the hated Grover Cleveland. His minion, "Buck" Hinrichsen, even predicted a bolt should the national party fail to nominate a pro-silver candidate. Reflecting upon the as-yet ambiguous public position of his supposed ally, the governor also made a statement that expressed his hope that the former mayor would yet remain on the side of the angels: "Mr. Hopkins," he proclaimed, "like every other man will do exactly as he sees fit, but the story [of his defection to the Honest Money League] is too ridiculous to be noticed. While he may differ with us in some ways, he is opposed to a single gold standard." Others within the silver faction were not so generous; one insider had already attributed the ex-mayor's increasingly ambiguous stance to a selfish interest in creating a "Hopkins party."[27]

It was against this backdrop of fragmentation, tempered by the transcending hope that the Democrats could remain united, that the State Central Committee met on April 20, 1896, in Springfield for the purpose of determining the location and date of the state convention. Things were cordial. To avoid confrontation it was decided by the dominant Altgeld/Hinrichsen silver faction, who made up sixteen of the nineteen committee members, to forego the introduction of a resolution in favor of free silver. There was also a general accord—or so it appeared—as to the distribution and method of electing the 1,063 delegates who were to meet on June 22 in Peoria.[28]

However, behind the scenes both the silver advocates and the sound moneymen were caucusing and preparing plans for control of the party. State Committeeman Hopkins heartily endorsed the decision to avoid any formal statement on the free coinage of silver, but still declined to clarify his own position. As it turned out, just three weeks after the state committee adjourned, all cause for doubt was at last dispelled with the news that John P. Hopkins (assisted by, among others, Roger C. Sullivan) would oversee the campaign for the gold cause in the city and Cook County[29]

After this point such good feeling, feigned or real, as had yet remained between the two camps quickly evaporated. When a formal call to elect the representatives to the Peoria State Convention was issued on May 21, it was greeted with howls of anger from the Honest Money League. Roger Sullivan called it an "infamous outrage," being like his compatriots dismayed at the distribution of delegates, which was designed to guarantee an overwhelming silver majority. Although they were actually helpless to do much about it, a radical scheme was briefly floated by the Honest Money League to induce the pro–Cleveland Democratic

National Committee to step in and replace the state committee because of alleged violations of a recent state primary law, "the dishonesty and unfairness of party rules," and the assertion of a supposed subornation to the Populists. Nothing came of this, so the League called its own convention to meet on June 13 in Chicago. It was directed to reorganize the Cook County Convention, to elect an alternate slate of delegates to the Democratic National Convention, and to take all steps necessary to take control from the "hordes of the political bosses!" Hopkins now openly signaled his disdain for Altgeld and what he labeled his "machine," making clear that he would never under any circumstances vote for the governor. Washington Hesing assured everyone that he, at least, would leave the party if the national convention nominated a silver advocate. It was now unquestionable that "war is declared!"[30]

The primaries for the Peoria convention were held, but were boycotted in protest by the gold Democrats. The subsequent convention was infused with both the spirit and presence of John P. Altgeld, who at this moment was probably the single most prominent silver Democrat in the country. He was renominated without opposition. The governor was also elected to head an almost exclusively pro-silver delegation to the national convention. A.S. Trude's brother, George, received the nod for attorney general. The attacks upon Cleveland were fiery and immoderate; government by "injunction" was condemned, and the national administration received much of the blame for the ill effects of the depression. Not least, the convention voted a strong endorsement of the free coinage of silver.[31]

Now the future for all causes and personalities depended upon the outcome of the Democratic national convention, scheduled to convene in Chicago in the first week of July. It promised to be lively. Cleveland refused any thought of running again but designated no successor. There was no other single leading candidate, and the ideological division over the currency question was poisoning and polarizing the party. It seemed that regardless of what happened or who was nominated, disintegration would be unavoidable. However, many on both sides remained hopeful that despite everything, party harmony would be restored, and that the streak of three years of virtually unremitting Republican victories could be at last terminated. Condemned to live in interesting times, the holders of these desperate longings would in the event pine in vain, doomed instead to have their deepest fears realized in one of the greatest political spectacles in the history of the republic. The circus was coming to town.

All agreed that tumultuous spring of 1896 that something extraordinary was underway. Breaking almost all precedent in American political history, an ideologically driven faction was seizing control of one state Democracy after another in a blatant repudiation of their own sitting president and his policies. By June, of twenty-three states holding conventions, eighteen had gone for silver, and elsewhere the tide was equally decisive. Almost spontaneously, the frustrations of those dissatisfied with the power of the "interests" and what they saw as their imposition of the gold standard now burst forth to inundate everything in their path. Such was the unchallenged and diffuse nature of the movement, however, that no single leader or presidential candidacy emerged from its ranks. Nonetheless, myriad politicians sought the honor.[32]

Former Governor John P. Altgeld in these months received most of the press attention as the mouthpiece of the silver cause, but his foreign birth disqualified him for the presidency. He, and therefore the Illinois delegation, was leaning towards Richard "Silver Dick" Bland, a former Congressman from Missouri responsible in part for the Bland-Allison Act of 1878 (that originally included free coinage but was greatly weakened in the Senate), and a passionate advocate of free silver. Bland, however, enjoyed far from universal acclaim, and as late as the eve of the national convention a broad assortment of other men was attracting speculation and support. Among these were Horace Boles, a former governor of Iowa; Vice-President Adlai Stevenson of Illinois; Henry M. Teller, idol of the West and a Republican senator from Colorado, who would become a leader of the Silver Republican Party; former secretary of the Navy and Cleveland loyalist William C. Whitney of New York; Claude Matthews, and David Turpie, respectively governor and senator from Indiana.[33]

One name that made few lists (and among those that did, it appeared as almost as an afterthought) was a former congressman from Nebraska named William Jennings Bryan. His relative obscurity was soon to end, as he was to become one of the most significant figures in American history, a giant in a generation of giants who would rank in the company of Theodore Roosevelt and Woodrow Wilson. To many, he would embody the Jeffersonian spirit as a champion of American rural values and of the people, sent as a savior to confront the negative encroachments of industrialization, urbanization, and modernity. To others, he was a small-minded and ignorant bigot, who was perfectly willing to stoke and take advantage of the fears of farmers and others to promote his own ambitions—the often cited contemporary adage being that he, like the Platte River back in his state of Nebraska, was "six inches deep, and six miles wide at the mouth." He was also soon to be the implacable enemy of Roger C. Sullivan and John P. Hopkins.[34]

Bryan was born on March 19, 1860, the son of Silas and Mariah Bryan in Salem, Illinois. His father, a prominent farmer, served extensive tenures in the state Senate, rubbing shoulders with Abraham Lincoln and Stephen Douglas. He was later elected as a circuit judge. Bryan would later attribute to his father his attachment to the soil and its tillers, as well as his mistrust of those with power. Initially home-schooled with the Bible and the *McGuffey Readers*, he embraced the moral lessons of both, rejecting for life sinful pursuits like loose women, gambling, and alcohol. Although his parents were Baptist and Methodist, he would be drawn to the more rigid piety of the Presbyterian Church, which he joined in his adolescence. His formal education began at age ten with his attendance at an academy associated with Illinois College in Jacksonville. Following his graduation as valedictorian, he studied jurisprudence at the Union College of Law in Chicago. Between 1883 and 1887, he practiced as an attorney back in Jacksonville before moving to Lincoln, Nebraska, to seek new horizons.

There he subordinated his law practice to a political ambition that brought his election in 1890 as a Democrat to the United States House of Representatives. Over the next four years in Washington, he became increasingly vociferous in his support of lower tariffs, and, as the populist movement began to make its presence felt, of the free coinage of silver. While still a congressman, he attempted to secure his own election to the United States Senate by the Nebraska legislature. Failing in this, he accepted the post as editor of the *Omaha World-Herald*. Gifted with great energy, a projecting and pleasing voice, an impressive appearance, a flair for both composing and delivering speeches, and a burning conviction of the righteousness of his causes, he dedicated himself to becoming one of the leading advocates of free silver.

By the time the Democratic National Convention met in 1896, he had been engaged for over a year in numerous speaking tours across the nation building grass-roots recognition and appreciation among silver advocates and local leaders. Former Governor Altgeld, however, did not find him particularly impressive and publicly "questioned [his] qualities as a thinker," while privately considering him a "damn fool." He was not pleased when Bryan had shown up, apparently without an invitation, at the Illinois Currency Convention in 1895, and it was perhaps for this reason that the Nebraskan's speech received only passing and relatively tepid praise in the meeting's journal. When the forty-eight Illinois delegates caucused immediately before the convention, only one opted for the man from Nebraska.[35]

As Chicago filled with delegates, the press, and onlookers from across the United States in the days before the convention was to convene on Tuesday, July 7, 1896, the excitement and sense of the extraordinary became almost palpable. Frantic meetings were held at the Sherman House by the silverites and at the Palmer House by those still hoping for at least a compromise on the money issue. In these unprecedented circumstances, nothing seemed certain. Despite this, the newspapers offered confident pontifications that were repeated in the streets and halls, and all concluded that the nominee would be either Richard Bland of Missouri, Altgeld's choice, or the favorite of the Populists and the Western wing of the Democratic Party, Henry Teller.[36]

The doors of the Coliseum opened promptly at 10:00 a.m. A boisterous crowd of over a thousand rushed in, having waited for hours for admittance to the guest galleries. Some paid as much as $50 for a ticket, and it required a corps of over a hundred ushers and police officers to maintain control. At noon, as the hall was still filling, a huge brass band made up of dozens of local musicians specially organized for the occasion, and led by "a great, gold-bedecked drum major with hair awry, and enthusiasm bursting from every seam," struck up the strains of "The Suwannee River," followed by "Dixie" as they began to march in, accompanied by general cheers and acclaim. Shortly afterwards, the convention was declared in session.[37]

From the beginning, it was clear that the silver advocates were in charge and unprepared to compromise. The first test came with the selection of the temporary chair. The Democratic National Committee favored Senator David Hill of New York, and he was duly nominated. Anticipating this, the silver forces, including Altgeld, had met earlier at the Sherman House and decided to support Senator John W. Daniel of Virginia. He was easily elected by a margin of 556 to 349. In the same spirit, a resolution introduced by Hill praising President Grover Cleveland was rejected by 534 to 357 votes. These results were also echoed by ballots sustaining the Committee on Credentials' decision to seat silver delegations from Michigan, Nebraska, and elsewhere. William Jennings Bryan testified before the Committee as an affected delegate on behalf of the Nebraska silverites. This appearance, combined with the effect of his months of politicking and speech-making for the cause around the country, helped bring him the chairmanship of the Platform Committee, which under his guidance returned a majority report emphatically in support of the free coinage of silver at a 16 to one ratio to gold.[38]

On July 9, 1896, William Jennings Bryan sprinted forward from his seat in the hall to speak in defense of the pro-silver majority report he had helped compose. His was but another of a series of speeches already presented on the issue, most of which inspired boredom and restlessness. He had been preparing for this moment for his entire adult life. For years he had been perfecting his dramatic oratorical style and cultivating his rich and powerful baritone that could overcome even the poor acoustics of the Coliseum. The hundreds of hours of oratory he had devoted around the country to the cause of free silver provided him with ample material from which to cull and collect his most effective statements and devices. No single speech in American history was to have a greater immediate impact.

He spoke of the divisions in the country emerging between East and West, of rural life as the bedrock of American values, of the defining nature of the gold/silver issue as a sacred cause that spoke to the preservation of democratic institutions, of the hypocrisy of those who were now advocating gold but who had supported bimetallism in the past (i.e., the Republican Party), and of the "interests" who were attempting to seize control of the American economy and society for their own selfish ends. He concluded with a war cry and warning to these same interests and leaders, famously proclaiming that you "shall not press down upon the brow of labor this crown of thorns; you shall not crucify mankind upon a cross of gold!"[39]

Throughout, the crowd was his, a "trained choir," and as he concluded, pandemonium ensued. He was lifted onto the shoulders—on a "platform of living flesh and bone"—of enthusiastic delegates who crowded around as he left the platform (snapping his suspenders in the process). State delegations, especially those from the South, seized their banners and inched their way through the cheering mob to stand beside the Nebraska contingent. Disheveled, Bryan at last managed to return to his seat, but the demonstration continued unabated. There was a real possibility that the convention would nominate him spontaneously, and the Bland managers frantically sought an adjournment after things calmed

down sufficiently for the majority report to be accepted. Bryan graciously agreed, and the exhausted but still cheering delegates began slowly to exit. The following day it would take five ballots, but the Democratic Party nominated William Jennings Bryan for the presidency of the United States. He was but 36 years old. A few weeks later, his standing as the new idol of the silver movement was reaffirmed when the Populists (or most of them, anyway; one group splintered off) and an aggregation calling themselves the National Silver Party (an organization of pro-silver Republicans) also proclaimed him their standard-bearer.[40]

The unprecedented emergence of Bryan at the 1896 convention was rooted in the insurrection that was the silver movement. Almost to a man, the Democratic advocates of silver had determined more-or-less at once in the spring of 1896 to seize control of their party from what

William Jennings Bryan, 1896 (Library of Congress LC-USZC2-6259).

they considered to be a reactionary Cleveland regime, so as to bring about radical change in its and their country's direction. Like the French *sans-culottes* of an earlier era, they would stand no compromise, brook no opposition. Aristocratic Cleveland ally William C. Whitney recognized this with distaste when he observed: "For the first time I understand the scenes of the French Revolution." But the silverites had everything but a leader. For all of the attempts by Altgeld, Bland, and others to take charge, none had captured their imagination. Bryan, charismatic and handsome, in the minutes of his "Cross of Gold" oration became the dominant figure, not just of the silver cause within and without his party, but also of Democratic national politics over the next decade and a half. Now it fell upon him to take the crusade to the American people, a task he took up with relish.[41]

But the final ballot was not unanimous and many in the hall and elsewhere were appalled by events. William Allen White, editor of the *Emporia* (Kansas) *Gazette* and famous for his social and political commentary, who was present in Chicago, regarded Bryan as the "incarnation of demagogy, the apotheosis of riot, destruction, and carnage." The conservative *New York Sun* put it more crudely, characterizing the nominee as "an ugly little anarchist from Illinois." Grover Cleveland in Washington took the nomination personally, writing: "Those who controlled the convention displayed hatred of me and wholly repudiated me." Democrats who yet supported the president and gold were now confronted with a crucial decision.[42]

Even as delegates were arriving in Chicago, the gold Democrats were holding themselves apart, organizing, and hinting that a bolt might be possible. John P. Hopkins, as a leading "sound money man," took it upon himself to engage in "corralling" delegates of like mind. On July 3, the Cook County gold men appointed an official reception committee for those coming to the convention. Principal among its membership were Hopkins, Roger Sullivan, Adolf Kraus, William C. Avery, and William J. Bogle. Meanwhile, the Illinois executive committee of the state Honest Money League established headquarters at the clubroom of the Palmer House, where most sympathetic delegates chose to stay. That night a massive rally was held at the Auditorium at which Hopkins, New York Senator David Bennett Hill, the Empire State's former governor Roswell Pettibone Flower, William C. Whitney, and others spoke. Illinois' Democratic national committeeman, Ben T. Cable, and Washington Hesing also shared the platform. Not surprisingly, when Altgeld's name was mentioned, it evoked hisses and other rude noises.[43]

Not content with mere words, the gold men pondered a desperate action—or so it was reported by the newspapers—to seize control of the convention machinery and then force the silver backers to bolt. Given that the advocates of the white metal were in a huge majority, the plan was tenuous at best. The first step of the conspiracy, so it was reported, was to nominate "some strong man" (probably Senator David B. Hill) for the temporary chairmanship, and then for Daniel Harrity, chair of the Democratic national committee, together with "other influential members" who would oversee the election, to refuse to recognize any silver demand for a roll-call on the grounds that it was unclear which delegates were legitimate (!) because the status of some of the states' representation was contested. Thereupon the gavel would be handed to the strong man, who would deliver a speech in favor of gold, prompting the silver men to walk out and abandon the party. Nothing came of this fantastic scheme aside from the failed nomination of Hill.[44]

Other attempts by the gold men to influence the convention, its platform, and its nominee would prove to be equally pointless. With Bryan's nomination, the discussions about bolting became much more serious. Within a couple of days after adjournment, sixteen leaders of the sound moneymen of Illinois (including Hopkins) issued a manifesto calling for a new Democratic convention. They claimed that the one just concluded was rendered illegitimate by (1) its rejection of Hill as temporary chair, (2) its recognition of a Michigan delegation that favored silver over one that supported gold, (3) its refusal to endorse "the honesty and fidelity of the current administration," and (4) its repudiation of the "time-honored democratic principle which demands the strict maintenance of a sound and stable national currency."[45]

On July 21, William Bynum, chair of the Indiana delegation, was delegated to send out telegrams inviting delegates from Kentucky, Indiana, Illinois, Iowa, Michigan, Minnesota, Missouri, Nebraska, and Wisconsin to gather at the Auditorium in Chicago to discuss the details of organizing. In all, thirty-seven men met on July 23, with John P. Hopkins and John M. Palmer of Illinois in attendance. For five heated hours they conferred, the principal point of contention being whether to move forward immediately or to wait until further support could be cultivated. In the end, it was decided to appoint a committee of nine to prepare a call for another convention. The counterrevolution had begun.[46]

Events now moved forward rapidly. On August 5, 1896, a committee representing eight states (Alabama, Illinois, Indiana, Kentucky, Missouri, New York, Ohio, and Wisconsin) came together at the Denison Hotel in Indianapolis under the chairmanship of Bynum. Three decisions were made: (1) to hold the convention on September 2 in the Indiana capital, (2) to turn the composition of the platform over to John M. Palmer, assisted by John P. Hopkins, and (3) to elect an executive committee (to include both Palmer and Hopkins). Within days, a letter was sent to President Grover Cleveland asking for his endorsement (which was rendered), a permanent Indianapolis headquarters was established, and the new executive committee was gathering at the Palmer House in Chicago to work out details.[47]

Meanwhile in Illinois, gold Democrats moved to create a state organization and to convene their own conclave. Hopkins declined the chairmanship of the new state central committee, but agreed to assist, and joined Frank S. Peabody and Chester Babcock, a lawyer from Adams County, in composing the platform. This endorsed gold, but also attacked Governor Altgeld and his administration as "mischievous, scandalous, reckless, and vindictive," while taking the "silverites" to task for their tactics in securing control of the Cook County and state Democratic parties. By the time the gold convention opened on August 25 at the Battery "D" headquarters in Chicago, a consensus had emerged around the gubernatorial candidacy of General John C. Black, United States Attorney for the Northern District of Illinois, and a general in the Civil War, who was active in the politically powerful veterans' organization, the Grand Army of the Republic. Candidates were also nominated for lieutenant governor, secretary of state, attorney general, auditor, treasurer, and the board of trustees for the University of Illinois. In some districts gold Democrats were selected to run for Congress. Delegates for the national convention were identified, and among the delegates-at-large were John M. Palmer, John C. Black, Ben T. Cable, Charles Ewing, John P. Hopkins, and Roger C. Sullivan.[48]

On September 2, 1896, the conclave of the "National Democratic Party," as the gold men were styling themselves (to the protests and lawsuits of the regulars across the country), opened its first session at Tomlinson Hall in Indianapolis. Built in 1886, the auditorium was admittedly "plain," but was elaborately decorated with flags, bunting, streamers, potted plants, and pictures of Jefferson, Jackson, Samuel J. Tilden, Grover Cleveland, and others. Dominating everything was a massive golden eagle emerging from a sunburst over the podium. Bankers, merchants, lawyers, and railroad executives made up the majority of the delegates, with relatively few professional politicians present (though a major Tammany leader and future boss, Charles F. Murphy, was there). In all, the assemblage was "as a body comprised of a higher class of men than generally forms the file of a national convention." Forty-four states and territories sent men, with only Idaho, Nevada, Utah, and Wyoming, all solidly in the silver camp, absent. The doors opened at 11:00 a.m., and at 12:29 p.m., Palmer as chair opened the proceedings. Ex-Governor Roswell P. Flower of New York delivered a rousing welcoming speech, and the rest of the day was largely given over to ever more lengthy oratory.[49]

For all the talk and enthusiasm, the real center of interest was in the presidential nomination. Since July, Senator Palmer had been the man most discussed, but having announced previously his impending retirement from politics, and having reiterated this intention, he appeared to be unavailable. President Cleveland was frequently referenced, but he made it clear that he was not interested. John P. Hopkins with a few others had made public their inclination towards Henry Watterson, editor of the *Louisville Courier-Journal*, a former congressman and a passionate advocate of the gold standard. The journalist's cause was undercut, however, when Cleveland let it be known that he was "not at all friendly" to the idea.[50]

On the second day, most speculation and support became centered upon Wisconsin's General Edward Stuyvesant Bragg, an ex-congressman and diplomat, and Simon Bolivar Buckner of Kentucky, a prominent former Confederate general who served as his state's governor after the war. In the Illinois delegation, on the other hand, Hopkins was organizing a "draft" of Palmer. Recognizing that the senator did not wish to seem to be pursuing the nomination, and that, indeed, he actually may well have been disinclined to undertake the burdens of candidacy, Hopkins judged that "if the [gold] Democrats of the United States demand that Senator Palmer lead this movement, I believe he will not refuse."[51]

He was right. Under pressure, Palmer allowed the Michigan delegation to present his name, having pointedly asked the Illinois men to forgo the honor so it would not appear that they were acting at his direction. Bragg was also in the running, but it was no contest; on the first ballot Palmer received 757½ votes to 124½ for his Wisconsin opponent. Before the balloting was completed, Bragg asked for the vote to be made unanimous. Buckner was given the nod for the vice-presidency by acclamation, and subsequently much would be made of the fact that both nominees had been general officers on opposite sides in the Civil War, having actually faced each other in combat in 1864 during Sherman's destructive raid through Georgia and the Carolinas. Now, so it was loudly proclaimed, the esteemed heroes and former enemies were joined together in a new fight for the nation's survival.[52]

The platform of the National Democrats, while better written than that produced by the gold men in Illinois, included most of the same themes. Foremost, it explained that a new organization was necessary because the nomination of Bryan represented an "attack [upon] the individual freedom, the right of private contract, the independency of the judiciary, and the authority of the President to enforce laws," through the "reckless" advocacy of debasing the national currency and the censure of the president for his repression of the Pullman Strike. The regulars were also condemned for abasing the Democrats' traditional cause of a reduced tariff by demanding it be for revenue only. Naturally, a central focus was the endorsement of the gold standard, but the platform also advocated the development of American shipping, and of international arbitration (like that which occurred in 1895, when Cleveland intervened in a dispute over boundaries between British Guiana and Venezuela).[53]

While convening Democratic dissidents and creating a new political entity—or restoring one that had become corrupted, as the participants preferred to believe—was relatively simple, there were daunting challenges to actually staging a national campaign. Not the least of these concerned the name National Democrats, a moniker that the silver forces were unwilling to concede. Contending that the use of the name was "illegal, deceitful, [and] fraudulent," because it could be easily confused with the name of the "real" Democratic Party, the "real" Democrats fought its use throughout the country. In some states, like New York, complicated court cases were necessary to resolve the dispute, but in Illinois the gold advocates eventually agreed to a compromise and ran their tickets under the banner of the "Independent Gold Standard Democrats."[54]

Nor were the "real" Democrats willing to forgive or tolerate those who had joined the rebellion. Even before the Indianapolis convention convened, the regular Illinois Democratic Central Committee, expelled (or allowed to resign) five members. John P. Hopkins was among them and was replaced by Alfred S. Trude. Others cast into the outer darkness were R.E. Spangler (whose seat was given to Carter H. Harrison, Jr.), William S. Forman, A.A. Goodrich, and Ben T. Cable, who would be replaced by Thomas Gahan as the state's national committeeman. In September, the regular Cook County Democratic Committee followed suit and expelled from its ranks Frank S. Peabody and four others. A week later, they enacted a resolution that "strongly condemn[ed]" those "scabs" who had entered into a conspiracy to destroy the Democratic Party by attending the gold convention. As a further dishonor, many of the more prominent leaders of the party who had defected (Cleveland and Hopkins among them) were to suffer the indignity of having their photos either turned to the wall or removed altogether from the county party headquarters![55]

Hopkins, ever optimistic, appeared quite unaffected by this abasement of his image. In October, he accepted an appointment as vice-chairman of the National Democrats' nine-member campaign committee. Because it was headed by Bynum, who was otherwise busy with the tasks of being national chairman, Hopkins was in "virtual control." He promised a "vigorous and lively campaign," with special emphasis upon the states of Illinois, Indiana, Kentucky, Michigan, Missouri, Wisconsin, Iowa, and Minnesota.[56]

Actually, the Gold Democratic campaign was unremarkable, especially in comparison to the efforts of the regulars and their standard-bearer; Bryan would travel over 13,000 miles and address crowds totaling more than five million. With no expectations of victory, Palmer, Hopkins, and the other Gold Democrats concentrated upon providing an alternative for those who could not stomach Bryan, but were too bound to their party to vote for the Republican candidate, William McKinley. However, aided by a national press that overwhelmingly opposed the man from Nebraska, they were successful in attracting some strong publicity in the beginning.

In September, much was made of the official notification ceremony, which took place in Louisville, Kentucky. The Bluegrass State was the home of their vice-presidential choice, Buckner, and Palmer had served there as military governor during the period of occupation following the Civil War. A couple of weeks later a large rally was held at Madison Square Garden in New York City. In attendance was a crowd of over 10,000 people, including representatives from Tammany Hall and most of the rest of the Eastern Democratic establishment. Palmer, Buckner, Flower, and Bynum made grandiloquent speeches that were greeted with an emotion matched only by the pandemonium that was evoked by any mention of the president, who by this point had officially bestowed his blessings upon the cause. In the Windy City, the most public moment of the Gold Democratic campaign came on Chicago Day, observed on October 9, 1896, which featured a massive parade of "68,307" watched by a crowd estimated to exceed 750,000. Beyond this, the Gold Democrats across the nation were to confine themselves chiefly to local politicking, augmented by a few interstate speaking tours arranged by Hopkins for Palmer and Buckner.[57]

Meanwhile, Illinois' regular Democrats were relying chiefly upon John P. Altgeld, who opened the campaign with a tour that began with a speech in the town of Girard on August 30. He was greeted around the state by ardent and enthusiastic audiences who applauded his attacks on McKinley, Palmer, and the gold standard. The regulars also had their own parade on Chicago Day (but on a different route). According to the hostile local press, it attracted considerably fewer onlookers than that of their rivals. Sometimes there was violence between the two rival Democratic camps, as happened when something called the Sound Money Equestrian Club staged their own nighttime procession in Oak Park. It had hardly begun when they were attacked by an organized group of silver "hoodlums." The gold men on horseback managed to beat off their attackers with their torches. However, the regulars' sound and fury seemed to be having little impact upon the voters; by the end of September, the Bryan men had all but conceded their probable loss of Illinois.[58]

This turmoil was but a subplot to the riveting drama between Bryan and McKinley. Increasingly emotional, the contest became in the end a metaphor for an unvarnished struggle between classes and sections. With evangelistic fervor, the young and energized Bryan strove to bring his message directly to as many as possible. Beginning with his own massive rally in Madison Square Garden, where he officially received notification of his nomination, he embarked upon a series of seemingly endless speaking tours. He was seconded by others, most especially John P. Altgeld, who also exhausted themselves for the cause.

In contrast, McKinley, at the behest of his campaign manager, Ohio's Senator Mark Hanna, conducted a more traditional "front porch" campaign. This was a revival of a practice from an earlier time when it was felt to be undignified for a man openly to seek the presidency. Its use was meant to communicate a message of tradition and safety. Over the course of the next months, thousands of supporters, some with their expenses paid by the Republican Party, made the pilgrimage to McKinley's home in Canton, Ohio, to meet the candidate and to listen to bromidic talks. This relatively decorous approach was made possible because the Republican campaign chest of as much as $3,500,000 (as compared to the Democrats' $650,000), together with the support of most of the national press and almost all of the business community, assured that their message would be heard.[59]

In the end, democracy turned back the "revolution." William McKinley won with 7,102,246 votes, or 51.1 percent, to Bryan's 6,492,559, or 47.7 percent of the total. In the

Electoral College, the Republican received 271 to his opponent's 176, with the bulk of the Democrat's strength concentrated in the South and West. Palmer and the National Democrats (who managed to get on the ballot in thirty-four states) appear to have been a negligible factor in the outcome, attracting the endorsement nationally of only 131,529 voters and no electors. In the states that Hopkins had especially targeted, the results were seemingly equally unimpressive. Indiana returned 1,117 or .10 percent; Iowa 4,516 or .9 percent; Kentucky 5,019 or 1.19 percent; Missouri 2,355 or .04 percent; Minnesota 3,230 or .94 percent; and Wisconsin 4,584 or .29 percent of the ballots cast. In Illinois, which went for McKinley, Palmer attracted only 1,147 or .1 percent of the votes. In Chicago most wards returned figures of under a hundred for the Gold Democrats, and even Roger Sullivan's bastion in the Thirteenth Ward provided just 74 votes for Palmer.[60]

On the other hand, the Gold Democrats felt they had some justification for self-congratulation. For one thing, Palmer's margin in Kentucky had denied Bryan the state. For another, the point of the campaign had never been victory, but rather to provide a rallying point for those Democrats opposed to Bryan who did not want to vote Republican, and, of course, also to help elect McKinley and assure the gold standard. These things had been accomplished. John Hopkins was pleased to note, "The outcome of the election is an affirmation of the truth that the people of the United States do not believe in revolutionary methods or anarchy."[61]

The contribution of the National Democrats was acknowledged at a massive victory dinner held by the GOP in Chicago shortly after the election. A number of Gold Democrats attended. Most prominent was Washington Hesing, who gave a well-received talk about the merits of Grover Cleveland. However, few other important gold leaders were present—both Hopkins and Sullivan were absent; sitting, dining, and celebrating publicly with the Republicans was not only bad politics but contrary to the habits of a lifetime.[62]

At first it seemed that this disinclination to feast with the opposition might signal some degree of reconciliation among Democrats. W.H. "Buck" Hinrichsen, a recently declared candidate for the chairmanship of the regular state committee, made conciliatory noises toward the "goldites" in early December. A few weeks later there was even an abortive attempt by the County Democracy (the marching club of Cook County Democrats currently led by Alderman Johnny Powers and an original source of support for Hopkins, who served as its president for a number of years) to bring the factions together. On December 20, 1896, it held a "love feast" at the county headquarters. President Cleveland's photo was featured (although it had to be repaired because of damage by an unknown party or parties), and even John Hopkins's picture was restored to the wall, though in a less prominent location than before. Speeches were delivered and a good time was had, but it was all for naught.[63]

In fact, few leaders on either side were inclined to forgive and to forget. Grover Cleveland helped set the tone by exacting vengeance upon federal appointees, including several Illinois postmasters, who supported Bryan. Altgeld also actively encouraged retribution against the Gold Democrats, while calling for sanctions to be imposed upon some leaders who had demonstrated insufficient ardor. At his behest, for instance, the regular Cook County Democratic Central Committee expelled six of its members, one of whom was P.J. Donahoe of the Thirteenth Ward, who was cast out for "having yielded too much to the influence of Roger C. Sullivan." Later, in 1900, William Bynum had his appointment as general appraiser of the Port of New York blocked in the Senate by silver Democrats with long memories.[64]

Clearly, neither the bitterness nor the fundamental ideological division that was its source were altered by the elections. Nationally, Cleveland proclaimed in an open letter his satisfaction with the defeat of Bryan and silver, while the Gold Democrats' central committee announced that they would continue the fight. Echoing this, Hopkins and the gold leadership met after the elections in early November and resolved to remain outside of the regular organization. However, this was only after negotiations, overseen by Sullivan, failed because of the intervention of Altgeld. Bryan and the silver forces retained control of the regular Democratic Party, and the fact that the Nebraskan believed (whether true or not) that the Gold Democrats had cost him the election through interfering with his momentum only strengthened his antipathy. In Illinois the silver cause was becoming inseparably entwined with the ambitions of the soon-to-be ex-governor (Altgeld having gone down to defeat for reelection), who was openly asserting his determination to seize control of the state central committee and achieve a personal hegemony over the Illinois Democratic Party. Without the opposition of Hopkins, Sullivan, and their circle, who remained outsiders, it proved to be a relatively uncomplicated challenge; in early January 1900, his candidate for party chair, Dwight Wilson Andrews, easily defeated Altgeld's former ally and now one his most ardent enemies, "Buck" Hinrichsen.[65]

Nationally, the Gold Democrats were to struggle on as an organization for years. However, Hopkins and Sullivan soon lost interest. In November 1896, John Hopkins offended many of the other members of the gold national committee by speaking too openly to the press, and Chair William Bynum unsuccessfully sought his expulsion from the governing board. John attended a national committee meeting in December 1896, but he did not attend a conference in January 1897, and, like most of the other members, he failed to respond to a call to gather in July the following year. Nonetheless, a skeleton organization was maintained that first elected General Charles Tracey as its chair in 1897, and then three years later, George Foster Peabody.[66]

By that point, the National Democratic Party had become moribund, with most of its remaining leaders supporting McKinley. In 1903, Simon Buckner, the party's 1896 vice-presidential nominee, broke ranks and joined the Republicans, and by the next year, Tracey could be found in the lobbies of Washington, D.C., hotels soliciting opinions about how to dissolve the party. By that point, few, if any, cared. Within the various states, however, the gold men after the elections of 1896 retained power in party politics, and the battle against silver and "Bryanism" would continue to divide Democrats, including those in Illinois.[67]

Thus it came to pass that John P. Hopkins, Roger C. Sullivan and the rest of the leadership of the Gold Democrats were to remain technically exiled from their party for the next three years. To be sure, they never became entirely divorced from internal Democratic struggles, nor did they ever lose completely their influence among the leaders and the rank and file. Sullivan especially would be credited for "not closing the gate behind him," and for preparing the way for their eventual return. However, for the immediate future, their position was now diminished, and so it would remain as long as Bryan, Altgeld, and the silver Democrats were in ascendancy.[68]

These circumstances helped create the opportunity for the rise of a new local force, and it was one that would ultimately bedevil Hopkins and Sullivan for over a decade. Carter H. Harrison, Jr., had been hovering on the fringes of power in the Chicago Democratic Party since his father's death in 1893. Born on April 23, 1853, in Chicago (he would be the first mayor of the city to be actually born there), at the age of 13 he went with his mother to the German Confederation, where he was educated at Altenburg, then in the Duchy of Saxe-Altenburg. Returning to Chicago in 1876 following his mother's death in Europe, he attended St. Ignatius College (now Loyola University), and then Yale University, where he obtained a degree in law. He practiced in the Windy City until 1888, when with his brother, William Preston Harrison, he took charge of his father's newspaper, the *Chicago Times*. For financial reasons this had to be sold in 1895 to Adolf Kraus, previously the editor and his father's ally of long standing. Harrison the younger, more urbane and personable than his father, was known for being an avid cyclist in an era when a bicycle race could outdraw a major league baseball game (in early campaigns he distributed photographs of himself posed with his safety bike and doing his best to appear athletic).[69]

He was also imbued with much of his father's political ambition and ability. These qualities, however, were to emerge slowly. During the Hopkins administration, Harrison sought some political consideration, but nothing came of this; however, in 1896, he was selected as an alternate to the Democratic national convention, where he managed to secure appointment as an assistant sergeant-at-arms. During the 1896 campaign, he supported Bryan, but was not prominent; and tellingly, in the fall of that year, the Harrison Club, founded by his father as a base for a political machine and in mothballs since his death, was reformed. Bright, charismatic, and with a magical name, he began attracting the support of a number of political operatives as a possible mayoral candidate in 1897.

Although it can be overstated, Harrison's emergence can be reasonably interpreted as a resurgence of Chicago's older ruling combination of native elites and the sometimes shady figures from saloon rings, which predominated before the advent of the younger business-man politicians of mostly immigrant stock. He was of English descent, and much of his base inherited from his father was native-born and from among those who could claim economic advantage of long standing. However, his immediate source of support came from professional operatives in the wards with little or no parallel entrepreneurial achieve-ment—many of whom would be specific targets of reformers. His greatest catch from among these was "The Little Dutchman," Robert Emmet "Bobby" Burke.[70]

Initially Burke had backed Judge John Barton Payne of the superior court for the mayor's office. Payne was widely liked, but inspired little enthusiasm and was subject to criticism for his lukewarm support of Bryan. Burke and his friends quietly switched their allegiance and began working on Harrison's behalf, who claimed that this was without his permission or encouragement. Soon, however, Harrison joined with Burke to organize something called the William J. Bryan League, ostensibly to keep "alive the flame" of the great cause, but which in addition had the potential (never realized, as it soon disappeared) of serving as a rallying point for a run for the mayor's office. Moreover, much was made of Harrison's delivery of the opening speech on January 8 during the annual Jackson Day Cel-ebration (of the regulars; the gold men had their own celebration). This inspired such a positive response as to sink Payne's hopes entirely.[71]

But a far more potent rival candidacy remained to be addressed. Alfred "A.S." Trude boasted a long record of service to the party, he was on the "right" side of the money question, and he apparently enjoyed the esteem of now former Governor Altgeld. He thus appeared to be an ideal alternative to Harrison, who, for many, conjured fears of a new machine modeled on that of his father and dominated by Burke. The ex-governor, however, proved to be fickle, and initially declined to offer his endorsement. Although initially threatening to bolt the party should he not be nominated, Trude would come to accept realities of the situation and shortly withdrew.[72]

Now the real race for the nomination began as Burke masterminded an open statement of support of Harrison by the remnants of the Populist Party, the majority of which had already amalgamated with the (regular) Democrats. Altgeld at last jumped on the bandwagon, and this also helped create the impression of an irresistible momentum. At the city convention of the regular Democrats, Harrison faced no open opposition. A.S. Trude introduced the name of the man who had been lately his rival for nomination by acclamation. Cynics, however, found the new candidate's promises of reform and change questionable, delivered as they were before a body that included 123 saloonkeepers! Also raising reformist eyebrows was Harrison's running mate for city clerk, William Loeffler.

Unlike so many Democratic leaders, Loeffler was not Irish but was born on January 1, 1857, in the Bohemian section of the Austrian Empire. At the age of nineteen he came to Chicago, where he started out as a butcher's helper, but quickly rose to become a millionaire specializing in real estate manipulation and development. He achieved prominence among the city's Bohemians (Czechs), and by this point was securing control of a number of West End wards. Over the years, until his death in 1909, he would become an increasingly potent force in the party as well as one of the straw men created as symbols of infamy by the emerging reformers. His presence on the ticket was a clear signal that Harrison the younger was as fully willing as his father to deal with the political professionals of dubious reputation.[73]

Carter Harrison would need all the help he could find as the number of his opponents in the campaign became legion. His Republican rival was not sitting Mayor George Swift, who declined to run again, but Nathaniel Clinton Sears, yet another Superior Court judge. Like Harrison, he was partially educated in Germany (as was common in this time, even as American universities were being structured on the German model), but unlike Harrison he was born not in Chicago, but in Gallipolis, Ohio, on August 23, 1854. His family soon moved to Elgin, Illinois, where he was initially educated at the Elgin Academy. He then earned bachelor's and master's degrees from Amherst College, followed by two years of legal study at the University of Berlin, which, however, did not result in a law

Mayor Carter H. Harrison, Jr. (*Illinois Political Directory, 1899*).

degree. Instead, he was admitted to the Illinois bar only after study with local attorneys. In 1893, he was elected a Superior Court judge, and four years later, he was appointed an associate justice of the Appellate Court of Illinois. He would serve there for five years before going into private practice at Sears, Meagher & Whitney. (Underscoring the interconnected nature of Chicago's political and business cultures, Boetius Sullivan, Roger's son, began his legal career as a clerk for this firm in 1912 and retired a partner in 1945.) A somewhat colorless figure attracting only dutiful support, he was chosen after it became clear that the potential fight among the leading candidates (among whom was Congressman William Lorimer, a growing power) could fracture the party.[74]

However, there were more. At the beginning of the year, the *Chicago Times-Herald* judged that there were 23 Republicans, 12 Democrats, three independents, two populists, and a Prohibition Party candidate interested in making a bid. Of these, two were important advocates of reform. John Maynard Harlan was a Republican alderman who had run before and championed regulation of the city's privately owned streetcar systems.[75]

When Charles Yerkes, who controlled the most important traction companies, attempted (without success) to induce the state legislature to pass what was known as the Humphrey Bill, which would have given the companies fifty-year franchises to use the streets of Chicago at what were almost universally judged to be disadvantageous terms for the city, there was outrage. It was this popular upheaval that was the basis for an earlier independent campaign by Harlan, and now he was prepared to try again. In a similar spirit, Washington Hesing, postmaster of Chicago and Cleveland loyalist, began preparing for the race in the fall of 1896 on a very liberal platform that promised an administration modeled on that of Detroit's progressive mayor, Hazen Pingree. However, Hesing's passionate advocacy of civil service reform, the curbing of machine politics, traction revision, and the use of vacant lots by the poor for the raising of beans and other vegetables failed to attract the backing of many of Chicago's reformers, who generally rallied behind Harlan (the Municipal Voters' League, for example, offered what was effectively an unofficial endorsement of the Republican).[76]

Hopkins, Sullivan and the other gold men still on the outs did not become involved to any extent in the mayoral election. Some like Adolf Kraus joined Harrison, while the remainder eventually issued a statement of support for Hesing, which came very late in the campaign and was noticeably tepid. By that point, it was becoming certain that either Harrison or Harlan would win, and it made little sense to expend resources and influence upon a losing cause.[77]

With four major and several minor aspirants, the mayoral campaign was destined to be contentious. As the apparent front-runner, Harrison endured the most mudslinging as his opponents attempted to characterize him as a machine politician (which he was), who was the creature of the streetcar companies (which he was not), who opposed civil service reform (which to a certain extent he did), and who was the puppet of Bobby Burke and other career politicians (which at this point he had become). In the end, the rhetoric did not seem to mean much. Carter H. Harrison, Jr., won decisively with 148,880 votes to Harlan's 69,730, Sears's 59,542, and Hesing's 15,427. Returning prosperity and Republican disunity had both contributed to the victory, it was true, but it was to Harrison as a candidate and his superior organization that much of the credit belonged. The Democrats were at last back in control, but the wounds inflicted by the gold/silver controversy remained unhealed.[78]

5

Taking the Reins
(1897–1901)

The emergence of Carter H. Harrison as a major new player immediately altered the dynamics of the state and local Democratic parties. Although considerably more cosmopolitan than his father, he proved to be no less ruthless in his drive to create his own united party organization. Using municipal patronage, he built his own "city hall crowd" into an important faction. At this point openly disdained by most self-styled reformers in the city, the new mayor was not above including within his ranks such notorious figures as the First Ward's aldermen, "Bathhouse" John Coughlin and Michael "Hinky Dink" Kenna, and others fully willing to profit from government. His key ally, lieutenant, tutor, mentor, and strategist was Robert Emmett "Bobby" Burke, one of the most important party operatives in the city.

By this point, Burke was a senior politician, feared and hated to be sure by many, but also widely respected. Born in Chicago in 1858, he never moved from the North Side neighborhood where he spent his childhood. His family was relatively poor and he began his career as a printer working for the *Chicago Times* and as a union activist. By 1885, he was the chief clerk for the city attorney, and in 1891, he became bailiff and the secretary of the Cook County Democratic Committee. He was a close friend and supporter of Carter Harrison, Sr., and managed his patron's successful mayoral campaign in 1893. As a reward, he became city sealer. In 1896 and early 1897, he initially backed Judge John Barton Payne for mayor, but soon shifted to become the leading force behind the nomination of Harrison Jr. Following the election, he accepted an appointment as chief oil inspector, a minor but very lucrative post. He also was once again chosen as secretary of the Cook County Committee. He was described as "caring for the small potatoes in a pile," and as a "polite and adroit … roly-poly, red-faced, little stout man." His skill, however, as a politician was not matched by his business acumen; his personal wealth always suffered by comparison to the young businessman politicians becoming so omnipresent in Chicago politics. Despite this, during the early years of the second Harrison's administration there was no more powerful figure in the party.[1]

Directly opposing the ambitions of the new mayor and his organization were those of John Altgeld. Since early 1896, he had maintained a tenuous dominance over the party based upon his advocacy of the silver issue and his pro-labor record as the state's chief executive. With the nomination of Bryan, he became the state's most publicly prominent Democrat. He still controlled the state Democratic Central Committee, and its chair, James Orr, was his creature. He also enjoyed the support of most of the reform-minded in the city including Clarence S. Darrow, Judge Murray Tuley, and Judge Edward F. Dunne. He could count also upon the loyalty of a considerable body of labor leaders and other Chicago politicians. He, too, shared the vision of one great unified Democratic organization, only with himself as its fulcrum.

It was, therefore, perhaps inevitable that Harrison and Altgeld would become factional opponents, not so much based on ideology (Harrison also supported silver and Bryan), but more simply because of competing cravings for power. The new mayor was already being touted as a possible candidate for governor and even for the White House. Although Altgeld could never be president, he was determined to maintain and even enhance his status as a national leader and kingmaker.[2]

For most of the remainder of 1897, a semblance of harmony was retained, although the former governor took public exception to Harrison's deliverance of a series of speeches in New York City. The mayor went at the request of Tammany Hall on behalf of the Democratic mayoral candidate running against Altgeld's old friend and founder of the Single Tax Movement, Henry George (who died before the election, in any case). By December, the first rumblings of antipathy were becoming apparent, and by early 1898, the conflict was open and public. The immediate issue between the two that spring was the scheduling of the state Democratic convention, control of which was a necessary first step towards shaping the Illinois delegation to the national convention two years hence.[3]

Robert Emmet Burke (*Illinois Political Directory, 1899*).

The state committee originally selected the date of May 17, 1898, for their meeting to decide the question. This was unacceptable to the Harrison people, who wanted it to be delayed until summer to provide them with additional time to organize. In March, the Harrison crowd gained control of the Cook County Central Committee through victories in the wards, demonstrating the mayor's growing ascendency. Moreover, as it was announced soon afterwards, Harrison negotiated a formal alliance with Richard Croker, head of Tammany Hall in New York (much to the consternation of the Altgeld camp), based upon a "common fidelity to sacred principles of Democracy," including the belief in limited government! This was especially portentous for Altgeld, as it seemed to presage a unified attack against silver, which Tammany had opposed in 1896. The former governor hit back with the creation of something called the "Bryan and Altgeld Democracy," augmented with a series of speeches excoriating those who were not truly committed to the great cause of silver and Bryan, a thinly veiled allusion to Carter Harrison. In the end, the state central committee agreed to postpone the state convention until mid–July, chiefly because there was general desire within the party to avoid a debilitating factional fight.[4]

Just as one dispute seemed to be fading—at least for the moment—another was emerging, underscoring the volatile nature of Democratic politics in Cook County. Timothy E. Ryan (who would be the great-uncle of the movie actor, Robert Ryan, 1909–1973) was a politician of growing influence with a firm base of power in West Town. Born in Ireland in 1848, he came to Chicago at the age of eighteen and initially worked as a ship caulker. Later he became wealthy in real estate and then entered Democratic politics. In 1891, he was elected assessor in West Town, and now he aspired to gain control of the Cook County Democratic Committee by becoming its chair.[5]

His chief obstacle was Thomas Gahan, who was in his third term as county chairman. Gahan was a formidable opponent. Born in the village of Greening (now Arlington Heights), Illinois, in his youth he worked in the stockyards, eventually gaining promotion to an executive position. Physically intimidating because of his size and strength, he first made a name for himself as a policeman and later as chief of the department of the town of Lake in Cook County. Soon, he would be elected town supervisor, and following Lake's annexation to Chicago, he became an alderman. His political career was to culminate with eight years (before his death in 1905) as Roger Sullivan's predecessor on the Democratic National Committee. Meanwhile, he became a sewer contractor, propelling him into the ranks of Chicago's numerous business multimillionaires. Following a term on the state Railroad and Warehouse Commission under Altgeld, Gahan enjoyed the windfall of being included in the formation and initial operation of the Ogden Gas Company. However, he was able to avoid being tarred with the brush of scandal, and he continued to remain politically prominent, sometimes on the side of Sullivan and Hopkins, with whom he was personally close, and sometimes supporting Altgeld, but always as an independent power in his own right.[6]

The fight for the chairmanship was short and bitter. Gahan enjoyed the backing of Carter Harrison and his machine. Altgeld, seeing an opportunity to undermine the mayor, quietly worked for Ryan. Roger Sullivan, and presumably Hopkins as well, were in Ryan's corner, a fact that unsettled Burke and Harrison, who feared the implications of the reemergence of the gold Democrats within the party. There were negotiations, and Gahan and Harrison offered to back Ryan for the Board of Assessors if he withdrew, but this proved to be unacceptable. Instead, Ryan demanded the nomination for country clerk, and when this was not forthcoming, put up his own complete county slate in the primaries where the issue was decided. Gahan won a decisive victory, securing 516 to his opponent's 252 delegates to the Cook County Convention. This met on July 9 (the date having been moved up a week), and it promptly reelected

Thomas Gahan (*Illinois Political Directory, 1899*).

Gahan chair of the Cook County Central Committee, while also nominating him for county treasurer. This was a victory of sorts for Carter H. Harrison, though not entirely—the contemporary wisdom being that the mayor's backing would have been insufficient without the additional strength of Gahan's own power base in Lake and Hyde Park. Nor was it a total defeat for Ryan, whose position within the party was strengthened, as was that of his loose associate Roger C. Sullivan, who for the first time since 1896 was going to the upcoming regular state convention as a delegate.[7]

When the Democrats met in Springfield on July 13, all the diverse elements of the party seemed to share a determination to achieve some kind of unity. Naturally, neither Harrison nor Altgeld was entirely pleased with the results. Harrison left Chicago for the capital city accompanied by 350 boisterous politicians, among whom was Sullivan, who was briefly in a loose alliance with the mayor. Providing the usual noise and spectacle were a brass band and the Cook County Democracy marching club. Harrison also went armed with a speech designed to galvanize the gathering and to promote his possible candidacy for higher office. Much to his chagrin and that of his followers, he found himself "frozen out" by deliberate delays until the convention adjourned reportedly (somehow) to maintain the appearance of harmony. This omission was especially galling because Altgeld not only spoke, but at such length that even his supporters grew restless. It was his usual tirade, though this time much more of his focus was upon castigating the Gold Democrats.[8]

For all of that, there was relative unity. The candidate for state treasurer, Millard Fillmore Dunlap of Jacksonville, and Perry O. Silver, the nominee for superintendent of public instruction (both loyal Bryan men), met with almost no opposition. Similarly, the party platform, like that of the Cook County convention, endorsed the free coinage of silver and the renomination of the Commoner in 1900. The only controversy came with the selection of the next state central committee—not because those chosen favored either Harrison or Altgeld (it was the general judgment that the body would be about evenly divided between the two camps), but because included were Gold Democrats, Roger Charles Sullivan as representative of the Fifth District, and Ben Cable for the Tenth. Cable especially excited heated imprecations, but in the end, after a lengthy debate and his abject public confession of error, the delegates agreed to his selection. Remarkably, Sullivan was not required publicly to embrace the Chicago platform of 1896 favoring silver, and unlike Cable's, his nomination and election evoked almost no open comment.[9]

Sullivan and Cable's selection was consistent with the growing demands for peace among Democrats in Chicago and Illinois. The gold men never considered themselves as having bolted their party—they retained, for instance, control of the Iroquois Club, a key component of Cook County Democratic culture. Rather it was their position that the Democracy had been captured by forces and beliefs alien to its traditions, and that they had simply organized themselves to keep the true faith until the other members of the party had come to their senses. The aspirations of a few of the national leaders like William Bynum aside, most gold Democrats, therefore, had no ambitions of permanently creating a new party, and implicit in their activities was a belief that at some point there would be a reunification. Indeed, this process could be said to have already begun when in May, Frank S. Peabody, with considerable fanfare, rejoined the "regular" party to be embraced and forgiven. Hopkins and Sullivan were also being importuned to return, inspiring public concern from the gold leadership about their fidelity. These fears had some basis, as it was very probable that a deal concerning Sullivan's elevation had been privately struck well before the state convention.[10]

Neither Hopkins nor Sullivan ever entirely severed his ties with the regulars. Even in 1897, both continued the practice of attending party picnics and social gatherings, and Hopkins made a point of accompanying his old friends of the County Democracy marching club on trips around the country. Symbolically, his photograph was placed on the wall when the new Cook County Democratic headquarters at 122 La Salle Street opened. Both men clearly retained a degree of power and influence among leaders as well as the rank and file that compelled respect. Sullivan's position was further strengthened by his association with Timothy Ryan, himself a potent force in the party, and the evidence suggests that Roger received the backing of the Harrison forces in the convention in part as a means to co-opt and thus undermine the West Town assessor's strength.

It was also sensible that it was Sullivan and not Hopkins who first migrated back into the fold; unlike his partner, Roger was not nearly so publicly identified with the cause and the national leadership of the National Democrats. Moreover, he, again unlike John, had not incurred the personal enmity of Altgeld. While it is speculative as to whether they did so, it would have been, in addition, politically astute under the circumstances for the partners to maintain a presence in both factions for the immediate future until events unfolded. Lastly and probably most importantly, the selection of Sullivan and Cable for the state central committee reflected the growing desire among Illinois' Democrats to end at last the debilitating factional struggles.[11]

However, all such hopes proved to be short-lived. John Altgeld, displeased with the Cook County ticket and with the return of Sullivan and Cable, initially declined to campaign. Eventually he was prevailed upon to support his party, and in September he began a series of speaking engagements, among which was one that awkwardly put him on a platform with Mayor Harrison. As usual he argued for free silver in his speeches, but he could not restrain himself from left-handed compliments about his factional opponents, taking the tack that while the Cook County ticket might include undesirable men, it was still better than the Republicans! At about the same time, he made the questionable decision to oppose a Peace Jubilee in Chicago to celebrate recent victories in the Spanish-American War. Arguing that it would only serve the interests of the Republicans who were taking credit for the national triumph, he induced the state central committee to issue a call for a postponement until after the election. Recognizing the political hazards of this, the Cook County Central Committee and Carter Harrison endorsed the ceremony and its original date. Altgeld found himself, much to his discomfiture, bypassed. Meanwhile, Sullivan kept working for harmony, while at the same time cultivating his alliance with the Tim Ryan faction with an eye towards strengthening the growing coalition of those outside of the Harrison and Altgeld alliances.[12]

The elections on November 8 did not go well, as the Republicans once again swept the state and county. The only bright spot was a slight increase in the number of Democrats in the state legislature. Recriminations followed. Richard Croker, the Tammany chief, came to Chicago shortly after the results were tabulated to confer with the mayor—a disturbing event for Altgeld. But even more divisive was Croker's announcement of his belief that the elections were a referendum on the current ideological posturing of the party and that they proved that "silver is dead." Another, less self-serving view held by many was that the party's factional fights, like those between Gahan and Ryan, had undercut the collective effort, as certainly had Altgeld's foot-dragging during the campaign. In truth, it would have been very difficult for the Democrats to have conjured up a victory in an election year dominated by the Spanish-American War for which President William McKinley and his party were being popularly acclaimed.[13]

Altgeld did his best to identify the disappointments of the election with the supposed failures of Carter Harrison, and within days, he used them to justify an announcement of his candidacy for the mayor's office. Ostensibly, his campaign issues were to be the "trusts or the multiplying monopolies in the American economy," and the municipal ownership of the city's street railways. The latter was an issue of current potency based upon an attempt by traction magnate Charles Yerkes to force disadvantageous franchises for his companies upon Chicago as authorized by the Allen Law recently enacted by the state legislature. This had engendered widespread popular outrage that Harrison sought to shape by vetoing the ordinance to implement the statute. Altgeld, unimpressed, argued that the authorization had only passed the city council because of the mayor's incompetence. A further ploy used by the ex-governor was to take on the role of ideological inquisitor to accuse the mayor of accommodating the Gold Democrats and their heresy.[14]

The actual points of contention between the two men remained power and a now reinforced personal antipathy—"our differences were personal," Harrison would later admit. If Altgeld defeated the mayor or even managed to throw the election to the Republicans, Harrison and his city hall crowd's power would be broken, or at least severely attenuated. This would destroy any ambitions the mayor may have held for the governorship or beyond. Moreover, with no other faction sufficiently robust to challenge a victorious Altgeld, he could dictate the state platform for silver, and control the Illinois delegation to the 1900 Democratic convention. This, in turn, would allow him to exercise an overarching influence in the party and the nation. Any thought of compromise, so clearly desired by the mass of Democrats, would inevitably be tossed aside in a contest between two men who, the *Chicago Tribune* judged, could not be "the friend of the other until he can view his tombstone."[15]

As both Harrison and Altgeld could call upon considerable resources, it promised to be a messy fight. Harrison controlled city patronage and the Cook County party. He also boasted a generally good record as mayor, and had paid at least lip service to the free coinage of silver and William Jennings Bryan. Altgeld was believed to retain his influence over at least half of the members of the incoming state central committee, and he enjoyed support among the ward leaders of Chicago's North Side and a sizable number of downstate operatives. Almost as importantly, his reputation as the champion of labor and reform remained untarnished. The only group of regular Democrats not fully in one camp or the other was the loose Ryan faction, which overlapped in part the mostly exiled but still important gold men. However, neither was to be a decisive element in this election cycle.[16]

For all of his resources, however, Altgeld recognized the potency of the hold of the city hall gang over the party's city organization, and he decided to forego the Democratic primaries as unwinnable. Instead, he ran as an independent. The wisdom of this was affirmed by the setbacks he shortly experienced when the new state central committee organized in early January 1899. His downstate supporters, it was true, were able to ram through a resolution endorsing free silver and the nomination in 1900 of Bryan. But this came about only after a bitter debate lasting hours until it was at last unanimously ratified (to retain the appearances of unity)—with a smiling Sullivan cheered as he announced his vote in the positive. This result was initially scored as an important victory for the former governor. However, Harrison's men on the committee had no intention of coming out against the candidate and platform of 1896 at this point—especially as the Great Commoner himself was present in Springfield, and scheduled to put in an appearance at the end of the meeting. Moreover, when they elected officers and an executive committee the results were decidedly unfavorable for Altgeld. The new chair was Walter Watson from Mount Vernon, with Thomas Gahan as vice chair, and Fred Eldred as secretary. None of the men were committed allies of John Altgeld, and what was broadly viewed as a repudiation of the former governor was compounded when Watson packed the executive committee with men like Gahan, Bobby Burke, and William Loeffler, who were friendly to Harrison.[17]

Undiscouraged, John Altgeld moved forward with energy and determination. Soon it would be announced that he was to be joined by a complete city ticket that included candidates for the city council under the slogan of "Municipal Ownership and the Chicago Platform." This decision was later ratified by a special convention held in March and attended by 4,000 cheering delegates. His campaign themes focused upon a mixture of local and national issues. Paramount was his urgent call for fidelity to the Chicago Platform of 1896 and its champion, both of which he felt were under attack by a vast right-wing conspiracy that featured Tammany Boss Richard Croker, the financier J. Pierpont Morgan, *Chicago Tribune* owner Joseph Medill, and Mayor Carter H. Harrison. Altgeld dismissed the state committee's resolutions and the mayor's repeated pledges to Bryan and silver as mere subterfuges. He also found reason to assail the mayor for his friendliness towards former Gold Democrats like Peabody, Cable, and Sullivan.[18]

However, his efforts in this direction were undercut somewhat by repeated statements during the campaign by Bryan (who was affecting a strictly neutral stance) welcoming back all those who admitted the errors of their ways. Locally, the ex-governor promised to bring about the lowering of streetcar fares from five to four cents, while also pledging to work for immediate municipal ownership of the street railways, something Harrison dismissed as impractical. A master of vituperation and invective, Altgeld besmirched Harrison mercilessly. Not only was the mayor the tool of the traction baron Charles Yerkes for agreeing to the twenty-year franchises, or so the rhetoric rang, but he was also an implacable opponent of reform, as illustrated by his well-known antipathy to civil service.[19]

Altgeld's campaign quickly took on the aspect of a crusade, and the faithful turned out with enthusiasm. From February through the election in early April, the former governor spoke to ever larger and more boisterous crowds. Nor was he alone. A bevy of orators swarmed throughout the city on his behalf. However, among the lengthy list of advocates were only two major Democratic figures, William Prentiss and Clarence S. Darrow. The remainder were either unknown or relatively minor politicos. Still, a number of groups joined his fight, including Chicago's own rather insignificant Tammany Society, the devotees of Henry George's single tax clubs, as well as various labor organizations.[20]

For all of the energy expended, there were few expectations—at least initially—that Altgeld could win the election outright. William Prentiss, one of his advisors, explained in January that their actual goal was merely to sabotage Harrison by throwing the election to the Republicans. As he explained, "Mr. Harrison as a private citizen has no political influence." With the mayor gone and the city hall gang dispersed, Altgeld could once again become the directing force in the state and local parties—or at least so it was believed. According to Prentiss, Altgeld would take from 20,000 to 50,000 votes, enough, he felt, to bring the mayor down.[21]

It was a threat that Carter H. Harrison took seriously. In the early weeks of the New Year, his campaign seemed to flounder. Repeatedly he and his allies tried to convince Altgeld to withdraw by appealing to his loyalty to silver and Bryan. They even promised that the Illinois Democratic delegation to the convention of 1899 would be composed of committed silver men—a proposal that was dismissed out of hand. With a touch of what looked like desperation, Harrison also began to seek allies, approaching Timothy Ryan and others for their support. Sullivan was already technically in the Harrison camp, though apparently he was not directly involved except in his own home Thirteenth Ward, where, by this time, he was recognized as the "boss." Hopkins's endorsement was also solicited but he declined to back either man. He explained: "I am taking no part in the fight this time, nor do I intend to. When the party gets around to its senses on public issues, then I may go into politics again."[22]

However, within a few weeks Bobby Burke had gone into action, and the prospects of the Harrison candidacy improved considerably. The city convention, held on March 16, was described as an "old fashioned Democratic love feast." The mayor was nominated by acclamation and the platform, reflecting the determination to ignore national issues and thus subvert Altgeld's strategy as much as possible, centered upon the Harrison administration's accomplishments. The slate was carefully crafted to include men from the Ryan and other minor factions. Even the Populists, or that portion known as the "middle of the road" Populists, who had not joined the Democrats after 1896, voted to back the mayor (though this brought yet another split in their ranks). Another unexpected statement of support came from John Maynard Harlan, long recognized as a leading expert on the traction issue in the Republican Party (who ran his own independent mayoral campaign back in 1897). Harrison and his allies now took to the stump in a schedule that more than matched that of the former governor—as many as five speeches a day. Declining to address the silver issue, he focused upon mayor's achievements in bringing better street lighting to Chicago, and in vetoing the implementation of the Allen Law. At the same time, they belittled Altgeld as a hypocrite for proclaiming his devotion to municipal ownership of the street railways after having ignored the question for years as governor, and for being (somehow) the actual tool of Charles Yerkes. By early April, the Harrison campaign was bristling with confidence.[23]

There was actually also a Republican candidate, although this time relatively few in the press seemed to care. His name was Zina R. Carter. He had been nominated amidst much factional struggle, and he inspired little enthusiasm even in the nominally Republican press. For the most part, both Harrison and Altgeld ignored him, a favor he generally reciprocated in his attempt to run a positive campaign premised upon returning business values to city government.[24]

By the official count, Harrison was reelected on April 1, with 148,439 votes to Carter's 107,439, while the former governor received only 47,162. Two weeks later the impact of the election upon the political contours of the state and local parties became apparent at a Jackson Day Banquet organized by the Milwaukee Democrats. Initially, Altgeld and Harrison were both invited to make addresses as opening acts for William Jennings Bryan.

However, following the mayor's victory, the ex-governor's name disappeared from the speakers' list. On the appointed day, Harrison and Bryan traveled separately to the Wisconsin city from Chicago, probably because in the Commoner's large party was John P. Altgeld. He would sit glowering and silent while his rival spoke to great applause on "Corruption in Politics, Dangerous to Free Government" followed by a talk by the Nebraskan upon "Democracy." It was a Shakespearean moment: the man who would make kings now reduced to service in a pretender's court.[25]

Another of Bryan's principal themes that night was the issue of territorial expansion, which was to play a major role in shaping the coming 1900 elections. When Congress, on April 19, 1898, declared the existence of a state of war between the United States and Spain, the stated goal was the liberation of an oppressed Cuban people, who had been seeking independence for decades. This determination to secure a free Cuba was codified in the war resolution by the Teller Amendment, introduced by Colorado senator and silver advocate Henry Moore Teller. On this basis, Bryan overrode his pacifist instincts and supported the conflict, even going so far as to serve as colonel of a Nebraska regiment. Sadly, he and his troops never made it nearer to the scene of the conflict than the swamps of Florida, where Bryan valiantly waged and won his own personal battles against typhoid and diarrhea.

Within weeks of the war's beginning, the United States enjoyed a series of crushing and relatively bloodless (for the Americans anyway) victories: on May 1, Admiral George Dewey, in the course of six hours and with no losses, destroyed the enemy fleet in Manila Bay in the Spanish colony of the Philippines; on June 20, the island of Guam surrendered; on July 3 the Spanish naval contingent off Cuba was defeated; on July 15, the Spanish forces quit on the island following sharp fighting; ten days later the Spanish colony of Puerto Rico was occupied by American troops. By then, the Spanish were ready for peace and the fighting ended.

When the smoke cleared, it became apparent that what had begun as a war of liberation had developed into one of territorial acquisition. Cuba, it was true, would become free (though under American "protection" until the 1930s), but even before the conflict's end, Congress annexed Hawaii, something that President Cleveland had refused to sanction back in 1893. When the Treaty of Paris was signed on December 10, 1898, it included provisions that provided for the transfer to American sovereignty of the Philippines, Guam, and Puerto Rico. In a typically American gesture, Spain was to be paid twenty million dollars for their already conquered and largest Pacific colony.[26]

This venture into European-styled imperialism was something new in the American experience; never before had the nation acquired so much territory inhabited by so many people considered to be so racially incompatible for citizenship. Moreover, being noncontiguous to the United States, the new lands were viewed as permanently ineligible for eventual statehood. It was also something deeply resented by the nationalists of the Philippines, who resisted American occupation until they were overwhelmed in 1902. This overseas expansionism was rooted in contemporary trends in Western civilization. Europeans had been eagerly dividing up Africa since the famous Berlin Conference of 1884–85, where the concept of the "sphere of influence" was formally recognized, and Asia too (and China in particular), was considered fair game for ruthless economic exploitation.

In part, they were acting under the influence of an American naval theorist, Alfred T.

Mahan, who in *The Influence of Sea Power on History* argued for the economic and nationalist necessity for large navies and colonies. Mahan had his followers in the United States as well, notably Theodore Roosevelt, who emerged with Admiral Dewey as one of the chief heroes of the war through his exploits as second-in-command of the famous Rough Riders, and his close friend, Henry Cabot Lodge, United States senator from Massachusetts. Roosevelt and Lodge were part of a generation of youngish men, latter-day "war hawks," who envied European colonies and international power and who, having never experienced the horrors of sustained combat, believed warfare to be the font of glory and manhood. They were consequently eager for an opportunity to demonstrate national economic and military strength by extending American influence around the world. American imperialists also built upon the country's sense of mission, present since colonial times. The Protestant writer Josiah Strong in his influential work *Our Country*, for instance, argued for both purifying American society and fulfilling the nation's divine destiny by controlling and restricting internal "alien" elements (like southern and eastern Europeans, African Americans, Asian Americans, and Mormons), while continuing expansion westward into the Pacific regions.[27]

Bryan and many who initially backed the war were appalled. It was not just a question of fairness and hypocrisy towards the peoples of the Philippines, Puerto Rico, and Guam, but in a time in which there was a widespread fear of plutocratic subversion of representative institutions, the precedent of the government exercising power over people outside of the national boundaries and the protections of the Constitution (something the Supreme Court would eventually uphold) was disturbing. Accordingly, Bryan embraced anti-imperialism. However, he took the seemingly incongruous posture of also supporting the Treaty of Paris. This was not—a popular historical cliché aside—a ploy merely to create a useful campaign plank for the elections of 1900. Rather, Bryan viewed ratification, rather naively, as part of a program to "end the bloodshed" and "detach the Philippines from Spain," to be followed by the granting of "the Filipinos independence by congressional resolution"—something that would not actually happen for forty-seven years![28]

Bryan in Milwaukee also reiterated his commitment to the free coinage of silver at the sixteen to one ratio. This, together with opposition to imperialism, and a general antipathy towards the "trusts," or industrial monopolies, was to be among his issues in the coming presidential campaign. For many Democrats in Chicago, Illinois, and elsewhere, his insistence upon free silver was bad politics. Since 1896, the economy had improved dramatically, thanks in part to an increased demand for American wheat by Europe, and also to an expansion of the money supply occasioned by massive gold discoveries in the Klondike of Alaska (recognized and codified in the law by the Gold Standard Act of 1898). Now what had been a cause rooted in the desperation of so many four years earlier had become merely ideological and academic. Moreover, it did not take political genius to conclude that an issue that had failed to bring victory during the last election, when circumstances were almost revolutionary, would be much less likely to bring success in the relatively stable conditions now prevailing. In addition, reemphasizing silver could keep the party divided, and would only serve to alienate the East, where anti-imperialism seemed to be making inroads on the Republican base possible. It was impeccable political logic that the currency issue should be dropped. But it was to have little impact upon the determinations of the Great Commoner, who was a true believer and whose hold on the national party was close to absolute.[29]

Such was Bryan's current stature that there was no thought of looking elsewhere for a candidate, even by those with such apprehensions. As a consequence, many Chicago and Illinois Democrats, among whom were many who had jumped on the free silver bandwagon without any ideological conviction, choose the middle course of vociferously supporting Bryan, while working to downplay silver in the hope that the issue could be somehow buried during the national convention and campaign. This was the route chosen by Mayor Carter H. Harrison and the men of his organization who were earnestly working for unity now that they seemed, with the defeat of Altgeld, to be poised to establish themselves as paramount in the party of the city, county, and state.

Their optimism, however, was ill-founded; for all the strength of the "city hall gang" (now defined as the Harrison crowd) in the Chicago and Cook County organization, and for all of their proclamations of loyalty to Bryan, they were failing to attract the support of most downstate Democrats as well as a significant body of urban politicos. In part, this was simply a natural reaction by many outside of the Windy City against a sitting mayor becoming the party's leader. It was also a function of Harrison's and Burke's tendency towards strong-armed methods based upon a false assumption that control in Cook County was sufficient for primacy statewide (a mistake Sullivan and Hopkins were never to make). This proclivity and the anger it engendered became clear when the mayor attempted in the spring of 1900 to force the gubernatorial nomination of his handpicked candidate.

Whether through ignorance, arrogance, or just bad political judgment, his choice could not have been worse. His man was virtually unknown outside of Chicago, had no significant record of public service, and was clearly intended be little more than the catspaw of Harrison and Burke. Adam Ortseifen was the Chicago treasurer, and a Harrison insider who had managed the McAvoy Brewery before taking office. The city hall gang went to work at first with real efficiency. Meetings were held, and most important Chicago politicians, including Roger Sullivan, went through the motions of support. After the local primaries, Ortseifen could claim the backing of all of Cook County's delegates save one. In the weeks before the convention, Bobby Burke began proclaiming his selection as inevitable.[30]

However, downstate Democrats were "resentful," and viewed with "bitterness" this attempt at dictation by the mayor of the Windy City. Not only was Ortseifen part of a "machine" judged to be remote from and even hostile to the interests of rural Illinois, but many found him unacceptable because of his former occupation. In 1900, the movement for prohibition, led by the state's chapter of the Anti-Saloon League, was a potent force, particularly in "Egypt" (the most southern part of the state) and elsewhere outside the environs of Cook County. A negative reaction set in. Many who opposed the consumption of alcohol, together with those who recognized that to nominate a former brewer might well guarantee a lost election, came out against his candidacy. The state central committee declined to vote a clear endorsement, and even members of the Cook County delegation began to balk. A pivotal moment came when virtually all the candidates for the nominations to the various other state offices indicated their unwillingness to run on a ticket with Ortseifen.[31]

His candidacy, and such hopes as Harrison and company may have entertained of electing their own governor, thereupon collapsed. The other leading contenders were General Alfred Orendorff of Springfield and Samuel Alschuler of Aurora. Orendorff was unacceptable to Harrison, so Alschuler, who had entered the convention with the fewest delegates of the three, was nominated.[32]

If events demonstrated that Harrison and Burke were far from their goal of domination, they also made clear that so was John P. Altgeld. As the last sitting Democratic governor, as a man who could call upon the important labor vote, as a "confidant" of the great Bryan, as a person of German descent in an election in which that group was being particularly courted away from the Republicans, and as the only Illinois Democrat with an imposing national reputation, it would have seemed appropriate to have had his name at least considered. However, by this point the former governor had alienated so many regular Democrats that he was given no thought at all. This underscored that for all of the machinations of Harrison and Altgeld over the previous three years, there remained a vacuum of power in the party. John P. Hopkins and Roger C. Sullivan now moved in to fill the void.

Since Sullivan's return to the regulars two years before, it was becoming clear that the pair were staging a comeback. What was remarkable was how easily and without public rancor it was being achieved—though it has to be recognized that Sullivan's rejoining the regulars first, consistent with his relatively less important status as a Gold Democrat when compared to Hopkins, was a brilliant ploy to dampen potential protest. All of the principals who might have opposed them by now had some interest in their return.

William Jennings Bryan, convinced that the Gold Democrats were decisive in his lack of success in 1896, was more than willing to accept Hopkins and Sullivan, lukewarm about him and his platform though they might have been, to help undercut the possibility of another opposition candidacy from within the party. As it proved, Bryan's reasoning was sound; Hopkins made clear his antipathy towards any thought of resurrecting the moribund National Democrats, arguing that times no longer dictated such a radical approach.

Since his loss at the polls in 1899, John Altgeld's priorities had changed, and he was currently more concerned about seeking allies against Harrison than with enforcing ideological purity. Mayor Harrison at this point (his unexpected contest with Altgeld aside) was not seeking battles, but rather consensus (to be sure, behind his own leadership). As he had done with Tim Ryan and initially with Sullivan, so the mayor was willing to do with Hopkins.[33]

There was not much else that Harrison *could* do, actually. Hopkins remained a popular celebrity with a strong following who was not to be disposed of easily. He was still the dapper young man who evoked smiles of admiration across the city—at the upcoming national convention, for instance, he would be proclaimed appreciatively "one of the best dressed men" present. Moreover, there was a tendency now to look back upon his mayoral term as a golden era for party governance, one that was generally free of factional fighting and in which a level of fairness in the distribution of perquisites had been achieved. For those in Cook County and downstate who were tired of Altgeld, his silver fanaticism, and his unceasing self-promotion, as well as for those who were leery of Harrison, Burke, and their gang, Hopkins was becoming an ideal alternative and rallying point. Additionally, he enjoyed an important asset in his partner Roger Sullivan, who commanded his own legions particularly in the Thirteenth Ward, and who was recognized as "having worked hard to prepare the way" by "getting involved inside soon after 1896 and taking an active hand in committee work." Though the details are elusive, it is certain that his role was decisive in forging the alliances necessary for the reentry of the two into the inner circles of power.[34]

Thus it was that in early January 1900, Hopkins made the bold announcement of his return to the regulars and his expectation to be elected a delegate to the state gathering in late June. He got his wish, and he and Sullivan were then, without ceremony or debate, chosen in Peoria to represent Illinois in Kansas City at the national convention. Even more remarkably, and reflective of the pair's growing support around the state, Hopkins and his partner were elected to serve on the new state committee, scheduled to take office in January 1901. Bolstering the perception that the return of the prodigals was finely orchestrated was the complete absence of dissent. Contrasting sharply were the howls of protest that met the announcement that Ben Cable, the other important returning gold apostate, would also be going to Kansas City (Cable was a downstater from Bryan country, and his bolt had inspired a special anger there). Such was the strength of the tide for Hopkins that it was openly "predicted" by "his friends" that before long he would "again be back in control."[35]

Like Harrison and most "practical" Democratic politicians, Hopkins and Sullivan soon revealed their discomfort with any attempt to recommit the party to the Chicago platform and sixteen to one. Beyond all philosophical objections, it was a question of "expediency," to "put victory ahead of futile declamations in behalf of a lost cause." The pair added their voices to the growing chorus urging Bryan to change his mind.[36]

The Commoner was having none of it. On July 4, as the national Democratic convention was convening in Kansas City, Missouri, he sent an open letter to the *New York World* declaring that defeat in the election was preferable to any sublimation of the currency question or the Chicago platform. He would have his way; the campaign would be based upon planks that denounced imperialism and called for the independence of the Philippines, that urged the breakup of the trusts, and that reaffirmed the party's absolute commitment to the free coinage of silver at the sixteen to one ratio. The only sop to those opposing the reiteration of the silver issue was their success in preventing Bryan from selecting Charles A. Towne, a silver Republican, as his running mate. Instead, Illinois' own Adlai Stevenson, a former vice-president with cordial relations with the Cleveland wing, but known as a moderate silver man, was nominated for the second place. Harrison would claim some of the credit for his selection, but unlike 1892, when Hopkins and Sullivan managed Stevenson's bid for the vice presidential nomination, neither became especially involved.[37]

Nor, given the outcomes of the convention, is it surprising that they also did not participate significantly in the campaign. They remained, it was true, in the elite circles of power of the party, as demonstrated by their inclusion in the committee to greet and chaperone Bryan when he visited Chicago in early August. However, beyond this and such local influence in their own wards and elsewhere as they were accustomed to exercise, they did little. Indeed, it was probably a matter of far greater concern to both when John fell suddenly ill in early September and underwent an emergency appendectomy (an operation that was still dangerous in 1900).[38]

In truth, they had little vested interest in a Bryan victory, which could only empower Altgeld and make their goal of party hegemony elusive. Far more would be gained from a national defeat, which would—or so it seemed—torpedo the predominance of the Nebraskan and his causes permanently. Others were coming to a similar conclusion, and were strengthened in their resolve by a growing belief that Bryan had no chance in either Illinois or Cook County. By October, it was reported that the Chicago Democratic Campaign Committee was advising its operatives to avoid promoting Bryan, silver, and anti-imperialism, and to focus instead upon local issues and candidates.[39]

Illinois voted for President McKinley's reelection by a margin of 597,985 votes, or 52.83 percent, to Bryan's 503,061, or 44.44 percent. In Cook County the results were somewhat more favorable, with the Republican taking 50.8 percent and the Democrat 46.4 percent. Alschuler did better, but still lost with only 46.05 percent of the state vote, and the Republican, Richard Yates II, became governor. Even worse, the GOP once again won all of the county offices on the ballot, including state's attorney and president of the County Board.[40]

For the true believers and those who had gambled their political careers on Bryan and the cause of silver, the results were devastating. Defeat in 1896 was in their minds but the first battle—a test of strength—in a cause destined for victory. This time there could be no doubt, as Bryan himself subsequently admitted, that what had seemed an irresistible imperative just four years earlier had been reduced to a mere ideal in face of the return of prosperity. On election night, John P. Altgeld sat with his head bowed listening to returns at the national campaign headquarters in Chicago. When approached by the press, he had nothing to say.[41]

For the former Gold Democrats, the election was a kind of redemption; the results justified their original antipathy to Bryan and silver, and this enhanced their stature within the party. For Hopkins and Sullivan the outcome only added momentum to their rise; within days of the election, it was widely reported that the two intended to take control of both the Cook County and state Democratic committees. Facilitating this was a newly revealed alliance with Thomas Gahan, county chair since 1894 (a post to which he was easily reelected on December 8) and now national committeeman. Although in the past he had been sometimes Hopkins and Sullivan's political opponent, he was also their personal friend and a business partner in the Ogden gas concern. With his own political base, he carried considerable weight in the party's ruling circles. Much more surprising, and for the Harrison-Burke faction perhaps even more galling, was an announcement by Altgeld on December 4, 1900, that he was now backing Hopkins for state chair! The former governor argued that "great principles" were not involved, but rather it was simply a question of a leadership that could bring victory. Apparently, too, he could not pass up the chance to thwart the hated Harrison and Burke. Nor was Altgeld alone, as party leaders all over the state began lining up behind Hopkins.[42]

Mayor Harrison and Bobby Burke, in face of this sudden tide, became desperate. They responded with the unorthodox tactic of expelling Hopkins, Sullivan, and Gahan from the county party, and thus rendering them ineligible for higher leadership. This plan was implemented by the Committee of Contests and Appeals (a subordinate body of the Cook County Committee), which was controlled by the mayor's friends. A body of four was appointed to investigate the pair's "disloyalty" and then to recommend their separation from the party. The success of this bizarre scheme was predicated upon Harrison's influence over the county committee, an influence that proved to be now illusory when it met in Chicago on January 7, 1901. Despite everything its secretary, Bobby Burke, could do, he was thwarted by Gahan, who, as chair, compelled an adjournment of the meeting after fifteen minutes without any consideration of the matter. Fistfights nearly erupted, and there were promises to bring up the question in the future, but subsequent events soon made all of this irrelevant.[43]

Concurrent with the county committee drama, another wrangle was taking place concerning the date of the next convocation of the state central committee. Under the constitution of the state party, it was set to gather on January 7 of the New Year. However, there was the danger that the Harrison faction would seek a delay for a few days. This was important because on January 8, William Jennings Bryan was scheduled to make a speech in Chicago. Since losing, he had been sending mixed signals about the party's future; on one hand, he urged an end to factionalism, and on the other, he called upon his followers to keep Cleveland Democrats from taking control of party machinery. If while visiting he were to condemn Hopkins and Sullivan, then there was a possibility that downstate Democratic leaders, who had generally remained loyal to the Peerless Leader, but who were at this moment mostly flocking to John and Roger's banner, might be convinced to change their minds. To block this, Hopkins, Sullivan, and Gahan sought to force the issue with a letter signed by ten members of the committee (this number being sufficient under the party charter to compel a meeting) to the state chair, Walter Watson, demanding that the state committee convene on the seventh in Springfield.[44]

Not to be outdone, Harrison and Burke induced Watson to call his own meeting on the ninth of January in Chicago, claiming that he alone could actually implement any such petition, and this he declined to do. Things became uncertain for the moment, and the possibility of two reorganizations of the state committee taking place within days of each other and having the issue forced into court loomed. In fact, the Springfield meeting was held, with eleven city hall committeemen declining to attend. Although a clear majority was present, it was decided to forgo any action to prevent any questions of legality and to reorganize instead at the scheduled Chicago assembly. This reflected a confidence that Bryan would not interfere—suggesting that some degree of foreknowledge of his intentions had been obtained. Bryan's speech at the Sherman House on the night of the eighth was full of pathos as he tearfully "abdicated" his position as party leader to a sympathetic crowd that included Harrison (but not Hopkins or Sullivan), even as he took the time to attack Grover Cleveland. However, he did not address the situation in Illinois.[45]

The following day, even as the Great Commoner was boarding his train for Nebraska, at 11:40 a.m., the state committee came together at the Sherman House. For several days previously, contradictory reports had appeared in the press about whether Hopkins and Sullivan were bluffing or whether they actually had the votes to take control. Bobby Burke confidently assured Chicago repeatedly that it would never happen. Words, however, proved to be very cheap. It was, as the *Chicago Tribune* observed, "a sweeping victory—a massacre." John P. Hopkins was elected state chair by a vote of eighteen votes to just nine for the incumbent (and Harrisonite) Walter Watson, and three for Ben Cable (two of which were reported as willing to switch to Hopkins should the necessity arise). So confident were the victors that Sullivan was not even present and was represented by a proxy (ex–Alderman John McGillen). Hopkins made an appearance of graciousness by voting for Watson, claiming rather speciously that he, himself, actually was not a candidate![46]

Sweetening the victory was the new chair's appointment of a Committee on Legislation with nine members (among whom were Sullivan and Gahan) to oversee the activities of Democratic legislators. Facilitating their task was the subsequent election of a new Democratic minority leader in the Illinois House, Roger's youngest brother, Representative Frank J. Sullivan, a 26-year-old attorney.[47]

The key to this unmitigated triumph that seemed to turn back the tides of 1896 and repair the fractures that followed in Illinois was the backing of a large majority of downstate Democratic leaders. The most prominent of these was Charles Boeschenstein of Edwardsville, who was elected vice-chair. He would become one of Roger Sullivan's most reliable allies as well as an important political force in his own right. Boeschenstein was, with a considerable body of downstaters, to remain loyal and to help make the state committee a virtually unassailable bastion of power for Hopkins and Sullivan. It, and eventually the Cook County Central Committee as well, were to be the two essential components of what would be ultimately labeled the Sullivan machine.[48]

No one could doubt that the capture of the state committee was an impressive victory and a tribute to the political skills and appeal of both John and Roger. However, the conquest was also to be but the first of many battles with the Harrison faction, still secure for the moment behind the walls of Chicago's city hall. The factional wars were far from over.[49]

6

At Home, at the Office, and at War
(1901–1903)

On the third of February 1901, Roger Sullivan turned forty years of age. He may well have marked this milestone, made especially compelling by the fact that it was also now the first year of the new century, with introspection. There was much from which he could take satisfaction. In each of the three spheres of his life, he had already accomplished more than most men achieve during their entire tenure on earth. In politics, he was one of the two most powerful men in one of the two most powerful factions of the Illinois, Cook County, and Chicago Democratic parties. Moreover, his stature was now at last being recognized in the press and by the public. In business, he was a millionaire, helped no doubt by his political contacts, but with his success being largely a result of his own hard work and acumen.

It was in his private life, however, where he could find the greatest personal satisfaction, for Roger Sullivan was a family man of a type idealized in his era. As a paterfamilias, he took responsibility for an extended clan of Sullivans and other relatives that stretched back to the old country. His rectitude also shaped his personal behavior both within and outside his home. In sharp contrast to the stereotype of the rough-talking, hard-drinking, big city boss, Roger Sullivan was a gentleman. One contemporary admiringly explained: "He is not addicted to profanity. No one has ever heard him tell a smutty story or use vulgar language. He never drinks [not entirely true], and seldom smokes. His life is as clean as the cleanest life in his community."[1]

Since Roger was "decidedly a home person," his moral compass was always his wife, Helen Marie Sullivan (née Quinlan). The couple was blessed with five children, a son and four daughters: Boetious (14 in 1901), Mary (12), Helen (10), Frances (9), and Virginia (5). Mrs. Sullivan was described as "a statuesque beauty" and "queenly." Although the sources are limited, they create the impression of a strong and devout woman whose chief focus was her family. As she would later explain when interviewed at the 1908 Democratic Convention in Denver: "Mr. Sullivan and I decided years ago that he should do the politics, and that I would take care of the family. He never has placed politics before our home interests, for our word has always been law to him." However, she did admit "of necessity, the children have been left mostly to my care." Her model as a wife and mother was President Grover Cleveland's young wife, the elegant and demure Frances Folsom, and like many of her generation, she did not believe "in women in active politics." Nor was she especially

Roger C. Sullivan, c. 1901 (*A Biographical History with Portraits of Prominent Men of the Great West*).

interested in the women's clubs so popular in the era: "I belong to five women's clubs," she admitted in 1912, "and don't attend the meetings of a single one." "If I have a hobby outside my home, it would be charity," she once said, though even this had practical limitations: "I joined a philanthropic club once, but I withdrew when it began paying out $100 for lectures."[2]

Nor was she impressed with the benefits of higher education for women, especially if it interfered with a woman's traditional role: "I think there is such a thing as overeducation. I don't approve of girls going to school too long. Girls in my opinion should make good as housewives and mothers." But she also admitted to being "old fashioned." Even more interesting

Helen Quinlan Sullivan and her daughters (courtesy Sullivan Family).

were her reflections on her husband's interests and motivations: "I remember Mr. Sullivan told me that if he were a millionaire he would be a politician. He loves the game for the game's sake." However, somewhat wistfully she also expressed the expectation that at some point he might slow down and retire.[3]

By 1901, Roger was already a wealthy and powerful man, something his family's lifestyle reflected. They had come to reside in a comfortable abode located at 842 Walnut Street, but in 1903 the Sullivans moved to a turreted mansion at the considerably more prestigious address of 1269 Washington Boulevard (2950 Washington after the city changed street numeration in 1909). Two servants were necessary to keep the household running. Both homes were originally located in the Thirteenth Ward, but a redistricting in 1901 placed them into the Fourteenth Ward, which became Roger's redefined personal base. The family was apparently happy, and loved to celebrate birthdays and holidays elaborately. It was rooted in solid middle-class values with strong emphases upon education and close ties to the Catholic Church.[4]

Like many Irish immigrants and first-generation Irish Americans, Roger Sullivan had maintained an affinity for the church and its priests since his childhood, and he would always count among his closest friends at least one member of the clergy. Although he would regularly associate with some of the roughest customers in a political culture notorious for being "wide open" and loosely tied to those who sought sustenance outside the strict limits of the law, there is no evidence—nor even the suggestion—that in his personal life he was anything other than completely devoted to his wife and family. His pleasures were simple and few; given the dimensions of his political and business activities, they could have been little else. He enjoyed reading and he shared his wife's love of traveling (especially when they became older). He would also become an aficionado of that defining upper middle-class pastime, golf, at the Elleserlie Golf Club, and of the rich man's passion of yacht racing in his *Apache*.[5]

Beyond his immediate family were his brothers and sisters. There were originally nine siblings, but by 1901, two had passed: Maurice in 1879 at age eleven from diphtheria, and Catherine Sullivan in 1899 at age 35 from organic heart disease. With the eldest brother, Boetious (1859–1910), in South Dakota, it fell to Roger to watch over the remainder of the clan, all of whom now lived in Chicago. His almost paternal interest and support was a presence in each of their lives. John J. Sullivan (1862–1941) was to serve as a police detective for nearly fifty years, and, alone among his brothers, did not become involved in enterprise. However, in an era when police work and politics were entwined, he could not have helped benefiting from Roger's importance, and perhaps occasionally suffering as well from his notoriety.

Eugene (1865–1911) was closest to Roger, serving as a business partner in various concerns and as a loyal political friend and ally. His brother secured him an appointment as a special United States revenue agent from President Grover Cleveland, and at the 1908 Democratic National Convention, he was the chief sergeant-at-arms. At the time of his death at age 45 from "rheumatism of the heart," he was representing his brother on the state committee.

Mark's (1866–1915) career was more varied. After completing his degree at Northwestern University, he spent four years in the 1890s working for the *Chicago Post* under noted publisher James W. Scott. He next turned to education as a vocation and became principal

Sullivan Home on Washington Boulevard (courtesy Sullivan Family).

of the Hayes Evening School, though not without controversy thanks to Roger's high profile. Tiring of this, he went into a profitable partnership with Roger and Eugene, concentrating his efforts thereafter upon the development of Sawyer Biscuit Company as its president and secretary. Mark was politically involved at least to the extent of representing Hopkins and his brother's interests at the tumultuous West Town Convention (representing the West Side wards) in 1895 as an assistant secretary of the gathering, and where, at one point, he distinguished himself by punching a supporter of William Loeffler. He, too, died early, at the age 47 from bronchial pneumonia.

Mary "Mame" Sullivan (1870–1955) grew up to marry William F. McCarthy, a "manufacturer's agent." "About 1910," she and her husband demonstrated typical Sullivan "gumption" (as it was known at the time) in moving East and constructing and managing a hotel and golf course in the resort city of Delaware Water Gap, Pennsylvania. Retiring in 1935, she eventually returned to Chicago to a comfortable life nearer her family. It was there that she died at the hale old age of 84, having celebrated in 1945 the fiftieth anniversary of her nuptials with a party meriting press.

Youngest sibling Frank J. Sullivan (1874–1941) would become a prominent attorney and would work closely his brother. In 1901, he was elected to the first of two terms in the Illinois House of Representatives, and would be (thanks to Roger) his party's unsuccessful candidate for the speakership, and consequently minority leader. He, too, secured his financial future by partnering with his siblings.

Roger Sullivan was also devoted to his pets, some of which participated in shows. His favorite was a Scottish terrier named Mike, a gift from close friend Frank Stuyvesant Peabody. He enjoyed promenading with his dog, which he adorned in an expensive brass collar. Once when Mike went missing, the entire Chicago police force was alerted. Regrettably, it is not recorded whether the beloved canine was ever located.[6]

As was typical of Irish immigrants and their children, Roger "was unwilling or unable to sever 'clannish connections,'" and was always prepared to lend support and help to his kindred. The 1910 Census, for instance, includes three of his Irish cousins (Nora, David, and Thomas) as members of his large household, and there was usually at least one recent arrival from Ireland residing with the family. His generosity extended back across the Atlantic, where he became something of a hero to at least a few of the home folks in Kerry, who described him as "flahoolagh" (or open-handed). However, for all of his familial devotion, his most profound relationship, save only those with his wife and children, was his remarkable friendship with John P. Hopkins.[7]

On the surface, John and Roger differed significantly in personal style. John the dapper dandy, known for being a bon vivant and for his relationship with the ladies (although he never married and maintained a home with his mother and sisters), seemed a clear contrast to Roger, the solid Victorian husband, father, and patriarch. In matters of substance, however, the two were much alike. They shared a *Weltanschauung* and the common experiences of self-made men from immigrant backgrounds with similar ambitions in politics. Indeed, their stylistic differences may well have been one source of their mutual admiration.

The remarkable fact was that John and Roger remained allies for decades in a political culture in which today's intimate could become in the course of weeks a despised enemy. They clearly enjoyed each other's company and made a practice of often traveling and vacationing together, usually with families in tow. While they could disagree, such disagreements never intruded upon either their mutual affection or political alliance. Roger would call John "one of the biggest, truest, and best men I ever knew."[8]

Nor was their community of interests limited to politics. Both men built impressive financial empires that in their own right would have assured them a place among Chicago's elite. It was some measure of how Roger defined himself that in 1895–after leaving office as probate clerk and before assuming one of the various positions he was to hold officially in his companies—he chose to list himself in the city directory simply as a "capitalist," a title that ably summarized both his and John's career goals and endeavors.[9]

Sometimes they were partners in business as well. Roger was a shareholder and eventually a director in Hopkins's very successful Great Lakes Dredge and Dock Company (GLDD), which was founded in 1891 as Lydon & Drews. Lydon was William A. Lydon, a graduate of Lehigh University, municipal civil engineer from 1886 to 1891, yachtsman, and (though only five years younger) John Hopkins's nephew (William's brother, Harry Lydon, was vice-president of the firm until his death in 1903). In 1905 the company was reorganized and renamed. Roger C. Sullivan was among those who contributed funding, and he served on the board of directors. By 1908, the GLDD was a major concern with branch offices in Cleveland, Detroit, Duluth, Buffalo, and Soo City, Michigan. Besides dredging and building docks, the company also excavated submarine rocks, and constructed canals and breakwaters. After John P. Hopkins and William Lydon died within two weeks of each other in October 1918, Roger was elected to succeed Lydon as president of the GLDD.

In another venture, Hopkins and Sullivan in 1893 joined with John D. Hurley to create the Aurora Automatic Machinery Company, which eventually was reorganized in 1918 as the Independent Pneumatic Tool Company, of which Sullivan also became a director. Its first product was a pneumatic hammer that could efficiently drill holes and pound rivets to hold railroad locomotive fireboxes. In 1953, the company became the Thor Power Tool Company (named after the Aurora Company's Thor pneumatic hammer and Thor motorcycles, manufactured by the firm until 1918). An even more lucrative investment by the two friends was in the enterprise that became the Union Carbide and Carbon Company, which in 1917, reorganized and absorbed three other companies to become the nation's largest producer of "carbon, oxygen, and acetylene products." Later, Sullivan also would serve as director of the People's Trust and Savings Bank, and at least one other bank.[10]

As this suggests, Sullivan's capitalist ventures over the years were complex and diverse, and included considerable real estate investment. However, the firm that occupied most of his time and attracted the most public attention in the first decade of the twentieth century was the Ogden Gas Company. The company was founded in 1895, amidst severe controversy as discussed above, and it was a testimony to Sullivan's business prowess (and those of his various partners) as well of his power and patience that it survived at all; the very name of the company became a watchword in Chicago and Illinois—roughly analogous locally to the term *Watergate* in the later years of the next century—of governmental corruption and boodle. This made it and Sullivan regular targets of politicians' opportunism and reformers' opprobrium as the onus it bore became exaggerated and increasingly symbolic. Ignored were the facts that the company did actually begin operations, and that it did provide the only meaningful competition to the local gas monopoly, even managing to bring consumer prices down for a time in some areas. Naturally, this also helped inspire the antipathy of the reconstituted Gas Trust (legalized again by the legislature in 1901), which continued to control all the other gas operations in the city.[11]

In the early years after the Ogden's chartering in 1895, its most profound challenges were legal attacks from Mayor George B. Swift's administration. In 1896, these took two strategies: (1) the revocation of the company charter by the city council, together with an attempt to deny a license to the company to tear up the streets to lay pipe (a privilege included in its franchise), and (2) an endeavor led by the Civic Federation to have the company charter declared illegal because city council procedure had been violated by its not having been introduced properly and by its passage without any committee report. Both issues ended up before Cook County Circuit Judges Murray Tuley and Francis Adams, who ruled that the Ogden charter was legal and binding because the procedures of the Board of Aldermen did not have the force of law and could be overridden at will.[12]

With this victory, the company at last built a small gas plant on Chicago's North Side (where its entire customer base would be located). By the end of 1896, it was up and running.

The following year, the company invested $1.25 million in purchasing land and constructing a much larger gas facility on Thirty-First Street. This enabled it to offer its product at eighty cents per 1,000 cubic feet, underselling the Gas Trust, whose standard charge was a dollar (later the Ogden rate would be raised to ninety cents). A "gas war" ensued between the two, climaxing in 1900, when the Trust organized a new rival company on the North Side, the Mutual Gas Company, specifically in response to the Ogden's incursions into its markets.[13]

However, even as this commercial conflict unfolded, negotiations were underway to merge the Ogden into the Gas Trust. It is not clear if this were the plan all along. It was the conventional wisdom back in 1895, when the city council first acted, that the Ogden was just a charade to create profits for the new company's shareholders by compelling the Trust to buy out the new franchise. This did not happen, though whether because of the associated political controversy, or because it was never intended, is not certain. However, what is clear is that by 1900, though the Ogden Company was making a profit, its owners were more than willing to broker a sale.

Reports emerged early in the year that deals were being discussed with the Wall Street interests (among whom were said to be the Vanderbilt family) that controlled the Gas Trust, negotiations that Roger Sullivan did his best to deny were occurring. In January 1901, after an arduous course of tortuous talks, poses, and counterposes, an agreement was reported to have been reached between Sullivan and a negotiating team in New York providing for the purchase of the Ogden Gas Company for six million dollars to be paid with bonds.[14]

The city council immediately directed a court challenge to the presumed agreement. The basis for this was a provision in the original charter that forbade any transference of rights to another company without their approval. Accordingly, the aldermen declared the franchise as defunct and sued in court to take the company's assets—something John P. Hopkins, who was emphatic in his claims of having no direct connection to the company, characterized as "utter foolishness." The lawsuit dragged on into 1902. Along the way, the lawyers for the Ogden and the Trust succeeded in transferring the case to federal court, while Mayor Harrison, said to be motivated by his current battles with Sullivan and Hopkins for control of the party, did his best to undercut the deal and to rally the public by vetoing a bill that legalized the agreement. He also began harassing the Ogden. One of his tactics was to create embarrassment by unsuccessfully directing the City Controller to decline the company's franchise fees.[15]

The city's entire case soon fell apart when federal Judge Peter Grosscup agreed to a "temporary" injunction (that effectively became permanent) restraining the city from seizing the property of the Ogden Company. This victory was followed by the questionable "revelation" that the purchase that stirred such controversy was in fact not scheduled to be completed until March 4, 1945, when the franchise was set to expire. Once again, it is not definite whether this was a response to the city's lawsuit, or the intention from the beginning. In any case, for the moment the issue was resolved, although, as was revealed years later, the Gas Trust began quietly in 1899 to acquire Ogden assets and property, bypassing the restrictions of the original charter by having its directors purchase shares personally.[16]

This interest was to expand still further on January 1, 1907, when the Trust leased all of the Ogden's remaining facilities. In 1912 and 1913, in a different political environment, the company at last officially became part of the Gas Trust under the control of Samuel

Insull, who after 1905 came to dominate the city's public utility industry (he also would become a close personal friend of Roger Sullivan). Until then, the Ogden continued its officially independent, but after 1907, largely paper existence because it began selling its product exclusively to the Trust. Sullivan remained as its leading officer, serving between 1897 and 1905 as its secretary, and (following President Thomas Gahan's death in May 1905) from 1906 and 1909 as president. Brother Gene Sullivan was also involved and held at different times the offices of secretary and treasurer.[17]

In the same period, Roger Sullivan became closely associated with the Cosmopolitan Electric Company. Enfranchised with the Ogden, the Cosmopolitan was very much the poor relation of the two. Where the gas concern became an important player among the city's utilities, the electric company was barely functional. It did manage to construct a small plant, assessed at a value of only $100,000, on Grove Street; in 1908, it was doing only about "$15,000 to $20,000 a month," mostly supplying "small concerns" on the West Side. However, the Cosmopolitan had a major asset in its broad franchise rights for fifty years to string lines above and below the streets virtually without restriction. This prompted an apparent deal (the terms were not public) in 1908 that gave the Commonwealth Edison Company (the primary local electrical utility) a majority interest. Later in 1913, the company also became part of the Insull empire. Meanwhile, Roger Sullivan served as its secretary between 1909 and 1913, with Gene Sullivan earlier holding the same position.[18]

A far less controversial business endeavor was the Sawyer Biscuit Company, created in 1901. Its incorporators were Roger's brothers, Mark and Frank, with Charles S. Sawyer. Although he never became an officer, Roger controlled the company and probably provided most of the original stated capital of $50,000. Among the company's products during Sullivan's lifetime were Crispo grahams, ginger snaps, and soda crackers, all in distinctive striped tin boxes that are now very collectable. "Better Biscuits Made the Better Way," Sawyer and Crispo became popular national brands. In 1919, the company expanded its operations with an additional plant on Long Island, New York. In 1925, five years after Sullivan's death, Sawyer became part of a newly formed conglomerate, the United Biscuit Company, which was ultimately absorbed by Keebler, today a division of the Kellogg Company.[19]

For Sullivan there was probably little real difference between his political and business ventures; both called upon similar interpersonal skills: flexibility, judgment, the ability to gamble and to improvise, as well as a willingness to engage in a degree of ruthlessness. Doubtlessly too, the two sets of interests overlapped and were mutually self-serving. Still it is a remarkable fact that just as Sullivan was devoting so much energy to expanding his commercial enterprises in the first years of the new century, he and Hopkins were engaged in a legendary life-or-death factional struggle with Mayor Carter Harrison, Jr., and his organization.

The mayor was no paper tiger and could call upon several important assets. He boasted a magical name, and he could rely upon most of Chicago's hardcore political operatives like Robert "Bobby" Burke and the First Ward's notorious aldermen, "Bathhouse John" Coughlin and Michael "Hinky Dink" Kenna. With the vast patronage of his office, Harrison was able to make himself an overshadowing presence in city and county Democratic politics; included in his camp, for instance, were most of the Democratic members of the city council. Being independently wealthy (though much of his prosperity came not from his inheritance—which was fairly limited—but from profits made after he entered politics), he also could afford to be especially generous in the distribution of political plums.

Moreover, Harrison, who was at first viewed with extreme skepticism by the city's reform-minded, developed a generally positive reputation (at least when an election was not being held) as an able administrator and as an advocate of the people's interests in his fight against what were perceived as the abuses by the streetcar companies and other utilities,. His repute locally and nationally grew to the extent that he was repeatedly touted as a possible presidential or vice-presidential candidate.

For all of the mayor's power and influence, his very position of strength also worked to build his opposition. In Chicago, Sullivan brilliantly set down a policy to gather up the political scraps left by the Harrison faction by cultivating the Democrats in Republican wards who, therefore, received relatively little in the way of city plums. He could offer perquisites and jobs through his influence in the city and county parties, and in this way, he was able to augment his own support and influence in the Windy City. It centered upon his own Fourteenth Ward, where he was already the "boss," and eventually included most of the wards extending westward from the two branches of the Chicago River. Generally involved were those that included large Irish-American populations, among whom Sullivan exerted considerable appeal (he was, after all, a role model of upward mobility and family values for many of the city's "lace curtain" Irish). Indeed, it was largely due to the success he enjoyed in this regard that he began emerging as the more visible political leader in his partnership with Hopkins during this period of from about 1901 to 1905; it was he who would usually work directly with the Democratic politicians of Cook County. By 1899, Sullivan regained sufficient prominence to be elected to the County Committee.[20]

Similar tactics of playing upon the fear of the Harrison/Burke machine and appealing to those Democrats left out of patronage distribution in Republican counties also helped build downstate support, where Hopkins, as state committee chair, tended to be the active partner at this point. John also added to the alliance's strength through his own prestige in Chicago, particularly in Hyde Park and the Third Ward.[21]

A significant development for Roger and John was the emergence of a major ally and partner in George E. Brennan. He became with the "silent member of [the] 'triumvirate'" of himself, Hopkins, and Sullivan that directed the incipient machine. His skill as a political tactician would excite even the admiration of Carter Harrison, who would later write of Brennan's "uncanny ability" and "political finesse." He was born on May 20, 1865, at Fort Byron, New York, as the son of Patrick and Anastasia Hines Brennan, both recent Irish immigrants. When he was a child, his family moved to Illinois. As a boy in the burg of Braidwood, he went to work in a mine, and at the age of thirteen tragically lost a leg while chocking cars. Such was the nature of the injury that in order to save his life, his limb was amputated on the spot without anesthesia. The injury would remain painful and would plague him for the rest of his life (the complications would eventually kill him). However, it provided a motivation to resume his education, and he became a country schoolteacher (one of his students was Anton Cermak, who would succeed Brennan as "boss" in 1928). His intelligence and common sense soon brought him a promotion to assistant superintendent of the Joliet, Illinois, schools. It was during this period that he became active in politics, and he secured an appointment as chief clerk (1893–97) for Governor John P. Altgeld's secretary of state and sometimes ally/sometimes enemy, William H. "Buck" Hinrichsen. Brennan was also soon elected a member of the Sangamon (Springfield) Democratic County Committee, and it was in this position that he first encountered Chicago's political leaders.[22]

About 1897, he relocated to the metropolis on Lake Michigan to manage Tom Gahan's unsuccessful bid for the office of county treasurer. From this point on, he was an important player in municipal Democratic politics, and he soon joined with Hopkins and Sullivan, becoming eventually their heir at Sullivan's death in 1920. In 1901, Hopkins, as chair, appointed him as the state committee's secretary to serve as an important liaison for Sullivan and Hopkins with downstate Democrats. Like so many politicians in this time and place, he also became a business millionaire. He rose to become the Chicago manager of a branch of United States Fidelity and Guaranty Company,

George Brennan (Library of Congress LC-B2-6537-14).

which did a booming business bonding for the city. He was devoted to his wife, Jessie Fogarty Brennan (who always preferred to be known as Mrs. George E. Brennan, even after her husband's death in 1928, when she dabbled in politics herself). The two had one daughter, Mary W. Brennan.[23]

Sullivan and Hopkins would need all possible assistance in their rivalry with the Harrison faction. This remarkable political fight was to become the fulcrum of the course and context of the Illinois Democratic Party. The two groups enjoyed nearly equal strength, and absolute victory seemed always elusive, with stalemate being the more usual state of affairs. Often referred to as a "war," the conflict at its heart was little more than a contest to attract the greater support from Illinois and Chicago's professional Democratic politicians. In practice, this was a complex even artful endeavor. The favorite tactic was straightforward deal-making, characterized by exchanges of promises of favors and support, or, if necessary, threats of punishments and retaliation. The ability to offer or withhold patronage and to exert influence over government was therefore crucial. Also important was the capacity to identify and utilize communities of interest, and to negotiate alliances accordingly. In the complex and volatile world of Chicago and Illinois politics, this could be like building sand castles in a tide, and it demanded constant attention and effort. Tactics could also become rougher with hints of what can only be described as blackmail and intimidation, descending at some times in some places (allegedly) to the level of violence.

Neither faction possessed a monopoly on strategic genius and tactical brilliance. This in itself virtually guaranteed the incessant character of the struggle. Added to this, however, were the influences of outside forces that staked claims upon the affairs of the state and city parties. Sullivan and Hopkins at this point would continue to profit from a connection with the more conservative wing of the party, still symbolically led by Grover Cleveland. Harrison was careful to cultivate the support of William Jennings Bryan, who already

identified Hopkins and Sullivan as enemies. Moreover, both factions would struggle to cope with the rising surge of reformism in American politics, the strength of which would undercut the best-laid plans.

As 1901 began, the Hopkins/Sullivan group had taken the reins of power in the state party. However, any illusion that a mortal wound had been delivered to the Harrison/Burke faction was soon shattered as the mayor and his cohorts came roaring back to reassert their dominance in Cook County and Chicago. In February, Burke, in a highly symbolic move, took charge of the annual County Democracy (the marching club) Ball, bringing the organization that had once belonged to Hopkins and Sullivan into his camp. In March, Harrison, despite the open opposition of an increasingly irrelevant John Altgeld, handily won an impressive majority of the delegates to the city convention, where he was renominated by acclamation. There was some discussion that Hopkins and Sullivan might field an opposition candidate. However, Harrison's strength and their own relative weakness dictated at least token support of the mayor. Despite Altgeld's and his followers' continued and pointless opposition, for a brief moment a general appearance of imposed harmony prevailed.[24]

The mayor's Republican opponent was Elbridge Hanecy, a judge of the Cook County Circuit Court. Throughout his career, Hanecy was the creature of one of the rising leaders of the local GOP, former Congressman William Lorimer (who would return to the House of Representatives in 1901). Like Sullivan's, Lorimer's base was in the wards extending westward from the branches of the Chicago River. Also like Sullivan, he was at times the target of reformist focus and anger. Most recently Republican reform types exhibited considerable disgust with Lorimer's strong-armed imposition of Hanecy over their favorite, John Maynard Harlan, who had conducted an independent candidacy in 1897 on a platform of addressing the city's public transportation issues.[25]

The Republican nominee did his best to present himself as a positive alternative to Harrison, advocating change of the fee system practiced by some city officials and stronger measures to control the street railway companies, but he was handicapped from the beginning by his association with Lorimer. Some Republicans even sought to induce Harlan to enter the race as an independent, but this he declined to do. Harrison took his opponent very seriously and campaigned hard. He was reelected on April 2, 1901, by a margin of 156,756 votes to Hanecy's 128,413, a clear, even decisive, victory in the context of Chicago politics at the time.[26]

Sullivan did his part by delivering, or at least not inhibiting, a narrow margin for the Democrat in the Fourteenth Ward. Harrison's position was naturally strengthened. It was just a month since William McKinley had been triumphantly inaugurated for his second term as president, and in Illinois, Republican Richard Yates II had recently assumed the governor's office; Democratic victories in general were relatively scarce across the nation. It was natural, therefore, that speculation emerged about a possibility of higher office for the newly reelected mayor. In Chicago, too, Harrison and Burke confidently began to reinforce their position. In June, their organization swept and gained control of almost all of the Democratic ward clubs. The annual Democratic Cook County picnic held in July was therefore little more than a celebration of Harrison, with his mentor, Burke, presiding and holding court for fawning politicians from across the city.[27]

However, it was not in the nature of Cook County Democratic politics in 1901 that any victory could long go unchallenged. The Hopkins-Sullivan-Brennan alliance continued to work against what John Hopkins called Burke's "dictatorship." They retaliated by keeping Harrison's men from responsible positions in the state organization, and, though overwhelmed in the ward clubs, they were able to put up a spirited fight. Moreover, as often happened in Chicago, Cook County, and Illinois Democratic affairs, national interests began intruding upon the local political culture. On June 20, a new body grandly titled the Samuel J. Tilden Democratic Association was organized. Its formation was a conscious emulation of an identically named aggregation created six months earlier in New York City by conservative Cleveland Democrats to subvert the influence of William Jennings Bryan and Bryanism. The evidence strongly suggests that Hopkins and Sullivan were involved.[28]

The group claimed former president Grover Cleveland's blessing and support, while attracting broad backing among former Gold Democrats and others discouraged by the Great Commoner's leadership and record of defeat. Its moniker attracted some criticism by those who remembered Tilden chiefly as the man who acquiesced to the "theft" by the Republicans of his presidential victory in 1876 (not a strong symbol of Democratic determination). Still, they could hardly name it after Cleveland, as this might be misinterpreted as the initiation of a reelection campaign on his behalf. Besides the president, Tilden was the nearest thing that the Democrats had to a national victor since the Civil War. Moreover, having been a relatively conservative governor of New York, he seemed to embody well the spirit of the new group. For the next three years, the Tilden Association would be a focal point for a conservative resurgence within the party, and it was particularly successful in drawing younger Democratic leaders. It would generally fall to Sullivan to exercise his faction's influence among the Tildenites, underscoring again his growing public profile as a leader in his own right.[29]

In October, the Tilden club formally began its assault upon Harrison and Burke with a mass meeting attracting a crowd estimated at 20,000. Officers were elected, and a complete ward organization was outlined. For all of its grandiose plans, however, the organization had little impact upon the next major battle, the selection of a new chair for the Cook County Democratic Committee. The sitting chair, Thomas Gahan, had his own following, particularly in his home Sixth Ward, and he wanted reelection. Moreover, he was Illinois' national committeeman, and had been loosely allied recently with Sullivan and Hopkins. However, many, particularly among the younger and more passionate members of the Tilden society, believed that he was too willing to work with Harrison and Burke.[30]

On the other hand, the city hall crowd of Harrison and Burke disliked Gahan as too independent and wanted their own man. There had been some discussion about Wenter, who was still of some importance, but he declined to become the focal point for the factional controversies that were sure to follow. Instead, the mayor and his chief advisor settled upon Ninth Ward Alderman Thomas Carey, a man upon whom they could rely in every circumstance. He had cultivated a close relationship with the local labor movement and this would contribute to his selection as chair of Chicago's relatively feeble and declining Tammany Society. He was also known for his love of horseracing; he eventually owned a racetrack and a string of horses. Like so many young politicians in both parties, he was a business millionaire. He had been loyal to the elder Carter Harrison, and he was a reliable ally of the son, who would recall him fondly, if somewhat cynically, as "one of my leading henchmen."[31]

As things stood, however, Thomas Gahan's comfortable majority among the members of the Cook County Democratic Committee made him appear invulnerable. Included among his backers was his ally and fellow county committeeman, Roger C. Sullivan. Despite this, Gahan recognized the potential threat posed by Harrison and Burke, and moved quickly to take the initiative by issuing the call for a meeting of the committee to elect officers. This seemingly innocuous action was in reality a blow against Burke, who, as secretary of the committee, normally performed this task, which gave him the de facto power to define the membership and therefore the votes. And it was the actual composition of the committee around which the conflict would turn. Gahan might have a majority, but Burke controlled its executive committee, and under a provision in the county constitution, it decided who comprised the full committee. Opponents were ruthlessly purged by Burke (particularly from the towns outside of Chicago), with many replaced with his own cronies. At the last convention 122 had been selected, but now the committee was reduced to just 98 . Burke next attempted to deliver a coup de grâce by using the authority of the executive committee to depose Gahan.[32]

The end result of these machinations was two separate meetings of two separate county committees, both held on December 2, 1901, to elect officers. At about 1:00 p.m., Gahan and his 65 backers, among whom was Sullivan, attempted to take possession of the party's county headquarters, but were met by an iron partition that had been rigged across the narrow stairway leading to the meeting room. They convened instead at the nearby Leland Hotel, where they promptly reelected Thomas Gahan as chair and chose two of their number as secretary and treasurer. An hour later, Burke and Harrison's version of the committee met at their headquarters and selected Carey. Burke was retained as secretary. "Open War" ensued over the next weeks. An agreement was finally reached in January by which Gahan reluctantly accepted Carey as chair in return for his own continued membership on the county committee as well as that of a number of his allies. Also appeased was Roger C. Sullivan, who with the Tilden Association had been generally supportive of Gahan, and who was empowered to choose one of his minions from the Fourteenth Ward (Thomas Little) to join him on the county committee. Mayor Harrison, apprehensive about Sullivan's expanding influence among Chicago's Democrats, acquiesced with great reluctance.[33]

Others were also unhappy with the compromise, particularly the Samuel J. Tilden Association, which vowed on January 17, 1902, to continue the struggle against Burke and Harrison. They also were disappointed with Gahan for accepting the deal. Among those speaking that night was Sullivan, whose speech is unrecorded, but doubtlessly concerned the foibles of Burke and Harrison. In response, the mayor denied Roger his choice of the Democratic election judges and poll watchers in the Fourteenth Ward, which under the rules of the game was his right as ward boss.[34]

During the conflict, reports began to emerge of a compromise between the factions to overthrow Bobby Burke, the mayor's personal Svengali, closest advisor, and the architect of his success. Harrison vetoed the idea, but the subtext of the proposal lingered—for Bobby rather suddenly was in big trouble. Although a strategist and tactician of the first order, he was virtually unique among the leading contemporary politicians in not having achieved success in business. Consequently, when Harrison became mayor, he asked for appointment as city oil inspector, a post that offered lucrative prospects for financial reward through a percentage of fees. The only obstacle was a standing city ordinance requiring that all charges be turned in to the treasury in return for compensation of $300 a month. Each successive oil inspector had signed an agreement to this effect upon taking office. However, this provision had been often ignored, and it became the long-standing practice to underreport all the collected charges. However, Burke found himself a victim of what the mayor would later call "a new set of public morals" when on October 5, 1901, he was indicted for embezzlement for failing to report and remit.[35]

Specifically the two counts of the indictment asserted that a discrepancy of $22,000 in 1900, and $8,000 subsequently, existed between the charges he took in from the Standard Oil Company and others and what was disclosed. Burke immediately sent to the city treasury a check for $30,000 (raised from his friends) to cover any "mistakes," but the ambitious Republican state's attorney and future governor, Charles S. Deneen, and the grand jury were not appeased. Burke was booked and released on bail of $25,000. He faced the possibility of imprisonment for up to fourteen years. His troubles were soon compounded when the grand jury also returned charges of conspiracy to defraud, and this time included his chief deputy, Max Praeger. Panic ensued, and Burke turned to Alfred S. Trude to conduct his defense.[36]

Trude immediately filed a motion of habeas corpus against the original indictment. Appearing before Circuit Judges Theodore Brentano, Marcus Kavanagh and Edward F. Dunne, who met as one court, he argued that the city ordinance requiring the city oil inspector to remit his fees was superseded by the state law originally creating the position. This had included a provision that allowed for the collection and retention of all fees by the oil inspector, and, as it had precedence over a city ordinance, Burke could not be charged. At most, he could be merely sued for violating a civil contract. The court agreed, and on October 25, 1901, quashed the indictment. However, they did not address the conspiracy allegations, and these stood until January 1903, when Judge Brentano threw them out on the same grounds.[37]

At first, Carter Harrison gave every indication of supporting his friend and mentor; they recently had worked in harness during Bobby's offensive against Gahan. By February 1902, however, things began to change rapidly as the County Democracy (the marching club) now under Burke's control, suddenly announced a withdrawal of its support from Harrison. For most, this was a major surprise. Even more distressing to some were the reports that the club was being transformed into an active political organization within the party to promote Burke's ambitions. Retaliation was not long in coming. In April, Mayor Harrison began firing Burke loyalists. In May, the mayor orchestrated the reduction of his erstwhile ally's influence on the county committee by chipping away at Burke's prerogatives as secretary. These had made him heretofore the body's actual leader and facilitator. Now he was confined to merely clerical duties, while real power was shifted to the chair (and Harrison's man), Tom Carey. From this point on, Burke and Harrison were bitter enemies and the configuration of power in the Chicago party was thereby altered. While the importance of this unexpected breakup is clear, its sources are less so. Harrison would claim that at the heart of their estrangement was Burke's belief that the mayor had abandoned him during the indictment crisis.[38]

Burke offered no explanation either then or later, but what is certain is that there were many in the Harrison camp that judged the secretary to be a liability; it is also possible that the mayor simply recognized an opportunity to become his own man. Perhaps informing this was the mayor's decision to replace Burke as his chief lieutenant with his city controller, Edward Maguire Lahiff. Born in Ireland, Lahiff was popular among the city's Irish. Most of his career had been spent in journalism. However, he was a loyal Harrison soldier, having also served as the mayor's secretary, and, not incidentally, was someone with no independent base or views.[39]

Another unexpected change in the political world of Illinois in the spring of 1902 came with the sudden death of John P. Altgeld. Since his defeat for mayor by Harrison in 1899 and the subsequent dimming of the influence of William Jennings Bryan and the cause of silver, he had ceased to be an important player in state and local politics. However, among reformers in Illinois and around the nation, he remained a popular figure whose status was embellished by an aura of martyrdom rooted in his defiance of Cleveland during the Pullman Strike, and his defeat for reelection following the pardons of some of the anarchists convicted after the Haymarket Riot. Moreover, his energetic advocacies never diminished as he continued to speak throughout the country for reformist causes. Most recently he had begun focusing again on the public ownership of utilities, and just days before he was struck down, he delivered a vigorous address excoriating those who would profit from the people's need for utility services. However, it would be another issue that would frame his final public appearance.

On the night of Tuesday, March 11, 1902, he was the featured speaker at a large rally in Joliet, Illinois, on behalf of the Boers, who were engaged in the final throes of a vain war of independence against the aggression of British imperialism in South Africa. The former governor was received well. As he was leaving the stage to the cheers of his audience, he suddenly fell over in a faint from what would be diagnosed as "apoplexy"—a medical term of the period to indicate either a stroke or a brain hemorrhage. He soon regained consciousness and was carried to the Hotel Munroe watched over by several physicians, who happened to be nearby at a Will County medical meeting. By midnight, he was pronounced as being "out of danger," but at about 1:30 a.m., he suffered another attack and sank into a coma from which he never awakened. By 3:00 a.m., the doctors had given him up for lost, and telegrams were sent to his family and to his law partner and close friend, Clarence S. Darrow. He died at 7:09 a.m.[40]

He had become a controversial figure, but his death inspired an outpouring of praise and grief. William Jennings Bryan labeled him "a true American, a true defender of the interests of the people." Mayor Harrison and the city council ordered flags to half-mast, and the *Chicago Tribune*, which had fought him at every step, praised his dedication and honesty. State Committee Chair John P. Hopkins, who had overseen the arrangements for Altgeld's gubernatorial inauguration, was also profuse in his statement of admiration: "I cannot command words suitable to express the esteem in which I held John P. Altgeld," he stated, going on to characterize the former governor as "the greatest man of his generation," while noting that he had not been nearly as radical as popularly perceived. Clarence Darrow felt it appropriate that his friend's final public words were on behalf of the women and children of the Boers of South Africa, calling him "a true loyal friend." Judge Edward F. Dunne, a rising star among Chicago's reform advocates, labeled him "honest and fearless."[41]

He was brought back to the city by train, and services were held on Friday, March 14, 1902, at his home. Among the eulogizers were Darrow and Jane Addams, the founder of the Hull House, a "settlement home" for immigrants, and a prominent local advocate of improved municipal conditions (particularly garbage collection). The following day, his mortal remains were placed in state in the north corridor of the City Library on a catafalque decorated with an American flag and an arrangement of roses and violets. There, between eleven in the morning and ten that night, as many as "95,000"people (by a "conservative estimate") passed in review. On Sunday, March 16, 1902, at about 11:00 a.m., the library doors were closed, and a short service was conducted that featured a choir of 250 German singers representing several of the Turner Societies (German-American fraternal organizations) from around the city, and eulogies by William Jennings Bryan and Charles A. Towne. The casket was then taken to Graceland Cemetery in a procession graced with the presence of Governor Richard Yates, Mayor Harrison, the Cook County Democracy marching club, Robert Burke, and other prominent Democrats like Darrow and Dunne (and based upon news reports, probably Hopkins, but not Sullivan). Among the pallbearers was Elmer Kimball, an Altgeld law partner, and the initial president of the Ogden Gas Company. At Graceland, John P. Altgeld, a man who might have been president—had his birthplace been but otherwise—was remitted to the earth. Bryan extolled him with a few more poetic phrases before the crowd of about 2,500: "[Like] the waters that run murmuring down the mountainside," the Peerless Leader rhapsodized, "and then help to form the river's majestic current at last make their contribution to the sea ... so his words and thoughts have contributed and still contribute to that public opinion that molds human action and shapes the destiny of men."[42]

The death of the former governor and the breakup of Harrison and Burke simplified the local political culture. The Altgeld grouping—they were too loosely organized by this point to label a faction—would fade after their leader's death and be absorbed in the progressive upsurge that would inundate city politics in 1904 and 1905. Burke continued to play an active but generally secondary role in city politics, remaining a special challenge for Harrison. However, the primary dynamic of state and local Democratic power for the next year and a half would be in the stalemate between the mayor, who maintained his control of the Cook County committee, and the broader coalition of Hopkins, Sullivan and other allies based in the state organization.

The rancor between the two groups was very much in evidence during the state convention held on June 17. There were many "harsh words" exchanged, and at one point things threatened to escalate into a physical confrontation. In the morning John was defeated for reelection to the state committee by a caucus of the delegates for his home First Congressional District committee largely through Harrison's influence. Immediately afterwards, an infuriated Hopkins confronted Harrison in the corridor outside the committee room. The mayor extended his hand in greeting. Red-faced, Hopkins called him a "pinhead" and accused him of having never earned "an honest dollar." Harrison retorted that Hopkins was just a "boodler," and a fistfight was only narrowly averted when Roger Sullivan led his friend away. That afternoon, Hopkins was restored to the committee as a delegate-at-large in a vote by the full convention, while the relative strength of the two factions was made clear when the Hopkins/Sullivan ticket for the state delegation to the national convention received 728½ votes (of which 209 came from Cook County) to Harrison's 523½ (with 252 from Cook County). Within a few days, William Jennings Bryan, pausing between his almost obsessive denunciations of Grover Cleveland, responded to the events in Illinois by characterizing Hopkins as nothing more or less than a "republican [sic]"![43]

Much of the immediate antipathy against Hopkins was rooted in the state committee's takeover (and the distribution of funds) of the Cook County campaign for the November elections. Not surprisingly, there was subsequently little enthusiasm for the elections among the "city hall crowd" of Carter Harrison. Given this fact, plus the recent increase in strength of the Republicans (as augmented by the presence of the increasingly popular Theodore Roosevelt in the White House after the assassination of William McKinley on September 6, 1901), it was almost inevitable that the results would be disappointing. The Democrats did manage to increase their numbers in the Illinois legislature, but in Cook County, only their candidate for sheriff won. This was Thomas Barrett, a "sportsman" who had been a clerk and broker at the Board of Trade, but who was chiefly known for a string of racehorses and membership on the Whitings, a local baseball team. He was popular with the "boys," but was not closely affiliated with either faction in particular. Indeed, he may well have been given the nomination in the expectation that no Democrat could capture the sheriff's office that year. His plurality was only about 6,000 votes, but he ran well enough ahead of the Republicans in the Fourteenth and other wards with large Irish populations.[44]

However, Barrett aspired to even greater things, and shortly began cobbling together his own organization to challenge independently the mayor for control of the county committee. His candidate for chair was John McGillen, while city hall supported the incumbent, Thomas Carey. McGillen was a close friend of John Hopkins. Born on November 13, 1861, in Chicago, to a political family (his father had been an intimate of Stephen Douglas), he achieved an early business success as a partner in the contracting firm of Agnew & Company. He then served eight years as an alderman, and he was selected to be temporary mayor following the assassination of Carter H. Harrison père and chair of the Cook County Democratic Committee between 1893 and 1894.[45]

Not one to miss an opportunity and pleased to advance his old friend, Hopkins offered his support to Barrett and took "full command" of this most recent attempt to undercut Harrison. Bobby Burke soon came on board and became the group's nominee to succeed himself as secretary of the committee against Harrisonite Edward M. Lahiff. After weeks of preparation, the battle was joined on the morning of December 1, 1902, at the Democratic county headquarters on Randolph Street. Both sides were confidently predicting victory, but the tension in the room was thick. The votes of 57 of the 113 members were necessary for election, and Barrett was claiming 63. With equal confidence, Carey proclaimed his certainty of the support of 64 committee members.[46]

Although there was a small group "on the fence" counted by each side as its own (reportedly holding out for the best deal), Harrison need not have worried; Carey was elected chair by the narrow yet comfortable 61 votes. Similar results were returned for Edward Lahiff for secretary and William Loeffler for treasurer. Roger Sullivan and Thomas Gahan, as expected, supported Hopkins and the McGillen-Burke ticket. Barrett claimed a victory of sorts in coming so near to thwarting the mayor, and he promised to fight until he and his friends received their just due in patronage. In truth, this would translate into the new sheriff and his followers becoming an appendage of the Hopkins-Sullivan faction. For the party and the public, however, the significance of the outcome was unquestionable; Harrison had won an impressive victory, one that now set him up for yet another run for reelection in the spring of 1903. The sources of his unexpected strength against the combination of the state chair, the sitting county committee secretary, and the newly elected sheriff of Cook County were not immediately clear, but it was speculated that the mayor might have suggested to certain committee members that police interest in certain gambling operations would doubtlessly increase should his friends not win.[47]

As the election of 1903 held special challenges, securing the nomination was just a step in Carter Harrison's difficult quest to keep his office. For the first time in over thirty years, when the voters selected Joseph Medill on the "Fireproof Ticket" in 1871 following Chicago's great conflagration, issues were beginning to transcend the usual organizational patterns of Windy City contests. Since the 1890s, reform had become an increasingly potent force, and it now actually threatened to intrude upon the mayor's plans for another term. Of most immediate concern was a movement based in the Chicago Federation of Labor to convince Clarence Darrow to mount an independent labor candidacy.

What would ultimately become a short-lived new party organized itself in October 1902 at a clandestine meeting at the Retail Clerks Association hall. Present were representatives from the unions of retail clerks, male elevator operators, streetcar workers, freight handlers, and others. Their stated purpose was to bypass the usual "machine politics" and bring greater democracy and efficiency to city government.[48]

Darrow was not yet the most famous lawyer in American history, but he was among the most respected of local Democratic operatives, and a working-class hero as well. He had been born in Kinsman, Ohio, on April 18, 1857, to parents who were committed to the abolition of slavery and women's suffrage. He attended Allegheny College in Pennsylvania and the University of Michigan law school. In 1878, he began practicing in Youngstown, Ohio. Nine years later, he came to Chicago, where he became corporation counsel for the Chicago & Northwestern Railroad. In 1894, he first attracted national attention as a lawyer for Patrick Eugene Prendergast, the assassin of Carter H. Harrison I (but he was unsuccessful in having Prendergast declared insane so as to avoid execution), and then as the lead attorney for Eugene Debs in federal court following the Pullman Strike. He had also become involved in Democratic politics, but never formally joined any faction. However, he was a very close friend and advisor of John P. Altgeld, and was considered by many to be the former governor's logical heir. In November 1902, he was easily elected, technically as an independent (but organizing with the Democrats), from the Seventeenth District to the Illinois state legislature.[49]

As the new year of 1903 began, Darrow was being importuned to run on his own for mayor—the collective judgment of his erstwhile supporters being that the Democratic primary was too much under the thumbs of Harrison and other professional politicians for him to have much of a chance. An anti–Harrison coalition began to emerge among the trade unions and the Chicago Federation of Labor, Bobby Burke's followers, the Tilden Democracy, and also from among the remnants of what had been the Altgeld faction now led by George Schilling. Neither Sullivan nor Hopkins was directly involved, at least publicly, and John was at pains to declare his disinterest. He did feel moved to reveal—rather gleefully—his belief that "nothing can stop that movement now."[50]

But Darrow vacillated. From Philadelphia (where he spent most of these weeks as an appointed arbitrator on a federal Anthracite Commission investigating conditions in the local coal fields), he sent a public telegram on January 27, 1903, addressed to his good friend, labor leader, and major booster Daniel L. Cruise. He asked to be allowed to defer judgment until he was back in Chicago, declaring he had never given any thought to being a candidate. Nevertheless, after his return, he continued to temporize. His friends forged ahead, ordering campaign buttons and holding a mass meeting on the evening of February 16 on Darrow's behalf at the Auditorium. The object of their affections spoke, as did noted reform advocate Henry Demarest Lloyd. Though Darrow would insist that the gathering had no political meaning (as underscored by his tedious speech on matters in the coal industry), to many observers the gathering was effectively a nominating convention. Still he pleaded for more time.[51]

Finally, on February 20, breathless reports appeared in the press that he had at last agreed to run, and a formal announcement would be forthcoming on the morrow. Jubilation reigned among his supporters, and the Harrison camp fell into deepest gloom. Neither should have bothered, as Darrow continued to procrastinate, refusing even the entreaty of a formal committee sent on the evening of February 21 by the incipient independent labor party to make his declaration. Still optimism prevailed that he would in the end consent. Two days later, Darrow stunned everyone by abruptly withdrawing his name from all consideration. He explained that he had consulted with major national labor leaders like Samuel Gompers of the American Federation of Labor, and they had urged him not to make a run that would probably result in a Republican victory. He frankly saw no compelling necessity for his candidacy as a way to assure organized labor its voice in city government (a clear supportive reference to Harrison). Moreover, the cause of municipal ownership of public transportation, the driving issue of 1903, would be better served with him outside of public office. He also speculated that in office he would likely in any case disappoint his friends. Darrow probably also remembered the fate of Altgeld's independent bid in 1899, and its impact upon the former governor's career. Moreover, he was constitutionally unsuited for the tedium and responsibilities of public service, a fact underscored by his resignation from the legislature before his term was completed.[52]

Consternation followed, and the executive committee of the United Labor Party, as the group now styled itself, nominated Cruise, who was given little chance nor much subsequent attention. For Mayor Harrison, Darrow's announcement was an unexpected gift. Despite his effort to co-opt the rising issue of public transportation, Harrison had not resolved the contentious matter and had resisted the popularly perceived panacea of immediate municipal ownership of the street railways. In addition, as an incumbent for going on six years, he bore the resentments for all points of dissatisfaction with municipal government, including its system of "political machines," and its growing reputation as a Mecca for gambling, saloons, and prostitution. Harrison would later admit that at the time he felt the election was probably unwinnable, an assessment broadly shared.[53]

However, as winter turned into spring, the outlook began to improve, if initially only slightly. Though still beset with factional discord, most Democrats of Chicago, with the exception of Bobby Burke, managed to pull together behind the mayor's candidacy. Having a Republican would hurt everyone, and, in any case, no one else much wanted the nomination. Harrison handily won the city primaries, with his supporters defeating Burke's men and allies (including Thomas Gahan), in the election of the city convention. Hopkins declined to run as a delegate, and Sullivan was chosen easily from his Fourteenth Ward stronghold. Harrison would be renominated without opposition. However, despite his hope to rouse emotions with a stirring address defending his administration, the conclave was "singularly devoid of enthusiasm."[54]

Adding to the mayor's burden was a united and confident Republican ticket, headed by Graeme Stewart. The GOP candidate was a businessman, who, with a sterling reputation for honesty and public service, appeared to embody all the virtues required for victory. Long discussed as a possible mayoral candidate, in February 1903, Stewart won the Republican primaries by a two to one margin over his principal opponent, John M. Harlan. Like the mayor, he was nominated in convention by acclamation. Harrison would always insist that Hopkins, Sullivan and their friends "to a man" secretly supported Stewart—an assertion that may have been based in truth. However, if it were so, their activities were so clandestine as to escape the attention of an otherwise vigilant press.[55]

The campaign was the usual full schedule of frantic meetings around the city colored by name-calling. Harrison did his best to intimate that Stewart was the tool of the corporations and the "interests," including most importantly the streetcar companies. Not to be outdone, the Republican accused the mayor of enabling corruption, and under the slogan, "six years, nothing doing," of accomplishing little of substance for the city. Late in the contest, Darrow entered the lists as a speaker for the Democrat, angering many of those supporting Cruise, but undeniably influencing much of the labor vote. The contest was close. Harrison managed to pull out the win with 146,208 votes to Stewart's 138,548. Though Cruise won only 9,947 ballots, he was able to deny the mayor the Fourteenth and other wards where Democratic candidates usually won. The Republicans, too, had some reason for self-congratulation, having managed to elect a city clerk (by a couple of hundred votes) and the city attorney.[56]

It may have been simply relief, a somber assessment of his political strength, a desire for fresh fields of conquest, or some mixture of all of the above, but the newly reelected mayor announced that he would not seek another term. This, however, did not mean that he was planning to leave politics. Within days, there was talk that Harrison was contemplating a possible 1904 presidential bid. Interestingly, John Hopkins was at pains not to dismiss these ambitions: "Everyone knows I am not for Harrison," he explained in a newspaper interview, "but I must admit that he is the most available man the democratic party [sic] has in the west for the presidential nomination."[57]

Underscoring his seriousness were Harrison's continuing attempts to whittle away at the strength of the Hopkins-Sullivan-Brennan faction on the state committee. This would prove frustrating. His rivals' influence proved to be formidable, especially among most downstate Democrats, who were remarkably resistant to the city hall faction's blandishments. Remarkable, too, was that Sullivan responded to the animadversions against his partner and the efforts to diminish his own position by working with greater public diligence at achieving harmony. In July, Roger Sullivan arranged a meeting with Harrison, who was vacationing in the Huron Mountains of Michigan's Upper Peninsula. Accompanying Sullivan were Hopkins and George Brennan. However, the personal antipathy between Hopkins and the mayor now ran so deeply that compromise proved impossible. Still, Sullivan kept trying, and for this, as there was a wide desire for harmony in the party, he gained considerable political capital in the city and state as a "peacemaker." This culminated in suggestions in November 1903 that he might be the ideal compromise candidate in the spring for county chair. It was an honor he vigorously declined.[58]

Added to the mix was the still viable wild card of Bobby Burke. The mayor had done his best to ignore his former advisor, and as late as February 1903 would only admit publicly that a parting of ways had occurred. Nonetheless, he continued to fire Burke men, the last being a hapless city hall janitor named John Gildea, making it clear that there were to be no dual loyalties. Burke had shown surprising resilience and strength since his falling-out with Harrison. Using the County Democracy (the marching club) as a base, he had created his own factionette. The city hall crowd, rather weakly, responded with the creation in April 1903 of its own brief-lived parading organization called the City Democracy. While no longer exercising anything like the prevailing power he displayed when partnered with the mayor, Burke remained politically important. Sharing a common enemy, Sullivan and Hopkins became generally friendly, but he was never to be fully part of their organization.[59]

However, it was Harrison's ambition itself and the obstacle of Sullivan and his partners that were most responsible for making party unity impossible. And this was not just a function of the rivalry for local and state power. Following the second defeat of William Jennings Bryan in 1900, the former Gold Democrats, represented in Illinois most obviously by John and Roger, seemed poised to call the shots at the Democratic national convention scheduled for the summer. Harrison, as a Bryan man and factional rival, knew he could not count on their support, and that should he be unable to wring some kind of endorsement from his own state delegation, his chances for the White House would become unlikely. For all these reasons, 1904 promised to be a time of fierce battles. However, what none of the professional politicians in any of the factions and parties of Chicago and Illinois appeared to have foreseen was that the coming year was also to witness the bursting forth of a local reformist tide that would—briefly—change the rules, and threaten to sweep all before.

7

Hopkins, Harrison, and Hearst
(1904)

It was billed as a "fight for political life." Standing in one corner was the mayor of Chicago, Carter H. Harrison, Jr., undisputed champion in the last four elections and supreme leader of the city hall crowd; in the other stood John P. Hopkins, former mayor, chair of the Democratic state committee, and a leading member of the most powerful statewide alliance in the party. Both men commanded extensive organizations, and both were determined at all costs to gain control of the Illinois delegation to the National Democratic Convention. This time the stakes seemed to be inordinately high. Many judged a victory for one as politically fatal for the other. The sparring over the past two years was to be but the preliminary to the big fight that everyone knew was now coming. However, as often happens in human affairs, expectations can be complicated by the unexpected, and in the political culture of Illinois that spring the unexpected had a name: Hearst.[1]

By the end of the twentieth century, the public perception of William Randolph Hearst, once one of the most powerful men in America, was reduced to little more than the caricature of Charles Foster Kane sketched in the famous 1941 motion picture *Citizen Kane*. Like that of the emotionally constipated character of actor-director-writer Orson Welles's imaginings, Hearst's life was enveloped by a vague aura of misdirection, and like that of Welles himself, of unfulfilled potential. In the early years of the twentieth century, however, Hearst was a potent force, and he would be an important player in Chicago and Illinois Democratic politics.

He was born wealthy in San Francisco on April 29, 1863, as the only child of George Hearst, "a rough-and-ready mining man" who made his "pile in Nevada," and was now a prominent local citizen. "Willie" lacked for nothing; doted upon by his mother Phoebe, he enjoyed his privileged life. He had access to the best education, St. Paul's School in Concord, New Hampshire, and Harvard (from which he was expelled after a series of pranks). Much against his better judgment, his father passed over to him control of the *San Francisco Examiner*, a failing newspaper. To general surprise, Willie demonstrated an aptitude for journalism, or for being able at least to increase circulation by working hard, emphasizing the sensational, and taking up local political causes. It was while editor of the *Examiner* that Hearst first came into unaffected contact with the ordinary folk who made up his staff and customers, and he developed an almost messianic sense of noblesse oblige that for a time would shape him politically.[2]

In 1891, his father died, freeing Willie from all curbs upon his obsessions and ambitions. He moved to New York City and acquired the *Morning Journal*, and turned it around to become a real rival of Joseph Pulitzer's popular *New York World*. The *Journal*, like the *World*, specialized in what became known as "yellow journalism," a reference to a series of political cartoons that appeared in Pulitzer's sheet that featured a child in a huge yellow nightgown (the first sustaining colored cartoon in America). Circulation boomed as Hearst delighted in what would later be called tabloid journalism, specializing in the shocking and titillating, including sex scandals and the supernatural. Before the Spanish-American conflict, Hearst became famous for his jingoism, beating the drum for war with unabashed exaggeration and distortion.[3]

As a rich man with a string of newspapers, who, moreover, was imbued with the addictive drug of national influence, Hearst's thoughts turned to politics. His father, after all, had died a United States Senator from California. In 1902, with the backing of New York City's Tammany Hall, the younger Hearst was elected to the United States Congress for the first of two terms. He left little mark in the House of Representatives, and was mostly known for being absent. Nonetheless, he felt this to be a basis upon which to begin a quest in 1904 for the White House.[4]

Throughout most of the country, his campaign inspired only a mixed response. However, in Illinois his candidacy assumed the proportions of a political phenomenon. He had prepared well in the Sucker State. In 1902, he began publishing two newspapers in Chicago, the afternoon *American*, and the morning *Examiner*. He also sent one of his chief lieutenants, Andrew Lawrence (who became technically the owner of the *Examiner*) to oversee his interests in the Windy City. Even more importantly, Hearst's agents spent prodigious amounts of money. Virtually overnight, he became a political force.

Hearst's appeal was manifold. Some saw him as a kind of Democratic Theodore Roosevelt. Like the president, he was a wealthy man from America's elite, who counted himself as a New Yorker. Also like the president, he was young, boasted a vigorous work record, and advocated progressive change that targeted in particular the large corporations and the interests. Others saw him as the heir to William Jennings Bryan, who would take up the mantle, so tattered from the defeats of 1896 and 1900, and move the cause forward. Presumably, too, he could appeal, unlike Bryan, to Eastern workers. However, neither the professional politicians nor most reformers were entirely comfortable with Hearst. Many found him to be opportunistic and untrustworthy. In 1901, for example, Cleveland's Mayor Tom L. Johnson, one of the leading

William Randolph Hearst (Library of Congress LC-USZ62-83833).

advocates of municipal reform in the nation, wrote John P. Altgeld privately that he did not "believe you can depend on him." Bryan, too, was mistrustful of the rich man who was laying claim to his base.[5]

For once, Harrison and Hopkins/Sullivan were in agreement: both sides did their best in the early months of 1904 to ignore Hearst, and when this did not stem the rising tide of the publisher's support, to counter his appeal among their followers. But in the larger Illinois Democratic Party, at least, the Hearst movement was unstoppable. At its head was Millard Fillmore Dunlap of Jacksonville, now Hearst's Illinois manager and long an opponent of Hopkins and Sullivan.

Born in Morgan County, Illinois, in 1856, and raised in Jacksonville, where he resided for all of his life, Dunlap attended the Whipple Academy, which was attached to the Illinois College in Jacksonville. There he was a school friend of William Jennings Bryan. Upon graduation, he went into banking, and rose to become president of the Ayers National Bank. Eventually he founded his own firm, Dunlap, Russell, and Company, which controlled three financial institutions. He ran twice unsuccessfully for state treasurer, and he served as treasurer of the Democratic State Committee between 1897 and 1901, and then in the same position thereafter until 1904 for the national committee. Dunlap had been close to Altgeld, even lending him $15,000 in 1894. He also was a friend of former Illinois Secretary of State William H. "Buck" Hinrichsen. Throughout his career, Dunlap remained devoted to Bryan; he was, for example, a companion of the Peerless Leader in 1896 during his campaign in Illinois.[6]

Bolstered in his efforts by undisclosed but clearly large influxes of cash from New York, Dunlap led a parade of Democrats, particularly in downstate Bryan territory, who rushed to jump on the Hearst bandwagon. As the publisher's strength became clear, John P. Hopkins attempted to reach an understanding, but his peace proposals were publicly rejected. Nonetheless, both Hopkins and Harrison came to conclude that opposition to Hearst was pointless and self-defeating. For the mayor, the success of Hearst in the state was especially frustrating. Now that the state's presidential choice was being preempted, he was compelled to lower his sights to the post of national committeeman. In the end, both factions conceded the Illinois delegation to Hearst, and focused upon their fight for the state machinery.[7]

The city hall crowd of Carter Harrison initially planned their next offensive as a battle for control of the state convention. In April, just before the primary election to select delegates, the mayor called together nearly 2,000 precinct captains in a special meeting to ask for support "on the eve of battle," reminding his enthusiastic listeners of his record of victories.

Millard Fillmore Dunlap (*Illinois Political Directory, 1899*).

First lieutenant Edward Lahiff also spoke, warning that there would be no compromise with "trimmers and traitors."[8]

The actual primary results were not clear. Each of the three sides initially found reasons for satisfaction. Harrison's people insisted that they controlled 750 delegates to Hopkins's 831. However, any remaining hopes the mayor might have entertained about receiving the Illinois party's endorsement for the White House were dashed; even in Cook County, Hearst counted 295 state delegates pledged to his candidacy against Harrison's 205. However, the local conventions that implemented these mandates also tended to elect their usual leaders, whose primary loyalties were generally with Hopkins, Sullivan, etc., or with Harrison. It was felt that when the various delegations met in their congressional districts to select their representatives to the national convention, as was the rule, the mayor could count on a number of his men being included—perhaps even a number sufficient to challenge Hopkins, Sullivan, and Brennan for control of the state party. Eventually these hopes collapsed. As they dominated the state committee, which could assert vast powers including overriding precedents and rules, Hopkins and his allies decided that it, and not the districts, would make the final selection of the national delegation for subsequent approval by the state convention. Since the state committee expected to control that assemblage, they would be well placed to dictate the results. The mayor came to recognize the futility of his cause. "I am not interested in the state convention," he forlornly conceded on May 12, admitting that "the other crowd is in control."[9]

When it met in Springfield on June 13, 1904, however, all sides still did their best to pack the galleries. Hopkins arranged for 27 train carloads to carry his followers from Chicago, while the Harrison crowd (despite their leader's official lack of interest) filled 14 cars, with the Hearst men riding in two. From the beginning everything was scripted by Hopkins, Sullivan, Brennan, and the state committee. John, as state chair, convened the convention at about noon, and immediately presented the name of Frank Quinn, a Peoria attorney and an ally, as the state committee's choice for temporary chair. He then handed Quinn the gavel. The Hearst and Harrison forces had attempted earlier to induce the committee to select Congressman Henry T. Rainey, but in a test of strength, he was defeated by a vote of 23 to 11. Quinn continued to preside until he was formally elected at 5:00 p.m. following the presentation of the report of the Committee on Permanent Organization. The state committee had also decided to temporarily seat most of those disputed delegates who were loyal to Hopkins (but only a few of the Harrison or Hearst men, a majority of whom were being challenged), until a special subcommittee (that included Roger Sullivan) made its recommendations to the full convention. This meant that for the moment, these extra votes strengthened their control.[10]

Despite these provocations, the convention was initially relatively sedate. This changed abruptly at about 6:00 p.m. when Quinn introduced the report of the credentials subcommittee. It, predictably, affirmed the action of the state committee and seated almost all of the Hopkins men, while ruthlessly discounting a number of the results in districts that had voted for Harrison supporters. These included the Twenty-first and Twenty-third districts, where the mayor's forces seemed to have unquestionably won. The uproar that followed only deepened when Quinn called a quick voice vote and then even more quickly declared the subcommittee's report as accepted. The catcalls (among which were taunts of "Ogden Gas") and din increased when the proposed platform was read. However, even more provocative was the selection of the national delegation based upon the recommendations of the state committee.[11]

Made up mostly of Hopkins and Sullivan's men, but also including some representation for the city hall crowd and the Hearst forces, the slate was elected over vociferous opposition. The one apparent defeat of the Hopkins-Sullivan-Brennan steamroller came with the debate over the phrasing of the endorsement of Hearst. The state committee presented for approval a statement requiring the national delegates to vote for the New York editor and to use "all honorable means" to secure his nomination. Clarence S. Darrow took charge of the fight to make the instructions more ironclad, and succeeded in persuading the convention, by a margin of 936 to 382, to alter the phrasing to require support for Hearst as long his name was before the delegates in St. Louis. Most of the Hopkins-Sullivan loyalists actually voted for the change, primarily, it seems, because few took the issue of their party's choice for president that seriously (especially as William Jennings Bryan was not a candidate). Probably even fewer doubted that the popular President Theodore Roosevelt would fail to secure reelection regardless of whom the Democrats nominated. Nor was there much more optimism concerning the elections in Illinois. The state ticket (also preselected), which was headed by Lawrence B. Stringer as the gubernatorial candidate, was nominated by acclamation on a motion by Sullivan, but was greeted with lassitude and resignation.[12]

Still Hopkins and Sullivan had every reason to be pleased. Both, of course, were going to St. Louis as delegates—Roger from the Seventh District and John as a delegate-at-large. Moreover, Hopkins's control of the state committee had been again affirmed, and he was handily reelected as chair. Sullivan could be confident that the Illinois delegation as it stood would choose him as national committeeman in St. Louis. He was even granted the privilege of personally selecting the Democratic candidates for trustees of the University of Illinois. John could not help but gloat: "We controlled the convention," he crowed, "and nominated our friends." There could be no longer any doubt that "we are still in charge of the organization." Harrison and his supporters were disappointed, but promised, as did some of the Hearst people, to fight at the national convention the state committee's ruthless decisions on the state delegation. The mayor attempted to find some comfort as well in the binding endorsement of Hearst, which he believed would doom Hopkins and Sullivan: "It will be a pleasing spectacle to see John P. Hopkins [and] Roger Sullivan," he asserted, "manacled by instructions, going down with the Hearst ship in St. Louis."[13]

A week later Harrison exacted a measure of revenge at the Cook County convention, held on June 20, where it was his turn to control the machinery. Under the gavel of Tom Carey, and the watchful management of William Loeffler, the convention did all that the mayor could have wished. Of course, it ratified his predetermined slate of candidates. But more importantly, Harrison's control was ruthlessly displayed when, taking a page from the Hopkins-Sullivan book, a resolution was steamrolled through that stipulated that the existing executive committee (the operational body of the county committee that was very much the mayor's creature) would select all new county committeemen. This vitiated the modest gains Hopkins-Sullivan's men had made locally in the recent primary. After the appointments were made, 97 of the 118 members were counted as being in the mayor's pocket. Tom Carey was once again chair, and Edward Lahiff returned as secretary. Robert "Bobby" Burke was ousted from his Twenty-first Ward seat, as was George Brennan in the Thirty-second. Sullivan and his minion, Thomas Little from the Fourteenth Ward, were allowed to return. This was not altruism or a peace offering—Harrison continued to spurn all attempts at harmony—but, rather, recognition that Sullivan enjoyed such support and power in the city that he could not be left out without disrupting the operation of the local party. For similar reasons, Roger was granted the prerogative of naming the candidate for the clerk of the Superior Court.[14]

Now all eyes and thoughts turned to St. Louis, especially when it became known that William Jennings Bryan had decided to make the Illinois controversy his own. Without any expectation of receiving the nomination, the Nebraskan was determined to demonstrate his relevance and power against the so-called "reorganizers" (this being the moniker adopted by and applied to those conservative elements in the party led by Cleveland and New York's former governor and now United States Senator David B. Hill, who sought to eliminate the impact of Bryan and Bryanism). To this end, though the Great Man's stated purpose were principle and justice, it soon became clear that revenge and a desire to strike out against the former Gold Democrats in Illinois, "to wipe out the record of Hopkins and his machine," were also key motivations.[15]

The Peerless Leader came to Chicago to confer and organize with Mayor Harrison and Millard Fillmore Dunlap of Jacksonville, leader of the Hearst movement but long a loyal Bryan man and Hopkins-hater. Interestingly, Dunlap went to some lengths to make clear to the press that they were not targeting Roger Sullivan's own delegate seat, because they recognized that he had in fact received a majority of votes in his district. Perhaps as well, they had some hope to separate the powerful Chicago Democrat, who was known for his irenic skills from "his friend" and their immediate antagonist John P. Hopkins. Instead, the plan was to attack those delegates from twelve congressional districts that they claimed were fraudulently seated by the state committee. In addition, Hopkins and Ben Cable as delegates-at-large were also to be challenged, again on the basis that others would have been selected if the legally elected representatives had been seated, and, moreover, because allegedly their appointment was never formally affirmed by the state convention.[16]

John quickly went to work, and Roger just as quickly made his allegiances known. Hopkins enjoyed the advantage of being "on intimate terms with a large majority of the [national] committeemen," a circumstance which he was more than willing to exploit as he began lobbying for their support (though national chair James K. Jones was known to be "not a friend of John P. Hopkins"). Sullivan issued some verbal blasts, questioning the loyalty to Hearst of Dunlap, Harrison, and the others on their team by pointing out that the potential outcome of these challenges could be to delegitimize the state convention and its instructions to vote for the publisher. Nor was Roger impressed with the claims of principle. Where was that principle when the Cook county convention met, and the will of so many of the rank and file was ignored? Moreover, both Hopkins and Sullivan pointed an accusatory finger at Bryan for intruding into a local matter and potentially undermining party unity solely for the benefit of his own selfish ends.[17]

Two days before the convention was to convene, M.F. Dunlap submitted to the national committee a petition from a purported 872 of the 1,321 state convention delegates asking for the seating of "only such persons as received a majority of votes as cast in caucus in their respective Congressional districts." In dispute were those of twelve congressional districts, as well as the at-large seats of Hopkins and Cable. The national committee selected a special subcommittee of five, headed by Senator William J. Stone of Missouri, to investigate and to report. With the jarring noise of Fourth of July fireworks echoing in the room, Hopkins and Frank Quinn delivered their arguments. The opposition case was presented by Major Edgar Bronson Tolman, Harrison's corporation counsel (and an officer in the Spanish-American War, hence the title), and Judge Owen Thompson. During the hearings, however, it was suggested that Clarence Darrow, who was a delegate but not present, was "the man behind these contests." Hopkins used this suggestion to question the contention that the state convention was "boss managed." After all, Darrow's more binding instructions for Hearst were accepted despite being contrary to the recommendation of the state committee and its chair.[18]

Following "a long and patient hearing," the subcommittee reported: "It appears that the delegates selected by the district conventions were replaced by delegates who were not selected … and in some instances it is at least doubtful whether the substitutions were properly made." However, the report also concluded, "it would require a long and exhaustive examination to ascertain the real facts," an examination it felt was "impractical," and "beyond the province of this committee." Accordingly, it voted to sustain the results of the state convention with the exception of the case of one delegate, General Alfred Orendorff of the Twenty-first district, whose removal from the rolls was said by some in the Hopkins-Sullivan camp to have been a "mistake," but by others to have been deliberate because "he got too smart." The full national committee accepted the report and agreed to seat the designated Illinois representatives temporarily, until the convention's Committee on Credentials investigated the matter.[19]

Now Hopkins and Sullivan could organize the Illinois delegation. John was chosen chair by a vote of 40 to 8 over his opponent, Andrew M. Lawrence, Hearst's Chicago publisher. Roger was elected national committeeman by 45 of those present over M.F. Dunlap, who received only three votes (including Sullivan's as an act of courtesy). Fred Kern, a Hopkins ally, was elected to the convention's Committee on Credentials, while Ben Cable was placed on the Committee on Resolutions. All the remaining offices, including sergeant-at-arms and the several honorary vice-presidencies, also went to friends of John and Roger.[20]

On July 6, immediately following the convention's daily adjournment, the Committee on Credentials prepared for its hearings. That evening there was a long and arduous session lasting from 7 p.m. to 3 a.m., in which multiple witnesses including Hopkins, Sullivan, and Quinn testified. Tolman and Thompson once again appeared in opposition. Bryan at some point joined the audience but did not participate. Finally, the Committee, by a margin of 30 to 13, upheld in all regards the report of the subcommittee. This, however, did not conclude the matter; a minority report was hastily composed, for which William Jennings Bryan quickly assumed the role of chief advocate.[21]

On Thursday, July 7, 1904, at 2:00 p.m., the delegates reconvened for the afternoon session of the National Democratic Convention. The environment in the recently built Coliseum was "thick, moist, heavy, and hot." In the galleries was a sizable herd of Bryan supporters who, with some sympathetic delegates, began the meeting with a noisy demonstration in support for their hero. The Great Commoner himself was on the verge of illness, pale and sweating; within days he would be confined to bed with pneumonia. But he was determined to exorcise the evil that he saw possessing the Illinois Democratic Party. He hoped that a great speech could undercut the legitimacy of the state's delegation, and achieve a victory that would go far towards demonstrating his continued influence over the party.

At the very least, should he lose, he would have left his mark. Everyone waited patiently as the Committee on Credentials report was read. It affirmed that irregularities had occurred, but also that they did not rise to a level that could justify overturning the outcomes of an official state convention and committee.[22]

Following some discussion about the disputed delegations of Puerto Rico and the Philippines, Bryan rose to "demand" a separate vote on the Illinois matter. This was granted, and he then read into the record the minority report of the Committee on Credentials, which characterized the action of the state convention and committee in replacing numerous delegates as "illegal, unsupported by any evidence, the hearing farcical, [and] the claim absurd." The report then explored the circumstances associated with delegate selection in the twelve contested congressional district caucuses, and found, or purported to find, evidence proving that in each mostly Harrison and Hearst men had won, but in violation of the rules were disallowed.[23]

Next, it addressed the issue of John P. Hopkins and Ben Cable's status as delegates-at-large, asserting that, contrary to the official record and newspaper reports, no actual vote took place on the delegate slate in the state convention. Instead, it was urged that Judge Edward F. Dunne should replace Hopkins, and Silas Cook of East St. Louis should replace Ben Cable, on the rather specious basis that the state convention would have elected them if given the opportunity. Earlier Dunlap and others had been asked why they were not also contesting the two other delegates-at-large, Samuel Alschuler and Andrew M. Lawrence (both Harrison men). Their answers were vague, unconvincing, and to the effect that they should remain as delegates because they enjoyed broad popular support in Illinois. The minority report concluded by addressing the operation of the state convention itself, which, it argued, had been corrupted by a "conspiracy" that was "deliberate" and was designed "to override the will of the voters as expressed in the various district caucuses."[24]

Now Bryan rose to speak. For all of his passion, spurred on by frequent interrupting applause, it was not one of his greatest perorations. He began quietly, attempting to build the argument that the proceedings in Illinois were illegal and that the violations of the sacred principle of majority rule were the acts of "train robbers." In detail, he presented his interpretation of events. In the process, he personalized his arguments with frequent references to John P. Hopkins. Eventually, the real emotional core of his presentation emerged in his richly expressed loathing for the former Gold Democrats (so-labeled) who directed the Illinois convention, and who in 1896 had turned their backs on the party (and him). He warned that if the convention did not restore legitimacy to Illinois' representation, it would be placing the state party in the hands of the betrayers, which would convince the voters that the Illinois party was unworthy of their support. He concluded by falling back upon one of his usual quasi-religious bombasts (not unlike the conclusion of his "Cross of Gold" speech in 1896), proclaiming the results of the state convention a "sin," that would be "put upon the Democratic Party of the nation" (presumably by God) should it not be overturned. His supporters applauded and cheered wildly, but almost everyone else in the hall appeared unimpressed.[25]

First up in rebuttal was Indiana's G. V. Menzies, a member of the Committee on Credentials. He noted that Bryan was absent for most of the committee's hearing on the matter, an absence he felt called into question the sincerity of the claims of high principle: "Great as [Bryan] is, he is not so omniscient that he can know a case without having heard it (applause)." He then reviewed in depth the procedures that were followed in addressing the controversy before defining what he saw as "the heart of this contention": "[W]hether the action of the constituted authorities of the Democratic Party of Illinois shall be trampled upon by bare assertions of fraud, unsupported by evidence, and whether the regular action of the duly chosen and elected convention of the party ... is to be ignored because of pique, chagrin, and disappointment." The supposed evidence was *ex parte* and founded upon little more than "bare assertion." Moreover, even the credibility of the petition introducing the matter was now rendered suspect by the numerous telegrams and other communications denying participation from many of those supposedly among the 871 signers.[26]

Frank Quinn, the chair of the Illinois state convention, was next to speak. Emotionally, he took umbrage at Bryan's attempt to characterize the Illinois leadership as lacking in Democratic principles. Quinn reminded the convention that he had remained loyal in 1896 and had campaigned for Bryan. Like Menzies, he questioned how the Great Commoner could possibly reach a measured judgment after having been present for the Credentials Committee's hearing for only about forty-five minutes of a session lasting nearly eight hours. Why, he asked, did Bryan and his allies wait until the last minute to file any kind of contest if they were so offended? No, these are not legitimate grievances, he proclaimed, but were designed merely "to advance the personal spleen of Millard Fillmore Dunlap, who sits here upon the stage prompting Mr. Bryan."[27]

Following a very short rebuttal by Bryan that said nothing new, James R. Head from Tennessee, chair of the Committee on Credentials, also spoke in favor of the majority report. He, too, affirmed the arduous efforts of the committee to arrive at the truth, and he, too, denied that there was adequate support for such a radical course as discarding the results of the Illinois convention. Not only was there insufficient evidence, but just a tiny minority of the committee had even questioned the majority, and even they did not raise the issue of fraud during the meeting. At the conclusion of his talk, something of the drastic implications of what Bryan was demanding of the convention was then pointed out by delegate Leonard Rosing of Minnesota, who asked what would happen to the Hearst instructions should the Illinois convention be delegitimized? Was it possible that should Bryan succeed, the Illinois Democratic electors might lose their legal status?[28]

With this, the debate ended. Bryan demanded a roll call. When it came around to Illinois, Thomas Carey rose to protest "the wrecking crew" who had seized the Illinois party. But all protests were by now unavailing, and by a vote of 299 yeas to 647 nays, the minority report met defeat.[29]

Bryan was either standing forth courageously for his principles and his place in the party, or his stance represented "the inglorious eclipse of a man of one time brilliant promise," whose efforts were those of "the pettifogging police court lawyer indulging in untruths, abuse, vilifications, and malice," demonstrating "a complete lack of intellectual integrity." While the former interpretation would resound in the years ahead, in the summer of 1904, it was the latter that seemed to most Democrats to be the more accurate.

The convention was virtually an unmitigated triumph for the reorganizers. Any hopes that Bryan might stampede the convention and be renominated yet again were dashed as the controlling forces chose Alton B. Parker for president. He had been lately the chief judge of the New York Court of Appeals and the protégé of conservative Senator David B. Hill. Parker had also been endorsed by Grover Cleveland, who declined himself either to seek or accept the nomination. Further discouragement for the Nebraskan and his backers came with the selection of Tom Taggart of Indiana as national chairman. Taggart, whom Bryan despised, was a political boss and a friend of Sullivan's. Even the Nebraskan's one shining moment, convincing the Committee on the Platform to not endorse specifically the gold standard, became meaningless when his party's presidential nominee made his acceptance of the nomination conditional upon the understanding that he regarded "the gold standard as firmly and irrevocably established." Mayor Harrison had even less to celebrate, and in the end, he contented himself with the claim of a "moral victory" in helping to bring the Illinois delegation controversy before the party and the nation.[30]

As gold men of long standing, Hopkins and Sullivan were gratified with the convention's outcomes. Neither showed much interest in the identity of the nominee—again, just so long as it was not Bryan—and the Illinois delegation cynically continued to vote as a unit for William Randolph Hearst to the end. For all of the publisher's success in Illinois, which was largely a function of what was now reported to be as much as $1.4 million spent in the state (an unimaginably large sum for the time), he was only able to attract 181 of the 1,000 votes cast. He did have the consolation of a spirited and well-received speech by Clarence Darrow seconding his nomination. Roger and John became briefly involved in the selection of a vice-presidential candidate, attempting to secure it for someone from Illinois, and for Marshall Field in particular. Instead, Henry G. Davis, an octogenarian conservative banker from West Virginia who was very wealthy and would presumably help finance the campaign, and who served as a delegate to the Pan-American Conference of 1901, was chosen by acclamation.[31]

Sullivan and Hopkins could also take satisfaction from the demonstration and affirmation of their power in Illinois. This in turn set the stage for a significant and deliberate handoff of the leadership of their organization. Just weeks after the convention, on July 22, 1904, the state committee of the Democratic Party gathered in Chicago to elect new officers and to prepare for the campaign. Hopkins formally surrendered his post as state chair to his friend, Charles Boeschenstein of Edwardsville. The new vice-chair was another ally, Arthur Charles of Carmi, and the remainder of the officers was handpicked. All were elected without opposition, and all of them came from downstate Illinois.[32]

This statewide inclusiveness was brilliant strategizing by Sullivan and Hopkins; the primary tension between Chicago politicians and those of the rest of Illinois was founded in a fear of domination by those controlling party affairs in the great metropolis. One of Carter Harrison and Bobby Burke's chief mistakes had been their attempt to create a statewide organization so obviously headquartered in the Chicago mayor's office that it evoked almost instant suspicion and opposition. In contrast, what would become known as the Sullivan machine would function in Illinois as more of a mutually beneficial association of political leaders. Placing Boeschenstein and Charles at the head of the state committee was a demonstration of this power sharing, and was one source of the remarkable loyalty Sullivan would be able to command throughout Illinois—even in traditional Bryan country. At the same time, however, Chicago men, including Sullivan (at the insistence of John), Hopkins, Brennan, and Tom Gahan, packed the executive board of the state committee, assuring that no policy could be implemented without their advice and consent.[33]

Even more importantly, the meeting was, in effect, an informal inauguration of Roger Sullivan as leader in place of John Hopkins. This had all the appearances of being the outcome of a concerted plan. By 1903, Sullivan had begun noticeably to develop a public reputation as a harmonizer, independently of Hopkins. This bolstered his image and helped move him further out of the shadows. With the state, county and national convention, he successively became more prominent, and his election as national committeeman was a clear proclamation of his enhanced status. Now working with Boeschenstein, Sullivan, as a national committeeman, as a new member of the executive board of the state committee, and as the most important representative of his political circle on the Cook County committee, would take full charge in the months ahead. Hopkins's role, on the other hand, became clearly secondary, and within a couple of years, he was to retire entirely from the public aspects of politics—refusing even to serve as a delegate to national conventions and other such honors.

The sources of this public transfer of leadership are not certain; there is no good evidence as to why or when it was conceived. However, it is unquestionable that in large measure, Sullivan's rise was due simply to his own robust ambition and desire to lead. Certainly, there is no proof or suggestion that Hopkins was in any way "overthrown"; it is difficult to imagine a figure as dynamic and powerful as John Hopkins involuntarily foregoing his position of leadership even to Sullivan, his best friend. In addition, John's paramount role in promoting Roger as well as his quiescent, even eager, acceptance of a steadily more obscure public profile would argue against this and suggest instead that he may have been wearying of being the lightning rod of the alliance. It is even possible that health issues played a part, as John suffered from recurring throat problems. At the same time, it is important to remember that Sullivan was never Hopkins's subordinate, and that the shift was a logical extension of the more prominent role Roger already played behind the scenes in recent years, and especially in Chicago's wards. Also important were Hopkins's personal antagonisms with Bryan and Harrison. These had developed to the point where he personally could be judged as an obstacle to any hope of party unity. Sullivan, in contrast, was the one man in the organization who had been able to work with the mayor, albeit with difficulty, and he was not as yet a personal target for the Commoner.

For these reasons, Roger Sullivan became, after July 22, 1904, steadily the more active of the pair, and within a year, he was broadly acknowledged as paramount leader. Hopkins, while the darling of the faction, was never considered its "boss"—even by the press. However, it became quickly commonplace to apply the title to Sullivan, who, though hating the epithet, nonetheless did introduce an increasingly direct and orderly leadership of the burgeoning organization that more than justified its use. In part this was a function of Sullivan's personal style of leadership, which was always more direct and "hands-on" than that of Hopkins.

Also, the years ahead of unceasing conflict with the Harrison organization naturally lent itself to greater structure and hierarchy. Important, too, was the business ethos of efficiency, which was already permeating society and progressivism in this age of industrialization, and which Sullivan and his associates, as successful businessmen, brought to their political activities as well. As a result, the sets of political alliances that made up the Hopkins-Sullivan faction before 1904 would develop into an expanded and increasingly structured Sullivan machine.

Roger Sullivan's new status became unmistakable in the campaign ahead. Initially both the Harrison and Hearst crews remained bitter, vowing to continue to fight on. As often happens in politics, however, resolution soon faded in the face of expediency. Bryan announced his support of Parker, and without his leadership, any local reluctance to support Democrats in the campaign or appearance of attempting to thwart the work of the sitting state leadership would be viewed as a tacit bolt. Thus, when the state committee met in late July to organize itself and the election effort, Harrison was intentionally on vacation—a clear signal of his grudging acquiescence. This in turn had the effect of isolating the Hearst men and dampening any thought for the moment of their continued resistance.[34]

Just after his selection, the new state chair, Charles Boeschenstein, appointed a campaign committee led by Sullivan, Hopkins, Cable, Frank Quinn, and Bobby Burke. A week later Sullivan and Hopkins traveled to New York City to confer with members of the national committee. It was decided there that Chicago, as it had been during the last two national elections, should be the site of the western campaign headquarters (later amended to being just the headquarters of the Midwest). An office was rented at the Auditorium Annex near the Republican command center. Roger, acting out his new more visible role, publicly dismissed all thought that the Democrats in Illinois would drag their feet for Parker: "We believe the chances this year are largely in our favor," he assured the city when asked about the matter by reporters, "consequently it rests with us to take advantage of the situation, and do all we can to elect our national ticket."[35]

Others were doubtlessly more cynical about the likelihood that the state's bitterly antagonistic Democratic factions would pull together. But the miracle occurred. All sides, as it proved, had an interest in victory, or at least in avoiding all appearance of responsibility for defeat. Sullivan and the state's other reorganizers were eager to prove they could better Bryan's 1896 and 1900 totals and carry the state for Parker. The Nebraska Democrat probably had little faith in a Parker triumph, but he recognized the need to demonstrate party regularity if he were ever to resume his leadership in the future. For similar reasons, neither Harrison nor the Hearst men, most of whom were Bryan loyalists at heart, had anything to gain by ignoring the calls for harmony and sitting out the election. This "love feast" among Illinois Democrats was strongly encouraged by the national leadership, which placed the state in the "hopeful column," and was willing to spend substantial sums to secure it for Parker. In the hope of placating everyone, Mayor Harrison was chosen to distribute funding in Cook County, while Sullivan and Hopkins oversaw the financing in the rest of the state.[36]

Roger Sullivan was seemingly unlimited in his enthusiasm for harmony and the campaign. He even extended a personal invitation to Bryan to come speak in Illinois. It was, after all, his first opportunity to demonstrate openly his new status. In a remarkable change from his usual shadowy presence (in the press at least), he now, as national committeeman, took a more central and publicized posture. In August, with Charles Boeschenstein in tow, he attended a Chicago Democratic picnic at which Lawrence Stringer spoke, as did Harrison and Judge Owen Thompson. This was a highly symbolic move, effectively a visit to the enemy camp, and one that merited press attention. On December 19, the national chair, Tom Taggart, and Sullivan sat down to discuss the campaign at a meeting called by the state committee. To help present a united front, such implacable enemies as M.F. Dunlap, Owen Thompson, and Tom Carey were convinced to attend. An even more astounding event occurred a month later when Taggart returned to Chicago. This time he was accompanied by Bryan, just completing a tour of Indiana. Waiting at the train station were Sullivan and Boeschenstein. Not only did Bryan shake their hands in front of witnesses, but, he even deigned to call Illinois' national committeeman (the man he had labeled just months before as a train robber) "Roger"! The Peerless Leader then took time off to attend a horse show, after which he boarded a train for his home in Nebraska. Taggart joined Roger and Boeschenstein for a midnight meeting with John Hopkins, who had been discreetly waiting for Bryan's departure.[37]

While Sullivan was focusing upon the mechanics of the campaign, insisting among other things that a Democratic candidate appear in each county race regardless of Republican predominance, Harrison did a journeyman's service speaking throughout the state for Parker. His principal themes were the dangers of industrial combination and imperialism—both pet saws of Bryan. At one point, the mayor attracted some criticism by comparing Filipino guerrillas, who resisted American occupation until 1902, to the patriots of 1776. However, his hard work was rewarded with an invitation late in the campaign from the chair of the Democratic national executive committee, William F. Sheehan, to come to New York City to consult with Parker himself.[38]

By election eve, however, unpleasant realities began to intrude. The press turned to Sullivan for a prognosis. He tried to be optimistic, noting that the reelection of President Theodore Roosevelt was in "no wise so certain as the political correspondents ... would have the public believe." Parroting the statements of the national headquarters, he went on to profess that he believed that Parker would be able to add to the block of the usual Southern Democratic electoral votes those of New York, Indiana, West Virginia, Delaware, Connecticut, Colorado, New Jersey, Montana, Idaho, and Nevada, and thereby achieve election. However, he was too much of the master politician to blind himself to the Republican momentum in Illinois. Struggling to be positive, he pointed out that the state had fooled people in the past, most recently in 1892 when it unexpectedly went Democratic, but argued that it did not really matter anyway, as "Illinois is not needed to elect Parker this year!"[39]

However, the elections proved to be a disaster of a magnitude that even Sullivan probably did not foresee. The country may well have been distrustful of the perceived radicalism of William Jennings Bryan and Bryanism, but neither did it want the return to the days of William McKinley and Grover Cleveland that Parker represented. Theodore Roosevelt was elected by the landslide margin of 336 electoral votes to 140 for the Democrat. Parker failed to carry a single state outside of the deep South, solidly Democratic since the traumas of military occupation during Reconstruction. In New York, the president received 53.12 percent of the vote to 42.28 percent for Parker, in Connecticut 58.12 percent to 38.14 percent, in Colorado 55.11 percent to 41.7 percent, and in Idaho 65.84 percent to 25.46 percent. Illinois' returns were no better; the president took 632,645 votes or 58.77 percent to Parker's 327,606 or 30.43 percent. In Cook County, the outcome was even worse; Roosevelt was given 68.89 percent. All of the county's ten congressional seats went Republican. Cook County also elected three Republicans and no Democrats to the Illinois Senate, and to the House, 57 members of the GOP to 23 Democrats. This created heavy Republican majorities of 42 to 9 in the upper house and 91 to 57 in the lower. In the county elections, Roosevelt's coattails helped secure every elected office for the Republicans except that of sheriff. Statewide, Charles Deneen, the state's attorney from Cook County, buried Lawrence Stringer for the governorship, taking with him to Springfield almost the entire Republican ticket.[40]

The election was a major blow for all Democrats, but especially for the reorganizers, who premised their argument for power upon the assumption that without the burden of Bryan the party could win. Instead, they had actually done worse than in 1896 and 1900. Of course, this was chiefly a matter of the popularity of Theodore Roosevelt, as well as the nomination of the completely uninspiring Parker to be his opponent. Nonetheless, the election would provide a very potent argument for the return of Bryan in the years ahead.

If there was anyone less happy with the results than Roger Sullivan and his cohorts, it had to be Carter Harrison. His grand plans to run for the presidency (or vice-presidency) that had seemed so plausible at the end of 1903 had been thwarted by the Sullivan-Hopkins triumphs in the state and national conventions. Now, any hope he might have harbored to secure reelection as mayor (or some appropriate federal job) was sabotaged by the electoral disaster. He might have been able to overcome even this—after all, in 1903 he had beaten the odds—but a new and more potent force in Illinois and Chicago politics than even Roosevelt was emerging as the election campaign was underway. This was the progressive movement, which would now burst forth to overwhelm the local political culture and elect, in the spring of 1905, Chicago's only completely reformist mayor.

By 1904, progressivism had become as pervasive as to be a defining element of the nation's life and the Zeitgeist of the period. Reform was in the air, and virtually everyone would claim to be a reformer on some issue. The term itself became a watchword of the age, and it was not uncommon for dairies, laundries, and other businesses to include the word "progressive" in their monikers. Though progressivism could mean different things to different people, and it could include contrary and even contradictory methods and goals, in its broadest form it was a Janus-like movement that looked both backwards and forwards.

In the past it found a comforting model of middle-class and native-born predominance in American life. Much of this, which would be a kind of collective atavism, was founded in a fearful chauvinism directed against the multitudes of recently-arrived eastern and southern European immigrants crowding into the Eastern and Midwestern municipalities. They seemed to defy all hope of assimilation. Though generally discounted or overlooked by historians, immigration reform was an important and revealing political theme of the progressive period that would find final fruition in rigid restrictions implemented in the 1920s.

At the same time, progressivism was inspired by the business economy and culture of the late nineteenth and early twentieth centuries. With an emphasis upon efficiency and growth fueled by the new technologies, it had brought not only mass production and consumption, but an affirmation of mankind's ability to control its own destiny. It is important in this context to remember that for Americans of this period, the tremendous economic, technological, and social changes brought not just the daunting challenges of industrialization and urbanization (including for a time vast human misery among workers), but also the promise of the perfectibility of man and society. Married to a vigorous, even adolescent, nationalism, progressivism was eternally optimistic and proactive.

While private activism was one characteristic of the movement, it was to government that progressives as a rule looked to be key mechanism of reform. Only an enhanced government, but also one bolstered by greater democracy, could take on the problems of monopoly, urban squalor, industrial violence, and corruption that confronted the country. When Theodore Roosevelt became president in September 1901, the national government, or at least the executive branch, became a progressive institution overnight. The new president brought a wider vision of governmental responsibility than had existed previously, and it was he, through his notion of the "Square Deal," who facilitated the redefinition of government as a referee of American society. Roosevelt, for instance, was the first chief executive not to instinctively favor business over labor, the first to seek more rigorous enforcement of the regulation of business monopoly and practices, and it was he who put the federal government permanently in the business of supervising the nation's natural resources.

However, the reformist impulse of this period did not originate on the national stage, but earlier in Eastern and Midwestern urban centers, where the social impact of the new economies and population growth was first felt. In general, these municipal reform movements tended to conform to the pattern first proposed by historian Melvin Holli, who identifies two categories of urban progressives: "structural" and "social" reformers. Structural reformers were generally native-born, upper-middle or upper class, and tended to congregate in the Republican Party. Highly organizational, these groups, sometimes derisively called "goo goos" for being for "good government," came together to counter the influence of political machines and to bring efficiency to municipal governance in the forms of lower taxes and better services. To this end, they actively sought to eliminate politically individuals and situations they felt were hindrances to their goals, and in some places, they experimented with new structures of urban government (hence "structural reformers"), including superseding or replacing the traditional mayor and city council with a professional city manager or a set of trained commissioners to oversee specific operations of government like roads and sewers.

Social reformers had a different and broader agenda. Inspired to some degree by the collectivism being espoused by socialists and the followers of Henry George, and appalled at the living and working conditions of the urban working masses, they were less concerned with corruption and efficiency than with transforming government into an agency of the people's welfare to directly alleviate the challenges of the new industrial environment for workers and other citizens. Generally Democratic, this group was less clearly defined in terms of ethnicity and class and included young social activists, reformist judges and lawyers, labor leaders, and even some politicians.[41]

It was the structural reformers of the Windy City, however, who began the agitation for change through their Civic Federation of Chicago (founded on February 3, 1894). Its object was to support "all of the forces for good, public and private," and it was to be "nonpartisan, non-political, and non-sectarian." More specifically, it sought "to promote honesty, efficiency, and economy in the administration of the public business." It was the Federation that led public outrage over the Ogden franchise, but more usually, it confined itself to more prosaic matters like public sanitation and sidewalks.[42]

The primary political agency of the structural reformers in Chicago was to be instead the Municipal Voters' League. Created by the leading lights of the Federation in 1896, the League's state purposes were (1) "to secure the nomination and election of aggressively capable men to all city, town, and county offices, (2) to secure the efficient and business-like administration of municipal, town, and county affairs, and the strict enforcement of civil service laws, (3) to secure a just and equitable assessment of property..., and (4) to protect the rights of the people to the streets." George E. Cole was its first permanent president (he had also served at one time in that capacity for the Civic Federation), and would become identified more than anyone as the leading activist of this type in Chicago. He was also a personal friend of Roger C. Sullivan.[43]

Like so many structural reformers, Cole was native-born and a successful businessman, heading George E. Cole & Company, a printing firm. He had been active in the Civic Federation, and in the years ahead would expand his battle for better government by also undertaking the leadership in 1901 of the Citizens Association (founded 1874) and the Legislative Voter's League (founded in 1902 in large part through his efforts). His strategy and, therefore, that of the Municipal Voters' League was to focus upon Chicago's city council, and to convince voters to elect good men while expelling the "roaring rascality" of members identified as "gray wolves," or aldermen felt to be espe-

George E. Cole (*Illinois Political Directory, 1899*).

cially corrupt. Throughout this period, every local election would be graced by recommendations from the League. Though it would enjoy some success, such was the embedded nature of political practice and power in Chicago that some highly desirable targets proved to be beyond even their most persistent efforts.[44]

Alderman Edward Cullerton was typical of those in the League's sites, and like many others, he manage to survive its wrath. Born in 1842 in Chicago, "Sly Ed" had a career that summarized what the League saw as the malignancy infecting city government. Unlike the officers of the Civic Federation and Voters' League, he was of working-class origins, and had received only a common school education. His first employment was as a canal boat driver, where he soon saved enough to buy his own boat. Not long afterwards, he procured an appointment as a federal gauger (like Roger Sullivan in his early career) before moving for two years to Canada.[45]

Upon his return in 1871, he was elected to the city council as a Democrat. Here he served several terms as chair of the finance committee, then the council's highest position, but he was compelled to leave when an "independent movement" discovered that his ward residency was nominal. In 1898, he secured reelection (this time having legally established his residence), and remained intermittently the council until his death in 1930. In office, he was always found on the side of those the Federation and League identified as boodlers, and he was one of those who supported the Ogden and Cosmopolitan franchises. Cullerton's business dealings were somewhat shady, and he identified himself variously as "a detective, a real estate broker, and as the president of the 'Chicago Tax Adjusting Company.'" He was alleged to have criminal connections and would always be in the sights of the Voters' League, which in 1903 launched an investigation into his affairs and his taxes, to no meaningful

outcome. He was long identified as a leading "gray wolf" and the intimations of corruption and dishonesty always followed him but were never legally addressed.[46]

The advent and impact of Chicago's social reformers were initially more subtle. Unlike their structural counterparts, they were not organizational, and their influence and public profile were more often linked to a specific individual or cause. However, by 1904, some of the leading social reformers such as Clarence S. Darrow and George Schilling were already active. Many were former supporters of Governor John Altgeld. Others came from the local labor movement. Prominent among these were John J. Fitzpatrick of the Chicago Federation of Labor, and most especially Margaret Haley of the Chicago Federation of Teachers. Social activists like Jane Addams of Hull House fame, Raymond Robins, and Louis Freeland Post also became leaders. Still another group emerged from Chicago's judicial machinery. Since the fourteen Circuit and twelve Superior Court judges were all elected, and since they commanded some patronage, they were inevitably political, and the Cook County judiciary was always a fertile source of candidates. Moreover, since the judges enjoyed some degree of independence from factional politics, they tended to be more politically autonomous (Roger Sullivan made it a policy that judicial candidates should always be well qualified), which in turn allowed them the luxury of reformist activity without the direct threat of retaliation. Among the judges, one the most widely recognized promoters of reform was Murray F. Tuley. He became the "grand old man" of Chicago's social reformers, and was very active as a stump speaker, as a delegate to the various Democratic conventions, as president of the Iroquois Club, and as a proponent of change, including celebrated advocacies of improved drainage (such was his ardor and success that he earned the sobriquet of the "white-headed eagle of drainage reform") and of the municipal ownership of public transportation. Jane Addams would remember his "high sense of justice," but his most important contribution to the cause of social reform was his promotion of his protégé, future mayor and governor Edward F. Dunne. It was to be Dunne who would do the most to bring the influence of the social reformers and their agenda into the city's government.[47]

Like Sullivan and Hopkins, Dunne was born as the child of Irish immigrants. Unlike Sullivan and Hopkins, however, Edward F. Dunne had the advantage of a father, Patrick William "P.W." Dunne, who was an entrepreneur with a talent for making large amounts of money (much of which he donated to the cause of Irish independence). In 1855, when "Eddy" was but two years of age, P.W. moved his family from Connecticut to Peoria. There he prospered in a number of businesses. The elder Dunne also became involved in local and state Democratic politics, and was for a time a member of the state legislature. His prosperity made it possible for his son to study at Trinity University in Dublin, Ireland (one of his classmates was Oscar Wilde). In 1877, the entire family moved to Chicago, where Edward attended and graduated from the Union School of Law.[48]

He practiced as an attorney for the next few years until 1892, when thanks to the patronage of Tuley (which was probably secured through his father's influence and connections), he was nominated by the Democrats to fill a vacancy on the Circuit Court. He was elected easily and became a popular figure. As the son of an activist for Irish freedom, he inherited a natural sympathy for those oppressed by economic and social disadvantage. He soon earned a reputation on the bench for justice and humanity. At the same time, he developed close personal friendships with such important social reformers as Clarence Darrow, Jane Addams, and Henry Demarest Lloyd; he was, for instance, one of those who spoke at the funeral of John P. Altgeld. Moreover, he had worked passionately for Bryan, and at one point led a secession of Democrats from the Iroquois Club (of which, upon his return, he would serve a term as president) in protest of its control by gold men.

Generally, however, he had avoided all involvement in the factional fights; Dunne never embraced Sullivan or the type of machine politics he represented, but he also never made a point of openly joining his opposition or speaking out against him—an intelligent policy for anyone with political ambitions. Dunne became the one man in Chicago who had the advantage of both party regularity and a close association with the social reformers. His standing was further enhanced by the frequent speeches he delivered around the city for various reformist causes including free silver, anti-imperialism (especially concerning Ireland, the Philippines, and South Africa), and the rights of working men and women.

However, the great issue that was to propel him to power was to be the municipal ownership of public transportation. This was at once the defining element of the city's social reformism, and the single most important issue in Chicago in the years straddling the turn of the century. The controversy it engendered would become so powerful that not only would it briefly supersede the existing political culture, but it would also, much to Sullivan's satisfaction, drive Carter Harrison from office and the field of combat.[49]

8

"I was born a Democrat"
(1904–1908)

It was entirely sensible that public transportation should temporarily alter the political landscape in Chicago during the first years of the new century. The two decades between 1890 and 1910 alone accounted for a 57 percent growth in the population of the city. Meanwhile, in Cook County, beyond the municipal borders the modern phenomenon of the suburbs was beginning to emerge. There the increase was an even more impressive 113.8 percent in the same period as greater numbers sought a more bucolic home environment. Both this vast expansion in the number of people and their ever-wider dispersion were only possible because of new technologies of mass transit, and in particular the development of the railed streetcar.[1]

The first recorded mechanism of public transportation in the United States was the omnibus, horse-drawn wagons that began service in New York City in 1827. These were largely replaced by horse cars on rails appearing in 1832, which brought far greater efficiency in terms of payload and comfort. Horses, however, were expensive to maintain, had to be replaced periodically, and also contributed to the mounds of filth then pervading the streets. An additional challenge was the limitations of horsepower. This could be a special problem for hilly locations like San Francisco, and it was there, in 1873, that the first cable cars were installed. Vehicles were moved attached to miles-long cables that ran under the street powered by huge central engines. When everything worked, this solved the problem of moving large numbers of people over difficult terrain. On the other hand, to keep everything working meant constant and expensive maintenance, especially of the cable, and construction required replacing the streets. Nonetheless, Chicago embraced cable enthusiastically, and on January 28, 1882, commenced to run what would become the largest fleet of cable cars outside of the City by the Bay itself.[2]

Cable systems would continue to serve in Chicago into the twentieth century and in San Francisco into the twenty-first. However, they were soon superseded by the new wonder power-source of the age, electricity. The first workable electric motors appeared in the 1830s, but it was not until the 1880s that the associated technology had advanced to make it practical to put a motor on a streetcar. In 1888, Frank Sprague built the first functional electrical transportation system in Richmond, Virginia, and other cities soon followed. Usually, electricity was provided from a trolley that ran overhead on a wire; hence the name trolley cars. Sometimes, however, power also could be accessed from a third rail on the street. Chicago's streetcar companies opened their first electrical line on October 2, 1890, and by 1904, they dominated all systems.[3]

For all of its improved efficiency, the challenges of public transportation remained something that Chicago's government found difficult to address. In large part this was due to the state's arrogation to itself of the power to regulate all municipal franchises. Since the majority of state legislators were from outside of Chicago, and therefore were not accountable to the local voters, they were frequently more responsive to the blandishments of the business concerns that sought to profit from the streets than to the apparent interests of the population. This could, and did, have some very unfortunate results. In 1853, the legislature divided Chicago for the purposes of franchises into three divisions based upon the two branches of the Chicago River. This led to multiple streetcar companies, each with a different charter with different terms creating a tangle of legal obstacles to any kind of municipal oversight.[4]

Nor did it end there. In 1865, a state law extended the franchises of the three largest companies from the original twenty to ninety-nine years. The prospect of the city's being locked into a binding agreement until 1964 was greeted with bitter protests in Chicago and an overridden veto from Governor Richard Oglesby. However, the legality of extensions came into question when the 1870 Illinois Constitution was ratified. A constitutional provision specifically withheld from the legislature the right to grant these lengthy franchises without the consent of the municipality concerned. Since Chicago had never agreed to the Ninety-nine Year Act, this seemed to resolve the matter. Accordingly, in 1875, when a new city charter was introduced, it specifically limited all such contracts to twenty years. However, in 1883, the whole issue reappeared when two of the streetcar companies' original twenty-year charters expired. Corporation Counsel Francis Adams ruled that the Ninety-nine Year Act was probably valid. Not wishing to recognize these unimaginably lengthy claims to their streets, but also wishing to avoid expensive lawsuits, the city council set a policy of extending all streetcar franchises by twenty years whenever they became due.[5]

The dearth of regulation and the precipitous growth of population and area of the city helped create a Wild West economic environment of sharp practice and competition that was especially glaring in public transportation. Fortunes were made; in 1900 more than a million and a quarter passengers rode streetcars provided by ten surface railway companies, two of which grossed more than a million dollars a year (huge sums at the time). With money came power, and the companies became associated in the public mind with the worst kinds of predatory capitalism and related corruption of government. Personifying these evils was the man most Chicagoans grew to love to hate, Charles Tyson Yerkes.

He was born on June 30, 1837, outside of Philadelphia as the son of Charles Tyson Yerkes, Sr., a banker and a Quaker who had been expelled from the church when he took a nonbeliever as his wife. Charles Jr. completed a two-year course in high school but left at 17 year of age. Five years later, he founded his own brokerage firm and went to work at the Philadelphia stock exchange. He soon branched out to selling governmental bonds, and achieved a degree of local prominence. This all ended abruptly when a stock manipulation of his failed, thanks to the great Chicago Fire. Unfortunately, the capital he was using (to which he had obtained access as the financial agent for Philadelphia's treasurer) belonged to his city. Unable to make restitution, he was convicted of larceny and sentenced to thirty-three months in the notorious Eastern Pennsylvania Penitentiary. He tried to avoid prison by blackmailing two local politicians, and while this scheme failed, the information was so damaging to them that he won a pardon after seven months by promising to refute it publicly. He then went to the Dakota Territory to obtain a divorce from his wife of twenty years, and to wed Mary Adelaide Moore, who was just twenty-four years of age.[6]

In late 1881, Yerkes arrived in Chicago and went to work as a stock and grain broker. This brought sufficient prosperity to help finance a consortium he organized in 1886 to purchase the North Side City Railway. Soon he expanded his interests by securing control of the Chicago West Division Railway Company as well. Investing with him were such prominent locals as George Pullman and Marshall Field. He also began acquiring a number of suburban companies including the Chicago Electric Transit, the Chicago and Jefferson Urban, the Cicero and Proviso, the Evanston Electric, the North Chicago, and the Ogden Street railway companies. His eventual goal was a monopoly. However, the largest traction concern in the city, the Chicago City Railway (operating on the South Side), always eluded his grasp. Moreover, in face of the uncertainty associated with his companies' rights to use the streets, he felt the need to convince the state legislature to bring clarity to the situation, and (allegedly) he was not above using manipulation, blackmail, and bribery to achieve results. His questionable methods would prove one major source of the outrage that fueled the traction issue.[7]

Chicago, State Street, 1905 (Library of Congress LC-USZ6-133).

In 1897, thanks in part to Yerkes, the Humphrey Bill was introduced into the Illinois House of Representatives. It would have guaranteed extension of his companies' charters to fifty years. The intensely negative response this evoked led to the bill's defeat. However, it did not prevent the passage the following year of the seemingly more innocuous Allen Law, which boasted what appeared to be ample provisions for compensation to the city. But it also included many aspects felt to be exploitive, and essentially gave the city the choice of disadvantageous fifty- or twenty-year extensions. Where the Humphrey Bill inspired mass meetings and protest, the Allen Law ignited open rebellion.[8]

The Civic Federation and Mayor Carter Harrison, Jr., led the opposition, but they failed to block either the bill's passage or its approval by Republican Governor John Tanner. The fight then shifted to the Chicago city council, which needed to approve all franchise extensions. Yerkes and his associates were unrestrained in their attempts to convince the aldermen that it was in their interest to acquiesce. For well over a year, the controversy festered. The traction magnate did his best, even acquiring control of an important newspaper, the *Inter-Ocean*, to help manipulate public opinion. Finally, on December 5, 1898, an ordinance ratifying the law was introduced. Mass meetings were organized, and the Civic Federation and the Citizens Association vociferously supported the mayor as he sought to block passage. Others who joined the outcry included George Cole and John P. Altgeld. There were even threats of lynching should the aldermen not respect the popular will. Mayor Harrison observed "only half seriously" that a real possibility existed of "some hanging done in the streets of Chicago." Not wishing to test the seriousness of the threat, the city council voted by 36 to 27 to table permanently the proposed ordinance.[9]

Mayor Harrison's prospects for reelection soared after his fight against the Humphrey Bill and the Allen Law, and his stance against both was one basis for his claim—trotted out whenever efficacious—of being a reformer. Yerkes, on the other hand, became discouraged. Within a year of the failure of his ordinance, he began preparing to liquidate and leave the city. In 1899, he consolidated his suburban interests into Consolidated Traction Company, and in 1900 sold it, with the Northside and Westside Street railroads, to a new entity controlled by eastern investors called the Union Traction Company. This syndicate also oversaw systems in Philadelphia, New Jersey, Baltimore, and Pittsburgh. Yerkes profited greatly, but as it proved, he was about the only one; in 1903, the Union Traction Company went into receivership in large part because of financial irregularities hidden within the structures of the promoter's former companies. With his fortune in hand, however, the master manipulator left Chicago and moved to New York for a short rest. He then sought greener fields in Great Britain, where he gained fame and additional fortune overseeing the construction of the main components of the London Underground.[10]

But it was not Yerkes's manipulations, nor even the substantial profits the traction companies harvested from the use of the streets without satisfactory compensation, that so infuriated the people of Chicago. Rather, it was the daily experience of riding the cars that so many found frustrating and unacceptable. There was limited cooperation among the streetcar companies, meaning that transfers were not always an option. A working man or woman could potentially pay up to three fares going to and coming from work. Added to this were the general unreliability of schedules, the dirty and overcrowded cars, the frequently rude and incompetent employees (the job of streetcar conductor was poorly paid and subject to rapid turnover), and the accidents that seemed to occur weekly—sometimes with the loss of life. Not surprisingly, an emotionally driven movement for municipal ownership began to erupt.

It took its inspiration from the European experience with the municipal ownership of utilities, as well as from the more direct examples of publicly run streetcar systems in Berlin, Germany, and Glasgow, Scotland. Without the private profiteering and the alleged corruption of city officials that followed, surely "MO" (as it was labeled by its advocates) could create an efficient and consumer-oriented mechanism of public transportation. It was not even an entirely new idea in Chicago either; the city had owned and operated its own waterworks since 1857, and beginning in 1887, had run a lighting plant. Additionally, there were precedents in other American cities like Detroit, where Mayor Hazen Pingree had worked earlier for Immediate Municipal Ownership (or IMO), and Cleveland, where Mayor Tom L. Johnson was becoming known as one of the idea's leading advocates.

In Chicago, a Municipal Ownership League emerged as early as 1898, with William Prentiss as its first head. John Altgeld, who was governor at the time, made his sympathies clear, but he never did much for the cause until the following year, when it was the basis of his independent campaign to replace Carter Harrison as mayor. Altgeld lost, but MO began to take on a life of its own. The year 1902 saw the organization of what would become an unsuccessful effort to draft Clarence S. Darrow to run for mayor on a public ownership ticket. He declined, and his friend Daniel Cruise ran instead. Like so much of the agitation for municipal ownership, this initiative originated among Chicago's labor circles, and indeed, the Chicago Federation of Labor and its leaders were always leading proponents. Much more important, however, were two advisory referenda in April 1902 on the issue of MO. The results were resoundingly in the positive. By a margin of 142,826 to 27,998, the voters endorsed a municipally owned and run streetcar system, and by a majority of 104,743 votes, also registered their approval of public gas and electric lighting.[11]

For the social reformers, support of municipal ownership was a defining article of faith. Made up almost universally of followers of William Jennings Bryan, they shared his fear of unfettered capitalism and the "interests." Public proprietorship seemed to promise a solution that would at once vitiate the predatory proclivities of the streetcar barons, and, more importantly, fulfill the social reformist vision of government as a disinterested social actor. With an almost fanatical belief in the efficacy of the collective will in overcoming all barriers, they were prepared to move forward immediately. However, others among the city's leadership did not share either their confidence or their vision.

After 1900, it was true, both major parties routinely endorsed the concept of municipal ownership, and virtually every public figure paid lip service as well. However, while almost everyone supported the idea in theory, many were less sanguine about the ramifications of immediate acquisition. The obstacles, legal and otherwise, were intimidating and led a sizable number to adopt a more cautious advocacy that looked to a long and meticulous transitory process. Among those adhering to this position were most of the structural reformers and Carter Harrison. Following the 1902 referenda, the mayor helped to check the momentum of the movement by making his consent to any form of municipal ownership contingent upon the passage of a new state statute concerning the actual purchase and operation of the street railways. The result of this demand, echoed by others, was the Mueller Law.

Introduced by Senator Carl Mueller, it permitted the city to "own, construct, acquire, purchase, maintain, and operate street railways." However, another referendum was mandated, where approval by three-fifths of the voters would be necessary. Moreover, further referenda were authorized by which a simple majority could overturn any existing franchises. Lastly, a two-thirds vote in referendum was required for the issuance of interest-bearing bonds for financing. In the April 1904 elections the immediate implementation of the Mueller Law was endorsed by Chicago's voters by a margin of nearly five to one.[12]

Harrison now came under growing pressure to obey the stated will of the people, particularly from a relatively new but vociferous organization, the Municipal Ownership Delegate Convention. Founded in 1903 by Henry Demarest Lloyd, a major national social reformist figure who passed away shortly afterwards, the Convention featured among its membership Darrow, Cruise, and Margaret Haley of the Chicago Federation of Teachers. It was unrelenting in its insistence that there be no delay. However, Harrison vacillated. From his perspective, and increasingly that of the structural reformers, putting the law into practice was a much more complex proposition than any of the advocates recognized. Most importantly, federal Judge Peter Grosscup had recently ruled that the Ninety-nine Year Act still had a legal life. Until this issue was resolved, in Harrison's view, the city could not reasonably move forward. Also daunting were the costs of purchase and improvement, as were the prospects of creating the governmental agencies to operate a municipally owned mass transit system without political corruption. Consequently, the mayor began urging a policy of twenty-year renewals of all traction franchises as they came due. These would include the right of purchase by the city after ten years and the creation of a sinking fund to provide eventual financing for acquisition. Moreover, each company would be required to renounce any rights under the Ninety-nine Year Act. Finally, there would be yet another referendum, this time to approve any new franchises. This approach became known as the "Tentative Ordinance" and would signal Harrison's political downfall.[13]

By the time the city council's Committee on Local Transportation issued its report on Harrison's proposal in November 1904, the political climate had become so violently charged with emotion that nothing further could be done. Instead, the mayor and his plan were swept away by the tide of opinion within and outside his party that would find focus in a man most came to see as the city's great champion of transportation reform, Judge Edward F. Dunne. He recently had become publicly prominent as an advocate of municipal ownership by working closely with the mayor on the issue over the last two years; for instance, he was among those Harrison chose to contribute ideas for what became the Mueller Law. The Judge's reputation for honesty, his strong ties to the social reformers, and his Democratic Party regularity made him an ideal candidate in this extraordinary moment. On September 4, 1905, Dunne delivered a critical speech at one of the Fortschrift Turner Societies, in which he broke with the mayor and denounced the Tentative Ordinance. Daniel Cruise and William Prentiss also spoke, but it was Dunne who inspired Chicago, and in the following weeks, he was applauded wherever he appeared publicly.[14]

The effect of Dunne's speech, together with electoral setbacks for the Democrats in the November elections, torpedoed any hopes that the mayor might still have retained about his future in office. On November 21, he announced his intention not to run in the spring. Three weeks later, on January 15, 1905, Judge Murray Tuley issued a formal letter calling upon his protégé, Edward F. Dunne, to seek the mayor's office. With this, the party en masse jumped onto the bandwagon, and the judge was nominated by acclamation in

February 1905, to run upon a self-composed platform that featured immediate municipal ownership.[15]

His opponent was John Maynard Harlan, who also was counted as an expert on the traction situation. In 1897, he ran as an independent for the mayor's office, and in 1903, he was an unsuccessful candidate for the Republican mayoral nomination. On both occasions he argued for traction reform, and remained one of the most respected voices on the issue. His current platform hedged on the question of immediate municipal ownership, demanding that the city first demand rehabilitation of the street railways, with greater compensation for use of the streets. He also urged that this "should contain ample provision for municipal ownership and operation," with the qualification that this could only be implemented when "the city can be legally and financially able to successfully adopt it." It was, in essence, the same approach as that previously advocated by Carter Harrison.[16]

But the voters were angry, and the appeal of immediate municipal ownership was pervasive. Dunne was elected by a margin of 163,189 votes to 138,671, the largest mayoral plurality to that point in the city's history. Moreover, in referenda, the Tentative Ordinance with Chicago City Railway, and "any ordinance granting a franchise to any street railway company" short of municipal ownership, was decisively defeated by margins that approached three to one. Just a few days after his inauguration, the new mayor was feted at the annual Jefferson Day Banquet. Among those present at the grand event were William Jennings Bryan and Cleveland's Mayor Tom L. Johnson. Both praised Dunne, and rhapsodized about what they supposed to be a watershed moment in the history of Chicago and the nation; it seemed to some that a new era had dawned in the city's governance, an era that would have little place for political machines or their leaders.[17]

The events of the spring of 1905 could only inspire mixed feelings on the part of Roger Sullivan and other businessman politicians. He could not be unhappy, of course, that Carter Harrison had been knocked off his perch, and even now the former mayor was making plans to abandon the city and relocate to California (though his influence would never entirely disappear, and he made frequent trips back to Chicago to consult with his followers). Nonetheless, it was undeniable that the Harrison faction was in disarray, and this, presumably, offered an opportunity for a greater consolidation of power by Sullivan—especially as the new mayor was not a political creature. At the same time, the movement at the heart of Dunne's election was the kind of phenomenon that made professional politicians uneasy. The structure and culture of politics in Chicago was premised upon relative voter apathy, which, in effect, represented a passive abdication of power to the professionals. Any event or concatenation of events that roused the populace, and inspired them to set aside their usual apathy, was understandably a source of concern.

However, neither municipal ownership nor the social reformist ideology offered anything like the direct threat that would have been present in a structural reformist crusade founded upon demands for a change in the city's political practices. Accordingly, Sullivan, Hopkins, and their fellow regulars of the party, in the face of the great reform crusade, did the only efficacious thing—lie low. Probably not coincidentally, in January 1905, just as the movement for Dunne and IMO was climaxing, Roger and John embarked upon a joint vacation to Mexico. When they returned, they offered a perfunctory endorsement of Dunne (as did Harrison), and their participation in the city convention and the campaign was minimal. This would become Sullivan's standard strategy for the immediate future in dealing with reform and reformers. He never publicly assumed a posture of opposition, and he was generally successful in dodging, deflecting, or ignoring attempts to make him a target of opportunity for reformist rage.[18]

Nor was the concept of municipal ownership something that would have intrinsically alarmed Sullivan. How could he be entirely unsupportive of expanding the public payroll, and thus patronage? Moreover, he took the time to visit the municipally owned traction system in Glasgow and elsewhere while seeing Europe in August and September 1905. Traveling with him were his wife, Helen Quinlan Sullivan, his son Boetious, and his daughter Mary. Also in the party were Julia Hopkins (John's sister), and attorney Michael L. McKinley, currently a representative in the Illinois General Assembly from the Sixth District. They had a good time making their grand tour, though Roger suffered the indignity of having his watch and a scarf pin (worth the substantial sum of $750, a measure of his prosperity) pickpocketed in London. He discovered the theft while traveling to a meeting with Sir Henry Campbell-Bannerman, who would become prime minister on December 5, 1905, serving in that position until resigning due to ill heath on April 3, 1908. The party arrived in New York from Cherbourg, France, on September 5 aboard the *Kaiser Wilhelm II*, but Roger, while admitting that he had looked over different transit systems, was careful to "reserve his decision" regarding municipal ownership.[19]

On the other hand, as an officer of the Ogden Gas Company, his more immediate interest was in fending off public acquisition of any of the public utilities, and gas service in particular. For this reason, in the spring of 1905, he testified in Springfield against a bill that was designed to empower Chicago to institute governmental proprietorship of gas production. While admitting the need for greater oversight of the industry, he warned that there was such opposition against municipal ownership, particularly in Chicago's business community, that it would undercut any implementing law. With Sullivan appeared other utility officials, including Samuel Insull, who made similar arguments. Whether because of their testimony, or because of Sullivan's backstage maneuvering (as his antagonists later would have it), the bill was defeated in the Illinois Senate. Almost immediately thereafter, the Illinois legislature did enact a measure providing for the direct *regulation* of the gas industry by Chicago. Sullivan urged acceptance upon his peers in the gas industry as the only viable alternative to public ownership. In response, Mayor Dunne, late in 1905, attempted to use the municipality's new authority to lower the cost of lighting and heating gas from 90 cents to 75 cents per one hundred cubic feet. Sullivan and the Gas Trust opposed this, and Roger, as Ogden's secretary, endured a heated grilling by Dunne and his allies before a committee of the city council. In the end, however, the aldermen accepted the industry's counteroffer of 85 cents, a result that reinforced reformist perceptions of Roger C. Sullivan as a gas baron.[20]

Another concern evoked by the election was the new mayor's closeness to William Jennings Bryan. Having a municipal chief executive who was an ideological liegeman of his most powerful enemy could have been challenging. Mayor Dunne, however, was not a schooled politician, and was at this point in his career still the idealistic amateur. It was true that he enjoyed a considerable measure of respect among the Democratic Party's rank and file, and that he had served in such party positions as the presidency of the Iroquois Club, but he had never been involved in the rough and tumble of Chicago's political life. Powerful friends secured his nomination for the circuit court back in 1892, and thereafter his primary political duty had been to accept renomination and reelection every four years. He certainly never had to campaign for himself. All of this freed him to assume a statesmanlike posture above the fray, and to make his name with frequent well-received speeches around the city on reform and other topics. It also permitted him the luxury of not having to be involved in factional politics or confronting entrenched political leaders.

However, William Jennings Bryan was encouraged by the election of Dunne to intervene directly into Chicago's and Illinois' factional dynamics in an effort to transform the Sucker State into a personal political fiefdom. Sullivan may have controlled the party machinery, and he may have lined up most of the professionals, but he had as yet to achieve anything like an overarching hegemony over the multiple factions and factionettes that still pervaded the city and county Democracies. The Harrison men were divided into a "half dozen" factions, though the former mayor, still living in California, would sometimes go through the motions for the cause of general unity in the year ahead. Far more disruptive were the activities of the Hearst and Bryan men, who at Bryan's behest created yet another organization specifically designed to undermine Sullivan. Grandly titled the Majority Rule League of Illinois, it had leaders whose names were familiar: M.F. Dunlap and Judge Owen Thompson. As secretary, the group chose Theodore Nelson of Chicago, but also prominently among its ranks was a man who would emerge for a time as one of the most important of Sullivan's antagonists: Congressman Henry T. Rainey, future speaker of the United States House of Representatives.[21]

Rainey was originally prominent in the Municipal Ownership League, which was even now, in the fall of 1905, cheering on Hearst in his ultimately unsuccessful bid for the mayor's office of New York in an election that proved to be extremely close. The League would continue to support Hearst in his next and last race, a vain attempt at the New York governorship as the Democratic nominee against Charles Evans Hughes. They applauded his calls for municipal ownership and support of labor, and they appreciated the benefits of his money, which he distributed lavishly, as well as his newspapers, which shifted their coverage and editorial stances with a discipline *Pravda* under Stalin would have envied. However, for virtually all of the Illinois and Chicago Hearst Democrats, the New York publisher was in reality little more than a stalking horse for their real hero, William Jennings Bryan. In a remarkably short time after the election of 1904, the Great Commoner had become once again the bride of the Democratic Party, wooed and worshipped. And there was no one in the nation more determined than Bryan to unseat Roger Sullivan and his faction, and no one who would contribute more to the disruption and electoral setbacks of the Chicago Democratic Party in 1906.

The emotional basis for the Peerless Leader's desire for revenge was understandable. In his total war on Roger Sullivan, Bryan seemed to be playing out an important scene in his personal passion play. His eager embrace of self-sacrifice and humiliation at the hands of the unbelievers during the 1904 national convention was the first act before a descent into the hell of political exile from which he was resurrected sanctified. Now he prepared to judge the sinners and to consign them to the pit.

He could have chosen another Gold Democrat as the focus of his wrath—the national chair and boss of the Indiana party, Tom Taggart, whom he loathed, would have seemed an obvious choice—but targeting Sullivan held a special attraction beyond symbols and emotions. Bryan wanted control of the Democratic Party of Illinois, which was the one industrial state east of the Mississippi River where he could count upon broad support, and where he had been born. If Sullivan and his faction were removed or their power greatly diminished, inevitably the new emerging leadership, whether it included Dunne, Harrison, Darrow, Dunlap, or others, would be closely tied to the Commoner. This would create a more-or-less permanent political base in the nation's number two or three state (Illinois was vying for place with Pennsylvania), which would improve his chances of securing the presidential nomination in 1908, as well as enhance his political influence thereafter even should he lose again. William Jennings Bryan was, therefore, preparing for the first time to become a direct player in the party wars of Illinois and Chicago.

Roger Sullivan, on the other hand, as the leader of the largest and most stable of the Democratic factions, and no longer significantly challenged by Harrison, had every interest in promoting peace; coordinating all the various fragments and splinters of the party could only redound to his favor. He was also a man who as a rule did not carry grudges, a character trait that was reinforced over the years by his experiences with Chicago's kaleidoscope of ever-changing political loyalties. Consequently, his instinct, as always, was to be a "harmonizer," something that would also serve the immediate cause of electoral success. While most of the regulars would come to appreciate and cooperate with him in this, others chose to flock to the banner of Bryan and Hearst.

On February 16, 1906, the state Democratic Committee gathered in Chicago to discuss factional peace. In charge were Sullivan, Hopkins, and Boeschenstein, but it was M.F. Dunlap, present as a guest, who dominated the proceedings. Abruptly, as the meeting began, he launched into a tirade. Continuation of the "present leadership," he argued, would "wreck the party" because of the crooked legacy of the last state convention. It was "two or three men here now" who were responsible not only for that travesty of gavel rule, but for depressing the potential Democratic vote with their boss rule. The two or three were, of course, "Mr. Hopkins, Mr. Sullivan, and Mr. Quinn." Dunlap's unexpected and ungentlemanly attacks inspired "red faced" sputtering anger among some of the participants, but Sullivan took the high road and continued to urge unity. "I am glad Mr. Dunlap has spoken," he mildly responded, "but let us have peace." "We don't believe in these wars of extermination," he assured everyone, and "we want Mr. Dunlap to put his feet under the table and be one of us." As Roger completed his brief statements, there were calls for adjournment, but the now usually taciturn John Hopkins (also there as a guest) was angry: "I want to talk to you plainly, Millard Dunlap," he began: "I want to tell you that you went over this state in 1904 with a slush fund of $200,000 and spent it in debauching the democratic [*sic*] voters of this state on behalf of a presidential candidate [Hearst]. You and your people caused the uproar and confusion in that state convention. You put a prizefighter next to me on the stage of the convention hall. If that convention were disgraceful, you made it so, Mr. Dunlap." With this outburst, the meeting fell apart. One committeeman wearily conceded: "Oh hell, let's adjourn. The only place you can find harmony is in the graveyard!"[22]

The Majority Rule League now began to work to overthrow Sullivan and to secure the Illinois delegation for Bryan in the 1908 national convention. Initially, however, they needed to resolve divided loyalties between those who still supported Hearst, and the vast majority who were for the Nebraskan. Most ambiguity seemed to have disappeared when the New York publisher on March 16 endorsed Bryan. Nonetheless, the Hearst forces, led by Andrew Lawrence, continued in the months ahead to muddy the situation.[23]

Sullivan, however, maintained his peace offensive. In April, he extended a special invitation to Hearst and his followers, expressing confidence that all could work together. Most regular Democrats supported him, some not so much out of loyalty, but because unity was necessary for any chance of victory. Among those signing on were Carter Harrison (still hovering on the fringes) and Edward F. Dunne, both of whom sent representatives to a joint caucus called to choose potential judiciary candidates. As a result, a general calm prevailed at the May 1 judicial convention, which merely ratified the earlier choices of the leaders. Sullivan ran the gathering, even going so far at one point as to walk the aisles demanding quiet. Mayor Dunne was less of a presence, and only one of his picks was nominated.[24]

On June 18, a truce until after the judicial elections was announced. This was the collective decision of a widely heralded meeting of virtually all the regular Democrats. Tom Carey and Alderman Johnny Powers represented Harrison, Alderman William Dever came on behalf of Dunne, and Clarence S. Darrow spoke for the Hearst/Bryan faction. Also present were Sullivan, William Loeffler, and Robert "Bobby" Burke. A "harmonizing committee" of 33 (including Sullivan, of course) was appointed, and for a brief moment it seemed that some degree of temporary stability had been achieved. Indeed, as late as July, Tom Carey would claim that the motto of the party had become "let us forget!" However, just two days after the conclave's optimistic conclusion, the Majority Rule League announced that M.F. Dunlap would depart for London in July for a conference with Bryan, a move that did not bode well for either Democratic unity or their longed-for success in Chicago.[25]

While exploring Europe in the last phase of a world tour, the Commoner finalized his plans for Illinois. The bombshell was dropped on July 31, 1906, by Judge Owen Thompson, who released Bryan's vituperative letter from Scotland demanding Sullivan's immediate removal as national committeeman. According to Bryan, Sullivan's supposed "corporate connections," and the allegation that the Chicago leader held his position through "fraud," were more than sufficient justifications. Should he refuse to resign, Bryan insisted, he should be compelled by Illinois' Democrats. Although this was, in effect, a tacit recognition of the replacement of Hopkins by Sullivan as leader, Roger found no reason to be pleased. After receiving the communication privately from Thompson, he retreated to the Sherman House with George Brennan and John McGillen, and quickly put together a scathing counterstatement arguing that Bryan was as "mistaken" in this as he had been "on the free silver question." However, it was not entirely the Peerless Leader's fault, so the press release asserted, as he had been "misled by men whose assumed friendship ... is not sufficiently great to prohibit them from attempting to place him in an awkward light." These men were "Millard Fillmore Dunlap and Judge Owen P. Thompson," leaders of the central Illinois "Jacksonville cabal," who had been "twice repudiated by the Democrats of the state." Sullivan went on to point out that his claim to legitimacy as a national committeeman was at least as valid as those representing the South, whom Bryan embraced with enthusiasm, and whose selection was based upon a system of legalized racial discrimination. In response, South Carolina Senator Ben Tillman, a vehement racist and impassionate Bryan supporter, suggested Sullivan should be "thrown out a window." But Sullivan's logic was impeccable: if his election was invalid, then so was that of "three fourths of the Democratic leaders in the country." Dunlap quickly issued a counterstatement denying his ability to influence Bryan against his will.[26]

Even as the Peerless Leader and his Illinois myrmidons were waging war against Sullivan, Democrats were rocked by the news (released on August 7, 1906) that the Hearst men were leaving the party. They subsequently organized themselves as the local branch of Hearst's Independence League, a national organization put together by the publisher to promote his agenda and his ambitions in cities where his newspapers allowed him a measure of influence. Hearst was seeking the governorship of New York, and, despite disclaimers, he apparently still harbored dreams of a presidential nomination in the coming year. The new League nominated a slate of its own local candidates, destroying any hope of Democratic victories.[27]

Another group making its presence known, and which also ran its own men, was something called the Progressive Alliance. Organized directly out of the Municipal Ownership League back in April 1906, it was a radical group closely tied to Chicago's laboring and union circles. Among its leaders was Daniel L. Cruise, but its president was P.T. Quinn, once head of the MO League and "a former anarchist, Knights of Labor member, and boyhood foe of T.R. [*sic*] Roosevelt." The Alliance was angry with just about everyone, including Hearst, and to a lesser extent Mayor Dunne for not achieving immediate municipal ownership of the street railways. Like the mayor, the Independence League, and Roger Sullivan himself for that matter (though doubtlessly more cynically), the Alliance was vociferous in its support of Bryan for president.[28]

The regular Democrats as a body were naturally distressed by the Hearst defection, and futile negotiations were conducted. On the other hand, they did their best to ignore the demands for Sullivan's resignation. At the Cook County Democratic Convention, held just days after Bryan's letter became public, Sullivan remained in charge, controlling about 65 percent of the delegates—an achievement made possible by a temporary alliance with remnants of the Harrison organization. The candidates had been pre-selected by the leaders months before, and just about everyone concerned, including the mayor and Bobby Burke, was pleased at the results. Sullivan, typically, permitted each faction adhering to the truce a voice in the selections, but reserved to himself absolute control of the delegation to the Peoria state convention.[29]

Bryan was not idle while Roger was consolidating and underscoring his and the organization's strength in the city and state parties. On August 11, still in Europe, he issued a new demand, this time through an open letter to former Congressman Benjamin Caldwell. Now he insisted that not only should Sullivan

William Jennings Bryan, 1907 (Library of Congress LC-USZ62-95709).

be divested of position and power, but that the state committee should demonstrate repentance for having backed him in the first place. If his "requests" were not heeded, he would decline to speak in support of any Illinois Democrat candidate in the November election campaign.[30]

Sullivan continued to blame Dunlap in particular for events (something Bryan directly denied—though the Boy Orator of the Platte River admitted later in his memoirs that Dunlap was a party in the decision to try to unseat Illinois' national committeeman), and responded with his own missive addressed to each of the 1,645 delegates to the impending Peoria meeting. As was usually the case with anything composed by Sullivan, it was crisp and logical. In the first place, he argued, it was a violation of well-established precedents in the party for any national figure to interfere directly in state and local matters: "Democracy ... governs itself by city, town, county, state, and national conventions. It recognizes no dictator, no matter what the name of the would-be dictator." In the second place, despite Bryan's statements to the contrary, this "false issue" was motivated by the personal ambitions of Dunlap and Thompson, two "political adventurers" who "by the misuse of Bryan's name" hoped, now that the Hearst money had dried up, to enrich and empower themselves by ostensibly fighting for principle. Sadly, for entirely selfish reasons, they were willing to sacrifice the interests of the party, which "is now united as it has not been for years." It was this duo who misled the Great Man "by the familiar arts of the sycophant," and by trading on the fact that Dunlap had been Bryan's school chum. For them to recreate divisions was a "party crime," but even if the Nebraskan were completely sincere, "I do not concede even to Mr. Bryan the right to question my democracy or my membership on the national committee." Sullivan then recited the facts of his election as he saw them, and again underscored that he held his office with as much legitimacy as any other member of the national committee. He also denied any "corporate connections" beyond his service as president and secretary of the Ogden Gas Company, and he made clear his lack of embarrassment because he profited from this association: "They are all honest dollars, as honest as any Mr. Bryan has made."[31]

While Bryan's subversion was not without some success—a number of downstate county conventions voted their support, even as the Democratic Majority Rule League proclaimed its loyalty—Sullivan was certain by mid–August that "the [actual] majority will rule" in Peoria. He was right. The Majority Rule League obediently did its best to influence the delegates, and introduced a motion calling on Sullivan to resign. Thompson spoke in favor, but was repeatedly interrupted, and only allowed to continue by the request of the Roger Sullivan. However, everything went the way of the "Chicago Boss" (as he was now regularly titled by the press). The resolution inspired fistfights, and loud cries of "no, no" and "Hurrah for Sullivan." It was tabled by a two to one margin. Bryan's ally, Congressman Henry T. Rainey, then abruptly withdrew his candidacy for the temporary chairmanship against Carroll D. Boggs (quite possibly, as was rumored, because he was warned that past political misdemeanors would be aired otherwise), and a state committee friendly to Sullivan was appointed.[32]

Perhaps most discomfiting for Bryan, the convention also formally endorsed his presidential ambitions and voted an effusive eulogy of his accomplishments. The Nebraskan was already making noises about not wanting the support of any gathering controlled by Sullivan, but no one doubted that he would welcome the votes of the Illinois delegation.

There was some friction and catcalling between the Bryan men and the regulars, but in the end, the vast majority were loyal to "de guy what put de hooks into de geezer dat put de Democratic Party on de bum!"[33]

That it was Roger C. Sullivan and not William Jennings Bryan who now mattered most in the Illinois Democracy was underscored by the Chicago leader's overthrow of Tom Carey as chair of the Cook County Democratic Committee. Accomplishing this with the cooperation of William Loeffler and elements of the Dunne and Harrison factions, Sullivan promoted William O'Connell as Carey's replacement. O'Connell was Mayor Dunne's advisor, but also close to Sullivan, and his appointment was explained as simply an implementation of "the spirit of harmony." While Roger did not as yet have the kind of absolute command in Chicago that he recently had demonstrated over the state party, his influence was unquestionably on the rise.[34]

The Illinois convention was an unqualified success: Sullivan declared himself to be "deeply grateful." However, Bryan remained obdurate. Sullivan was originally to have been among those delegated by the Cook County party to travel to New York City to "greet" the Nebraskan upon his return from Europe. Roger did in fact travel east, but, not surprisingly, he did not attend after learning he would not be welcomed. Following ceremonies of mass ecstasy that remained unsullied by Roger's presence, the Great Man boarded a train for Chicago. At the city limits, he debarked and was met by Mayor Dunne. The pair then undertook a triumphant automobile ride into the city accompanied by the mayor of Omaha and M.F. Dunlap. As Roger had done his best to ascribe the attacks against him to Dunlap, this was a clear "red flag." The following day a huge banquet was held in Bryan's honor at the Auditorium under the auspices of the Jefferson Club. Before an audience of 750, the Nebraskan again took the occasion to excoriate Roger Sullivan, declaring flatly: "Mr. Sullivan is not my friend!" Remarkably, his spleen was such that he advised Democrats not to vote for the state and county tickets: "No man is entitled to the support of Democrats in this crisis that either stands with Mr. Sullivan, or is afraid to oppose him." His reasoning was, as usual, that the Chicago boss had too many "corporate connections," had seized control through fraud, and secretly wished to deny him the presidential nomination. Under this pressure, Mayor Dunne, who was caught between his need for the backing of the Bryan loyalists and his fear of the boss, reluctantly also called for Sullivan's removal.[35]

Roger had had enough. His attempts at accommodation had gone nowhere, and there seemed to be no limit to Bryan's violations of political etiquette. Speaking from New York, where he remained waiting to meet John Hopkins (who, like Bryan, had been wandering about in Europe), he once again made accusations of "dictatorship" and "autocracy." Bryan was simply disloyal, and would "rather have his own way than have democrats [*sic*] elected to congress [*sic*] or any other office." It was especially galling to have his party loyalty questioned: "I was a democrat when Mr. Bryan was a populist in Nebraska!" Sullivan explained: "My father came to this country to find in the democratic party [*sic*] of the United States that political liberty which had been denied him in his native land. I was born a democrat [*sic*]!" He then turned his fire on his Illinois enemies. Theodore Nelson was "an unconvicted felon." Owen P. Thompson had "bought his nomination" for judge in 1896 at $50 a head, and Millard Fillmore Dunlap, the banker, gets "deposits of state funds when democrats [*sic*] are in office, [with] his republican [*sic*] partner, Russell, getting the deposits when the republicans [*sic*] are in power." Congressman Henry T. Rainey was no better, and had illegitimately claimed mileage money in 1903 from the state treasury. These were the men with whom Bryan chose to associate and dared to hold up as morally superior?[36]

Nor were insinuations of a "disreputable" link between himself and Ogden Gas reasonable or fair. "The only offense this corporation ever committed was to lower the price of gas ... it gave its customers for 90 cents what it had been paying $1.10 for." In addition, among his associates in this enterprise had been Governor John P. Altgeld and respected Judge Thomas A. Moran: "Does Mr. Bryan dare to impugn their memory?" It was hypocritical to criticize him for his wealth. Bryan, himself, was a rich man, who had made almost all of his fortune because of his political activities, so "if Mr. Bryan thinks it is wrong to make money out of politics, then he should stop making money!" Sullivan proposed a test: if a majority of delegates to the state convention of 1904 now believed he had been fraudulently elected to the national committee, he would resign. However, if they did not, then Bryan should withdraw from the presidential race for falsely accusing a fellow Democrat. "Call the roll," he demanded![37]

It was a strong performance, and his willingness to make such specific charges and publicly reveal the alleged foibles of his enemies (for such was not his usual style) was a measure of his anger and frustration. Even the Republican *Chicago Tribune*, known for its opposition to Sullivan, but no fan of Bryan's either, found his arguments cogent and deserving of a response. Bryan initially was a dismissive: "You can expect that kind of attack from that kind of people." Soon, however, he retreated, and in a rather weak statement, written in the third person, reasserted his claim that Sullivan did not represent the Democrats of Illinois, and questioned some of the details of his account. But the Commoner (wisely) refused to become involved further in a personal row. Judge Thompson labeled the accusation against him as "a malicious and unmitigated falsehood." Dunlap denied everything and passed off the attacks as from a man "whose general reputation is that of a professional boodler," who would "charge anyone he hates with any vice or crime to divert attention from himself or in his desire to drag others to his level."[38]

Theodore Nelson was even less sanguine, and sued Sullivan for his "unconvicted felon" remark. Though the legal action would soon fade away, Nelson made his own public attack by blaming the Chicago leader for the defeat of a bill the previous year providing for the municipal ownership of gas, and for working to keep gas rates high (neglecting to mention the uncertainty of its passage in any case, and Sullivan's subsequent support of state regulation). According to Nelson, Sullivan's entire political purpose was rooted in a desire to protect the Ogden Gas Company and its profits. Based upon half-truths and hyperbole, the aspersions summarized well the nefarious legend of Sullivan as boodler that were founded in events now thirteen years past. This would be the recurring theme of his opposition until the end of his public life (and one that would find their way into historical accounts). For the moment, however, Roger Sullivan, by surviving, was winning.[39]

It is not an unduly difficult task to ascertain why the man who was already being proclaimed as the inevitable presidential nominee of his party could suffer such a complete reversal. The Nebraskan's crusade against Sullivan failed to ignite much real passion among the party's national leadership, most of whom knew and respected Roger Sullivan. It was well understood that the broader context of Bryan's attacks was the ideological polarity between eastern and western Democrats. They also recognized that Sullivan and his allies' methods were common practice across the country. This, together with the absolute nature of Bryan's demands, were sources of concern for other political leaders like Tom Taggart, head of the Indiana Democrats, who feared a similarly biased standard might be applied to them. To illustrate this point, Sullivan publicly inquired about Bryan's intentions towards his own good friend and ally, Senator Joseph W. Bailey of Texas, who was allegedly connected to the Standard Oil Company. Bailey, affronted, passionately denied the accusation, but Bryan remained silent. Once he had made his point, however, Sullivan quickly let the matter drop.[40]

Another element at work in Sullivan's favor was an unarticulated rule of factional politics with foundations as least as far back as the medieval Byzantine Empire. This held that success in overthrowing the emperor was in itself evidence of divine sanction. So, too, if a political leader or organization could gain control of party machinery, that, in itself, could be interpreted as evidence of majority support, or at least the support of a majority of those who mattered. In short, Roger Sullivan had, by the standards of his time and place, done nothing especially unusual or untoward, certainly nothing that would justify among his peers his political ruin. In Illinois and Chicago as well there was little enthusiasm among Democrats for Bryan's intervention or his goals. Sullivan was popular with most leaders as a man of judgment and respect, who kept his word, who, when pressed, could be a highly effective political scrapper, and who valued and sought harmony.[41]

And there was a longing in the state for an end to the incessant political battles that had been so instrumental in the electoral defeats plaguing recent state and local party history. Real unity had not existed since John P. Hopkins's term as mayor over a decade before, while the elder Carter Harrison's near creation before that of a single organization was a fading memory. Sullivan offered a path towards reestablishing a united party that did not require the destruction of anyone's political career (if all cooperated), and that promised mutual benefit. There was, moreover, the fear and resentment of an outsider, even one with the ties to Illinois Bryan enjoyed, attempting to impose his will. No one, it seemed, aside from the more fanatical members of the Majority Rule League, was comfortable with the idea of Illinois' becoming a fiefdom of the Great Commoner.

The Bryan-Sullivan feud was followed with some interest by the national press. Some of those cynical about the Great Commoner found reason for amusement in the outcome. The *Duluth News-Tribune*, for example, wrote: "Mr. Bryan sent word to the Illinois convention that if Roger Sullivan were not ousted as national committeeman, he would decline its indorsement [sic] as the Democratic presidential candidate. The convention thereupon promptly indorsed [sic] Sullivan by a vote of two to one, and unanimously declared for Mr. Bryan in 1908. There is nothing more effective than this choking a man with his own words."[42]

Meanwhile, events in Chicago were also going Sullivan's way. With the Harrison faction fragmented, it might have been expected that a new rival could emerge in Edward F. Dunne, the Democrat elected in 1905 as mayor. However, Dunne was very much the idealist and political amateur, and he had no interest in creating his own city hall crowd or faction. His focus instead was upon implementing immediate municipal ownership of public transportation as mandated by the voters. However, even in this, he would soon find himself frustrated.

Initially having no clear plan, his momentum was slowed soon after his inauguration by a massive and violent teamsters' strike. It was not until June 1905, or two months after taking office, that he and his Special Traction Counsel, Clarence Darrow, at last proposed two alternative schemes to reform the traction lines. Neither found favor with a city council unimpressed with their practicality. By the end of November, Darrow had resigned and the mayor was left feckless. Worse, the council elections in April 1906 (while electing an additional three Democrats to the Board of Aldermen) failed to provide the majorities (required under the Mueller Law) needed for the funding of any acquisition by the city of the streetcar companies. Serious speculation followed that Dunne might resign.

Instead, Mayor Dunne sought to use his patronage powers to build support, but with only mediocre skill. More importantly, he now turned to several generally sympathetic councilmen for advice, and as a result appointed as his new Special Traction Counsel Walter L. Fisher, a Republican (he would serve under President William Howard Taft as Secretary of the Interior from 1911 to 1913), who enjoyed wide respect for his expertise in traction matters, but was no friend of municipal ownership. Fisher negotiated a new so-called Tentative Ordinance with the streetcar companies, which included upgrades of service, more remuneration for the use of the streets, and tighter regulation—but no meaningful plan for foreseeable municipal purchase.

Dunne at first trumpeted Fisher's accomplishment as his own. However, pressured by Hearst's Independence League, which threatened to run its own candidate in the next mayoral elections, and his social reformist allies, Dunne abruptly reversed his position. Nonetheless, the council, to much public approval, enacted the measure, subject to a popular vote in the April 1907 elections.

The "regulars" of the party were at first bemused, then perplexed, and then resentful of a chief executive so unschooled in the art of politics as practiced in Chicago and Illinois. It was difficult to take a mayor seriously who, through such indecision and misdirection, had frittered away popular support—support that could benefit all Democrats. Moreover, it was all well and good that Dunne was disinclined to challenge the existing party hierarchies, but how could they cope with someone who showed so little skill in passing out city jobs and other perquisites, someone who favored the diffuse collection of political outsiders comprising his circle of friends and allies, to the detriment of loyal sons of the party? To be sure, in his last year of office, Dunne attempted to be more accommodating, but the damage was done.[43]

The end result was that Roger Sullivan, as well as the increasingly orphaned Harrison men, essentially abandoned Dunne in his reelection campaign. For Sullivan and the other "regulars," a Republican mayor who recognized the rights of Democrats to some of the plums of government (and it was the long-standing practice that the party out of power would have its share) was preferable to a Democrat who was such "a child politically." After the election, one Democratic insider, William Loeffler, explained: "I voted for Dunne … my personal friends did. But we felt when we had done that we had done our entire duty." And the GOP standard-bearer, Postmaster Fred Busse, with his own "federal faction," was someone upon whom they could rely to abide by the rules. Dunne campaigned vigorously, and his social reformist allies strived mightily, but he lost the April 1906 election by a substantial margin even as the voters overwhelmingly endorsed the "Tentative Ordinance."[44]

With Busse in office, and the tide of the radical reformism of municipal ownership receding, order was restored. Candidacies and distribution of patronage and favors among the Democrats were virtually Sullivan's to bestow or withhold. The extent of his growing power was yet again dramatically illustrated at the state convention in April. In 1904, everyone knew he was in charge, but in 1908, he was visibly so. His now rotund figure—there had been recently some humorous comments to the effect that the narrow doors of the new party headquarters in Chicago would have to be widened for his benefit—was the center of all attention. His every frown and smile was noted, with the actual transmission of orders left to George Brennan, who slowly hobbled the aisles assuring conformity. Easily dealing with a few small challenges, Sullivan dictated the platform, and his distribution of the at-large seats to the national convention was done with typical inclusion and generosity.[45]

Adding to Sullivan's increasingly overarching influence was a new primary law enacted in January 1908 by the state legislature that brought greater centralization of party governance. Judged by some as designed to "make bosses," the measure was passed by a heavily Republican legislature with no direct evidence of the Chicago leader's influence. It is difficult, however, to construe that, as the state's leading Democrat, he was uninvolved. Regardless, the state and county central committees, redesigned to supervise election activities more directly, were now to become more like governing agencies, with much of their power concentrated in smaller "management committees." This was to be hereafter the formal mechanism of Sullivan's and his successors' control of the Cook County Democratic Party.[46]

In the fall of 1908, Roger Sullivan's closest ally, George Brennan, headed the panel appointed to draw up a new Cook County party constitution. The "power of Sullivan" was evident in the subsequent appointments to the state and county management committees. Sullivan served on both as an at-large member, and not surprisingly: "Foes of Roger were conspicuous by their absence." Although broad representation of the remaining Harrison men and others was arranged, gone were figures associated with Bryan's futile offensive.[47]

And by this point even the Great Commoner was coming to accept these new political realities. His decisive defeat in 1906 by Sullivan and his friends at first seemed to have done nothing to diminish his ardor; as late as February 1908, he was in Springfield, Illinois, still hoping to convince state Democrats that Sullivan was "not the right sort." However, even Bryan's conspicuous self-righteousness proved to be malleable for the sake of ambition.[48]

Following the debacle of 1904, with Democrats around the nation returning repentant to their discarded champion, Bryan's second renomination was as early as 1906 a certainty. However, unlike 1900, when he sacrificed expediency by insisting on retention of the commitment to the silver issue, in 1908, he was willing to do just about anything to win. Although there was no doubt of his selection as the nominee, he recognized the need for the active support in the election campaign of the leaders of the eastern Democrats, among whom was Roger Sullivan, whose hold on the Chicago Illinois parties could no longer be denied.[49]

Before the Democrats met in Denver in June 1908, and to the intense unhappiness of some of his more ardent supporters, Bryan negotiated a general détente that included Sullivan. Promised due consideration on patronage matters, and probably convinced that Bryan would lose in the national election, eliminating him as a threat, the Illinois leader entered happily into the arrangement. The Republican *Chicago Tribune* quipped: "Mr. Bryan and Mr. Sullivan are [now] walking hand in hand down the flowery paths of harmony while the tutelary genius of democracy hovers overhead and blesses them."[50]

And so it was to be. Sullivan was placed in charge of the arrangements committee for the convention, and it was under his supervision that the oft-referenced massive painting of George Washington, generally said to resemble William Jennings Bryan in a powdered wig, was prominently placed. He was easily reelected by the state delegation to the national committee, and Bryan let this pass without comment. The Commoner also declined to embrace yet another pointless challenge by former Mayor Harrison and the remaining fragments of his organization to the composition of the Illinois delegates. Moreover, in the coming campaign, Sullivan would play a conspicuous role.[51]

With even William Jennings Bryan recognizing the hegemony of Roger Sullivan in Chicago and Illinois, all local opposition skulked away into a sullen quiescence. Power in the state, county, and city Democratic parties was effectively cornered, something not entirely achieved either by the powerful "city hall crowd" of Carter H. Harrison, Sr., or even by the incipient "machine" during the administration of John P. Hopkins. Although he disliked the title (always claiming merely to exercise "influence"), Roger C. Sullivan was now and would be hereafter the "boss" and his organization "the machine." It had been a long and eventful climb from his youthful and starry-eyed aspirations during the days of the Nectar Club.

Between 1881 and 1908, Chicago underwent a remarkable transformation from a largish city into a major and sprawling metropolis. Riding a wave of industrialization that would make the United States the wealthiest society in history, its growth was unwieldy and unplanned. Almost from the beginning, previous political patterns of "segments" controlled by ward leaders and of the dominating but usually indirect influence of traditional native elites became hopelessly inadequate. As layers of sometimes-contrary structures were hurriedly improvised, politics and governance became ever more corrupt, problematic, and Byzantine.

The solution to the threat of chaos emerged from within the unfettered capitalism driving the city's growth. A new generation of businessman politicians, seeking opportunity in politics, rose to take charge of the Democratic Party (and to a less organized extent, the Republicans as well). Based more-or-less on business precedents of efficiency and organization, they would reshape party politics, and by extension government, into something more orderly and functional.

The formative careers of Roger C. Sullivan and his partner John P. Hopkins speak closely to this process. Their

Roger C. Sullivan, boss of the Illinois Democrats (Library of Congress LC-DIG-ggbain-06936).

rise into the elite circles of the local party, leading ultimately to positions as successively the two most powerful Democrats in the city and state, was a direct reflection of the ascendency of the businessman politicians. Their merger of extraordinary achievements as political leaders and entrepreneurs was more exalted but entirely typical. Moreover, it must be recognized that their personalities, skills, and actions were in and of themselves more than small elements in the course of events.

Sullivan's successful parrying of and ripostes to the Commoner's assaults in 1906 proved to be the rite of passage that brought his leadership into focus. The earlier downfall of Harrison in 1905, the subsequent political mismanagement and defeat of Dunne, and his turning back of Bryan in between, all assured an unprecedented and enduring paramountcy in the Democratic Party that he would pass on to his successor George Brennan. To be sure, his leadership hereafter would not go entirely unchallenged, but his position as "boss" of Illinois' Democrats was never again seriously in question.

Even more importantly, because of his success, Democratic politics after 1908 would be framed within the organizational outlines of the Sullivan model. Not a faction based upon a personal ambition and following, not a saloon or criminal ring, not an ideological grouping bent upon a specific agenda, the Sullivan organization was instead a strong structure focused upon collective empowerment and advantage for professional political operatives. Its "sovereignty," however, would be derived not just from control of the party machinery, but just as meaningfully from outcomes in government that met at least minimal public expectations.

Something of its tensile strength was made clear with the uncomplicated transfers of leadership in 1904 from Hopkins to Sullivan, and in 1920 from Sullivan to Brennan, but just as telling was its ability to survive, and even thrive, during the progressive surge of 1905 and beyond. For decades it would easily outlast and outmaneuver all reformist passions. By the 1930s, with Republican rivals reduced to irrelevancy, the descendant of the organization would become the actual governing body of Chicago, epitomizing a style of urban governance then prevalent in the nation's urban centers, informing an entire epoch of American political history.[52]

Appendix: The Gold-Silver Controversy

The passions associated with the fight over the metallic standard for money in the United States in the last years of the nineteenth century are virtually beyond the comprehension of someone not alive in the period. Yet this was the single most important issue of its time. It inspired the creation of new political parties and the reconfiguration of the Democrats, climaxing in 1896 with the remarkable emergence and campaign of William Jennings Bryan. The issue bridged the Gilded Age and the Progressive Era, and the associated ideologies of the gold and silver question are fundamental to understanding the political cultures of both periods.

The intense emotions of the controversy become clearer when it is understood that it became a metaphor for the fundamental divisions in American society. In effect, it evolved into a litmus test for two sets of competing visions of America's essence and future: of urban versus rural, of the factory versus the farm, of industrial versus agricultural, of the East versus the West and South, of the "interests" versus the "people," of capital versus labor, of the rich versus the poor, of native versus immigrant, and ultimately, for many, of good versus evil. This polarity had always been present (and continues to be so), and was articulated at the nation's inception by Thomas Jefferson, with his interpretation of the American promise in terms of middle-class yeoman farmers, and Alexander Hamilton, with his belief in a society made fruitful through the efforts of a prosperous economic elite. However, the broad changes that industrialization and urbanization wrought in a relative historical instant made the social gaps far more acute and for some even desperate. For many advocates on both sides, therefore, the issue of gold versus silver was nothing less than a holy battle for the soul of the nation.[1]

Most immediately, many of those supporting the unlimited or "free" coinage of silver based their crusade upon two facts: the undeniable fall of farm prices over the thirty years before the turn of the century, and the relative contraction of actual available money in the economy during the same period. Between 1870 and 1897, wheat fell from about $1.07 a bushel to 63.3 cents, corn from 43.1 cents a bushel to 29.7 cents, and cotton from 15.1 cents a pound to a mere 5.8 cents. Meanwhile the amount of money in circulation per capita that stood in 1873 at $18.19 had risen in 1896 to just $23.02, despite a massive expansion of the economy and population.[2]

For farmers this created an especially difficult situation as the value of long-term debts rose substantially in terms of the output of their crops, i.e., the amount of grain a farmer needed to produce to repay an obligation could in a few years as much as double from

Silver campaign poster (Library of Congress LC-DIG-pga-03796).

when it was originally contracted. Consequently, while agriculture suffered throughout the nation, it was the new producers in the Great Plains—who, between 1870 and 1900, populated and developed an area greater in acreage than had been settled in the previous three hundred years—who were particularly vulnerable. Bringing land into production cost money, and long-term debt was common. Added to this was a tendency towards overcapitalization in the boom years that came to an abrupt halt in the winter of 1886–87, when major climatic changes on the frontier brought depression and despair. Thus Western farmers, together with their brethren in the South, were a natural reservoir of support for expanding the money supply, and through making money "cheaper," raising farm prices, lowering interest rates, and lightening their burden of debt.

Historically, farmers were not the only proponents of deliberate monetary inflation. Nor was the expansion of the coinage of silver the only method envisioned. In 1876, the Greenback Party was created to advocate the continued issuance of legal tender paper money, a practice to which the Northern government had resorted to finance the Civil War. "Greenbackers," mostly headquartered in the East, believed that such "soft money" (as opposed to "hard," or gold and gold-based money) would lead to greater prosperity and create broader opportunity. This third party in the end achieved little; the number of legal tender notes was to remain roughly the same for the remainder of the century. In part, because of this, it was silver that became the focus of such strategies, and by 1888, the Greenback Party embraced free coinage.[3]

Before 1873, the United States did in fact adhere to a bimetallic standard, which meant that both gold and silver were required by law to be coined and issued if presented to the treasury. In practice, however, beyond small coinage, the use of the white metal was always vastly surpassed by the yellow in volume. This had never been a point of controversy. It was against this backdrop that in 1873, Congress, by a close vote in the House but unanimously in the Senate, adopted the Gold Standard and halted the coinage of all silver dollars except for a Trade Dollar for exclusive use overseas (and especially in China).[4]

The onset of depression following a panic on Wall Street just months later reinforced growing demands for a resumption of the coinage of silver. Representative Richard "Silver Dick" Bland, a Democrat from Missouri, introduced into the House a bill that provided for free and unlimited coinage of silver to expand the money supply and presumably counter some of the worst effects of the economic downturn. In the Senate, however, Senator William B. Allison and other legislators amended the bill to require the Treasury to purchase just two to four million dollars' worth of silver each month, to coin it as legal tender, and to issue silver certificates in denominations of ten dollars or more upon deposit of silver dollars. President Rutherford B. Hayes vetoed the measure, noting in his message that the price of silver was falling worldwide and that the proposed law required an expenditure of at least $24,000,000 a year. Nonetheless, the bill was passed over his veto, in large part because the opposition was appeased by promises of a Resumption Law (actually enacted in 1879), that would restore the payment of gold for Federal Bonds, a practice suspended during the Civil War.[5]

The Bland-Allison Act pleased no one—the expanding number of silver advocates still wanted unlimited coinage, and conservatives distrusted and disliked even the most limited expansion of legal tender based upon anything other than gold. Reflecting this, the Treasury initially had difficulty keeping silver dollars in circulation, as they were being exchanged for gold, but this problem in large part disappeared in 1879 when prosperity returned. However, in 1884, there was another economic downturn that created a growing surplus of silver in the Treasury as investors continued exchanging dollars for the surety of gold. This also increased the demand for free coinage. With further economic stresses in the American West in 1886–87, however, the calls for an inflated currency swelled to a roar that could not be ignored. In 1890, the American Bimetallic League was organized, and two years later, various farmers' alliances (political action groups among the tillers of the soil that began appearing in the 1880s) met with representatives of the Greenback Party and others in Omaha, Nebraska, to create the People's or Populist Party, which had as a leading plank of its platform the free coinage of silver at the ratio of 16 to one to gold.[6]

The 16 to one ratio was based upon the Currency Act of 1834 establishing the relative value of one grain of gold as worth sixteen of silver in coining dollars, a standard that had served as a rough gauge ever since. It became the mantra of silver advocates and a pervasive slogan of the age. All of this agitation, augmented by the entrance into the Union of a number of new silver-mining Western states that elected congressmen, bore fruit in 1890 with the passage of the Sherman Silver Purchase Act. It directed the Treasury to purchase and to coin 4,500,000 ounces of silver bullion a month (or roughly the monthly silver output in the United States) and to pay for it with legal tender certificates. This was still far short of free coinage. Much of the good will the act might have engendered was vitiated by the exchange of support necessary for its passage for the McKinley Tariff of 1890, which vastly increased duties on many goods entering the country—an issue also of great importance to Western farmers and other consumers.[7]

In March 1893, a new panic precipitated the worst depression to date in American history. President Grover Cleveland, reentering office in that month after a four-year hiatus following his first term, was a Democrat. But he was also a former Wall Street lawyer and financial conservative. He noted with alarm that the price of silver was steadily declining, facilitated by the announcement by the British government that it was closing its mints in India to the free coinage of the white metal. Even more unsettling was the related drain of the government's gold reserve to below $100,000,000—a magical figure, based upon nothing actually, but long held to be the minimum stockpile necessary—as investors and bond holders dumped their silver. Accordingly, at Cleveland's urging, the House on June 24, 1893, repealed the Sherman Act by a vote of 239 to 108. The Senate, after a vigorous and lengthy fight, agreed on October 1 by a narrow majority of 43 to 42 to implement the president's recommendation.[8]

The fierce battle in the Senate portended the angry response that greeted repeal. For silver advocates this was exactly the wrong strategy for dealing with the depression when greater amounts of capital seemed to be needed. Moreover, it reinforced a growing tendency among their number to believe in an ongoing conspiracy by "the interests" to despoil the people and the country for profit. By the 1890s, this devil's theory held that an "Aristocracy of Wealth" had begun coordinated efforts to subvert the American economy from as early as the Civil War. The presumed conspiracy's supposed sophistication and detail goes far towards explaining much of the desperate and even revolutionary spirit present in the free silver movement.[9]

It was in 1861, at the beginning of the great conflict, that "the money kings" made their first grab, so the theory ran, by seeking to create high interest rates for their own remuneration by cornering the supply of gold and silver. Failing in this because of the issuance of greenbacks, they made sure that the paper money could not be used as interest on the public debt or import duties. They were thus able to charge high returns on the hard currency they loaned for these purposes. When the banking system was revised in 1863, "Shylock" now arranged that investments in government bonds could be purchased with greenbacks (which "they" had been often able to purchase at a discount), and that 90 percent of the interest accrued would be paid in national bank notes to be issued by recognized and registered national banks across the country. These could be loaned out in turn for interest, giving the already wealthy a means to secure a double return on the same investment.

Nor was this end of their nefarious machinations. Next "they" brought about the act of April 12, 1866, that began the process of retiring greenbacks, which did not return interest (and which, of course, many of "them" had bought up at a discount), and replacing them with bonds, which did. The same sources, which some said included August Belmont as representative of the Rothschilds, were at work in the passage of the Credit-Strengthening Act of 1869, by which government bonds purchased by this elite group during the Civil War for depreciated amounts of as much as 60 percent were now to be paid in full with "coin." This was interpreted by the government to mean ever-more valuable gold, bringing even greater opportunity for more unwarranted profit. Then on July 14, 1870, the national debt was refunded instead of being easily paid off with an existing surplus. This maintained indefinitely the obligation of the government and the payment of interest to the conspirators' benefit, while also saddling the people with its burden indefinitely.

Having reaped millions from the war, the manipulation of bonds, and the national debt, the kings of Wall Street perpetrated "the crime of '73," the cessation of silver coinage itself. This not only caused the subsequent depression, so it was maintained, but it had the effect of deliberately lowering farm prices, causing farmers to have to work harder and produce more to pay off their debts to the benefit of the moneyed interests. It also meant that those who had stockpiled gold (and we all know who they were!) now could watch the value of their hoards increase with the contraction of money in the economy. Just two years later, on January 24, 1875, Congress replaced paper fractional currency of less than one dollar (originally printed during the war to compensate for the disappearance of coin during those dark and insecure days) with silver coinage. Although widely accepted and useful, the paper substitutes were deliberately withdrawn, so the logic of conspiracy ran, as a means to further enrich the wealthy by requiring the purchase of the necessary silver bullion with interest-bearing bonds of such high denominations as to be only accessible to the rich. Even such laudable laws as the Bland-Allison Act and the Sherman Purchase Act had been severely limited by the backroom lobbying of the shadowy masters of the economy, and the repeal in 1893 of the Sherman measure was just another denominator of the strength of their power and the evil of their intent.[10]

Such were the contentions in the account of the presumed economic pillage of the nation as embraced by many of those supporting the free coinage of silver. In the unsettled times after the onset of depression in 1893, these beliefs increasingly evoked anger and real fear of the advent of a genuine plutocracy—fear that, married to an environment of a wider disquiet over the rise of corporate strength in American life, seemed ever more possible. This analysis also had the popular effect of making the complex and obscure social science of economics accessible, and providing the emotional satisfaction of someone to blame. Moreover, as the use of the term "Shylock" and the reference to August Belmont and the Rothschilds underscore, there was also at least some subtext of anti–Semitism and apprehensions about vague international forces at work as well. Both themes were present in American culture at that time, but were especially pervasive among rural Americans, from whom the shock troops of the free silver movement were being drawn.[11]

An international context was also referenced by those more conservative and generally Eastern voices speaking out against the free coinage movement as a canard. Among their most powerful dialectical weapons was the fact that Europe and most of the remainder of the world were on the gold standard. Bimetallism might actually be desirable if handled correctly—even the pro-gold Republican platform of 1896 conceded this—but it would be impossible without international agreement, and this the United States had repeatedly and vainly sought at conferences in 1878, 1881, and 1892. To the argument that the United States should lead by example, they countered that such unilateral action would simply mean that gold would disappear from the American economy with disastrous effects, including difficulties in attracting foreign investment and decline of trade. Not the least of the reasons for this was that the silver in a coined dollar was worth by this time far less than one hundred cents (thanks to falling prices of silver relative to gold). In fact, in 1895 silver's intrinsic value was just fractionally more than sixty-five cents in comparison to the value of a gold dollar. Because of this, the idea of coining silver money at a ratio of sixteen to one was held to be just inherently wrong-headed as the actual ratio of value was by this time about thirty-two to one. Inevitably, then, should free coinage be realized, other nations would use their stocks of cheap silver to exchange for comparatively more valuable American gold dollars, creating not a bimetallic national standard, but in actuality one based entirely upon the less valuable metal. This would in turn reduce the United States—and American workers—to the economic level of the few other countries on the silver standard like Peru, Haiti, Siam, and China.[12]

Moreover, this belief was further legitimized by a venerable economic principle called Gresham's Law. Named after Thomas Gresham, an English Tudor economist, this theory divided tender into good money, which had an exchange value roughly equal to its worth as a commodity (i.e., gold), and bad money (e.g., silver), which did not. With the inexorable inevitability of the law of gravity, the introduction of bad money would drive out good money, leading to inflation, depression, and even collapse. Against the wisdom of the ages (since challenged by more modern economists), the silverites could only rejoin with the rather incoherent argument that after the initial outward migration of gold, Europeans would be so inundated with the yellow metal as to cause ultimately a free and equal exchange of both gold and silver.[13]

Nor were conservatives willing to accept that the gold standard was a source of the impoverishment of working Americans. The deflation brought by rising gold prices had actually had the effect, so the proponents of gold argued, of increasing the buying power of the wages received by workers. Moreover, agriculture's woes were in truth founded in the precipitous growth of foreign competition as new farm lands were opened (thanks in part to the new technologies developed for the American Great Plains), and the poor business practices of the food producers, who invariably increased production as prices fell.[14]

The Gold Bugs also had their own conspiracy theory. As time went by, they became increasingly fond of pointing out that rapidly declining silver prices had motivated some owners of the silver mines in the West to help finance the movement. These "silver barons" were said to include some of the leading political figures supporting free coinage, like Senator Henry Teller of Colorado, but also the inevitable Rothschilds. It was the one thing upon which both sides could agree: there were indeed dark and mysterious forces at large bent upon the exploitation and enslavement of the nation and its economy, forces that at all costs must be overcome to assure the survival of the republic![15]

Chapter Notes

Introduction

1. See Matthew Josephson, *The Politicos, 1865–1896* (New York: Harcourt, Brace, 1938).

2. Harold Zink, *City Bosses in the United States: A Study of Twenty Municipal Bosses* (Durham: Duke University Press, 1930); Richard Allen Morton, "'A Man of Belial': Roger C. Sullivan, the Progressive Democracy, and the Senatorial Elections of 1914," *Journal of the Illinois State Historical Society* 91 (Autumn 1988): 133–61.

3. *Chicago Tribune*, 26 July 1910, pp. C1; 16 January 1920, p. 4; 28 January 1920, p. 10; *Chicago Record-Herald*, 26 July 1910, pp. 1, 2; *Chicago Daily News*, 25 August 1910, pp. 1, 2, 26 June 1910, p. 8; *Chicago Evening Post*, 25 June 1910, p. 1.

4. *Chicago Tribune*, 7 May 1919, pp. 1, 6; Forrest McDonald, *Insull* (Chicago: University of Chicago Press, 1962), p. 82.

5. John A. Campbell, ed., *A Biographical History with Portraits of Prominent Men of the Great West* (Chicago: Western Biographical and Engraving, 1902), p. 333.

6. James Langland, ed., *The Chicago Daily News Almanac and Year-Book for 1920* (Chicago, The Chicago Daily News Company, 1919), p. 802.

7. James Langland, ed., *The Chicago Daily News Almanac and Year-Book for 1910* (Chicago: Chicago Daily News, 1909), p. 514; *Daily News Almanac, 1911*, pp. 491, 516; Daniel H. Burnham and Edward H. Bennett (Charles Moore, ed.), *Plan of Chicago, Prepared under the Direction of the Commercial Club, During the Years MCMVI, MCMVII, and MCVII* (Chicago: The Commercial Club, 1909); pp. xviii, 1, 31. Symbolic of the city's exalted status, the Merchants Club in October 1906 publicly initiated what would become known as the Burnham Plan (of which Sullivan, like other business leaders, would be one of the original subscribers) to "bring order out of the chaos incidental to rapid growth, and especially to the influx of peoples of many nationalities without common traditions or habits of life." It was eventually to transform the heart of the Windy City into something more consistent with Edwardian sensibilities.

8. Burnham and Bennett, p. xviii.

Chapter 1

1. Interview with Frank Sullivan (grandnephew), 17 July 2004.

2. *Ibid.*

3. *Ibid.*; *Belvidere Daily Republican*, 15 April 1920 (Collection of George M. Gibson, Boone County, Illinois, Historian); there is some dispute about the location of Roger Sullivan's birthplace. In 1920 one friend recalled that it was at the current site of the city waterworks, while another insisted that the home stood at the location of a downtown shoe store (Harnish & McCartney).

4. George W. Hawes, comp., *Illinois State Gazetteer and Business Directory for 1858–59* (Chicago: George B, Hawes, 1860), p. 13 (Boone County Historical Museum); *Belvidere Recorder*, 13 May 1915 (Gibson collection).

5. *Belvidere Daily Republican*, 15 April 1920 (Gibson collection); *Chicago Evening Post*, 15 April 1920, p. 1; 17 April 1920, p. 2.

6. James Langland, ed. *The Chicago Daily News Almanac and Year-Book for 1923* (Chicago: Chicago Daily News, 1924), pp. 169–75, 779 (hereafter cited as *Daily News Almanac*); *Daily News Almanac*, 1924, pp. 952–68; Lincoln Steffens, *The Shame of the Cities* (New York: McClure, Phillips, 1904 second impression), p. 234; Harold F. Gosnell, *Machine Politics: Chicago Model* (Chicago: University of Chicago Press, 1937), p. 25.

7. *Daily News Almanac*, 1922, p. 368–74, 817; *Daily News Almanac* 1924, pp. 719–20.

8. *Republican Northwestern*, 4 September 1906; *Belvidere Daily Republican*, 12 August 1914 (Gibson collection); Thomas Hutchinson, comp., *Lakeside Annual Directory of the City of Chicago*, 1879 (Chicago: The Chicago Directory Company, 1879, hereafter cited as *City Directory*), p. 1045.

9. Peter Clark McFarlane, "Is Roger Sullivan a Boss?" *Collier's Magazine* 53 (8 August 1914): 5–6; *United States Census*, 1870, Cook County, microfilm edition, series T9–1094, roll m593_207, p. 385; *D.B. Cooke and Companies General & Business Directory for Chicago, Illinois* (Chicago: D.B. Cooke, 1859), p. 83; *Edwards' Chicago, Illinois General & Business Directory for 1873* (Chicago: Richard Edwards, Publisher, 1873), p. 255.

10. *City Directory*, 1882; *Chicago Tribune*, 22 March 1881, p. 6; 23 March 1881, p. 3; 26 March 1881, p. 6; 27 March 1881, p. 7; 9 August 1914, p. 12; *Belvidere Daily Republican*, 17 April 1920 (Gibson collection). The other candidates in the Republican primary were Jesse Spaulding, Eugene Cary, and James T. Raleigh.

11. *Delavan Tri-County Times*, 1914 (Gibson Collection); Doane Robinson, *History of South Dakota, Together with Personal Mention of Citizens of South Dakota* (Logansport, IN: B.F. Bowen, 1904), p. 1605.

12. *City Directory*, 1883, p. 1195; 1884, p. 1275; *Chicago Inter-Ocean*, 1 October 1890, p. 4; *Chicago Daily News*, 5 April 1920, p. 1.

13. *Chicago Tribune*, 8 May 1881, p. 16; 3 December 1893, p. 25; 14 October 1918, p. 2.

14. *Chicago Tribune*, 3 December 1893; *Worcester Daily Spy*, 8 January 1894, p. 6; p. 25; *Illinois Political Directory, with Portraits and Biographical Sketches* (Chicago: W.L. Bodine, c. 1899), p. 265.

15. Robin L. Einhorn, *Property Rules: Political Economy in Chicago, 1833–1872* (Chicago: University of Chicago Press, 1991); William T. Stead, *If Christ Came to Chicago! A Plea for the Union of All Who Love in the Service of All Who Suffer* (Chicago: Laird & Lee, 1894), pp. 292–94.

16. *Illinois Political Directory, 1899* (Chicago: W.L. Bodine, 1899), p. 265; Charles E. Merriam, *Chicago: A More Intimate View of Urban Government* (New York: Macmillan, 1929), p. 253; Ralph R. Tingley, "From Carter Harrison II to Fred Busse: A Study of Chicago Political Parties and Personages from 1896 to 1902" (Ph.D. diss., University of Chicago, 1950). By Merriam's later count there were 408 "governments" in Cook County, and sixteen hundred in the metropolitan area.

17. John M. Allswang, *A House for All Peoples: Ethnic Politics in Chicago, 1890–1936* (Lexington: University of Kentucky Press, 1971), pp. 3–88; Humbert S. Nelli, "John Powers and the Italians: Politics in a Chicago Ward, 1896–1921," *Journal of American History* 57 (June 1970): 67–84.

18. *Chicago Tribune*, 22 May 1910, p. 1.

19. *Ibid.*, 25 March 1890, p. 4; 17 January 1891, p. 6; 25 June 1932, p. 18. Asay was appointed assistant city attorney in 1892, city prosecuting attorney between 1903 and 1905, and assistant attorney for the sanitary district between 1913 and 1919.

20. Edward F. Dunne, *Illinois: The Heart of the Nation*, 5 vols. (Chicago: Lewis, 1933), III. 274; *Harper's Weekly*, 6 January 1894: 117.

21. *United States Census, 1860*, New York, Erie, 8 WD Buffalo, microfilm edition, series M653, roll 747, p. 539; *United States Census, 1870*, New York, Erie, 8 WD, Buffalo, microfilm edition, series M93, roll 934, pp. 376–77; Eugene Tyler Chamberlain., *Early Life and Public Service of Hon. Grover Cleveland, The Fearless and Independent Governor of the Empire State, Also the Life of Hon. Thomas A. Hendricks* (Chicago and New York: Caxton, 1884), pp. 63–4.

22. Sullivan Family Collection.

23. *City Directory*, 1886, p. 1435; MacFarlane, "Is Roger Sullivan a Boss?," 6; *Chicago Inter-Ocean* 1 October 1890, p. 4.

24. Clare Sullivan (niece) to Helen Sullivan McKinley (granddaughter), 11 January 1981, Sullivan Family collection; *City Directory, 1886*, p. 1453; *1887*, p. 1509; *1889*, p. 1773; *Republican Northwestern*, 4 September 1906 (Gibson collection); *Chicago Daily News*, 15 April 1920, pp. 1, 2; *Chicago Inter-Ocean* 1 October 1890, p. 4; Macfarlane, "Is Roger Sullivan a Boss?": 6.

25. Stanley Bruder, *Pullman: An Experiment in Industrial Order and Community Planning, 1880–1930* (New York: Oxford University Press, 1967), pp. 112–13.

26. *Ibid.*; Stead, *If Christ Came to Chicago*, pp. 293–95; Ray Ginger, *Altgeld's America: The Lincoln Ideal versus Changing Realities*, reprint edition (New York: New Viewpoints, 1973), p. 147.

27. *Daily News Almanac* (1920), p. 941. For more on the annexation issues see Louis P. Cain, "To Annex or Not? A Tale of Two Towns: Evanston and Hyde Park," *Explorations in Economic History* 29, 1983: 58–72.

28. *Chicago Times*, 21 April 1889, p. 1; Bruder, *Pullman*, pp. 112–113.

29. *Chicago Times*, 28 April 1889, p. 5; 4 May 1889, p. 1; 5 May 1889, p. 10; 8 May 1889, p. 1; 12 May 1889, p. 1; 15 May 1889, p. 1.

30. *Ibid.*, 18 May 1889, p. 3; 24 May 1889, p. 5; 30 June 1889, pp. 1, 7.

31. *Ibid.*, 30 October 1889, p. 1; *Daily News Almanac* (1890), p. 157 (1891), p. 299.

32. *Chicago Tribune*, 29 January 1894, p. 11; 1 February 1894, p. 1; 20 August 1896, p. 1; 9 December 1917, p. 15; 18 April 1919, p. 1; 20 August 1922, p. 1; 28 August 1922, p. 1; 17 December 1925, p. 22; 19 February 1927, p. 1; 9 April 1931, p. 25; *The Pharmacist* 13 (April 1880): 130; Bob Skilnik, *Beer: A History of Brewing in Chicago* (Fort Lee, NJ: Barricade, 2006), p. 371.

33. *Chicago Tribune*, 15 May 1896, p. 8; 29 January 1898, p. 8; 23 March 1898, p. 6; 29 March 1901, p. 7; 11 December 1901, p. 1; 27 December 1901, p. 3; 4 January 1902, p. 5; Charles H. Hermann, *Recollection of Life & Doings From the Haymarket Riot to the End of World War I* (Chicago: Normandie House, 1945), p. 123.

34. *Chicago Tribune*, 24 August 1890, p. 6; 30 September 1890, p. 1; *Chicago Times*, 30 September 1890, p. 1.

35. *Chicago Tribune*, 5 November 1894, p. 1.3 December 1895, p.1; there is no evidence that the Nectar Club, Hopkins, or Sullivan were ever affiliated with McDonald, or at this time, with Johnny Powers— though there was a general unity among Democratic leaders referred to in the opposition press as a "machine." In December 1895, fist fights broke out between members of the factions in the Cook County

Democratic Committee over nominations. Neither Hopkins nor Sullivan participated.

36. *Chicago Times*, 1 October 1889, p. 1; *Chicago Tribune*, 30 September 1889, p. 1; 1 October 1889, p. 1; 18 January 1896, p. 4; *Chicago Evening Journal*, 30 September 1890, pp. 1, 2; *Chicago Inter-Ocean*, 30 September 1890, p. 6; *Chicago Daily News*, 30 September 1890, p. 1. Lawler was born in Rochester, New York, and came to Chicago in 1854. He worked for the railroad and became a caulker in the shipbuilding trade. He soon became active in union organizing. He then worked in the post office, before serving between 1876 and 1885 in the city council, followed by two terms as a United States representative from 1885 to 1891. Before his death on 16 January 1896, he was reelected to the city council.

37. *Chicago Times*, 24 August 1890, p. 5; 25 September 1890, p. 1; 28 September 1890, 1 October 1890, p. 2; *Chicago Tribune*, 18 September 1890, p. 5.

38. *Chicago Times*, 1 October 1890, p. 2; *The Lakeside Chicago, Illinois General & Business Directory for 1890* (Chicago: Chicago Directory, 1891), p. 1012.

39. *Chicago Daily News*, 15 April 1920, pp. 1–2.

40. *Ibid.*, 22 October 1890, p. 3; 30 October 1890, p. 3; 3 November 1890, p. 1.

41. *Ibid.*, 5 November 1890, p. 1; 7 November 1890, p. 1; 19 November 1890, p. 1; *Chicago Tribune*, 5 November 1890, p. 1; 19 November 1890, p. 1; *Historical Encyclopedia of Illinois* (Chicago: Munsell, 1904), p. 330.

42. *Chicago Tribune*, 29 October 1893, p. 10.

43. *Chicago Times*, 22 March 1891, p. 3; Claudius O. Johnson, *Carter Henry Harrison I, Political Leader* (Chicago: University of Chicago Press, 1928), p. 74.

44. *Chicago Times*, 14 March 1891, p. 1; 6 November 1892, p. 3.

45. *Ibid.*, 11 March 1891, p. 1; 19 March 1891, p. 1; 20 March 1891, p. 1; the use of the eagle imagery was common in this patriotic age. Governor John P. Altgeld was also known as the Eagle, and Judge Murray Tuley was referred to during the 1891 county convention as the "white-headed eagle of drainage reform."

46. *Ibid.*, 21 March 1891, pp. 1, 2; 22 March 1891, pp. 1, 4; *Chicago Tribune*, 22 March 1891, pp. 1, 2; Adolf Kraus, *Reminiscences and Comments* (Chicago: Toby Rubovits, 1925), pp. 59–63; Johnson, *Harrison*, op. cit., pp. 142–43.

47. *Chicago Times*, 28 February 1891, p. 1; 11 March 1891, p. 1; *Chicago Tribune*, 11 March 1891, p. 1.

48. *Chicago Times*, 2 April 1891, pp. 1, 2.

49. *Daily News Almanac* (1920), p. 864; Johnson, *Harrison*, op. cit., p. 74; *Chicago Times*, 8 April 1891, p. 1.

50. *Chicago Times*, 8 August 1891, p. 1.

51. *Ibid.*, 24 September 1891, p. 1; 27 September 1891, pp. 1–2; 29 September 1891, p. 1.

52. *Ibid.*, 31 October 1893, p. 2; 4 November 1891, pp. 1, 2; *Chicago Tribune*, 4 November 1891, p. 1, 2.

53. Allan Nevins, *Grover Cleveland: A Study in Courage* (New York: Dodd, Meade, 1934), p. 470.

54. *Chicago Times*, 19 April 1892, p. 1.

55. *Ibid.*, 19 June 1892, p. 2; 8 April 1892, p. 1l; 23 April 1892, p. 2; 25 April 1892, p. 1; 27 April 1892, p. 11; June 1892, p. 2.

56. *Ibid.*

57. *Ibid.*, 24 June 1892, p. 1; *Detroit Free Press*, 23 June 1892, pp. 1, 2; 24 July 1892, p. 20.

58. *Ibid.*, 19 July 1892, p. 2; 11 August 1892, p. 1; 12 August 1892, p. 2; 19 August 1892, p. 5; 20 August 1892, p. 1; 21 August 1892, p. 1, 2; *Chicago Tribune*, 20 August 1892, p. 1; 21 August 1892, pp. 1–2.

59. *Daily News Almanac* (1920), p. 864; *Chicago Times*, 13 November 1892, p. 1; 22 November 1892, p. 1.

60. *Chicago Times*, 11 December 1892, p. 2; *Chicago Sunday Post*, 11 December 1892, p. 3.

61. *Chicago Times*, 17 September 1892, p. 2.

62. *Ibid.*, 26 January 1893, p. 1; 31 January 1893, p. 1; 8 February 1893, p. 1; 12 February 1893, p. 116; 18 February 1893, p. 1; Cleveland to Harrison, 10 March 1893 in Allan Nevins, ed., *Letters of Grover Cleveland, 1850–1908* (Boston and New York: Houghton Mifflin, 1933), p. 321.

63. *Ibid.*, 24 February 1893, p. 2; 28 February 1893, p. 1; *Chicago Tribune*, 27 February 1893, p. 1; 28 February 1893, p. 1.

64. *Chicago Times*, 1 March 1893, p. 1, 2, 3; *Chicago Tribune*, 1 March 1893, p. 1, 2; Kraus, op. cit., pp. 63–4. One of those discussed to chair the convention was Clarence S. Darrow.

65. *Chicago Times*, 3 March 1893, p. 1; 10 March 1893, p. 1; 5 April 1893, p. 1, 18 April 1893, p. 1; *Chicago Tribune*, 5 April 1893, p. 1; 18 April 1893, p. 1; *Daily News Almanac* (1920), p. 864.

66. *Chicago Times*, 13 April 1893, p. 3; 22 April 1893, p. 2; 30 April 1893, p. 1; 12 May 1893, p. 2; 18 May 1892, p. 8; *Chicago Tribune*, 6 August 1893, p. 3; 2 October 1893, p. 2.

67. *Chicago Tribune*, 27 June 1893, p. 1; Chicago Times, 2 October 1893, p. 1; Charles Hoffman, "The Depression of the Nineties," *Journal of Economic History* (June 1956): 16, 137–64.

68. *New York Times*, 20 December 1893, p. 1; *Chicago Times*, 17 September 1893, p. 1; 22 September 1893, p. 1.

69. *Ibid.*, 16 September 1893, p. 4; 18 September 1893, p. 6; 2 October 1893, p. 2; 3 October 1893, p. 2; 3 October 1893, p. 1; 4 October 1893, p. 1, 2, 4; 5 October 1893, p. 1; 6 October 1893, p. 2; 11 October 1893, p. 2; 13 October 1893, p. 1; 14 October 1893, p. 4; *Chicago Times*, 22 September 1893, p. 1; 5 October 1893, p. 1; 6 October 1893, p. 2.

70. *Chicago Times*, 30 October 1893, p. 1–3; *Chicago Tribune*, 29 October 1893, p. 1; 31 October 1893, p. 3.

Chapter 2

1. *Chicago Tribune*, 2 November 1893, pp. 1, 2, 3; *Chicago Times*, 2 November 1893, pp. 1, 2. For the

full account of the assassination, the funeral, and the trial and execution of the assassin, see Richard Allen Morton, "A Victorian Tragedy: The Strange Deaths of Mayor Carter H. Harrison and Patrick Eugene Prendergast," *Journal of the Illinois State Historical Society* 96 (Spring 2003): 6–36.

2. *Chicago Tribune*, 3 November 1893, p. 1; *Chicago Evening Post*, 3 November 1893, p. 1. The term "businessman-politician" in this context first appears in Bill and Lori Granger, *Lords of the Last Machine: The Story of Politics in Chicago* (New York: Random House, 1987).

3. *Ibid.*, 4 November 1893, p. 1; *Chicago Times* 4 November 1893, p. 1; *Chicago Evening Post*, 3 November 1893, p. 2.

4. *Chicago Times*, 5 November 1893, pp. 1, 2; *Chicago Tribune*, 5 November 1893, p. 1; *Chicago Inter-Ocean*, 5 November 1893, p. 1; *Chicago Evening Post*, 4 November 1893, pp. 1, 2; *Washington Post*, 5 November 1893, p. 1; *Atlanta Constitution*, 5 November 1893, p. 15.

5. *Ibid.* It was reported that governor John P. Altgeld attempted to influence the Democrats' choice for temporary mayor in favor of one of his favorite local judges. This attempt was ignored.

6. *Chicago Times*, 7 November 1893, p. 1; Chicago *Tribune*, 7 November 1893, p. 1; *Chicago Inter-Ocean*, 5 November 1893, p. 1; Board of Aldermen, *Proceedings of the City Council of the City of Chicago for the Municipal Year 1893 and 1894, Being From April 17th, 1893, To April 14th, 1894 Inclusive* (Chicago: John F. Higgins, 1894), pp. 1027, 1031–36, 1039–41.

7. *Chicago Times*, 8 November 1893, p. 1; *Chicago Tribune*, 8 November 1893, p. 1.

8. *Chicago Tribune*, 3 December 1893, p. 1.

9. *Chicago Times*, 3 November 1893, p. 1; a leading "dark horse" candidate was Hiram Jones, Commissioner of Public Works.

10. *Ibid.*, 12 November 1893, p. 2; 15 November 1893, p. 1; 21 November 1893, p. 1.

11. *Ibid.*, 11 November 1893, p. 1; 16 November 1893, p. 1; 18 November 1893, p. 1; 27 November 1893, p. 1; *Chicago Tribune*, 16 November 1893, p. 1.

12. *Chicago Tribune*, 2 December 1893, p. 2.

13. *Ibid.*, 3 December 1893, pp. 1, 2; 18 January 1896, p. 4; Chicago *Times*, 3 December 1893, pp. 1, 2. "Our Frank" Lawler was one of the more colorful political characters of this period. He was born in Rochester, New York, on June 25, 1842, and with his parents moved to Chicago in 1854. As a young man he worked on the railroads as a newsagent and as a brakeman. He learned the craft of shipbuilding and became involved in union affairs and became president for a time of the Ship Carpenters and Caulkers' Association. This brought him some political influence, and between 1869 and 1877, he worked several jobs in the post office under Postmaster John McArthur. In 1876, he was elected to the city council from the Eighth Ward, where he served until 1885. There he was successful in the enactment of a local

child labor bill and other labor measures. In 1878, he became a liquor merchant, and he was a member of Congress from 1885 to 1891, when he was defeated for reelection. He would be defeated as sheriff in 1891 and for a return to Congress in 1895. He worked hard to secure the World's Fair for Chicago in 1893. In part because of this, he would be elected to the city council in 1896, a position he still held when he died the same year.

14. *Ibid.*, 5 December 1893, p. 4, 5; *Chicago Times*, 4 December 1893, p. 1; 5 December 1893, p. 1; 10 December 1894, p. 3; J. Seymour Curry *Chicago: Its History and Builders, A Century of Marvelous Growth*, 3 vols. (Chicago: S.J. Clarke, 1918): II: 38–39.

15. *Chicago Times*, 3 December 1893, p. 2.

16. *Chicago Tribune*, 3 December 1893, pp. 1, 2; 17 December 1893, pp. 1, 2; *New York Times*, 20 December 1893, p. 1; *Chicago Herald*, 3 September 1891, p. 9. The truth was that in 1891, after six years of engineering services including during two Republican administrations, William A. Lydon (age 28) had insisted that the city accept his resignation so that he could join his father's firm of Lydon & Drews. Capt. Michael B. Lydon was senior partner. William Lydon sought to superintend three upcoming contracts of this type: construction of the north shore inlet; the foundation for the pumps for the World's Fair; and the foundation for a government lighthouse.

17. *Chicago Tribune*, 15 December 1893, p. 5; 16 December 1893, p. 3; 23 May 1908, p. 1; 10 October 1929, p. 4; *Chicago Times*, 11 December 1893, p. 1; 17 May 1908, p. 1; 20 May 1908, p. 3; 19 November 1908; 30 November 1923, p. 10; 2 December 1923, p. 2. Frank Wenter was born in Germany in 1844, and in 1857 was brought by his parents to Chicago. In 1874, he married, and he would have nine children. At age 19, he went into business building furniture, and later bicycles. In 1902, he became a broker. From 1883 to 1890, served on the board of education, from 1889 to 1902, he was a member of the sanitary board, of which he served several terms as president. He died of heart disease on October 9, 1929. In 1908, he was involved in a scandal in which he was named as a co-respondent in the divorce of his friend James Stepina, a prominent Republican businessman, from his wife Anna. Wenter's first wife, at the same time, sued for divorce for his assignation with a different woman, a Mrs. Dell Myer. Following his divorce, Wenter convinced Anna to wed. Stepina, who became president of the American State Bank, never overcame his bitterness, and included a provision in his will that became public after his death in November 1923, for an annuity of $500 to go to his ex-wife to be increased to $1,200, if she should leave "the man who desecrated my home."

18. James Langland, comp., *The Chicago Daily News Almanac and Year-Book for 1920* (Chicago: Chicago Daily News, 1919), p. 864 (hereafter cited as *Daily News Almanac*); *Chicago Tribune*, 20 December 1893, p. 2.

19. *Chicago Times*, 26 December 1893, pp. 1–3.

20. *Ibid.*, 28 December 1893, p. 1–2; *Chicago Tribune*, 28 December 1893, pp. 1–2.

21. *Ibid.*

22. *Ibid.*

23. *Chicago Tribune*, 26 June 1894, p. 3; 30 October 1894, p. 3; Corkery died unexpectedly on June 25, 1894, at the age of 41 following an appendicitis operation. Although he always took "an active part in politics, he never held a salaried city office."

24. *Ibid.*

25. "Of this type" because even reformers like Robert Lafollette of Wisconsin and the Socialist Party of Milwaukee, Wisconsin, during this period created political machines. However, their goals were not entrepreneurial but ideological.

26. Joel A. Tarr, "The Urban Politician as Entrepreneur," *Mid-America* 49 (January 1967): 56.

27. Lincoln Steffens, *The Shame of the Cities* (New York: McClure, Phillips, 1904), p. 10.

28. Michael F. Funchion, "Irish Chicago: Church, Homeland, Politics, and Class—The Shaping of an Ethnic Group, 1870 -1900," in Melvin G. Holli and Peter d'A. Jones, *Ethnic Chicago*, revised edition (Grand Rapids, MI: William B. Eerdmans, 1984), pp. 14–45; Michael F. Funchion, "The Political and Nationalist Dimensions," in Lawrence J. McCaffrey, et al., *The Irish in Chicago* (Urbana: University of Illinois Press, 1987), pp. 61–97.

29. *Chicago Tribune*, 10 August 1914, p. 7; *Chicago Examiner*, 20 October 1909, p. 10; *Washington Post*, 1 July 1912, p. 4; Paul Michael Green, "Irish Chicago: The Multi-Ethnic Road to Machine Success," in Melvin G. Holli and Peter d'A. Jones, *Ethnic Chicago*, pp. 412–59. At the 1912 Democratic national convention, for example, one of Roger's daughters (Virginia) was noted as having a mild brogue.

30. Frank R. Kent, *The Great Game of Politics* (Buffalo: Economics Books, 1923, 1959).

31. Roger C. Sullivan to Robert E. Burke, 25 April 1900, *Sullivan Family Collection*. The letter was written on the stationary of the Ogden Gas Company, "N.E. Cor, Clark and Randolph Sts., Ashland Block."

32. Sullivan to Burke, 26 August 1899, Sullivan Family Collection. This was also written under the letterhead of the Ogden Gas Company.

33. *Chicago Tribune*, 26 May 1887, pp. 1, 2; 19 June 1887, p. 9; 22 June 1887, p. 4; 25 July 1887, p. 7; 6 August 1887, p. 10; 8 August 1887, p. 1; 8 November 1887, p. 1; for an engaging account of this side of Chicago's political culture in this period, see Richard Lindberg, *Chicago Ragtime: Another Look at Chicago, 1880–1920* (South Bend, IN.: Icarus Press, 1985).

34. *Ibid.*

35. *Chicago Tribune*, 7 January 1888, p. 1.

36. Charles Edward Merriam, *Chicago: A More Intimate View of Urban Politics* (New York: Macmillan, 1929), pp. 27–8.

37. Joel A. Tarr, "J.R. Walsh of Chicago: A Case Study in Banking and Politics, 1881–1905," *The Business History Review* 40 (winter 1966): 460; *Washington Post*, 13 May 1902, p. 3. Such loans were not confined to machine politicians. John P. Altgeld also took a loan from John Walsh in 1890, for the astronomical figure of $400,000 to rebuild his Unity Building. Unable to repay, or even make the payments, eventually the future governor was compelled to divest himself of most of his assets, and remained financially strapped for the rest of his life. To his apparent credit, he allegedly refused an offer (some said bribe) from Charles Yerkes, a notorious streetcar promoter, which would have relieved him of his debts.

38. Robert K. Merton, "The Latent Functions of the Machine," in Bruce M. Stave, ed., *Urban Bosses, Machines, and Progressive Reformers* (Lexington, MA: D.C. Heath, 1972), pp. 27–37; Elmer E. Cornwell, Jr., "Bosses, Machines, and Ethnic Groups," in Thorstein Sellin, ed., *The Annals of the American Academy of Political and Social Sciences*, Essay Index Reprint Series (Plainview, NY: Books for Library Press, 1964, 1975), pp. 27–39.

39. *Chicago Tribune.*, 22 December 1893, p. 2; 25 February 1894, p. 3; 26 February 1894, p. 1; 4 April 1894, pp. 1, 8; 5 April 1894, p. 2; *Chicago Times*, 21 February 1894, p. 1; 4 April 1894, p. 1; *Daily News Almanac* (1895), pp. 360–61.

40. *Ibid.*, 20 May 1894, p. 1; 12 June 1894, p. 10; *Chicago Times*, 10 June 1894, p. 1; 11 June 1894, pp. 1–2; 12 June 1894, p. 1; 13 June 1894, p. 1.

41. *Chicago Times*, 19 June 1894, p. 1; 27 June 18 1894, p. 1; 28 June 1894, pp. 1, 4, 5; *Chicago Tribune*, 26 June 1894, pp. 1, 12; 27 June 1894, p. 1; 28 June 1894, pp. 1, 5; *Illinois State Journal* (Springfield), 27 June 1894, p. 1; 28 June 1894, pp. 1, 6; O.M. Enyart, comp., *A Biographical Congressional Directory, 1774 to 1903. The Continental Congress: September 5, 1774, to October 21, 1788, inclusive. The United States Congress: the First Congress to the Fifty-seventh Congress, March 4, 1903, inclusive. With an Outline History of the National Congress, 1774–1911* (Washington, D.C.: Government Printing Office, 1911), p. 724.

42. *Chicago Tribune*, 17 March 1894, p. 1; 4 May 1894, p. 2; 11 June 1894, p. 1; *Chicago Times*, 16 March 1894, p. 1; 11 June 1894, p. 4; 12 June 1894, p. 1.

43. *Ibid.*

44. *Chicago Times*, 24 January 1894, p. 3; 3 April 1894, p. 1; 6 May 1894, p. 3; *Chicago Tribune*, 3 April 1894, pp. 1, 2.; 10 October 1910, p. 1; *New York Times*, 20 October 1910, p. 12. Lambert Tree was one of the grand old men of the Chicago Democratic Party, and a reliable conservative. He was born on November 29, 1832, in Washington, D.C. Subsequently educated in the law, in 1864 he was elected president of the Chicago Bar Association, and five years later a circuit judge. He resigned this post in 1875, and spent a number of years in Europe before returning to be an important and respected leader of his party. In May 1885, President Cleveland appointed him minister to Belgium, and in September of that year, minister

to Russia. When he died on October 9, 1910, his estate was valued at $4.5 million from his business activities.

45. *Ibid.*

46. William H. Carwardine, *The Pullman Strike* (Chicago: Charles H. Kerr, 1894), p. 25.

47. United States Strike Commission, *Report on the Chicago Strike, June-July 1894* (Washington, D.C.: Government Printing Office, 1895), pp. xxxii–xxxv; *Chicago Times*, 23 April 1894, p. 1. The contracts taken in the fall of 1893 were $52,069 below cost, but the wage cuts totaled an estimated $60,000.

48. *Strike Report*, pp. xxxv–xxxvi.

49. *Ibid.*, p. xxxvi; Carwardine, *Pullman Strike*, pp. 71–80.

50. *Strike Report*, p. xxxviii; Carwardine, *Pullman Strike*, pp. 29, 33–37; Ohio D. Boyle, *A History of Railroad Strikes* (Washington, D.C.: Brotherhood, 1935), pp. 46–47; *Chicago Times*, 23 April 1894, p. 1; 10 May 1894, p. 1; 12 May 1894, p. 1. In December 1893, there had been a brief strike among Pullman's blacksmiths that was quickly quashed.

51. *Chicago Tribune*, 11 January 1898, p. 1.

52. Stanley Buder, *Pullman: An Experiment in Industrial Order and Community Planning, 1880–1930* (New York: Oxford University Press, 1967), p. 153.

53. *Ibid.*, p. 170; Carwardine, *Pullman Strike*, pp. 41–44; *Chicago Times*, 10 June 1894, p. 3.

54. *Strike Report*, pp. xliii–xliv; Boyd, *History of Railroad Strikes*, pp. 57–9.

55. *Strike Report*, pp. 344–45.

56. Grover Cleveland, *The Government in the Chicago Strike of 1894* (Princeton: Princeton University Press, 1913), pp. 13–29.

57. *Strike Report*, pp. xlv–xlvi, 344–45, 365, 375; *Chicago Tribune*, 6 July 1894, p. 12; 7 July 1894, p. 1; *Chicago Times*, 7 July 1894, p. 1.

58. *Strike Report*, pp. 351, 591; *Chicago Tribune*, 12 July 1894, p. 1; 15 July 1894, p. 3.

59. *Strike Report*, pp. xli–xlii; *Chicago Tribune*, 14 July 1894, p. 1; 4 August 1894, p. 9; 2 September 1895, p. 6; 16 September 1895, p. 2; 17 September 1895, p. 12; 24 November 1895, p. 2; *Chicago Times*, 14 July 1894, p. 1.

60. *Chicago Times*, 2 August 1893, p. 1; 3 August 1893, p. 1.

Chapter 3

1. *Chicago Tribune*, 13 September 1894, p. 2; 20 September 1894, p. 5; 21 September 1894, p. 2; *Chicago Times*, 30 September 1894, p. 3; 6 October 1894, p. 3; *Chicago Times*, 30 August 1894, p. 4.

2. *Chicago Tribune*, 11 August 1894, p. 4; 14 August 1894, p. 6.

3. *Ibid.*, 18 August 1894, p. 1; 19 August 1894, pp. 1, 7; *Chicago Times*, 18 August 1894, p. 1; 19 August 1894, pp. 1, 2.

4. *Chicago Tribune*, 24 August 1894, pp. 1, 2; 25 August 1894, p. 1; 2 September 1894, p. 7; *Chicago Times*, 24 August 1894, p. 1; 25 August 1894, p. 1.

5. *Chicago Tribune*, 18 August 1894, p. 1; 13 September 1894, p. 2; 25 September 1894, p. 2; 28 October 1894, p. 1; *Chicago Times*, 7 September 1894, p. 1; 13 September 1894, p. 1; 15 September 1894, p. 1; 23 September 1894, p. 1; 27 September 1894, p. 2. However, the Independent American Party was careful to denounce some of the more extreme statements by the leadership of the APA.

6. *Chicago Times*, 30 September 1894, p. 1; *Chicago Tribune*, 4 September 1894, pp. 2; 30 September 1894, p. 3.

7. *Chicago Times*, 11 August 1894, p. 4; 22 August 1894, p. 4; *Chicago Tribune*, 5 September 1894, p. 1; 6 September 1894, p. 1; 8 September 1894, p. 1; 13 November 1894, p. 12. For some especially telling examples of the cartoons see: 11 September 1894, p. 1; 27 September 1894, p. 1; 16 October 1894, p. 1.

8. *Chicago Tribune*, 3 June 1894, p. 1; 22 September 1894, p. 1; 23 September 1894, p. 1; 24 September 1894, p. 1; 29 September 1894, p. 1; 18 November 1894, p. 1; *Chicago Times*, 21 September 1894, p. 30.

9. George E. Plum, comp., *The Daily News Almanac and Political Register for 1895* (Chicago: Chicago Daily News, 1895) (hereafter cited as *Daily News Almanac*), pp. 161, 169–72, 350–60; *Chicago Tribune*, 7 November 1894, p. 1; Howard W. Allen and Vincent A. Lacey, *Illinois Elections, 1818–1990: Candidates and County Returns for President, Governor, and House of Representatives* (Carbondale: Southern Illinois University Press, 1992), pp. 230–32.

10. *Ibid.*

11. *Chicago Tribune*, 13 November 1894, p. 12; 17 November 1894, p. 2; 24 December 1894, p. 2; *The Broad Ax* (Chicago), 6 September 1919, p. 2; 24 April 1920, p. 1. Roger Sullivan as Probate Clerk appointed William G. Anderson, an African American, as his private secretary. Though there was no political gain to be gotten, Sullivan personally was consistent in his verbal support of African American dignity and rights. In the 1904 National Democratic Convention, he and Hopkins, "boiling over in rage," vigorously opposed before the Committee on Resolutions a proposed plank calling for the repeal of the Fourteenth and Fifteenth Amendments. In 1906, he purchased for the considerable sum of $25 a box seat at the Orchestra Hall for a benefit for Union Hospital. Scheduled to lecture was South Carolina Senator Ben Tillman. When Sullivan learned that among night's subjects were to be a defense of lynching, he turned in his tickets without refund, and let it be known that he did not condone Tillman's advocacy of violence. Similarly, he condemned publicly the East St. Louis Race Riot of 1917. After the 1919 Chicago riots (he was in California when they broke out), he allowed the publication of an interview in which he expressed his friendship for African Amer-

icans, and called for peaceful coexistence. He also condemned "the rough and lawless element" involved in the riot. These were remarkable acts for an Irish urban leader in this the nadir of the Jim Crow experience in America.

12. *Ibid.*, 10 April 1894, pp. 2, 3; Weston A. Goodspeed and Daniel B. Healy, *History of Cook County, In Two Volumes Illustrated* (Chicago, The Goodspeed Historical Association, c. 1909), pp. 429–431.

13. *Chicago Tribune*, 31 January 1894, p. 12; *Chicago Times*, 29 July 1894, p. 1.

14. *Chicago Times*, 19 April 1894, p. 1; 9 August 1894, p. 4; *Chicago Tribune*, 1 April 1894, p. 6; 5 April 1894, p. 2; 12 April 1894, p. 4; 20 November 1894, p. 12; 2 December 1894, p. 5; 18 December 1894, p. 1; 29 December 1894, p. 1; 4 January 1895, p. 1.

15. *Ibid.*

16. Wallace Rice, *75 Years of Gas Service in Chicago* (Chicago: The People's Gas Light and Coke Company, 1925), pp. 1–6, 28–29, 34. This was "water gas," so called because hydrogen gas is created "by passing steam through incandescent beds of coal or coke," which is "then 'carbureted' or enriched by adding other elements derived from oil."

17. *Ibid.*, pp. 36–7.

18. *Chicago Tribune*, 18 February 1894, p. 4; 25 February 1894, p. 1; 11 March 1894, p. 1; 27 June 1894, p. 2; 31 August 1894, p. 1.

19. *Ibid.*, 8 February 1894, p. 511; February 1894, p. 6; 14 February 1894, p. 1; 15 February 1894, pp. 1, 7; 6 March 1894, p. 1; 11 March 1894, p. 1; 13 March 1894, p. 1.

20. *Ibid.*, 17 July 1894, pp. 1, 8; 21 July 1894, p. 4; 24 July 1894, p. 1; *Chicago Times*, 17 July 1894, p. 1; 24 July 1894, p. 4; 19 August 1894, p. 7; Illinois Bureau of Labor Statistics, *Biennial Report*, vol. 9 (Springfield: Bureau of Labor Statistics, 1897), p. 251; William J. Pringle, et al., *Investigation of the People's Gas and Coke Company for the Chicago Council Committee on Gas, Oil, and Electric Light* (Chicago: City of Chicago, 1911), p. 13; *Chicago Securities*, vol. 8 (Chicago: Chicago Director Company, 1898), p. 84; *Moody's Manual of Railroad and Corporation Securities, Twenty-third Annual Number*, Part 2: *Public Utility Section* (New York: Poor's Publishing, 1921), p. 967; Rice, *75 Years of Gas Service*, p. 37.

21. Chicago Board of Alderman, *Chicago Council Proceedings: 1894–1895*, part 2, *October 1 to April 2* (Chicago, 1895), pp. 2660–2661; *Chicago Tribune*, 26 February 1895, pp. 1, 5; 27 February 1895, p. 2; *Chicago Inter-Ocean*, 26 February 1895, pp. 1, 2, 4; *Chicago Evening Journal*, 26 February 1895, pp. 1, 2.

22. *Ibid.* It was James R. Mann who as a Congressman in 1910 sponsored the Mann Act, which prohibited transporting a woman across state lines for immoral purposes. The law was used against heavyweight boxing champion Jack Johnson.

23. *Ibid.*

24. *Chicago Council Proceedings*, p. 2665; *Chicago Tribune*, 26 February 1895, p. 5; *Chicago Inter-Ocean*, 26 February 1895, pp. 1, 4; *Chicago Evening Journal*, 26 February 1895, pp. 1, 2, 4.

25. *Chicago Tribune*, 27 February 1895, p. 2; 28 February 1895, pp. 1, 2; *Chicago Inter-Ocean*, 27 February 1895, p. 6; *Chicago Evening Journal*, 26 February 1895, p. 4.

26. *Ibid.*, 2 March 1895, p. 1; 3 March 1895, pp. 1, 5; 4 March 1895, pp. 1, 2; *Chicago Times-Herald*, 4 March 1895, pp. 1–3; *Chicago Daily News*, 4 March 1895, p. 1.

27. *Chicago Tribune*, 27 February 1895, pp. 2, 8; 2 March 1895, p. 1; 3 March 1895, p. 5; *Chicago Daily News*, 1 March 1895, p. 1; 4 March 1895, p. 1; 5 March 1895, p. 1; *Chicago Times-Herald*, 5 March 1895, p. 1. This was just the second issue of a combined *Times* and *Herald*; Adolf Kraus, the former Harrison leader, had taken over first the management, then the ownership, of the *Times* from the Carter H. Harrison family. He then sold the paper to the Herald company, with the result that Chicago was not to have a completely Democratic newspaper during this period.

28. *Chicago Tribune*, 5 March 1895, p. 11; *Chicago Times-Herald*, 5 March 1895, pp. 1, 2; *Chicago Inter-Ocean*, 26 February 1895, p. 1.

29. *Ibid.* The Chicago City Railway ordinance was probably part of a package of deals to obtain council support for the Cosmopolitan and Ogden proposals.

30. *Chicago Daily News*, 5 March 1895, p. 4; *Chicago Tribune*, 5 March 1895, p. 6.

31. *Chicago Daily News*, 7 March 1895, p. 1; *Chicago Times-Herald*, 7 March 1895, p. 1.

32. *Ibid.*

33. *Chicago Daily News*, 13 March 1895, p. 1; 14 March 1895, p. 1; 25 March 1895, p. 1.

34. *Chicago Tribune*, 3 March 1895, p. 3; 9 March 1895, p. 1; *Chicago Daily News*, 9 March 1895, pp. 1, 6.

35. *Chicago Tribune*, 10 March 1895, pp. 1, 2; *Chicago Daily News*, 10 March, p. 1; *Chicago Times-Herald*, 10 March 1895, p. 1.

36. *Ibid.*

37. *Chicago Times-Herald*, 11 March 1895, p. 1; *Chicago Tribune*, 1 April 1895, p. 1; *Daily News Almanac*, 1920, p. 864.

38. *Chicago Tribune*, 9 April 1895, p. 1; 4 April 1895, p. 1, *Wall Street Journal*, 27 March 1895, p. 1.

Chapter 4

1. *Chicago Daily News*, 11 April 1895, p. 1; 14 May 1895; 17 May 1895, p. 1; 19 June 1895, pp. 1,2; 20 June 1895, p. 1; 22 June 1895, p. 1; *Chicago Tribune*, 11 April 1895, p. 1. Much of this civil service law, however, would be overturned in court, as had happened with several previous attempts.

2. *Chicago Tribune*, 12 June 1895, p. 1.

3. *Chicago Times-Herald*, 30 April 1897, pp. 1, 4; Harry Barnard, *Eagle Forgotten: The Life of John Peter Altgeld* (Indianapolis: Bobbs-Merrill, 1938,

1962), pp. 64–5, 406–11. According to Carter Harrison, Altgeld would eventually sell his share of the Ogden company for "about $800,000." However, the figure may have been much less, as the Harrison book is replete with exaggerations and rumor presented as fact.

4. Howard W. Allen and Vincent A. Lacey, *Illinois Elections, 1818–1990: Candidates and County Returns for President, Governor, Senate, and House of Representatives* (Carbondale: Southern Illinois University Press, 1992); p. 224.

5. The best sources on Altgeld's life remain Harry Barnard, *Eagle Forgotten,* and Ray Ginger, *Altgeld's America, 1890–1905* (New York: Funk & Wagnall's, 1958).

6. Harvey Wish, "John P. Altgeld and the Campaign of 1896," *Mississippi Valley Historical Review* 24 (March 1938): 503–06.

7. *Ibid.,* p. 506; *Chicago Tribune,* 6 April 1895, p. 1; Paolo Coletta, *William Jennings Bryan,* vol. 1: *Political Evangelist, 1860–1908* (Lincoln: University of Nebraska Press, 1964), p. 96.

8. *Chicago Tribune,* 13 April 1895, p. 6; 4 May 1895, p. 2; *Chicago Times-Herald,* 5 May 1895, p. 1; 6 May 1895, p. 1; Charles R. Tuttle, *Illinois Currency Convention* (Chicago: Charles H. Kerr, 1895), pp. 36, 42.

9. Tuttle, *Illinois Currency Convention,* pp. 29, 62, 78, 100, 106.

10. *Ibid.,* 81, 140–41.

11. Allan Nevins, *Letters of Grover Cleveland* (Boston: Houghton Mifflin, 1935), p. 384; *Chicago Tribune,* 18 April 1895, p. 1; *Chicago Times-Herald,* 19 April 1895, p. 1.

12. *Chicago Tribune,* 19 April 1895, p. 2; 24 April 1895, p. 1; *Chicago Daily News,* 18 April 1895, p. 2.

13. *Ibid.*

14. *Chicago Daily News,* 25 April 1895, p. 1; *Chicago Tribune,* 16 June 1895, p. 2.

15. *Chicago Inter-Ocean,* 21 September 1895, p. 6; 22 September 1895, p. 2;

Chicago Tribune, 15 September 1895, p. 1; 22 September 1895, pp. 1, 2; *Chicago Times-Herald,* 22 September 1895, p. 1.

16. *Ibid.*

17. *Chicago Times-Herald,* 23 December 1895, pp. 1.

18. *Chicago Evening Post,* 16 April 1920, p. 4; *Chicago Tribune,* 12 October 1923, p. 8.

19. *Ibid.*

20. *Chicago Tribune,* 30 August 1891, p. 1; 20 October 1891, p. 2; 6 August 1893, p. 3.

21. Claudius O. Johnson, *Carter Henry Harrison I, Political Leader* (Chicago: University of Chicago Press, 1928), pp. 292–93.

22. *Chicago Times-Herald,* 8 November 1895, p. 5; 4 December 1895, pp. 1, 5; 15 December 1895, p. 5; *Chicago Tribune,* 26 April, p. 4; 16 January 1908, p. 3; 28 August 1922, p. 1; 3 September 1922, p. 13. Francis Stuyvesant Peabody was a longtime ally and

friend of Sullivan and Hopkins. He was born in 1859 in Chicago, and educated at Yale. He began work as a messenger boy for the Merchants Loan and Trust Company. His father, Francis B. Peabody, was a coal merchant who brought his son into the family coal business, and when he died in 1908, left the younger man his holdings in the Peabody Coal Company. At his death in 1922, Francis S. left an estate estimated to have been worth over ten million dollars. In 1894, he was an unsuccessful candidate for Cook County sheriff, and he followed Sullivan and Hopkins into the Gold Democratic fold.

23. *Chicago Tribune,* 7 November 1895, p. 1; *Chicago Times-Herald,* 16 January 1896, p. 12.

24. *Chicago Tribune,* 13 April 1896, p. 7.

25. *Chicago Tribune,* 3 February 1896, p. 3; 18 April 1896, p. 3; 19 April 1896, pp. 3, 5; *Chicago Times-Herald,* 18 April 1896, p. 2.

26. *Chicago Tribune,* 23 February 1896, p. 3; *Chicago Times-Herald,* 1 April 1896, p. 5.

27. *Chicago Tribune,* 13 April 1896, p. 7; *Chicago Times-Herald,* 20 April 1896, p. 1.

28. *Chicago Tribune,* 12 May 1896, p. 5.

29. *Ibid.*

30. *Chicago Tribune,* 22 May 1896, p. 3; 30 May 1896, p. 7; *Chicago Times-Herald,* 10 June 1896, p. 14; 11 June 1896, p. 1; 13 June 1896, p. 11; 14 June 1896, pp. 1, 8.

31. *Chicago Times-Herald,* 23 June 1896, p. 2; 24 June 1896, pp. 1–2; 27 June 1896, p. 4.

32. Paolo Coletta, *William Jennings Bryan,* vol. 1: *Political Evangelist, 1860–1908* (Lincoln: University of Nebraska Press, 1964), 115.

33. *Chicago Times-Herald,* 29 June 1896, p. 1.

34. Ben Shapiro, *Project President: Bad Hair and Botox on the Road to the White House* (Nashville: Thomas Nelson, 2008), p. 110. The quote is from Republican Senator Joseph B. Foraker of Ohio.

35. *Chicago Daily News,* 6 July 1896, p. 1; *Chicago Tribune,* 3 July 1896, p. 1; Coletta, *Bryan,* p. 115; Barnard, *Eagle Forgotten,* p. 367.

36. *Chicago Daily News,* 6 July 1896, p. 1; 7 July 1896, p. 1.

37. *Ibid.,* 7 July 1896, p. 1; *Chicago Tribune,* 3 July 1896, p. 2.

38. *Chicago Tribune,* 7 July 1896, p. 1; Genevieve Forbes Herrick and John Origen Herrick, *The Life of William Jennings Bryan* (Chicago: Grover C. Buxton, 1925), p. 103–4.

39. *Chicago Times-Herald,* 10 July 1896, p. 3; 11 July 1896, p. 1; William Jennings Bryan and Mary Baird Bryan, *The Memoirs of William Jennings Bryan* (n.p., 1925), p. 115; Herrick and Herrick, *Life of Bryan,* p. 124.

40. *Ibid.* To maintain an appearance of autonomy, the Populists nominated their own separate candidate for vice-president, Tom Watson of Georgia.

41. Quoted in Leroy Ashby, *William Jennings Bryan: Champion of Democracy* (Boston: Twayne, 1987), p. 5.

42. William Allen White, *The Autobiography of William Allen White* (New York: Macmillan, 1946), p. 278; Grover Cleveland, ed. Allen Nevins, *Letters of Cleveland, 1850–1908* (Boston, New York, Houghton Mifflin, 1933), p. 497; David B. Anderson, *William Jennings Bryan* (Boston: Twayne, 1981), p. 82.

43. *Chicago Tribune*, 1 July 1896, p. 2; 2 July 1896, p. 2; 4 July 1896, p. 1; 12 July 1896, p. 5; 25 July 1896, p. 1; *Chicago Times-Herald*, 5 July 1896, p. 4.

44. *Chicago Tribune*, 3 July 1896, p. 1; 7 July 1897, p. 1; 8 July 1896, p. 1.

45. *Chicago Times-Herald*, 14 July 1896, p. 1; 19 July 1896, p. 6.

46. *Ibid.*, 22 July 1896, p. 1; 24 July 1896, pp. 1, 10; *Chicago Tribune*, 21 July 1896, p. 2; 25 July 1896, p. 3.

47. *Chicago Times-Herald*, 6 August 1896, pp. 1, 2; 10 August 1896, p. 3; 11 August 1896, p. 5; 15 August 1896, p. 2; 18 August 1896, p. 1; *Chicago Tribune*, 2 August 1896, p. 1. Not involved was Senator David B. Hill of New York, who, despite his antipathy to the free silver movement, was unwilling to surrender his control of the Democratic state organization of New York by joining the secession of the Gold Democrats.

48. *Chicago Tribune*, 16 August 1896, p. 2; 22 August 1896, p. 2; 25 August 1896, p. 1; 26 August 1896, p. 2; *Chicago Times-Herald*, 13 August 1896, p. 1; 26 August 1896, pp. 1, 2.

49. *Chicago Daily News*, 2 September 1896, p. 1; David T. Beito and Linda Royster Beito, "Gold Democrats and the Decline of Classic Liberalism, 1896–1900," *The Independent Review* 4 (Spring 2000): 561.

50. *Chicago Times-Herald*, 30 August 1896, p. 5; 31 August 1896, p. 2; 1 September 1896, pp. 1, 2; Grover Cleveland, ed. Allan Nevins, Cleveland to D.B. Griffin, 2 September 1896, *Letters of Grover Cleveland, 1850–1908* (Boston: Houghton Mifflin, 1933), p. 456.

51. *Chicago Daily News*, 3 September 1896, p. 2; Beito, "Gold Democrats," 561–63.

52. *Chicago Times-Herald*, 4 September 1896, pp. 1, 2; Beito, "Gold Democrats," 563–64.

53. *Chicago Times-Herald*, 6 September 1896, p. 3.

54. *Chicago Tribune*, 7 October 1896, p. 1; 13 October 1896, p. 1.

55. *Ibid.*, 4 August 1896, p. 4; 2 September 1896, p. 3; 7 September 1896, p. 3; 3 October 1896, p. 3; 26 October 1896, p. 1.

56. *Ibid.*, 3 October 1896, p. 1.

57. *Chicago Tribune*, 12 September 1896, p. 3; 13 September 1896, p. 1; 23 September 1896, p. 1; 10 October 1896, p. 1; *Chicago Times-Herald*, 13 September 1896, pp. 1, 3; Herrick and Herrick, *The Life of William Jennings Bryan*, p. 128; Beito, "Gold Democrats," 565–66.

58. *Chicago Times-Herald*, 30 August 1896, p. 1; 20 September 1896, p. 1; 30 September 1896, pp. 1, 2; 10 October 1896, p. 1; *Chicago Tribune*, 7 October 1896, p. 5.

59. Eugene H. Roseboom, *A History of Presidential Elections, From George Washington to Richard M. Nixon* (New York: Macmillan, 1957, 1970), pp. 314, 316.

60. George E. Plumbe, ed., *The Daily News Almanac and Political Register for 1899* (Chicago: The Chicago Daily News, 1900), pp. 340–404 (hereafter cited as *Daily News Almanac*).

61. *Ibid.*; *Chicago Times-Herald*, 4 November 1896, p. 4; *Chicago Tribune*, 4 November 1896, p. 5.

62. *Chicago Times-Herald*, 7 November 1896, pp. 1–2; *Chicago Tribune*, 7 November 1896, p. 1.

63. *Chicago Tribune*, 7 December 1897, p. 5; 21 December 1896, pp. 1, 5; *Chicago Times-Herald*, 13 December 1896, pp. 1, 9; 21 December 1896, p 1; *Chicago Tribune*, 7 December 1897, p. 5.

64. *Chicago Times-Herald*, 6 November 1896, p. 5; 11 November 1896, p. 7; *Chicago Tribune*, 2 December 1896, p. 4; 4 December 1896, p. 4; *Washington Post,* 29 March 1900, p. 4.

65. *Chicago Times-Herald*, 4 November 1896, p. 4; 5 November 1896, p. 7; 26 November 1896, p. 1; 5 January 1900, p. 5; 6 January 1900, p. 5; 8 January 1900, pp. 1–2; 10 January 1900; pp. 1–2. The object of these negotiations was an unsuccessful attempt to secure the county party chairmanship for Alderman Powers against Altgeld's man, the current chair Thomas Gahan, who subsequently became also the vice-chair of the state central committee.

66. Bynum to W.B. Haldeman, 12 December 1896; Bynum to John P. Hopkins, 30 June 1897; William Dallas Bynum Papers, Manuscript Division, Library of Congress, Washington, D.C.; *Washington Post*, 26 April 1896, p. 3; 25 November 1896, p. 6; 11 December 1896, p. 1; 22 July 1897, p. 3; 29 July 1899, p. 1; 7 September 1900, p. 1; 8 September 1900, p. 6.

67. *Washington Post*, 17 September 1903, p. 6; 23 April 1904, p. 6; *New York Times*, 26 July 1900, p. 3; Beito, "Gold Democrats," 566–68.

68. *Chicago Times-Herald.*, 22 January 1900, p. 7.

69. Carter H. Harrison, *Stormy Years: The Autobiography of Carter H. Harrison, Five Times Mayor of Chicago* (Indianapolis: Bobbs-Merrill, 1935), p. 77.

70. *Ibid.*

71. *Ibid.*, pp. 81–83; *Chicago Tribune*, 1 February 1897, p. 4; 4 February 1897, p. 12; 11 February 1897, p. 7; 12 February 1897, p. 12; 24 February 1897, p. 7.

72. Harrison, *Stormy Years*, pp. 93–94; *Chicago Times-Herald*, 6 March 1897, p. 1; 8 March 1897, p. 1; 9 March 1897, p. 5; *Chicago Tribune*, 27 February 1897, p. 1; 28 February 1897, p. 4; 1 March 1897, p. 5; 7 March 1897, pp. 3, 28; 11 March 1897, p. 6.

73. *Chicago Times-Herald*, 11 March 1897, pp. 1–2; 12 March 1897, pp. 1–2; *Chicago Tribune*, 12 March 1897, p. 7; 23 June 1909, p. 6.

74. *Chicago Times-Herald*, 27 February 1897, p 1; *Chicago Tribune*, pp. 1, 4; Scott McMurray, *Meeting the Challenges: The History of Ross & Hardies, 1902–2002* (Chicago: Ross & Hardies, 2002), pp. 15–16.

75. *Chicago Times-Herald.* 26 February 1897, p. 1; 1 April 1897, p. 3; 30 March 1897, p. 3.

76. See Melvin Holli, *Reform in Detroit: Hazen S.*

Pingree and Urban Politics (New York: Oxford University Press, 1969). Hazen Stuart Pingree was elected mayor of Detroit in 1889 and exposed corruption in street paving contracts and the school board, while attacking the city's utility monopolies. He would later be elected governor of Michigan and is credited as among the very first of the Midwest's progressive mayors.

77. *Chicago Tribune*, 30 March 1897, p. 3.

78. *Chicago Times-Herald*, 26 March 1897, p. 3; *Daily News Almanac* (1916), p. 549.

Chapter 5

1. *Chicago Times-Herald*, 31 March 1897, p. 3; *Chicago Tribune*, 30 July 1921, pp. 3, 11; 14 July 1899, p. 2.

2. *Chicago Tribune*, 31 January 1898, p. 7.

3. *Ibid.*, 30 October 1897, p. 12.; 56 December, p. 2; *Chicago Times-Herald*, 21 June 1897, p. 3.

4. *Chicago Tribune*, 9 February 1898, p. 7; 14 February 1898, p. 5; 2 March 1898, p. 7; 7 March 1898, p. 7; 8 March 1898, p. 6; 9 March 1898, p. 8; 17 April 1898, p. 7; 18 April 1898, p. 7; 19 April 1898, p. 6; 24 April 1898, p. A12; *Chicago Times-Herald*, 14 April 1898, p. 5.

5. *Chicago Tribune*, 10 June 1898, p. 7; 11 June 1897, p. 9; 25 October 1914, p. A2.

6. *Chicago Tribune*, 10 July 1898, p. 5; 1 May 1905, p. 5.

7. *Ibid.*, 13 June 1898, p. 4; 28 June 1898, p. 12; 20 June 1898, p. 7; 1 July 1898, p. 7; 9 July 1898, p. 5; 10 July 1898, p. 5; *Chicago Times-Herald*, 24 June 1898, p. 7; 10 July 1898, p. 1.

8. *Chicago Tribune*, 12 July 1898, p. 10; 13 July 1898, p. 1; *Chicago Times-Herald*, 12 July 1898, pp. 1, 4; 13 July 1898, pp. 1, 4, 5; 14 July 1898, p. 5.

9. *Ibid.*

10. *Chicago Tribune*, 30 May 1898, p. 9; 13 June 1898, p. 4; *Chicago Times-Herald*, 25 March 1898, p. 1.

11. *Chicago Times-Herald*, 10 May 1897, p. 4; 28 August 1897, p. 4; *Chicago Tribune*, 9 January 1898, p. 2; 11 October 1897, p. 8; 9 May 1898, p. 9. William Jennings Bryan himself, at the Jackson Day Banquet in January, had struck the theme of unification, asking that the Gold Democrats pay only lip service to silver and his candidacy.

12. *Chicago Times-Herald*, 17 July 1898, p. 8; 7 September 1898, p. 4; 8 September 1898, p. 5; 25 September 1898, p. 1; *Chicago Tribune*, 3 September 1898, pp. 5, 6; 6 September 1898, p. 10. Interestingly, Roger's brothers, Mark, Eugene, and Frank, were also becoming politically active, actually becoming involved in a physical altercation at the Second District Democratic convention called in July to select legislative candidates over the choice of chair.

13. *Daily News Almanac* (1899), pp. 405–19; *Chicago Times-Herald*, 10 November 1898, p. 2; 14 November 1896, p. 3; 15 November 1898, p. 1.

14. *Ibid.*, 13 November 1898, p. 1; *Chicago Tribune*, 13 November 1898, pp. 12, 34; 6 December 1898, p. 2.

15. *Chicago Tribune*, 16 November 1898, p. 2; 18 November 1898, p. 7; 19 November 1898, p. 8; 20 November 1898, p. 34; Harrison, *Stormy Years*, pp. 125, 210. According to Harrison, the enmity with Altgeld began when the mayor, shortly after his election, chose Robert A. Waller, a man the former governor despised personally, as the city comptroller.

16. *Ibid.*, 13 November 1898, p. 12.

17. *Ibid.*, 4 January 1899, pp. 2, 7; 5 January 1899, p. 1; 7 January 1899, p. 2; *Chicago Times-Herald*, 6 January 1899, pp. 1, 2.

18. *Chicago Tribune*, 5 January 1899, p. 1; 8 January 1899, p. 2; 19 February 1899, p. 7; 11 March 1899, p. 4; 12 March 1899, p. 32; *Chicago Times-Herald*, 19 March 1899, p. 3; 20 March 1899, p. 2. Altgeld's concern about the sincerity of returning Gold Democrats was not entirely misplaced. F.S. Peabody privately let it be known that regardless of his statements of the previous year, he remained opposed to free silver.

19. *Ibid.*

20. *Chicago Tribune*, 7 January 1899, p. 7; 11 January 1899, p. 2; 28 January 1899, p. 6; 22 March 1899, p. 4; 23 March 1899, p. 3; 25 March 1899, p. 2; 28 March 1899, p. 1; 2 April 1899, p. 2; 3 April 1899, p. 2; *Chicago Times-Herald*, 31 March 1899, p. 1.

21. *Chicago Tribune*, 5 January 1899, p. 10.

22. *Ibid.*, 19 January 1899, p. 5.

23. *Chicago Times-Herald*, 17 March 1899, pp. 1, 13; 30 March 1899, p. 3; *Chicago Tribune*, 16 March 1898, p. 3; 19 March 1899, p. 2.

24. *Chicago Times-Herald*, 8 March 1899, pp. 1, 2.

25. *Chicago Tribune*, 2 April 1899, p. 1; 9 April 1899, p. 4; 12 April 1899, p. 7; 13 April 1899, p. 2.

26. See David F. Trask, *The War with Spain in 1898* (Lincoln: University of Nebraska Press, reprint edition, 1997).

27. Alfred T. Mahan, *The Influence of Sea Power upon History, 1660–1783* (London: S. Low, Marston, 1890); Josiah Strong, *Our Country: Its Possible Future and its Present Crisis* (New York: Baker & Taylor for the American Home Missionary Society, 1885); John M. Mackenzie, *The Partition of Africa, 1880–1900: European Imperialism in the Nineteenth Century* (London and New York: Methuen, 1983).

28. Coletta, *Bryan*, pp. 233–37. Nor was Bryan responsible for the treaty's ratification, as some would have it. Coletta argues convincingly that he simply did not enjoy that degree of influence over the Democrats in the Senate.

29. William Jennings Bryan, "The Issue for 1900," *North American Review* 170 (June 1900): 753–71.

30. *Chicago Tribune*, 25 May 1900, p. 2; 29 May 1900, p. 7; 9 June 1900, p. 2l; 11 June 1900, p. 2; *Chicago Times-Herald*, 25 June 1900, p. 4.

31. *Chicago Tribune*, 12 June 1900, p. 4; 22 June 1900, p. 5; 25 June 1900, p. 1.

32. *Chicago Times-Herald*, 27 June 1900, p. 1. Others spoken of as possible choices included Harrison,

who declined, and former Vice-President Adlai Stevenson. At this convention, Thomas Gahan was chosen to be a national committeeman.

33. *Chicago Tribune*, 8 July 1900, p. 3; 25 August 1900, p. 5.

34. *Ibid.*, 5 July 1900, p. 3; *Chicago Times-Herald*, 22 January 1900, p. 7.

35. *Chicago Times-Herald*, 22 January 1900, p. 7; *Chicago Tribune*, 25 January 1900, p. 4; 27 June 1900, pp. 1, 4. Cable, however, declined to be reelected to the state central committee.

36. Harrison, *Stormy Years*, p. 202; *Chicago Tribune*, 27 June 1900, p. 5.

37. *Chicago Tribune*, 4 July 1896, p. 4; 5 July 1900, p. 3; 8 July 1900, p. 3; *Chicago Times-Herald*, 4 July 1896, pp. 1, 2; 5 July 1896, p. 1; 6 July 1896, p. 2; Eugene H. Roseboom, *A History of Presidential Elections: From George Washington to Richard M. Nixon* (New York: Macmillan, 1970), pp. 326–27. Bryan had been also nominated by the silver Republican Party, and Towne was their nominee for the vice presidency. Stevenson was an alternate in the Illinois delegation as well.

38. *Chicago Times-Herald*, 8 August 1900, pp. 1–2; *Chicago Tribune*, 30 August 1900, p. 4; 3 September 1900, p. 5.

39. *Chicago Tribune*, 12 October 1900, p. 1.

40. Howard W. Allen and Vincent A. Lacey, eds., *Illinois Elections, 1818–1990: Candidates and County Returns for President, Governor, Senate, and House of Representatives* (Carbondale: Southern Illinois University Press, 1992), pp. 242, 244; *Chicago Daily News Almanac* (1901), p. 392.

41. *Chicago Tribune*, 9 November 1900, pp. 1–2; *Chicago Times-Herald*, 9 November 1900, pp. 1, 2.

42. *Chicago Tribune*, 8 November 1900, p. 2; 18 November 1900, p. 8; 5 December 1900, p. 2.

43. *Ibid.*, 4 January 1901, p. 2; 8 January 1901, p. 2.

44. *Ibid.*, 30 December 1900, p. 3.

45. *Ibid.*, 31 December 1900, p, 12; 7 January 1901, p. 3; 9 January 1901, p. 1; *Chicago Times-Herald*, 9 January 1901, p. 1.

46. *Chicago Tribune*, 9 January 1901, p. 2; 10 January 1901, p. 1.

47. *Ibid.*

48. *Chicago Tribune*, 4 July 1952, p. 16; Marquis Who's Who Inc., *Who Was Who in America, 1951–1960* (Chicago: Marquis Who's Who, 1966), III: 86. Boeschenstein had been born in Macon County, Illinois, on October 27, 1862, and was educated at Washington University in St. Louis. As a leading citizen of Edwardsville in Madison County, he pursued diverse careers in politics, business, publishing, and banking. Between 1897 and 1917, he was vice-president and treasurer of the Edwardsville Water Company, which he helped create. He was also the publisher of the *Edwardsville Intelligencer* for thirty-four years until 1917, when he organized the Edwardsville National Bank & Trust, of which he was president until 1951. His lengthy political career ranged from several terms as Edwardsville's mayor,

beginning in 1887, to a lengthy tenure on the Democratic National Committee between 1912 and 1924.

49. *Ibid.*

Chapter 6

1. *Belleville News-Democrat*, 6 January 1912, p. 1.

2. John A. Campbell, ed. *A Biographical History with Portraits of Prominent Men of the Great West* (Chicago: Western Biographical and Engraving, 1902), p. 333; *Fort Worth Star-Telegram*, 28 June 1908; *Washington Post*, 24 June 10, 1912, p. 4.

3. *Ibid.*

4. *Ibid.*; Reuben Donnelley (comp.) *Lakeside Annual Directory of the City of Chicago, 1901* (Chicago: The Chicago Directory Company), p. 1910; *1910*, p. 1286 (hereafter cited as *City Directory*); Bureau of the Census, *1910 Federal Population Census, Chicago Series*, National Archives Microfilm Publication, T-624, roll 256, p. 236 (hereafter cited as *Census, 1910*); Campell, *ibid..*; interview with Frank Sullivan (grand-nephew), 16 April 2007. Sullivan also owned a summerhouse at Fox Lake, Illinois.

5. *Ibid. Chicago Tribune*, 5 July 1905, p. 12; 8 December 1929, p. 16; *Chicago Evening Post*, 15 April 1920, p. 10; Hawthorne Daniel, "Golf and Good Health," *World's Work* 40 no. 4 (August 1920): 393–401; Kerby A. Miller, *Emigrants and Exiles: Ireland and the Irish Exodus to North America* (New York: Oxford University Press, 1985), pp. 332, 526; not to mention the numerous clubs to which he belonged including the Catholic Order of Foresters, the Menoken Club, the Sherman Club, the Royal Acanum, and the Knights of Columbus.

6. *Chicago Tribune*, 10 March 1895, p. 1; 30 October 1894, p. 1; 5 October 1900, p. 4; 10 January 1901, p. 2; 24 April 1901, p. 13; 3 May 1901, p. 2; 9 August 1906, p. 3; 10 August 1906, p. 4; 13 October 1906, p. 1; 15 April 1911, p. 9; 12 August 1915, p. 13; 7 January 1941, p. 21; 19 April 1941, p. 12; *Chicago Examiner*, 20 June 1915, p. 7; *Los Angeles Times*, 30 May 1909, p. 13; *Chicago Daily News,* 15 April 1920, p. 2; James Langland, comp., *The Chicago Daily News Almanac and Year-Book for 1907* (Chicago: Chicago Daily News Company, 1906), p. 360 (hereafter cited as *Daily News Almanac*).

7. *Census 1910*, p. 236; Miller, *Emmigrants and Exiles*, p. 272.

8. *Chicago Tribune*, 16 October 1918, p. 9; at his death in 1918, John still lived with three of his sisters, Adelia, Julia, and Kate.

9. *City Directory* (1895), p, 1687

10. *Chicago Tribune*, 13 June 1959, p. A5; 26 June 1961, p. C7; *Railway Age* 65 (July–December 1896): 828; *Daily News Almanac* (1909), p. 535; *Chicago Tribune*, 17 December 1893, p. 1; 24 November 1903, p. 1; 29 October 1918, p. 17; 10 February 1928, p. 11; 13 June 1959, p. A5; *Chicago Examiner*, 23 February 1910, p. 2; 15 May 1917, p. 16; *New York Times*,

3 October 1917, p. 21; *Wall Street Journal*, 15 November 1918, p. 8.

11. *Chicago Tribune*, 7 May 1897, p. 5; *The Broad Ax* (Chicago), 6 September 1919, p. 2.

12. *Ibid.*, 15 March 1896, p. 6; 19 March 1896, p. 71; April 1896, p. 7; 11 April 1896, p. 4; 19 April 1896, p. 4; *Wall Street Journal*, 20 July 1895, p. 1.

13. *Ibid.*, 21 June 1896, p. 29; 17 February 1897, p. 5; 24 April 1897, p. 37; May 1897, p. 5; 10 May 1898, p. 10; 30 August 1900, p. 35; September 1900, p. 3; *Wall Street Journal*, 15 December 1896, p. 1; 1 May 1897, p. 4; 12 August 1897, p. 4; 12 January 1899, p. 2.

14. *Ibid.*, 12 September 1900, p. 7; 17 October 1900, p. 1; 9 January 1891, p. 9; *New York Times*, 10 January 1911, p. 10; 11 January 1901, p. 12; 20 October 1900, p. 2; *New York Tribune*, 19 October 1900, p. 12; *Wall Street Journal*, 11 July 1896, p. 1; 13 August 1898, p.1; 15 September 1898, p. 2; 16 May 1900, p. 3; 9 July 1900, p. 5; Wallace Rice, *75 Years of Gas Service in Chicago* (Chicago: The People's Gas Light and Control Company, 1925), p. 40.

15. *Chicago Tribune*, 26 June 1900, p. 1; 13 January 1901, p. 13; 16 January 1901, pp. 1, 3; 17 January 1902, pp. 2, 16; *Chicago Record-Herald*, 16 January 1902, p. 1; *New York Times*, 16 January 1901, p. 1; 17 January 1902, p. 1; 30 January 1901, p. 1; *Wall Street Journal*, 11 August 1895, p. 1; 6 January 1904, p. 3.

16. *Chicago Tribune*, 17 January 1902, p. 16.

17. *Ibid.*, 25 May 1912, p. 2; 18 January 1941, p. 7; *New York Times*, 12 February 1907, p. 11; *Wall Street Journal*, 6 November 1911; *The American Gas Light Journal* 80 (1 January to 30 June 1905): 53: Illinois Bureau of Labor Statistics, *Biennial Report* 9 (Springfield: Bureau of Labor Statistics, 1897), p. 251; *Chicago Securities* 8 (Chicago: Chicago Directory Company, 1898), p. 84; William J. Pringle, et al., *Investigation of the People's Gas and Coke Company for the Chicago Council Committee on Gas, Oil, and Electric Light* (Chicago: City of Chicago, 1911), p. 13; *Moody's Manual of Railroad and Corporation Securities, Twenty-third Annual Number*, Part 2: *Public Utility Section* (New York: Poor's Publishing, 1921), p. 967; *City Directory* (1897–1909); Rice, *75 Years of Gas Service*, pp. 40–1; Werner Troesken, *Why Regulate Utilities? The New Institutional Economies, and the Chicago Gas Industry, 1849–1924* (Ann Arbor: University of Michigan Press, 1996), pp. 44–7.

18. *Chicago Tribune*, 25 September 1897, p. 1; 29 November 1908, p. 5; 15 April 1911, p. 9; 25 December 1925, p. 22; *City Directory* (1910–1913); *Electrical World* 52 (1908): pp. 922–23, 1213; *Electrical Review* 53 (1908): 932; *Electric World and Engineer* 36 (1908): 360. Hanecy would serve as Lorimer's attorney during his fight to remain in the United States Senate that would culminate with his expulsion in 1912.

19. *Chicago Tribune*, 24 April 1901, p. 13; 1 May 1915, p. 4; 14 April 1919, p. 13; 18 November 1925, p. 30; *New York Times*, 21 September 1919, p. 105; 18 November 1925, p. 33; 20 November 1925, p. 31; *American Business* 10 (1940): 14; *Moody's Industrial Manual*, vol. 2 (New York: Moody's Investor Service, 1929), p. 2420.

20. Paul Michael Green, "The Chicago Democratic party 1840–1920," Ph.D. diss., University of Chicago, 1975, p. 88.

21. *Ibid.*

22. Carter H. Harrison, *Stormy Years: The Autobiography of Carter H. Harrison, Five Times Mayor of Chicago* (Indianapolis: Bobbs-Merrill, 1935), p. 232; Walter A. Townsend, *Illinois Democracy: A History of the Party and Its Representative Members—Past and Present*, 5 vols. (Springfield: Democratic Historical Association, 1935), vol. 2, 34; *Chicago Tribune*, 8 August 1928, p. 1; *New York Times*, 8 August 1928, p. 19.

23. *Ibid.*

24. *Chicago Tribune*, 12 January 1901, p. 2; 13 February 1901, p. 2; 4 March 1901, p. 5; 5 March 1901, p. 2; 10 March 1901, p. 2; 12 March 1901, p. 1; 21 March 1901, p. 1; *Chicago Record-Herald*, 10 March 1901, p. 1.

25. *Chicago Tribune*, 3 March 1901, pp. 1, 2; *Chicago Record-Herald*, 3 March 1901, p. 1; Joel Arthur Tarr, *A Study in Boss Politics: William Lorimer of Chicago* (Urbana: University of Illinois Press, 1971), pp. 106–07. Elbridge Hanecy was born in Trenton, Wisconsin, on 15 March 1852. As a young man, he worked as a clerk in a dry goods store, while also studying law. In 1871, he was admitted to the Illinois Bar, and in 1893, he was elected to the circuit court, where he would serve two terms. In 1904, he would be appointed by Governor Richard Yates to fill a vacancy on the Superior Court.

26. *Chicago Tribune*, 5 March 1901, p. 5; 13 March 1901, p. 12; 19 March 1901, p. 4; *Chicago Record-Herald*, 3 April 1901. pp. 1, 2; *Daily News Almanac* (1902), pp. 285–93.

27. *Chicago Tribune*, 15 June 1901, p. 3; 17 June 1901, p. 2; 28 July 1901, p. 2; *Chicago Record-Herald*, 28 July 1901, p. 2.

28. *New York Times*, 5 January 1901, p. 8; 12 January 1901, p. 3; *Chicago Tribune*, 27 June 1901, p. 9; 30 June 1901, p. 4; 8 July 1901, p. 1.

29. *Ibid.*

30. *Chicago Tribune*, 24 October 1901, p. 9; 25 October 1901, p. 3; 26 October 1901, p. 2; 27 October 1901, p. 1; 29 October 1901, p. 3.

31. *Ibid.*, 2 September 1925, p. 12; Harrison, *Stormy Years*, p. 86. Born in 1860 in West Brookfield, Massachusetts, Thomas Carey moved to Chicago in 1881, where he found employment as a brickmaker. At the same time, he became involved in Democratic politics and did a journeyman's service for the party. In 1890, his work was rewarded when he was elected an alderman from what would be, after the 1901 redistricting, the Twenty-ninth Ward, a job he was to hold for years.

32. *Ibid.*, 11 November 1901, p. 4; 30 November 1901, p. 1; 1 December 1901, p. 3; *Chicago Record-Herald*, 30 November 1901, p. 1.

33. *Chicago Tribune*, 3 December 1901, p. 3; 28 December 1901, p. 7; 5 January 1902, p. 2; 8 January 1902, p. 4; 11 January 1902, p. 2; *Chicago Record-Herald*, 8 January 1902, p. 4; 11 January 1902, p. 1.

34. *Chicago Tribune*, 18 January 1902, p. 3; 24 January 1902, p. 9. In contrast, Gahan's list was accepted for the Sixth Ward.

35. *Chicago Tribune*, 24 December 1901, p. 9; Harrison, *Stormy Years*, p. 210.

36. *Chicago Record-Herald*, 6 October 1901, p. 1; 3 November 1901, p. 1; *Chicago Tribune*, 6 October 1901, p. 1; 1 November p. 3; 3 November 1901, p. 1. Burke had remitted to the city in the same period fees totaling $53, 225.04.

37. *Chicago Tribune*, 26 October 1901, p. 1; 23 December 1902, p. 7; 18 January 1903, p. 5.

38. *Ibid.*, 11 January 1902, p. 2; 16 February 1902, p. 7; 17 March 1902, p. 3;

39. *Ibid.*, 2 April 1902, p. 12; 9 April 1902, p. 6; 18 April 1902, p. 5; 11 May 1902, p. 5.; 12 April 1914, p. 9; Harrison, *Stormy Years*, p. 211.

40. *Chicago Tribune*, 9 March 1902, p. 6; 12 March 1902, p. 1; 13 March 1902, p. 2; *Chicago Record-Herald*, 12 March 1902, p. 1.

41. *Chicago Tribune*, 13 March 1902, p. 2.

42. *Ibid.*, 15 March 1902, p. 5; 16 March 1902, p. 2; 17 March 1902, p. 3.

43. *Chicago Daily News*, 24 May 1902, p. 3; *Chicago Tribune*, 18 June 1902, p. 1, 2; 24 June 1902, p. 1; 27 June 1902, p. 7; *Chicago Record-Herald*, 18 June 1902, p. 1.

44. *Chicago Tribune*, 15 June 1902, p. 8; 6 November 1902, p. 4.

45. *Chicago Tribune*, 2 March 1924, p. 10.

46. *Ibid.*, 27 November 1902, p. 7; 29 November 1902, p. 4; 30 November 1902, p. 8. As a tribute to his growing status, there had been some discussion in November that Sullivan might be a popular choice for treasurer and George Brennan for clerk. The mayor quashed all such thoughts.

47. *Chicago Tribune*, 1 December 1902, p. 3; 2 December 1902, p. 4; *Chicago Daily News*, 1 December 1902, p. 6; 2 December 1902, p. 2; *Chicago Record-Herald*, 2 December 1902, p. 4. Sullivan was selected as one of the two West Side committee members to serve on the formal nominating committee that morning. Outvoted, Sullivan opposed the committee's recommendation of the Harrison ticket.

48. *Chicago Tribune*, 21 October 1902, p. 7.

49. *Ibid.*, 5 November 1902, p. 4; see Irving Stone, *Clarence Darrow for the Defense* (Doubleday, Doran, 1941). A good political biography of Darrow has yet to be written.

50. *Chicago Tribune*, 2 January 1903, p. 7; 12 January 1903, p. 8; 20 January 1903, p. 3; 25 January 1903, p. 3; 5 February 1903, p. 4.

51. *Ibid.*, 28 January 1903, p. 3; 11 February 1903, p. 7; 16 February 1903, p. 3; 17 February 1903, p. 2.

52. *Ibid.*, 20 February 1903, p. 1; 21 February 1903, p. 5; 22 February 1903, p. 2; 24 February 1903, p. 1; *Chicago Daily News*, 20 February 1903, p. 1; *Chicago Record-Herald*, 20 February 1903, p. 1; Ray Ginger, *Altgeld's America: The Lincoln Ideal Versus Changing Realities* (New York: Funk & Wagnall, 1958), pp. 266–67.

53. *Chicago Tribune*, 10 March 1903, p. 2; Harrison, *Stormy Years*, p. 229.

54. *Chicago Tribune*, 15 March 1903, p. 1; 17 March 1903, pp. 1, 2; *Chicago Daily News*, 15 March 1903, p. 1; 17 March 1903, p. 1; 23 March 1903, p. 7.

55. *Chicago Tribune*, 7 March 1903, p. 2; 27 June 1905, pp. 1, 3; Harrison, *Stormy Years*, p. 249. Graeme Stewart had been born to Scottish immigrants in Chicago on August 30, 1853, and educated locally, taking his higher education at the first University of Chicago (a Baptist college founded by Stephen Douglas that operated between 1857 and 1886). As a young man, he began in business as an errand boy. At the age of 27, he joined the firm of William Hoyt and Company, a wholesale grocery concern. Five years later, he was on the board of directors, and not long afterwards, he was taken on as a partner. In 1874, Stewart became a captain of a company of the First Illinois National Guard Regiment, which he organized, and in 1882, the elder Harrison appointed him to the city board of education upon which he served (sometimes as its president) for six years. He also helped lead the movement against what were perceived to be abuses and legal attempts to steal the use of the streets by the streetcar companies. In 1900, he was elected to the Republican national committee, which placed him on its executive board. He also helped oversee the McKinley reelection campaign that year in the western United States.

56. *Ibid.*, 29 March 1903, p. 3; 2 April 1903, p. 5; *Daily News Almanac* (1904), pp. 328–36.

57. *Chicago Tribune*, 11 April 1903, p. 4; 22 September 1903, p. 4. Rural leaders were reported as "swearing by John P. Hopkins, because he runs the state committee without calling on them for money."

58. *Ibid.*, 10 February 1903, p. 5; 30 September 1903, p. 2; 4 November 1903, p. 16.

59. *Ibid.*, 8 November 1902, p. 11; 13 April 1903, p. 3; 27 April 1903, p. 3; 26 August 1903, p. 14.

Chapter 7

1. *Chicago Tribune*, 18 April 1904, p. 4.

2. Robert, L. Duffus, "The Tragedy of Hearst," *World's Work* 44 (October 1922): 623–30; W.A. Swanberg, *Citizen Hearst, A Biography of William Randolph Hearst* (New York: Scribner's, 1961), pp. 56–7, 61–5; John K. Winkler, *William Randolph Hearst: A New Appraisal* (New York: Hastings House, 1955), pp. 97–117.

3. *Ibid.*

4. Duffus, "The Tragedy of Hearst": 629–30.

5. Johnson to Schilling, 28 March 1901, box 2, George A. Schilling Papers, Abraham Lincoln Presidential Library, Springfield, Illinois.

6. *Chicago Tribune*, 18 December 1898, p. 5; Barnard, *Eagle Forgotten*, p. 416; William Jennings Bryan, *The First Battle: The Story of the Campaign of 1896* (Chicago: W.D. Conkey, 1896), pp. 302, 596; *Who Was Who in America, with World Notables*, vol. 4, p. 270.

7. *Chicago Tribune*, 6 June 1904, p. 1; 7 June 1904, p. 4; 8 June 1904, p. 2; 5 May 1905, p. 4; Barnard, *Eagle Forgotten*, p. 416; Bryan, *The First Battle*, pp. 302, 596; *Who Was Who in America*, vol. 4, p. 270.

8. *Ibid.*, 29 April 1904, p. 4; 30 April 1904, p. 7.

9. *Ibid.*, 3 May 1904, p. 2; 4 May 1904, p. 5; 13 May 1904, p. 3; *Chicago Records-Herald*, 4 May 1904, p. 1.

10. *Ibid.*, 14 June 1904, p. 2.

11. *Ibid.*, 13 June 1904, p. 1; 14 June 1904, pp. 1, 2; 15 June 1904, pp. 1, 2; *Chicago Record-Herald*, 13 June, pp. 1, 2; 14 June 1904, pp. 1, 2; 15 June 1904, pp. 1, 2; *New York Times*, 15 June 1904, p. 1.

12. *Ibid.*

13. *Chicago Tribune*, 16 June 1904, p. 7.

14. *Ibid.*, 20 June 1904, p. 1; 21 June 1904, p. 7; 23 June 1904, p. 8; *Chicago Record-Herald*, 21 June 1904, p. 2.; *New York Times*, 21 June 1904, p. 1.

15. *Chicago Tribune*, 26 June 1904, p. 5; 30 June 1905, p. 5; 29 June 1904, p. 8; *New York Times*, 25 June 1904, p. 1.

16. *Ibid.*

17. *Chicago Tribune,* 1 July 1904, p. 4; 2 July 1904, p. 4; *New York Times*, 5 July 1904, p. 2; *Chicago Record-Herald*, 4 July 1904, p. 3.

18. Milton W. Blumenberg, reporter, *Official Proceedings of the Democratic National Convention Held in St. Louis, Missouri, July 6, 7, 8, and 9 1904* (New York: Publishers' Printing, 1904), p. 101; *Chicago Tribune*, 5 July 1904, p. 3; *Chicago Record-Herald*, 5 July 1904, p. 3.

19. Official *Proceedings, 1904 Democratic National Convention*, p. 108; *Chicago Tribune*, 7 July 1904, p. 1; *Chicago Record-Herald*, 6 July 1904, p. 3; 7 July 1904, p. 4; 14 July 1939, p. 3.

20. *Chicago Tribune*, 6 July 1904, p. 3.

21. *Ibid.*, 7 July 1904, p. 1; 8 July 1904, p. 3; *Chicago Record-Herald*, 8 July 1904, pp. 1, 2.

22. *Ibid.*, 7 July 1904, p. 2; *New York Times*, 11 July 1904, p. 1; *Official Proceedings, 1904 Democratic National Convention*, pp. 56–85.

23. *Official Proceedings, 1904 Democratic National Convention*, pp. 87–95, 100.

24. *Ibid.*

25. *Ibid.*, pp. 103–08.

26. *Ibid.*, pp. 109–11.

27. *Ibid.*, pp. 111–12.

28. *Ibid.*, 112–16.

29. *Ibid.*, pp. 121–22; *Chicago Tribune*, 4 July 1904, p. 4.

30. *Official Proceedings, 1904 Democratic National Convention*, p. 274–318; *Chicago Tribune*, 8 July 1904, p. 4; 7 March 1929, p. 10; *New York Times*, 2 July 1904, p. 1; 10 July 1904, p. 1; 7 March 1929, p. 18; *Washington Post*, 2 July 1920, p. 1; Harrison, *Stormy Years*, pp. 233–35; James Philip Fadely, *Thomas Taggart: Public Servant, Political Boss, 1856–1929*; Richard Walter Haupt, "History of the French Lick Springs Hotel," Master's thesis, Indiana University, 1953. Taggart was one of Sullivan's staunchest political allies and friends. Thomas Taggart was born in County Monaghan, Ireland, on November 17, 1856, and his family moved to Xenia, Ohio, in 1861. Young Tom first began work on the railroads, and moved to Garrett, Indiana, in 1874, and then in 1877 to Indianapolis. He became engaged in the hotel and restaurant business, which would be his lifelong profession. He also began his political career with a term as auditor of Marion County, 1886–1894, as chair of the county committee in 1888, followed by service as mayor of Indianapolis, 1895–1901, and as a member of the Democratic National Committee, 1900–1916, of which he was chairman between 1900 and 1908. By this point, he was "boss" of the Indiana Democratic Party. In March 1916, he was to be appointed as a Democrat to the United States Senate to fill a vacancy, a position he held until the following year, having been defeated for a full term in the November 1916 elections. Later, after Sullivan's death, he worked closely with his successor, George Brennan. Meanwhile, his business interests prospered with an investment in a small hotel at French Lick, Indiana, which quickly grew into a major resort, and a meeting place for leading national Democrats. Taggart died in 1929 at seventy-two years of age

31. *Official Proceedings, 1904 Democratic National Convention*, p. 250; *Chicago Tribune*, 8 July 1904, p. 5; 9 July 1904, p. 4; *Chicago Record-Herald*, 10 July 1904, p. 2.

32. *Chicago Tribune*, 21 July 1904, p. 2; 23 July 1904, p. 2.

33. *Ibid.*, 12 July 1904, p. 2.

34. *Ibid.*, 22 July 1904, p. 5; 23 July 1904, p. 2.

35. *Ibid.*, 31 July 1904, p. 5.

36. *Ibid.*, 27 October 1904, p. 6.

37. *Ibid.*, 20 August 1904, p. 5; 20 September 1904, p. 6; 27 October 1904, p. 6; *Detroit Free Press*, 1 July 1904, p. 9.

38. *Chicago Tribune.*, 5 October 1904, p. 2; 16 October 1904, p. 5; 24 October 1904, p. 3; 27 October 1904, p. 6.

39. *Ibid.*, 6 November 1904, p. 3.

40. *Ibid.*, 9 November 1904, pp. 1, 2, 4; 10 November 1904, pp. 1, 5; *Daily News Almanac* (1906), pp. 224, 229–32, 255, 366, 397–98.

41. See Melvin G. Holli, *Reform in Detroit: Hazen S. Pingree and Urban Politics* (Oxford: Oxford University Press, 1969); Maureen A. Flanagan, *Charter Reform in Chicago* (Carbondale: Southern Illinois University Press, 1987), pp. 125, 182. Not all historians are comfortable with the division between social and structural reformers. Maureen Flanagan argues that separating those interested in reform into two distinct camps creates "an incomplete picture of the urban

context and the interaction among people of differing ideas." While this is a valid point, the same criticism can be levied against virtually any historical classification (when exactly did the Progressive Period begin, anyway?), which are inevitably arbitrary. Also, it is a fact that the distinctions in orientation among Chicago's reform-minded in this era do break down conveniently into the two classifications. Moreover, the division is also an accurate representation of the personal and political associations of the men and women involved in reform. Raymond Robins, a major social reformer, for example, did not work with and was not involved with the crusades of either Civic Federation or the Municipal Voters League, and the same can be said for other social reformers, like Jane Addams and Margaret Haley. This relative exclusiveness was also true of the structural reformers. Accordingly, as the classifications have been found to be generally accurate and reflective of the actual political orientations and interactions of Chicago's reformers, they are used here.

42. The Civic Federation of Chicago, *First Annual Report of the Central Council* (Chicago: R. Donnelley & Sons, 1895), p. 7.

43. *Chicago Tribune*, 21 January 1896, p. 3; 27 January 1896, p. 6; 14 February 1896, p. 4.

44. *Ibid.*, 22 February 1902, p. 7; 26 October 1911, p. 8; 19 October 1930, p. 5; 30 October 1930, p. 10.

45. *Ibid.*, 2 February 1920, p. 1. During the course of his career, Cullerton was alderman from the Sixth, Seventh, Ninth, and Eleventh wards.

46. *Ibid.*

47. Murray Tuley was born in 1827 in Kentucky to native-born Americans of Irish descent. After his father died, his mother remarried a well-established attorney in Chicago, where the family relocated. As a teenager, he returned to Kentucky to study law in a private office, but he moved back to Illinois to practice. When the Mexican War broke out, he immediately enlisted. After its conclusion, he became attorney general for the territory of New Mexico and then a member of its legislature. Upon returning to Chicago in 1853, he resumed his work as a lawyer, and also became involved in politics, serving as a delegate to the Illinois constitutional conventions of 1862 and 1870. In 1869, he was appointed the city's corporation counsel. In 1878, he was elected to the city council, and in 1879, to the circuit court, where he remained until his death in 1905.

48. For a more complete biography of Dunne, see Richard Allen Morton, *Justice and Humanity: Edward F. Dunne, Illinois Progressive* (Carbondale: Southern Illinois University Press, 1997).

49. *Ibid.*

Chapter 8

1. Charles Merriam, Spencer D. Parratt, and Albert Lepawsky, *The Government of the Metropolitan Region of Chicago* (Chicago: University of Chicago Press, 1933), pp. 11–12.

2. *Chicago Tribune*, 27 January 1882, p. 8;1 June 1886, p. 1; 7 September 1886, p. 8; November 1886, p. 1; Harry P. Webber, *Outline History of Chicago Traction* (Chicago: n.p., 1936), pp. 26–8.

3. James Langland, *Chicago Daily News Almanac and Year-Book for 1909* (Chicago: Chicago Daily News Company, 1908), p. 528 (hereafter cited as *Daily News Almanac*); see also James David Johnson, *A History of Chicago Streetcars, 1858–1958* (Wheaton, IL: Traction Orange Company, c. 1964).

4. By 1890, there were four major companies within the city: the Chicago City Railway, the Chicago West Division Railway, the North Chicago Street Railway, and the West Chicago Street Railway; Weber, *Outline History*, pp. 5–14.

5. *Chicago Tribune*, 22 January 1865, p. 2; 23 January 1865, p. 2; 25 January 1865, p. 4; 28 January 1865, p. 1; 29 February 1865, p. 4; 30 January 1865, p. 4; 5 February 1865, p. 1; 7 February 1865, p. 1; 24 February 1865, p. 2; 17 March 1875, p. 4; 6 July 1883, p. 6; Edward F. Dunne, *Illinois: The Heart of the Nation*, 5 vols. (Chicago: Lewis, 1933) 2:221; Robin Einhorn, *Property Rules: Political Economy in Chicago, 1833–1872* (Chicago: University of Chicago Press, 1991), pp. 217–24.

6. *American Street Railway Investments* 8 (1901): 58–84; *Street Railway Journal* 15 (1899): 77; John Franch, *Robber Baron: The Life of Charles Tyson Yerkes* (Urbana: University of Illinois Press, 2006), pp. 1–78, 89.

7. Franch, *Robber Baron*, pp. 128–29.

8. *Chicago Tribune*, 19 February 1897, p. 1; 20 February 1897, p. 9; 10 March 1897, p. 5; 18 March 1897, p. 7; 13 May 1897, p. 1.

9. *Ibid.*, 23 May 1897, p. 6; 28 May 1897, p. 1; 2 June 1897, p. 1; 4 June 1897, p. 1; 5 June 1897, p. 1; 10 June 1897, p. 1; 19 November 1897, p. 7; 6 December 1898, p. 1; 7 December 1898, p. 1; 9 December 1898, p. 2; 13 December 1898, p. 1; Franch, *Robber Baron*, p. 259.

10. *Chicago Tribune*, 21 May 1899, p. 42; 23 April 1903, p. 1; Franch, *Robber Baron*, pp. 266–71, 278.

11. *Chicago Tribune*, 14 February 1902, p. 1; 2 April 1902, p. 3.

12. *Ibid.*, 6 April 1904, p. 3; 1 May 1905, p. 5; *Daily News Almanac* (1904), p. 355 (hereafter referred to as the *Daily News Almanac*); Illinois House of Representatives, *Journal of the House of Representatives of the Forty-Third General Assembly of the State of Illinois* (Springfield: Philips Brothers, 1904), pp. 652, 965, 967, 987, 1044; Illinois Senate, *Journal of the Senate of the Forty-Third General Assembly of the State of Illinois* (Springfield: Philips Brothers, 1903), pp. 76, 497, 616, 636, 664, 659, 1023; the role of labor in the municipal ownership movement has been explicated in Georg Leidenberger, *Chicago's Progressive Alliance: Labor and the Bid for Public Streetcars* (DeKalb: Northern Illinois University Press, 2006).

13. *Chicago Tribune,* 12 April 1904, p. 1; Caro Lloyd, *Henry Demarest Lloyd, 1847–1903, A Biography* (New York: G.P. Putnam's Sons, Knickerbocker Press, 1912), p. 308; Chester McArthur Destler, *Henry Demarest Lloyd and the Empire of Reform* (Philadelphia: University of Pennsylvania Press, 1963), pp. 525–6. Another event that affected Sullivan was the sudden and unexpected death of former national committeeman Thomas Gahan on April 30, 1905.

14. *Chicago Record-Herald,* 5 September 1904, p. 1.

15. *Chicago Tribune,* 12 November 1904, p. 1; 21 November 1904, p. 8; 22 November 1904, p. 4; 16 January 1905, p. 1; 26 February 1905, p. 4. The only other man who received any support for the nomination before the convention was former Judge William Prentiss, first president of the Municipal Ownership League.

16. *Ibid.,* 15 January 1905, p. 1; 16 February 1905, p. 3; 24 March 1934, p. 4; Samuel Wilber Norton, *Chicago Traction: A History, Legislative and Political* (Chicago, n.p., 1907), pp. 94–97. John Maynard Harlan was born in Kentucky on December 26, 1864, as the son of future United States Supreme Court Associate Justice John Marshall Harlan. He entered Princeton College at the age of fifteen, completing his studies three years later. He spent the next two years in postgraduate study at Columbia University and the University of Berlin. He then went to work for his father as a law clerk, and in 1888 he came to Chicago to practice law. In 1896, he was elected alderman, and was responsible for the "Harlan Report," an authoritative assessment of legal issues associated with public transportation.

17. *Daily News Almanac* (1906), pp. 290, 292; *Chicago Tribune,* 14 April 1905, p. 1; *Chicago American,* 5 April 1905, p. 1.

18. *Chicago Tribune,* 21 January 1905, p. 3; 23 January 1905, p. 15.

19. *Ibid.,* 18 August 1905, p. 7; 7 September 1905, p. 16; *Daily Northwestern,* 12 August 1905; *London Times,* 12 September 1905, p. 8. The details of Sullivan's meeting with Campbell-Bannerman are not known. However, given events, it is highly probable that Irish affairs were discussed. Apparently, these were not encouraging, as upon his return to the United States, Sullivan told reporters that his advice to the young men of Ireland was to get out. Ellis Island Foundation, *Passenger Records.*

20. *Chicago Tribune,* 28 March 1905, p. 7; 7 April 1905, p. 7; 26 April 1905, p. 1; 27 April 1905, pp. 1–2; 6 May 1905, p. 1; 7 May 1905, p. 1; 15 December 1905, p. 4.

21. *Ibid.,* 5 May 1905, p. 4; 20 August 1934, p. 1; Robert Waller, *Rainey of Illinois: A Political Biography, 1903–34* (Urbana: University of Illinois Press, 1977); *Chicago Record-Herald,* 5 May 1905, p. 3. Henry T. Rainey was from Carrolton, Illinois, where he had been born in 1860 to a farming family. He attended Amherst College in Maryland, and earned

some acclaim as a runner. Rainey then took a law degree from the Union College of Law, returning home to practice. From 1887 to 1895, he was master in chancery for Greene County, and in 1903, he was elected to the House of Representatives. With the exception of one term from 1921 to 1923, he remained there until he died as speaker in 1934. He was always counted as among the most respected of Illinois politicians, and he was known for the honesty of his purpose.

22. *Chicago Tribune,* 17 February 1906, p. 4.

23. M.F. Dunlap to Owen Thompson, 6 August 1906, *Millard Fillmore Dunlap Papers,* Abraham Lincoln Presidential Library, Springfield, Illinois; *ibid..,* 12 March 1906, p. 1; 17 March 1906, p.1; *Chicago Record-Herald,* 12 March 1906, p. 1.

24. *Chicago Tribune,* 15 April 1906, p. 2; 1 May 1906, p. 5; 2 May 1906, p. 1; *Chicago Record-Herald,* 2 May 1906, p. 1, 2.

25. *Chicago Tribune,* 16 May 1906, p. 2; 19 June 1906, p. 7; 21 June 1906, p. 2; 27 July 1906, p. 5.

26. *Chicago Tribune,* 1 August 1906, pp. 1, 2; 6 August 1906, p. 2; *Chicago Record-Herald,* 1 August 1906, p. 3; *New York Times,* 1 August 1906, p. 4; 2 August 1906, p. 3; 6 August 1906, p. 1; 1 August 1906, p. 4; *New York Tribune,* 1 August 1906, p. 1; *Washington Post,* 1 August 1906, p. 3; *Detroit Free Press,* 1 August 1906, p. 8; M.F. Dunlap Statement, August 1906, *Dunlap Papers;* Coletta, *Bryan,* pp. 369–70.

27. *Chicago Tribune,* 9 April 1906, p. 4; 15 July 1906, p. 4; 8 August 1906, p. 1; 26 August 1906, p. 6; 28 August 1906, p. 6; 13 September 1906, p. 5.

28. Georg Leidenberger, *Chicago's Progressive Alliance, Labor and the Bid for Public Streetcars* (DeKalb: Northern Illinois University Press, 2006), p. 93.

29. *Chicago Tribune,* 6 August 1906, p. 3; 9 August 1906, p. 3; 10 August 1906, p. 4; 24 August 1906, p. 4; *Detroit Free Press,* 21 August 1906, p. 1.

30. *Chicago Tribune,* 12 August 1906, p. 4; *Chicago Record-Herald,* 12 August 1906, p. 3; *New York Times,* 14 August 1906, p. 3.

31. *Chicago Tribune,* 16 August 1906, p. 5; *Chicago Record-Herald,* 16 August 1906, pp. 1, 2, 5; *New York Times,* 15 August 1906, p. 4; *New York Tribune,* 16 August 1906, p. 1; William Jennings Bryan and Mary Baird Bryan, *The Memoirs of William Jennings Bryan* (Philadelphia: John C. Winston, 1925), p. 147l; Coletta, *William Jennings Bryan,* p. 1:117.

32. *Chicago Tribune,* 3 April 1906, p. 1; 10 August 1906, p. 4; 19 August 1906, p. 6; 21 August 1906, p. 1; 23 August 1906, p. 3; *Chicago Record-Herald,* 21 August 1906, p. 2; 24 August 1906, p. 2; 29 August 1906, p. 2; 8 September 1906, p. 2; *New York Times,* 22 August 1906, p. 1, 2; 3 August 1906, p. 3; 24 August 1906, p. 1; *New York Tribune,* 22 August 1906, p. 1; 23 August 1906, p. 6; 30 August 1906, p. 2; *Detroit Free Press,* 22 August 1906, p. 1; Coletta, *William Jennings Bryan,* p. I:380; Walter Clyde Jones, "The Direct Primary in Illinois," *Proceedings of the American*

Political Science Association 7 (1910): 138–62. The political conventions, which usually were held in the spring or summer, were delayed until early fall because of a new primary law passed in early 1906, to replace one enacted the year before that had been declared unconstitutional by the Illinois Supreme Court. The 1906 act would also be eventually declared unconstitutional as well. Roger Sullivan, unlike many other political leaders, but like Mayor Dunne, favored a direct primary by which candidates would be selected by popular vote, and not, as provided in 1905 and 1906, by elected congressional district conventions. Roger Sullivan never feared the verdict of the people at the polls.

33. *Ibid.*

34. *Ibid.*

35. *Chicago Tribune*, 1 August 1906, p. 1; 30 August 1906, p. 1; 4 September 1906, p. 4; 5 September 1906, p. 1; *Chicago Record-Herald*, 4 September 1905, pp. 2; *The Commoner*, 7 September 1906, pp. 7, 9; 14 September 1906, pp. 3, 14; *New York Times*, 21 August 1906, p. 4; 22 August 1906, p. 1; 26 August 1906, p. 5; *New York Tribune*, 14 September 1906, p. 3.

36. *Chicago Tribune*, 8 September 1906, pp. 1, 4; *Chicago Record-Herald*, 8 September, p. 1; *Detroit Free Press*, 1 August 1908, p. 2; 8 September 1906, p. 1; 14 September 1906, p. 1. Sullivan's passionate attachment to the Democratic Party was characteristic of Irish-Americans in this period. See Kerby A. Miller, *Emmigrants and Exiles: Ireland and the Irish Exodus to North America* (New York: Oxford University Press, 1985), pp. 523–26.

37. *Ibid.*

38. *Chicago American*, 8 September 1906, p. 4; *New York Times*, 5 May 1906, p. 4; *New York Tribune*, 14 August 1906, p. 1; 9 September 1906, p. 2.

39. *Chicago Tribune*, 9 September 1906, p. 5; 14 September 1906, p. 7; *Chicago American*, 8 September 1906, p. 4; *New York Times*, 5 May 1906, p. 4; *New York Tribune*, 14 August 1906, p. 1; 9 September 1906, p. 2.

40. *Chicago Record-Herald,* 17 September 1906, p. 1; 20 September 1906, p. 5; *New York Tribune*, 7 September 1906, p. 6; 8 September 1906, pp. 2, 6; 10 September 1906, p. 6; 18 September 1906, p. 6.

41. *Ibid.*

42. *Duluth News-Tribune*, 25 August 1906, p. 6.

43. For a more detailed account on the Dunne administration, see Richard Allen Morton, *Justice and Humanity: Edward F. Dunne, Illinois Progressive* (Carbondale: Southern Illinois University Press, 1997).

44. *Chicago Tribune*, 24 August 1905, p. 5; 11 September 1905, p. 3; 26 September 1905, p. 2; 25 July 1936, p. 12; 19 June 1906, p. 7; 3 April 1907, p. 1; Edward F. Dunne, *Illinois: The Heart of the Nation*, 5 vols. (Chicago: Lewis, 1933), 2:295.

45. *Chicago Record-Herald*, 22 April 1908, pp. 1, 5; 23 April 1908, pp. 1,2; *Chicago Tribune*, 24 April 1908, pp. 1, 2; 26 April, p. 5; 27 April 1908, p. 5.

46. *Chicago Tribune*, 31 January 1908, p. 5.

47. *Ibid.*, 1 September 1908, p. 2. Sullivan and county chair William O'Connell selected the men who wrote the new charter. Included among the membership of the first Cook County management committee was Roger Sullivan's next-door neighbor and special protégé, Patrick Nash (1863–1943). In 1933 Nash became "boss" of the organization in partnership with Mayor Edward J. Kelly following the assassination of Mayor Anton Cermak, who had been originally brought into politics by George Brennan.

48. *Chicago Tribune,* 22 February 1908, p. 3.

49. *Chicago Tribune*, 3 January 1908, p. 8; 18 January 1908, 7; 21 January 1908, 2; 22 January 1908, 8; 24 January 1908, 4; 22 February 1908, 3; 5 May 1908, 2; 28 June 1908, 4; 3 July 1908, 1, 2, 4; 1 November 1908, 1, 2; 2 November 1908, 3; *Chicago Record-Herald*, 21 January 1908, 4; 5 February 1908, 7; 11 February 1908, 7; 22 February 1908, 2; 21 April 1908, 2; 22 June 1908, 2; 4 July 1908, 4; 6 July 1908, p. 1; 1 November 1908, 1, 2; *Denver Post*, 2 July 1908, 2; 4 July 1908, 3; 5 July 1908, 1, 5; *Washington Post*, 28 June 1908, 6.

50. *Ibid.*

51. *Chicago Record-Herald*, 24 April 1908, p. 1; 4 July 1908, p. 4; *Denver Post*, 2 July 1908, p. 2; 4 July 1908, p. 3; 5 July 1908, pp. 1, 5.

52. See for example William V. Shannon, *The American Irish* (New York: Macmillan, 1964).

Appendix

1. Mark Sullivan, "Why the West Dislikes New York," *World's Work* 51 (February 1926): 406–11.

2. Ray Allen Billington, *Westward Expansion: A History of the American Frontier* (New York: Macmillan, 1949), p. 723; George E. Plumbe, comp., *The Daily News Almanac and Political Register for 1900* (Chicago: The Daily News Company, 1900), p. 80 (hereafter cited as the *Daily News Almanac*).

3. Davis Rich Dewey, *Financial History of the United States* (New York: Longman's, Green, 1931), pp. 360–67, 378–82.

4. *Ibid.*, pp. 403–04; Paul Studenski and Herman E. Kross, *Financial History of the United States: Fiscal, Monetary, Banking, and Tariff, including Financial Administration and State and Local Finance* (New York: McGraw-Hill, 1952), pp. 186–88; Margaret G. Meyers, *A Financial History of the United States* (Columbia University Press, 1970), pp. 202–06. The Trade Dollar ceased to be produced on order of the Secretary of Treasury in 1877, and the law authorizing it was repealed in 1887.

5. Dewey, *Financial History*, pp. 405–07; Studenski and Kross, *Financial History of the United States*, pp. 189–90.

6. Dewey, *Financial History*, pp. 407–09, 460–62; Studenski and Kross, *Financial History of the United States*, pp. 201–04; Meyers, *A Financial History*, pp. 208–10.

7. Dewey, *Financial History*, pp. 211, 436–40.

8. *Ibid.*, p. 445; *Daily News Almanac* (1900), p. 82; gold reserves minus outstanding gold certificates actually fell to $95,485,414 in 1893 and $64,873,025 in 1894. They would return to above $100,000,000 in 1895.

9. The term "Aristocracy of Wealth," reflecting the serendipity of historical research, appears on a sheet of paper on both sides of which were the notes for a talk on the financial and social problems of this era (including the "demoneyization [*sic*] of silver"). The paper, dated 1891, is clearly antique, and was found inserted in a copy of the 1891 *Chicago Daily News Almanac* between pages providing statistics about imports into the United States.

10. These themes of exploitation are common in populist and pro-silver literature and speeches. They are most directly articulated in Sarah E.V. Emery, *Seven Financial Conspiracies Which Have Enslaved The American People* (Lansing, MI: Lansing Review, 1896), also appearing in Kenneth Carpenter, ed., *Gold and Silver in the Presidential Campaign of 1896* (New York: Arno, 1974).

11. Emery, *ibid.*, pp. 19, 43–44. See Richard Hofstader, "The Folklore of Populism," in Leonard Dinnerstein, *Anti-Semitism in the United States* (New York: Holt, Rinehart, and Winston, 1971), pp. 58–62. Not all scholars agree that anti-Semitism was a significant force among populists and proponents of free silver; see Norman Pollack, "The Myth of Populist Anti-Semitism," *American Historical Review* 68 (October 1962): 76–80.

12. Kirk H. Porter and Donald Bruce Johnson, *National Party Platforms, 1840–1964* (Urbana: University of Illinois Press, 1966), pp. 67, 73, 81, 93, 108. Beginning in 1884, both parties routinely endorsed bi-metallism, and in 1888 the GOP platform condemned the Cleveland administration for attempting to demonetize silver: *Daily News Almanac* (1900), pp. 77, 79, 85; Edward A. Ross, *Honest Dollars* (Chicago: Charles H. Kerr, 1896), pp. 46–52; "To American Bread-Winners; A Word on Wages in Silver Countries," in Carpenter, *Gold and Silver in the Presidential Campaign of 1896*.

13. *Ibid.*, Ross, *Honest Dollars*; Arthur J. Rolnick and Warren E. Weber, "Gresham's law or Gresham's Fallacy," *Journal of Political Economy* 94, no. 1 (1986): pp. 185–199; Robert Giffen, "The Gresham Law," *Economic Journal* 1, no. 2 (1891): pp. 304–6; Louis R. Ehrich, *The Question of Silver* (New York: G. P. Putnam's Sons, the Knickerbocker Press, 1896), pp. 8–9.

14. *Ibid.*

15. "The Silver Plot," pamphlet in Carpenter, *Gold and Silver in the Presidential Campaign of 1896*.

Bibliography

Manuscript Collections

Addams, Jane, Papers (microfilm ed.). Manuscript Division, Library of Congress. Washington, D.C.

Alschuler, Samuel J. Papers. Abraham Lincoln Presidential Library. Springfield, Illinois.

Baker, Newton D. Papers. Western Reserve Historical Society. Cleveland, Ohio.

Bryan, William Jennings Papers. Manuscript Division, Library of Congress. Washington, D.C.

Bynum, William Dallas Papers. Manuscript Division, Library of Congress. Washington, D.C.

Cleveland, Grover S. Papers (microfilm ed.). Manuscript Division, Library of Congress. Washington, D.C.

Daniels, Josephus Papers. Manuscript Division, Library of Congress. Washington, D.C.

Darrow, Clarence S. Papers. Manuscript Division, Library of Congress. Washington, D.C.

Darrow, Clarence S. Papers. University of Chicago Library, Special Collections. Research Center, Chicago, Illinois.

Deneen, Charles S. Papers. Abraham Lincoln Presidential Library. Springfield, Illinois.

Dever, William E. Papers. Chicago Historical Museum. Chicago, Illinois.

Dunlap, Millard Fillmore Papers. Abraham Lincoln Presidential Library. Springfield, Illinois.

Dunne, Edward F. Collection. Abraham Lincoln Presidential Library. Springfield, Illinois.

Dunne, Edward F. Scrapbooks and Papers. Illinois Historical Survey, University of Illinois Library. Urbana-Champaign, Illinois.

Dunne, Robert Jerome Papers. Chicago Historical Museum. Chicago, Illinois.

Fisher, Walter L. Papers. Manuscript Division, Library of Congress. Washington, D.C.

Fitzpatrick, John J. Papers, Chicago Historical Museum. Chicago, Illinois.

Harrison IV, Carter H. Papers. Newberry Library. Chicago, Illinois.

Humphrey, Otis J. Papers. Abraham Lincoln Presidential Library. Springfield, Illinois.

Insull, Samuel Papers. Samuel Insull Collection, E.M. Cudahy Library. Loyola University, Chicago.

James, Edmund J. Papers. Archives, University of Illinois Library. Urbana-Champaign, Illinois.

Johnson, Tom L. Papers. Western Reserve Historical Society. Cleveland, Ohio.

Jones, Samuel J. Papers (microfilm ed.). Toledo-Lucas County Public Library. Toledo, Ohio.

Lowden, Frank O. Papers. University of Chicago Library, Special Collections Research Center. Chicago, Illinois

Merriam, Charles E. Papers. University of Chicago Library, Special Collections Research Center. Chicago, Illinois.

Municipal Voters League Papers. Chicago Historical Museum. Chicago, Illinois.

Palmer, John McAuley Papers. Abraham Lincoln Presidential Library. Springfield, Illinois.

Rainey, Henry T. Papers. Manuscript Division, Library of Congress. Washington, D.C.

Robins, Raymond Papers. Wisconsin Historical Society. Madison, Wisconsin.

Schilling, George S. Papers. Abraham Lincoln Presidential Library. Springfield, Illinois.

Schwartz, Ulysses Papers. Chicago Historical Museum. Chicago, Illinois.

Sherman, Lawrence Y. Papers. Abraham Lincoln Presidential Library. Springfield, Illinois.

Stringer, Lawrence B. Papers. Abraham Lincoln Presidential Library. Springfield, Illinois.

Thompson, Owen P. Papers. Abraham Lincoln Presidential Library. Springfield, Illinois.

Tree, Lambert Papers. Chicago Historical Museum. Chicago, Illinois.

Tumulty, Joseph P. Papers. Manuscript Division, Library of Congress. Washington, D.C.

Walker, John H. Papers. Abraham Lincoln Presidential Library. Springfield, Illinois.

Wilson, Thomas Woodrow Papers. Manuscript Division, Library of Congress. Washington, D.C.

Newspapers

Aberdeen Daily American (North Dakota)
Aberdeen Daily News (North Dakota)
Atlanta Constitution
Baltimore Sun
Belleville News-Democrat (Illinois)
Belvidere Daily Republican (Illinois)
Belvidere Recorder (Illinois)

Belvidere Republican Northwestern (Illinois)
Boston Globe
The Broad Axe (Chicago)
Carlinville Democrat (Illinois)
Champaign News-Gazette (Illinois)
Chicago American
Chicago Daily Journal
Chicago Daily News
Chicago Defender
Chicago Eagle
Chicago Evening Journal
Chicago Evening Post
Chicago Examiner
Chicago Herald
Chicago Herald-Examiner
Chicago Inter-Ocean
Chicago Record-Herald
Chicago Record-Herald and Inter-Ocean
Chicago Times
Chicago Times-Herald
Chicago Tribune
Chicago West Side Reporter
Cincinnati Inquirer
Cleveland Plain Dealer
Commoner (Lincoln, Nebraska)
Daily Illini (Urbana-Champaign, Illinois)
Daily Northwestern
Dallas Morning News
Delavan Tri-County Times (Delavan, Illinois)
Denver Post
Detroit Free Press
Duluth News-Tribune (Minnesota)
Fort Worth Star-Telegram (Texas)
Grand Forks Herald (North Dakota)
Los Angeles Times
New York Times
New York Tribune
Illinois Republican Northwestern (Belvidere)
Illinois State Journal (Springfield)
Illinois State Register (Springfield)
Indianapolis Star
News-Gleaner (Shawneetown, Illinois)
St. Louis Post-Dispatch
Washington Post
Worcester Daily Spy

Books

Allen, Howard W., and Vincent A. Lacey, eds. *Illinois Elections, 1818–1920; Candidates and Returns for President, Governor, Senate, and House of Representatives.* Carbondale: Southern Illinois University Press, 1992.

Allswang, John. *Bosses, Machines, and Urban Voters, an American Symbiosis.* Port Washington, NY: Kennikat, 1977.

_____. *A House for All Peoples: Ethnic Politics in Chicago, 1890–1916.* Lexington: University of Kentucky Press, 1971.

_____. *The Political Behavior of Chicago's Ethnic Groups, 1918–1932.* New York: Ayer, 1980.

Anderson, David B. *William Jennings Bryan.* Boston: Twayne, 1981.

Anti-Saloon League of America. *Yearbook,* various dates. Westerville, OH: The League.

Ashby, Leroy. *William Jennings Bryan, Champion of Democracy.* Boston: Twayne, 1987.

Bacon, Edwin, and Morrill Wyman. *Direct Elections and the Law-Making By Popular Vote.* Boston: Houghton Mifflin, 1912.

Bailey, Harry A., and Kate Ellis. *Ethnic Group Politics.* Columbus, OH: Charles E. Merrill, 1969.

Barnard, Harry. *Eagle Forgotten: The Life of John P. Altgeld.* New York: Bobbs-Merrill, 1938.

Bates, J. Leonard. *Senator Thomas J. Walsh of Montana: Law and Public Affairs from TR to FDR.* Urbana: University of Illinois Press, 1997.

Becker, Earl L. *A History of Labor Legislation in Illinois.* Chicago: University of Chicago Press, 1929.

Bennett, Fremont, comp. *Politics and Politicians of Chicago, Cook County, And Illinois.* Chicago: Blakely, 1886.

Biles, Roger. *Big City Boss in Depression and War: Mayor Edward J. Kelly of Chicago.* DeKalb: Northern Illinois University Press, 1984.

_____. *Richard J. Daley: Politics, Race, and the Governing of Chicago.* DeKalb: Northern Illinois University Press, 1995.

Billington, Ray Allen. *Westward Expansion: A History of the American Frontier.* New York: Macmillan, 1949.

Blum, John M. *Joe Tumulty and the Wilson Era.* Boston: Houghton Mifflin, 1951.

Bodine, W.L. *Illinois Political Directory, 1899, with Portraits and Biographical Sketches Of Party Leaders.* 2 vols. Chicago: John F. Higgins, 1898.

Bowers, Claude G. *The Life of John Worth Kern.* Indianapolis: Hollenbeck Press, 1918.

Boyle, Ohio D. *A History of Railroad Strikes.* Washington, D.C.: Brotherhood, 1935.

Bragdon, Henry Wilkinson. *Woodrow Wilson: The Academic Years.* Cambridge: Belknap Press of the Harvard University Press, 1967.

Brennan, John A. *Silver and the First New Deal.* Reno: University of Nevada Press, 1969.

Bright, John. *Hizzoner Big Bill Thompson.* New York: Jonathan Caper and Harrison Smith, 1930.

Brownell, Blaine A., and Warren E. Stickle. *Bosses and Reformers: Urban Politics in America, 1880–1920.* Boston: Houghton Mifflin, 1973.

Bryan, William Jennings, and Mary Baird Bryan. *The Memoirs of William Jennings Bryan* n.c.: n.p., 1925.

Bryce, James. *The American Commonwealth,* revised edition. Philadelphia: J.D. Morris, 1906.

Buder, Stanley. *Pullman: An Experiment in Industrial Order and Community Planning, 1880–1930.* New York: Oxford University Press, 1967.

Buelow, Paul A. "Chicago." *The 1918–1919 Pandemic*

of *Influenza: The Urban Impact in the Western World*. Edited by Fred R. Van Hartesveldt. Lewiston: Edwin Mellen, 1992.

Bukowski, Douglas. *Big Bill Thompson: Chicago and the Politics of Image*. Urbana: University of Illinois Press, 1998.

Burnham, Daniel Hudson, *Et Al. Plan of Chicago Prepared Under the Direction of the Commercial Club*. Chicago: The Commercial Club, 1909.

Campbell, John A, ed. *A Biographical History with Portraits of Prominent Men of the Great West*. Chicago: Western Biographical and Engraving Company, 1902.

Carpenter, Kenneth, ed. *Gold and Silver in the Presidential Campaign of 1896*. New York: Arno, 1974.

Carwardine, William H. *The Pullman Strike*. Chicago: Charles Kerr, 1894.

Catt, Carrie Chapman, and Nellie Rogers Shuler. *Woman's Suffrage and Politics: The Inner Side of the Suffrage Movement*. Seattle: University of Washington, 1969.

Cavanaugh, Helen. *Carl Schurz Vrooman: Self-Styled "Constructive Conservative."* Chicago: Lakeside Press, R.R. Donnelley and Sons, 1977.

Chamberlain, Eugene Tyler. *Early Life and Public Service of Hon. Grover Cleveland, the Fearless and Independent Governor of the Empire State, Also the Life of Hon. Thomas A. Hendricks*. Chicago: Caxton, 1884.

Champernowe, Henry. *The Boss. an Essay Upon the Art of Governing American Cities*. New York: Richmond, 1894.

Chicago Directory Company. *Chicago Securities, 1898: A Digest of Information Relating to Stocks, Bonds, Banks, and Financial Institutions of Chicago*. Chicago: Chicago Directory Company, 1898.

Church, Charles A. *History of the Republican Party of Illinois, 1854–1912, with a Review of the Aggressions of the Slave-Power*. Rockford, IL: Wilson Brothers, 1912.

Civic Federation of Chicago. *Fifty Years on the Civic Front, 1893–1943: A Report on the Achievements of the Civic Federation, Chicago*. Chicago: n.p., 1943.

_____. *First Annual Report of the Central Council*. Chicago: R. Donnelley and Sons, 1895.

Clark, Champ. *My Quarter Century of American Politics*. 2 vols. New York: Harper and Bros., 1920.

Cleveland, Grover. *The Government in the Chicago Strike of 1894*. Princeton: Princeton University Press, 1913.

Coletta, Paola E. *William Jennings Bryan*. 3 vols. Lincoln: University of Nebraska Press, 1959.

Comwell, Elmer E. "Bosses, Machines, and Ethnic Groups." In *The Annals of the American Academy of Political and Social Sciences*. Edited by Thorstein Sellin. Essay Index Reprint Series. Plainview, NY: Books for Library Press, 1964, 1975, 27–39.

Cook, Fred J. *American Political Bosses and Machines*. New York: Franklin Watts, 1973.

Coos, Leonard V. *The Junior High School*. Boston: Houghton Mifflin, 1920.

Counts, George S. *School and Society in Chicago*. New York: Harcourt Brace, 1928.

Croly, Herbert. *The Promise of American Life*. New York: Macmillan, 1909.

Cronon, William. *Nature's Metropolis: Chicago and the Great West*. New York: W.W. Norton, 1991.

Dalton, Kathleen. *Theodore Roosevelt: A Strenuous Life*. New York: Knopf, 2002.

Darrow, Clarence S. *The Story of My Life*. New York: Scribner's, 1932.

De la Roche, Roberta Senechal. *In Lincoln's Shadow: The 1908 Race Riot in Springfield, Illinois*. Carbondale: Southern Illinois University Press, 2008.

Destler, Chester McArthur. *Henry Demarest Lloyd and the Empire of Reform*. Philadelphia: University of Pennsylvania Press, 1963.

Dewey, Davis Rich. *Financial History of the United States*. 2nd ed. New York: Longmans, Green, 1903.

Dickson, Paul R. *Great Lakes Dredge & Dock Company: A Century of Experience, 1890–1990*. Oak Brook, IL: Great Lakes Dredge & Dock, 1990.

Donnelly, Reuben, comp. *Lakeside Annual Directory of the City of Chicago*. Chicago: Chicago City Directory, various dates.

Dorsett, Lyle W. *The Pendergast Machine*. New York: Oxford University Press, 1968.

Drake, St. Clark, and Horace Cayton. *Black Metropolis: A Study of Negro Life in a Northern City*. New York: Harcourt Brace, 1945.

DuBois, Ellen Carol. *Feminism and Suffrage: The Emergence of an Independent Women's Movement in America, 1848–1869*. Ithaca: Cornell University Press, 1978.

Duis, Perry R. *The Saloon: Public Drinking in Chicago and Boston, 1880–1920*. Champaign: University of Illinois Press, 1983.

Duncan, Otis Dudley, and Beverly Duncan. *The Negro Population of Chicago: A Study of Residential Succession*. Chicago: University of Chicago Press, 1957.

Dunn, Arthur W. *From Harrison to Harding: A Personal Narrative, Covering A Third of a Century, 1888–1921*. 2 vols. New York: G.P. Putnam's Sons, 1922.

Dunne, Edward F. *Illinois: The Heart of the Nation*. 5 vols. Chicago: Lewis, 1933.

_____. *Judge, Mayor, Governor*. Edited by William L. Sullivan. Chicago: Windermere, 1916.

Ebner, Michael H., and Eugene M. Tobin. *The Age of Urban Reform: New Perspectives on the Progressive Era*. Port Washington, NY: Kennikat, 1977.

Edwards, Richard. *Edwards' Chicago, Illinois Business Directory for 1873*. Chicago: Richard Edwards Publisher, 1873.

Ehrich, Louis R. *The Question of Silver*. 2nd ed. New York: G. P. Putnam's Sons, Knickerbocker Press, 1896.

Einhorn, Robin L. *Property Rules: Political Economy in Chicago, 1833–1872*. Chicago: University of Chicago Press, 1991.

Emery, Sarah E.V. *Seven Financial Conspiracies Which Have Enslaved the American People*. Lansing, MI: Lansing Review, 1896.

Fadely, James Philip. *Thomas Taggart: Public Servant, Political Boss, 1856–1929*. Indianapolis: Indiana Historical Society, 1997.

Fite, Gilbert C. "Irish Chicago: Church, Homeland, Politics, and Class—The Shaping of an Ethnic Group 1870–1900." In *Ethnic Chicago*, revised ed. Edited by Melvin G. Holli and Peter d'A Jones. Grand Rapids, MI: William Eerdmans, 1984.

Flanagan, Maureen A. *Charter Reform in Chicago*. Carbondale: Southern Illinois University Press, 1987.

Flexner, Eleanor. *Century of Struggle: The Woman's Rights Movement in the United States*. Cambridge: Harvard University Press, 1975.

Franch, John. *Robber Baron: The Life of Charles Tyson Yerkes*. Urbana: University of Illinois Press, 2006.

Funchion, Michael F. "The Political and Nationalist Dimensions." In *The Irish in Chicago*. Edited by Lawrence J. McCaffrey et al. Urbana: University of Illinois Press, 1987, 61–97.

Gardner, Joseph L. *Departing Glory: Theodore Roosevelt as Ex-President*. New York: Scribner's, 1973.

George, Alexander L., and Juliette L. George. *Woodrow Wilson and Colonel House: A Personality Study*. New York: Dover, 1964.

Ginger, Ray. *Altgeld's America: The Lincoln Idea Versus Changing Realities*. New York: Quadrangle Books, 1959.

Glad, Paul W. *McKinley, Bryan, and the People*. Philadelphia: J.B. Lippincott, 1964.

Goodspeede, Weston A., and Daniel B. Healy. *History of Cook County in Two Volumes Illustrated*. Chicago: Goodspeede Historical Association, c. 1909.

Gosnell, Harold F. *Machine Politics: Chicago Model*. Chicago: University of Chicago Press, 1937.

Gottfried, Alex. *Boss Cermak of Chicago: A Study in Political Leadership*. Seattle: University of Washington Press, 1962.

Gould, Lewis L. *The Presidency of Theodore Roosevelt*. Lawrence: University of Kansas Press, 1992.

Green, James R. *Death in the Haymarket: The Story of Chicago, the First Labor Movement, and the Bombing That Divided Gilded Age America*. New York: Pantheon Books, 2006.

Green, Paul M., and Melvin G. Holli, eds. *The Mayors: The Chicago Political Tradition*. Carbondale: Southern Illinois University Press, 1987.

Green, Paul Michael. "Irish Chicago: Multi-Ethnic Road to Machine Success." In *Ethnic Chicago*. Edited by Melvin G. Holli and Peter d'A Jones. Grand Rapids, MI: William Eerdmans, 1995.

Grossman, James R. *Land of Hope: Chicago, Black Southerners, and the Great Migration*. Chicago: University of Chicago Press, 1989.

Hachey, Thomas E. *Britain and Irish Separatism: From Fenians to the Irish Free State, 1867–1922*. Washington, D.C.: Catholic University of America Press, 1977.

Haley, Margaret. *Battleground: The Autobiography of Margaret A. Haley*. Edited by Robert Reid. Champaign: University of Illinois Press, 1982.

Harpine, William D. *From the Front Porch to the Front Page: McKinley and Bryan in the 1896 Presidential Campaign*. College Station: Texas A&M Press, 2005.

Harrison, Carter H., IV. *Stormy Years: The Autobiography of Carter H. Harrison, Five Times Mayor of Chicago*. Indianapolis: Bobbs-Merrill, 1935.

Hawes, George W., comp. *Illinois State Gazetteer and Business Directory for 1858–59*. Chicago: George W. Hawes, 1860.

Heddrick, Mary J. *The Chicago Schools: A Social and Political History*. Beverly Hills: Sage, 1971.

Herman, Charles H. *Recollections of Life and Doings from the Haymarket Riot to the End of World War I*. Chicago: Normandie House, 1945.

Herrick, Genevieve, and John O. Herrick. *The Life of William Jennings Bryan*. Whitefish, MT: Kessinger, 1970.

Historical Encyclopedia of Illinois. Chicago: Munsell, 1904.

Holli, Melvin G. *Reform in Detroit: Hazen S. Pingree and Urban Politics*. New York: Oxford University Press, 1969.

Hurley, Edward N. *The Bridge to France*, reprint. New York: Kessinger, 2004.

Hutchinson, Thomas. *Lakeside Annual Directory of the City Chicago, 1879*. Chicago: Chicago Directory, 1879.

Hutchinson, William T. *Lowden of Illinois: The Life of Frank O. Lowden*. 2 vols. Chicago: University of Chicago Press, 1957.

Huthmacher, J. Joseph. *Massachusetts People and Politics, 1919–1933*. Cambridge: Belknap Press of Harvard University Press, 1959.

Ickes, Harold L. *The Autobiography of a Curmudgeon*. New York: Reynard and Hitchcock, 1943.

Illinois Political Directory, with Portraits and Biographical Sketches. Chicago: W.L. Bodine, c. 1899.

Insull, Samuel, and Larry Plachno. *The Memoirs of Samuel Insull*. Polo, IL: Transportation Press, 1992.

Jensen, Richard. *The Winning of the Midwest: Social and Political Conflict 1888–1896*. Chicago: University of Chicago Press, 1971.

Johnson, Claudius O. *Carter Henry Harrison I*. Chicago: University of Chicago Press, 1926.

Johnson, Evans C. *Oscar W. Underwood: A Political Biography*. Baton Rouge: Louisiana State University Press, 1980.

Jones, Stanley. *The Presidential Election of 1896*. Madison: University of Wisconsin Press, 1964.

Karl, Barry D. *Charles S. Merriam and the Study of*

Politics. Chicago: University of Chicago Press, 1974.

Katz, William Loren, ed. *The Negro in Chicago: A Study of Race Relations And a Race Riot in 1919*. New York: Arno, 1958.

Keating, Ann Kurkin. *Building Chicago: Suburban Developers And The Creation of a Divided Metropolis*. Urbana: University of Illinois Press, 2002.

Kent, Frank R. *The Great Game of Politics*. Buffalo: Economics Books, 1923, 1959.

Kerney, James. *The Political Education of Woodrow Wilson*. New York: Century, 1926.

Kleppner, Paul. *The Cross of Culture: A Social Analysis of Midwestern Politics, 1850–1900*. New York: Free Press, 1970.

Kraus, Adolf. *Reminiscences and Comments*. Chicago: Toby Rubovits, 1925.

Lasch, Christopher. *Haven in a Heartless World: The Family Besieged*. New York: Basic Books, 1977.

Lear, Linda J. *Harold L. Ickes: The Aggressive Progressive*. New York: Garland, 1981.

Leidenberger, Georg. *Chicago's Progressive Alliance: Labor and the Bid For Public Streetcars*. DeKalb: Northern Illinois University Press, 2006.

Leonard, John W., ed. *The Book of Chicagoans, 1905*. Chicago: A.N. Marquis, 1905.

Lewis, Lloyd. *Chicago: The History of Its Reputation*, pt. 1. New York: Harcourt, Brace, 1929.

Lind, Alan R. *Chicago Surface Lines: An Illustrated History*. Park Forest, IL: Transport History Press, 1974.

Lindberg, Richard C. *King of Clark Street: Michael C. McDonald and the Rise of Chicago's Democratic Machine*. Carbondale: Southern Illinois University Press, 2009.

Lloyd, Caro. *Henry Demarest Lloyd, 1847–1903: A Biography*. New York: G.P. Putnam's Sons, Knickerbocker Press, 1912.

Lohr, Lenox R. *Fair Management: The Story of the Progress Exhibition*. Chicago: Cuneo, 1952.

Mackenzie, John. *The Partition of Africa, 1880–1900: European Imperialism In the Nineteenth Century*. London: Methuen, 1983.

Mahan, Alfred. *The Influence of Sea Power Upon History, 1660–1793*. London: S. Low, Marston, 1890.

Martin, Ralph G. *The Bosses*. New York: G.P. Putnam's Sons, 1964.

McCaffrey, Lawrence *Et Al. The Irish in Chicago*. Urbana: University of Illinois Press, 1987.

McDonald, Forrest. *Insull*. Chicago: University of Chicago Press, 1962.

McMurray, Scott. *Meeting the Challenge: The History of Ross & Hardies, 1902–2002*. Chicago: Ross & Hardies, 2002.

Merriam, Charles S. *Chicago: A More Intimate View of Urban Politics*. New York: Macmillan, 1929.

_____. *The Government of the Metropolitan Region*. Chicago: University of Chicago Press, 1933.

Merrill, Horace S. *Bourbon Leaders: Grover Cleveland and the Democratic Party*. Boston: Little, Brown, 1957.

Merriner, James. *Grafters and Goo Goos: Corruption and Reform in Chicago*. Carbondale: Southern Illinois University Press, 2008.

Merton, Robert K. "The Latent Functions of the Machine." In *Urban Bosses, Machines, and Progressive Reformers*. Edited by Bruce M. Stave. Lexington, MA: D.C. Heath, 1972, 27–37.

Meyers, Gustavus. *History of the Great American Fortunes*, vol. 3. *Great Fortunes from Railroads (Continued)*. Chicago: Charles Kerr, 1911.

Meyers, Margaret G. *A Financial History of the United States*. New York: Columbia University Press, 1970.

Miller, Kerby A. *Emigrants and Exiles: Ireland and the Irish Exodus to North America*. New York: Oxford University Press, 1985.

Miller, Kristie. *Ruth Hannah McCormick: A Life in Politics*. Albuquerque: University of New Mexico Press, 1992.

Miller, Zane L. *Boss Cox's Cincinnati: Urban Politics in the Progressive Era*. New York: Oxford University Press, 1968.

Moody's Manual of Railroad and Corporation Securities, Twenty- Second Annual Number, 1921. New York: Poor's Publishing, 1921.

Morton, Richard Allen. *Justice and Humanity: Edward F. Dunne, Illinois Progressive*. Carbondale: Southern Illinois University Press, 1998.

Moss, David A. *Socializing Security: Progressive-Era Economists and the Origins of American Social Policy*. Cambridge: Harvard University Press, 1995.

Mullen, Arthur F. *Western Democrat*. New York: Wilfred Funk, 1949.

Munro, William Bennett. *Personality in Politics: A Study of Three Types In American Public Life*. New York: Macmillan, 1924.

Nevins, Allan. *Grover Cleveland: A Study in Courage*. New York: Dodd, Mead, 1934.

_____. *Letters of Grover Cleveland*. Boston: Houghton Mifflin, 1933.

Norton, Samuel Wilber. *Chicago Traction: A History of Legislative and Political*. Chicago: n.p., 1907.

Nowland, James D., ed. *Illinois Major Party Platforms, 1900–1964*. Institute of Government and Public Affairs. Champaign: University of Illinois Press, 1966.

Oberholtzer, Ellis Parson. *The Referendum in America: Together with Some Chapters on the Initiative and Recall*. New York: Scribner's, 1912.

Ornig, Joseph R. *My Last Chance to Be a Boy: Theodore Roosevelt's South American Expedition of 1913–1914*. Baton Rouge: Louisiana State University Press, 1994.

Ostrogorski, Moisei. *Democracy and the Organization of Political Parties*, vol. 2. New York: Macmillan, 1902.

Pacyga, Dominic A. *Chicago: A Biography*. Chicago: University of Chicago Press, 2007.

Palmer, George T. *A Conscientious Turncoat: The*

Story of John M. Palmer, 1817–1900. New Haven: Yale University Press, 1941.

Parker, George F. *Recollections of Grover Cleveland*. New York: Century, 1909.

Passer, Harold C. *The Electrical Manufacturers, 1875–1900: A Study in Competition, Entrepreneurship, Technical Change, And Economic Growth*. Cambridge: Harvard University Press, 1953.

Paulson, Ross E. *Radicalism & Reform: The Vrooman Family and American Social Thought, 1837–1937*. Lexington: University of Kentucky Press, 1968.

Pettigrew, Richard F. *Imperial Washington: The Story of American Public Life from 1870–1920*. New York: Arno, 1970 [1922].

Platt, Harold L. *The Electric City: Energy and the Growth of the Chicago Area, 1880–1930*. Chicago: University of Chicago Press, 1991.

Porter, Kirk H., and Johnson, Donald Bruce. *National Party Platforms, 1840–1964*. Urbana: University of Illinois Press, 1966.

Proctor, Ben. *William Randolph Hearst: The Early Years, 1863–1910*. Oxford: Oxford University Press, 1998.

Reynolds, George M. *Machine Politics in New Orleans, 1897–1926*. New York: Columbia University Press, 1936.

Riordan, William L. *Plunkitt of Tammany Hall*. New York: E.P. Dutton, 1905.

Rice, Wallace. *75 Years of Gas Service in Chicago*. Chicago: The People's Gas Light and Coke Company, 1925.

Robinson, Doane. *History of South Dakota*. Logansport, IN: B.F. Bowen, 1904.

Roseboom, Eugene H. *A History of Presidential Elections: From George Washington to Richard M. Nixon*. New York: Macmillan, 1957, 1960.

Rothman, David. *Conscience and Convenience: The Asylum and Its Alternatives In Progressive America*. Boston: Little, Brown, 1980.

Salter, J.T. *Boss Rule: Portraits in City Politics*. New York: McGraw-Hill, 1935.

Salzman, Neil V. *Reform and Revolution: The Life and Times of Raymond Robins*. Kent, OH: Kent State University Press, 1991.

Sandberg, Carl. *Chicago Poems*. New York: Henry Holt, 1916.

Schmidt, John R. *"The mayor who cleaned up Chicago": A Political Biography of William E. Dever*. DeKalb: Northern Illinois University Press, 1989.

Shannon, William V. *The American Irish*. New York: Macmillan, 1964.

Skilnik, Bob. *Beer: A History of Brewing in Chicago*. Fort Lee, NJ: Barricade, 2006.

Snead, William T. *If Christ Came to Chicago!* Chicago: Laird and Lee, 1894.

Spear, Allan H. *Black Chicago: The Making of a Negro Ghetto, 1890–1920*. Chicago: University of Chicago Press, 1967.

Staley, William H. *History of the Illinois Federation of Labor*. Chicago: University of Chicago Press, 1930.

Stanton, Cady Elizabeth, et al. *A History of the Woman's Suffrage Movement*, 2nd ed. Rochester, NY: Mann, 1922.

Stave, Bruce M. *The New Deal and the Last Hurrah: Pittsburgh Machine Politics*. Pittsburgh: University of Pittsburgh Press, 1970.

_____. *Urban Bosses, Machines, and Progressive Reformers*. Lexington, MA: D.C. Heath, 1972.

Steffens, Lincoln. *The Shame of the Cities*. New York: McClure, Phillips, 1904.

_____. *The Struggle for Self-Government*. New York: McClure, Phillips, 1906.

Stein, C.A. *Resurgent Republicanism*. Ann Arbor, MI: Edwards Bros., 1963.

Steinberg. Alfred. *The Bosses*. New York: Macmillan, 1972.

Strong, Josiah. *Our Country: Its Possible Future and Its Present Crisis*. New York: Baker and Taylor for the American Home Missionary Society, 1885.

Stuart, William H. *The Twenty Incredible Years*. Chicago: M.A. Donohue, 1935.

Studenski, Paul, and Herman E. Krooss. *Financial History of the United States*. New York: McGraw-Hill, 1952.

Swanberg, W.A. *Citizen Hearst: A Biography of William Randolph Hearst*. New York: Scribner's, 1961.

Tansill, Charles. *America and the Fight for Irish Freedom, 1866–1922*. New York: Devin-Adair, 1957.

Tarr, Joel Arthur. *A Study in Boss Politics: William Lorimer of Chicago*. Champaign: University of Illinois, 1971.

Thomas, Charles A. *Thomas Riley Marshal, Hoosier Statesman*. Oxford, OH: Mississippi Valley Press, 1939.

Thompson, Charles Willis. *Presidents I Have Known and Two Near Presidents*. Indianapolis: Bobbs-Merrill, 1929.

Timberlake, James S. *Prohibition and the Progressive Movement*. New York: Athenaeum, 1970.

Townsend, Walter A. *The Illinois Democracy: A History of the Party and Its Representative Members—Past and Present*. 5 vols. Springfield: Democratic Historical Association, 1935.

Trask, David F. *The War with Spain in 1898*. Lincoln: University of Nebraska Press; reprint edition, 1997.

Troesken, Werner. *Why Regulate Utilities? The New Institutional Economies and the Chicago Gas Industry, 1849–1924*. Ann Arbor: University of Michigan Press, 1996.

Tuttle, Charles R. *The Illinois Currency Convention*. Chicago: Charles H. Kerr, 1895.

Tuttle, William M. Jr. *Race Riot: Chicago in the Red Summer of 1919*. New York: Athenaeum, 1971.

Van Devander, Charles W. *The Big Bosses*. New York: Ayer, 1974.

Walker, John K. *William Randolph Hearst: A New Appraisal*. New York: Hastings House, 1955.

Waller, Robert. *Rainey of Illinois: A Political Biography, 1903–1934.* Illinois Studies in Social Sciences, no. 60. Champaign: University of Illinois Press, 1977.

Weber, Harry P. *Outline History of Chicago Traction.* Chicago: n.p., 1936.

Weiss, Nancy Joan. *Charles Francis Murphy, 1859–1924: Respectability and Responsibility in Tammany Politics.* Northampton, MA: Smith College, 1968.

Welch, Richard F. *Big Tim Sullivan, Tammany Hall, and New York City from the Gilded Age to the Progressive Era.* Madison, NJ: Farleigh Dickinson University Press, 2008.

Wendt, Lloyd, and Herman Kogan. *Big Bill of Chicago.* Indianapolis: Bobbs-Merrill, 1953.

Whicher, George F. *William Jennings Bryan and the Campaign of 1896.* Boston: D.C. Heath, 1953.

White, William Allen. *The Autobiography of William Allen White.* New York: Macmillan, 1946.

Winkler, John K. *William Randolph Hearst: An American Phenomenon.* New York: Simon & Schuster, 1928.

Wooddy, Carroll Hill. *The Case of Frank L. Smith: A Study in Representative Government.* Chicago: University of Chicago Press, 1931.

Young, David. *Chicago Transit: An Illustrated History.* DeKalb: Northern Illinois University Press, 1998.

Zink, Harold. *City Bosses in the United States: A Study of Twenty Municipal Bosses.* Durham: Duke University Press, 1930.

Articles

Abbott, W.J. "The Carter Harrison Dynasty in Chicago." *Munsey* 24 (1898): 809–15.

Addams, Jane. "Why the Ward Boss Rules." *The Outlook* 58 (April 2, 1898): 879–82.

"Appointer General." *World's Work* 26 (October 1913): 616.

Barnes, James A. "The Gold Standard Democrats and the Party Conflict." *Mississippi Valley Historical Review* 17 (December 1930): 422–450.

Beito, David T., and Royster Beito. "Gold Democrats and the Decline of Classic Liberalism, 1896–1900." *Independent Review* 4 (Spring 2000): 555–75.

Block, Marvin W. "Henry T. Rainey of Illinois." *Journal of the Illinois State Historical Society* 65 (Summer 1972): 142–58.

Boxman, Burton A. "Adolph Joachim Sabath in Congress: The Early Years, 1907–1932." *Journal of the Illinois State Historical Society* 66 (1973): 327–40.

Bryan, William Jennings. "The Issue for 1900." *North American Review* 170 (June 1900): 753–71.

Buenker, John D. "City Ethics and the Politics of Accommodation." *Chicago History* 3 (Fall 1974): 92–100.

_____. "Dynamics of Chicago Ethnic Politics, 1900–1930." *Journal of the Illinois State Historical Society* 57 (1964): 175–99.

_____. "Edward F. Dunne: The Urban New Stock Democrat as Progressive." *Mid-America* 50 (1968): 3–21.

_____. "The Illinois Legislature and Prohibition, 1907–1919." *Journal of the Illinois State Historical Society* 62 (1969): 363–84.

_____. "The Urban Political Machine and the Seventeenth Amendment." *Journal of American History* 56 (September 1969): 305–22.

Cain, Louis P. "To Annex or Not? A Tale of Two Towns: Evanston and Hyde Park." *Explorations in Economic History* 29 (1983): 58–72.

Candeloro, Dominic. "The School Board Crisis of 1907." *Journal of the Illinois State Historical Society* 68 (1975): 396–406.

Darrow, Clarence S. "Chicago's Traction Question." *International* 12 (October 1905): 13–22.

Dernberg, Bernard. "The Ties That Bind America and Germany," pt. 2. *World's Work* 29 (December 1914): 186–89.

Dittey, Robert M. "Judson Harmon of Ohio—A Man of Deeds Not Words." *Editorial Review* 6 (April 1912): 316–24.

Duffus, Robert L. "The Tragedy of Hearst." *World's Work* 44 (October 1922): 623–31.

Dunne Edward F. "Chicago's Fight for Municipal Ownership." *Independent* 51 (October 18, 1906): 927–30.

_____. "How Chicago Will Do It." *World's Work* 10 (June 1905): 6265–66.

Fairlie, John A. "The Illinois Legislation of 1923." *Journal of Political Economics* 21 (1913): 931–7.

_____. "Municipal Functions in the United States." *Annals of the American Academy of Political and Social Sciences* 25 (1905): 304–8.

Fitch, George. "The Noiseless Suffragette." *Collier's* 51 (August 9, 1913): 4–6.

_____. "Politics in Illinois." *Collier's* 51 (August 9, 1913): 21–2; 29.

Fite, Gilbert C. "Republican Strategy and the Farm Vote in the Presidential Campaign of 1896." *American Historical Review* 55 (1960): 794–803.

Giffen, Robert. "The Gresham Law." *Economic Journal* 1 (1891): 304–06.

Gould, Alan B. "Walter L. Fisher: Profile of an Urban Reformer." *Mid-America* 57–58 (1975): 151–72.

Grosser, Hugo S. "The Movement for Municipal Ownership in Chicago." *Annals of the American Academy of Political and Social Sciences* 27 (1906): 27–90.

Hale, William Bayard. "Chicago, Its Struggle and Its Dream." *World's Work* 19 (April 1910): 12792–805.

_____. "Judson Harmon and the Presidency." *World's Work* 22 (June 1911): 14446–59.

_____. "Thomas Riley Marshall." *World's Work* 24 (October 1912): 630–38.

Hart, Rollin Lynde. "When the Negro Comes North: Ii, Future Results of the Migration." *World's Work* 48 (July 1924): 318–23.

Havig, Alan R. "The Raymond Robins Case for Progressive Republicanism." *Journal of the Illinois State Historical Society* 64 (1971): 401–18.

Hawthorne, Daniel. "Golf and Good Health." *World's Work* 40 (August 1912): 393–403.

Hayes, Samuel P. "The Politics of Reform in Municipal Government in the Progressive Era." *Pacific Northwest Quarterly* 55 (1964): 157–69.

Hendrick, Burton J. "The Recall of Justice Hughes." *World's Work* 32 (August 1915): 397–410.

Hoffman, Charles. "The Depression of the Nineties." *Journal of Economic History* 16 (June 1956): 137–64.

Huthmacher, J. Joseph. "Charles Evans Hughes and Charles Francis Murphy, the Metamorphosis of Progressivism." *New York History* 44 (January 1965): 28–34.

_____. "Urban Liberalism and the Age of Reform." *Mississippi Valley Historical Review* 49 (September 1962): 231–41.

"Interview with Mr. Dalyrumple." *Street Railway Journal* 26 (August 1905): 22–4.

Jones, Walter Clyde. "The Direct Primary in Illinois." *Proceedings of the American Political Science Association* 7 (1910): 138–62.

Kearney, James. "How Wilson Was Shown to the Nation." *Washington Post* (October 25, 1927): 1, 5.

Lindstrom, Andrew F. "Lawrence Stringer: A Wilson Democrat." *Journal of the Illinois State Historical Society* 66 (1973): 20–40.

Low, Theodore J. "Machine Politics—Old and New." *The Public Interest* 9 (Fall 1967): 83–97.

Lowry, Edward G. "The War in the Middle West." *World's Work* 33 (March 1917): 510–15.

Lyle, Eugene F. "Taft: A Career of Big Tasks." *World's Work* 14 (July 1907): 9135–44.

McCarthy, Michael P. "Prelude to Armageddon: Charles E. Merriam and the Chicago Mayoral Election of 1911." *Journal of the Illinois State Historical Society* 67 (November 1974): 5051–11.

McFarlane, Peter Clark. "Is Roger Sullivan a Boss?" *Collier's* 58 (August 8, 1914): 5–6.

McKitrick, Eric L. "The Study of Corruption." *Political Science Quarterly* 72 (December 1957): 502–14.

Middleton, James. "Are Americans More German than English?" *World's Work* 31 (December 1915): 141–47.

Miller, Kristie. "Ruth Hanna McCormick and the Election of 1930." *Journal of the Illinois State Historical Society* 63 (1968): 191–210.

Morton, Richard Allen. "Edward F. Dunne: Illinois' Most Progressive Governor." *Illinois Historical Journal* 83 (1990): 218–34.

_____. "'A Man of Belial': Roger C. Sullivan, the Progressive Democracy, and the Senatorial Elections of 1914." *Journal of the Illinois State Historical Society* 91 (Autumn 1998): 133–59.

_____. "A Victorian Tragedy: The Strange Deaths of Carter H. Harrison and Patrick Eugene Prendergast." *Journal of the Illinois State Historical Society* 96 (Spring 2003); 6–36.

Murphy, Majorie. "Taxation and Social Conflict: Teacher Unionism and Public School Finance in Chicago, 1889–1934." *Journal of the Illinois State Historical Society* 74 (1981): 242–60.

Nelli, Humbert. "John Powers and the Italians: Politics in a Chicago Ward, 1896–1921." *Journal of American History* 57 (June 1970): 67–84.

Pollack, Norman. "The Myth of Populist Anti-Semitism." *American Historical Review* 68 (October 1962): 76–80.

Powers, Stanley. "Chicago's Strike Ordeal." *World's Work* 10 (July 1905): 6378–84.

Price, Theodore H., and Richard Spillane. "Stalking for Nine Million Votes." *World's Work* 32 (October 1916): 663–77.

Roberts, Sidney I. "The Municipal Voters League and Chicago Boodlers." *Journal of the Illinois State Historical Society* 53 (1960): 117–40.

Rogers, Walter S. "The Embarrassing Mr. Sullivan." *Harper's Weekly* 59 (24 October 1914): 394–95.

"A Short Measure of What President Roosevelt Has Done." *World's Work* 17 (March 1909): 1311–12.

Smith, Herbert Knox. "Gifford Pinchot, Forester." *World's Work* 16 (July 1908): 10427–10430.

Sullivan, Mark, "Why the West Dislikes New York." *World's Work* 51 (February 1926): 406–11.

Tarbell, Ida. "How Chicago Is Finding Itself." Pts. 1 and 2. *American Magazine* 67 (1908): 29–41, 124–38.

Tarr, Joel A. "The Urban Politician as Entrepreneur." *Mid-America* 59 (January 1967): 56–63.

"Theodore Roosevelt." *World's Work* 37 (February 1919): 371–72.

Trout, Grace Wilbur. "Sidelights on Illinois Suffrage History." *Journal of The Illinois State Historical Society* 12 (1920): 145–79.

Waller, Robert A. "The Illinois Waterway from Conception to Completion, 1908–1913." *Journal of the Illinois State Historical Society* 65 (1972): 125–41.

West, Roy O., and William C. Walton. "Charles Deneen, 1863–1940." *Journal Of the Illinois State Historical Society* 34 (1941): 12–25.

"What the Council of National Defense Is Doing." *World's Work* 33 (April 1917): 629–36.

Wish, Harvey. "Governor Altgeld Pardons the Anarchists." *Journal of the Illinois State Historical Society* 31 (1938): 424–48.

Wrone, David R. "Illinois Pulls Out of the Mud." *Journal of the Illinois State Historical Society* 58 (1965): 54–75.

Unpublished Manuscripts and Theses

Beldon, Gertrude. "A History of the Woman Suffrage Movement in Illinois." Ph.D. diss., University of Chicago, 1971.

Callender, Richard W. "Walter L. Fisher, 1862–1935: The Regulation of Public Utilities." Master's thesis, University of Illinois, 1963.

Eisenstein, Sophia J. "The Elections of 1912 in Chicago," Master's thesis, University of Chicago, 1947.

Fisher, Walter L. "Autobiographical Sketch." [1932?] Illinois Historical Survey, University of Illinois Library, Urbana-Champaign.

Green, Paul M. "The Chicago Democratic Party, 1840–1920: From Factionalism to Political Organization." Ph.D. diss., University of Chicago, 1975.

Haupt, Richard Walter. "History of the French Lick Springs Hotel." Master's Thesis, Indiana University, 1953.

Lilly, Samuel A. "The Political Career of Roger Sullivan." Master's thesis, Eastern Illinois University, 1964.

McCarthy, Michael. "Businessmen and Professionals in Municipal Reform: The Chicago Experience, 1867–1920." Ph.D. diss., Northwestern University, 1970.

Morrison, Geoffrey F. "A Political Biography of Champ Clark." Ph.D. diss., St. Louis University, 1971.

Philip, William B. "Chicago and the Downstate: The Story of Their Conflict, 1870–1934." Ph.D. diss., University of Chicago, 1940.

Post, Louis F. "Living a Long Life Over Again." Louis Freeland Post Papers, Manuscript Division, Library of Congress, Washington, D.C.

Straetz, Ralph Arthur. "The Progressive Movement in Illinois, 1910–1916." Ph.D. diss., University of Illinois, 1958.

Thurner, Arthur W. "The Impact of Ethnic Groups on the Democratic Party in Chicago, 1920–1928." Ph.D. diss., University of Chicago, 1966.

Tingley, Ralph R. "From Carter Harrison II to Fred Busse: A Study of Chicago Political Parties and Personages from 1896 to 1907." Ph.D. diss., University of Chicago, 1950.

Warner, Mildred C. "The History of the Deep Waterway in the State of Illinois." Master's thesis, University of Illinois, 1947.

Weber, Robert David. "Rationalizers and Reformers: Chicago Local Transportation in the Nineteenth Century." Ph.D. diss., University of Wisconsin, 1971.

Index